# DARDANELLE AND THE BOTTOMS

# Dardanelle and the Bottoms

*Environment, Agriculture, and Economy in an Arkansas River Community, 1819–1970*

## Mildred Diane Gleason

The University of Arkansas Press
*Fayetteville*
2017

*In memory of*
*Mildred Boyce Gleason and*
*George Granville Gleason*

# CONTENTS

# DARDANELLE AND THE BOTTOMS

# PREFACE

*Continuity had always been the preferred and pre-*
*dominant emphasis among writers of Southern*
*history . . . down to the middle of the twentieth cen-*
*tury. Then . . . the emphasis swung to change and*
*discontinuity.*

C. VANN WOODWARD,
*"From the Old South to the New"*

*In the midst of winter, I finally learned that there*
*was in me an invincible summer.*

ALBERT CAMUS,
*"Myth of Sisyphus"*

The seeds for this book were planted on May 11, 1975. On that day, my father, George Granville Gleason, took me to the Dardanelle Bottoms. Seeing Carden Bottom for the first time, I was struck by its desolate beauty and sprawling landscape. Topping a small rise, I saw Carden Bottom High School, huge and majestic as it seemed to rise from the earth, a monolith representing something grand and undefined. At New Neely, near the location of my grandfather's plantation store and cotton gin, my father quietly commented that he had placed the bricks in the gin's foundation, and now they are tearing it down: it is almost all gone. Two days later, my father died. For four decades, his words played on my mind as I wondered what had happened and why.

Slightly more than forty years later, on August 15, 2015, I stood on Front Street in Dardanelle and watched as an entire block was engulfed in flames. One of the buildings destroyed belonged to my family, a building that had been in my family for sixty-two years and had housed two different family businesses. As the flames spread and the structures cracked, exploded, and collapsed, the front façade of the old Woodson's Department Store building fell away exposing the black glass panels installed there in the 1950s, which I remembered from my childhood. In minutes, they too were consumed by the flames.

The fire reminded me of the fragility of the history of Dardanelle and the Bottoms and how magnificently resilient its citizens had been. What a tough bunch of people they were. From the richest town merchant to the most deprived hardscrabble farmer, they believed in themselves, work, and their futures. They had endured floods, droughts, fires, death, disease, the Great Depression, the collapse of the cotton market, and two world wars, and yet their world has vanished. They live only now in memory—in history.

I watched as the concrete ledge in front of the old glass entryway of Williamson's Variety Store was destroyed and recalled that that very ledge had been the favorite perch for Short Lane, who, along with his brothers and family, farmed hundreds of acres of Bottom land. A respected sharecropper known for his skill and his honesty, Short Lane came to Dardanelle every Saturday as did hundreds of "country people." He was a rotund, stout man whose faded blue overalls, always unbuttoned on both sides, never seemed quite large enough, and, as he took his perch on Front Street, other folks would pass by and chat. "How the beans lookin', Short?" "What kind of fertilize' are you usin'?" "Are you still farmin' the Meeks place?" Saturday talk in Dardanelle from sixty years ago still plays in my mind.

Those country people, a few still driving wagons pulled by mules that were "parked" in the alley on Saturdays behind the Dardanelle Mercantile Company, came to town to buy their groceries and supplies, to shop and take in a movie at the Joy Theatre. Some went to the pool halls for a cold beer and entertainment. They stayed all day, usually not leaving until after the evening movie ended. The stores stayed open until at least midnight on Saturdays. Luther Banks's barbershop on Market Street was busy with customers, both African American and white. The African American shoe-shine man in the front corner of the shop slapped and buffed the waxy shine on worn shoes and boots. I was in awe of his skill, his dexterity, and the rhythm of his work.

Dardanelle was crowded on Saturdays. Parking space on Front Street was difficult to find and people roamed up and down the street, crowded shoulder to shoulder. The cafes, stores, and pool halls were busy; the Joy Theatre was packed both for the matinee and the evening double feature; and businesses did a booming trade. The sidewalks were covered in spit and chewing tobacco, and the pungent odor of bodies, sweat, and dirt was the town's Saturday bouquet. It was the smell of money, mutual interdependence, and success. Country women in worn cotton dresses with thin belts and men in overalls joined with the better dressed town people in forming the human kaleidoscope that was Dardanelle on Saturdays. With few changes through the decades, this was Dardanelle from 1880 to 1970, a mixture of rural and town.

Even in the 1950s, the reciprocal rural/town relationship was still intact. My father and my grandfather Jack Boyce relied heavily on the "country trade," and their business, the Dardanelle Mercantile, had a long history of extending credit to most, keeping prices low, and offering respect and appreciation to their customers. In the feed section—the back room of the store—I remember a farmer saying he had to have the 100-pound sack of oats that was on the bottom of a ten-sack-high pile of feed because his wife wanted a floral-pattern feed sack for her sewing. Much to the disgust of Frank Frazier, who worked in the store's back room, 900 pounds of oats had to be moved in order to retrieve the one floral sack of oats on the bottom of the pile because that was what the farmer wanted. Without the benefit of ever being told, I grew up somehow knowing that business success in Dardanelle required consideration and respect for that rural customer, that man in the Big Smith overalls whose sweat, hard work, and ingenuity gave him cash and whose honest reputation allowed him credit. He was the customer, the backbone of Dardanelle's business success.

So, as I watched the fire on August 15, 2015, take buildings down, my memories of Dardanelle and the Bottoms—their people, plans, work, struggles, and successes—all seemed crystalized. The past lives on only because those who know that past allow it to remain alive. It lives on in peoples' hearts as well as in their minds and serves one to better understand who and what one is and how one arrived at this present. Nonetheless, the past can never tell one how to move forward. For that, one must rely on his or her own intelligence, effort, courage, and grace.

The death of the rural/town reciprocity in the 1970s caused all of this to disappear. The destruction of that dynamic meant a way of life that had flourished through generations for at least ninety years had vanished. The rural world disappeared, the life of the town was profoundly altered, and a new reality was created. This is what happened and why it happened.

This book analyzes this rural/town reciprocity and the reasons this dichotomy both existed and vanished. The research comes primarily from newspaper accounts and first-person participants whose individual experiences and personal knowledge present the voices of Dardanelle and Bottoms residents. Thus, this work offers an insight into history from a local perspective, and as such represents both local and regional southern history. Dardanelle and the Bottoms in numerous ways were typical of most southern locations with towns serving as regional trade markets while their adjacent rural areas were performing production of agricultural goods. The transitions these locations endured are also typical of movement from the one-crop agricultural system centered on cotton production to a more modern economic model following World War II. Growing cotton drew settlers to Arkansas prior to the Civil War. Cotton production continued to be a mainstay of Arkansas agriculture until the 1960s and 1970s and still today is a major crop in the Delta region of eastern Arkansas. Traditionally, farmers and landowners marketed their crop to cotton merchants and factors, many of whom operated from Memphis, Tennessee, who then sold the product to various textile mills throughout the country. By the early twentieth century American cotton was part of a growing worldwide cotton/textile industry, a fact that resulted in catastrophe for many farmers following World War I as a worldwide glut in market supplies occurred.[1] In addition to a study of the economic influence of cotton, the characteristics of life in Dardanelle and the Bottoms as discussed in the following pages also involve the basic themes and dynamics dealing with race relations, health, education, and socioeconomic structure. Therefore, this work, while a historical monograph about the social and economic history of Dardanelle and the Bottoms, is also a study of life in an unknown number of other southern places whose social and economic features were similar.

While cotton production concerns and the functioning of regional trade centers were common to many southern locations, there is still and always has been something unique in Dardanelle and the Bottoms, some hint of outrageous optimism, some spirit born of southern sweat, independence, and wildness of character, some genuine, decent goodness and honesty that had always encouraged bold dreams and audacious activities leading to great successes, innovation, and sometimes to heartbreaking failures. The novelist Charles Portis called it grit, true grit. Some call it the spirit of the Free State of Yell. Those who have lived it, simply think of it as the appropriate attitude for addressing one's life. It is the Yell County way of living.

As Dardanelle and the Bottoms have quietly fallen into a backwater of progress, contaminated by modernity's homogenized mores, perhaps someone or some group shall be fortunate enough—wise and brave enough—to find and channel that spirit again and live through the flames of change with as much dignity and fortitude as did so many who preceded us in this place, Dardanelle and the Bottoms, thus creating a new reality forged on the true spirit of the place and its history. If strength, courage, and honesty are present, then perhaps this will happen. Perhaps.

# ACKNOWLEDGMENTS

Numerous individuals have been of great assistance in the preparation of this work. Several undergraduate and graduate students worked to photocopy newspaper files from the microfilm collections at Arkansas River Valley Regional Library, Dardanelle, Arkansas. Of particular assistance were the efforts of Marie Williams, whose work was of excellent quality and who became truly committed to the project. The staff of the regional library was also very helpful. Many individuals allowed interviews to be conducted and generously gave of their time and knowledge in order to further my research. My special thanks goes to Joe Grimes, who, in addition to several interviews, allowed access to his collection of photographs. Dr. Leslie "Skip" Stewart-Abernathy of the Arkansas Archeological Survey assisted with the gathering of maps. The resources of the Arkansas History Commission Archives and its staff were also consulted and assisted with my research. My colleagues in the Department of History and Political Science and from other departments at Arkansas Tech University offered their support and continued interest in this project. Dr. Jeff Woods, dean of the College of Arts and Humanities, was most helpful with the early conceptualization of the project. The administration of Arkansas Tech University allowed me an eight-month sabbatical during 2013, which allowed time for the writing of the first section of this manuscript as well as an opportunity for continued research.

I appreciate those who critically read initial drafts or portions of this manuscript: Dr. Jan Jenkins, Dr. Micheal Tarver, Carlos Marquez, Marcia Lawrence, and Lynne Murphy. Particularly my special thanks to Lynne Murphy, who assisted in reading hundreds of pages of newspapers, recording notes, and discussing this material with me. Her interest in this project has been without bounds and her enthusiasm for its completion has been inspirational and most helpful. The late Joe Murphy also offered his considerable assistance and demonstrated in various ways his unwavering support.

Also of great importance in the completion of this work was the assistance of two colleagues. Dr. Micheal Tarver gave many hours in the editing and refining of the manuscript and offered his experience as a historian and author to assist in numerous ways offering both technical expertise and historical insight. He was always available to answer my questions and offer his considerable knowledge of academic publishing. The manuscript would not have been as professionally developed without his kind and gracious assistance for which I am most appreciative. Also, Dr. Joseph Swain used his special skills to develop the maps that are included in this work, and they should be of great benefit to the reader's understanding of the area's geography. Both Dr. Tarver and Dr. Swain are valued as colleagues and friends, and each performed hours of scholarly work in the completion of this work. Their efforts and talents are greatly appreciated.

I would also like to acknowledge the mentoring I received under the graceful, enlightened hand of the late Dr. Willard B. Gatewood Jr., without which I would have never attempted to research and write anything. Likewise, I credit Dr. Elizabeth Payne for her role in developing my writing and inspiring me to carefully examine what I believe to be reality. Finally, I wish to acknowledge the late Dr. Gene Boyett for encouraging me to study American history and believing that I possessed the ability to do so.

The staff of the University of Arkansas Press has been of tremendous assistance. Particularly I must acknowledge David Scott Cunningham for his interest in and complete support for this project as well as his editing of the manuscript. David has provided substantial professional comfort as he has made the completion and publication of this work possible.

I wish to acknowledge the legacy presented by the previous residents of Dardanelle and the Dardanelle Bottoms. The history of their lives proved inspirational as well as intriguing and played a major role in maintaining my devotion to this work. I hope this work offers a fair historical rendering of their lives, struggles, and triumphs.

Merely mentioning the above groups and individuals unfortunately fails to transmit my deep appreciation to each of them and to countless others without whom this work could not have been completed. I hope this work is a credit to all who were involved in its completion.

## CHAPTER I

# The Beginnings, 1819–1879

*The idea of immortality . . . will continue . . . as long as love kisses the lips of death. It is the rainbow—Hope, shining upon the tears of grief.*

R. G. INGERSOLL,
*American attorney (1833–1899)*

*[A] good many of the Boomers have been killed since the war, some have left and now this is as peaceful country as any . . . The people are generally rough looking but honorable and generous and the wimen [women] are not pretty but they are clever . . . The Bottoms is a good place for a young man who will take hole [hold] to live but bring your wife with you.*

J. E. LINDSAY,
*March 1866*

*I pray God that I may never again witness such sights as were enacted on the streets of Dardanelle at that time . . . lawlessness continued . . . until 1874 . . . when the State was wrested from the hands of this lawless element and peace, law and order began to be restored.*

CHARLES H. MCGUIRE,
*September 1929*

# Introduction

Sometime during the spring of 1819 James Carden, in search of good land and a prosperous life, followed old Native American trails along the Arkansas River to the point of its convergence with the Petit Jean River. There he found scattered settlements of Cherokee farms. Given the rich land and its sparse settlements, Carden decided his travels were over and settled in an area that would become the extreme northeast corner of the Dardanelle Bottoms.[2] Carden was born in Ireland in 1780 and emigrated to the United States in 1806. He first settled in Missouri but left there in 1818 given the problems posed by the Sunk Lands, a result of the 1811–1812 New Madrid earthquakes. His search for a new beginning brought him the following year to an area immediately south of the Arkansas River and west of the Petit Jean River very near their point of convergence (see Appendix, fig. 3). At age thirty-nine, Carden wasted little time clearing one hundred acres of huge hardwoods and undergrowth and planting cotton. His homestead was profitable, the rich soil producing cotton that was shipped by steamboat from a landing he constructed on the banks of the Arkansas River, Carden Bottom's Landing. Within the next ten years, several additional white families settled in the area. Carden married Jace Tiner from Galley Rock, a settlement on the north side of the Arkansas River situated six miles southeast of the current-day community of Atkins, Arkansas. The Cardens prospered and had four sons: William H., George, James, and Tom.[3] Carden Bottom, the original settlement in the Dardanelle Bottoms, had been established.

# Native Americans

This was not virgin land, as Carden Bottom had a rich archaeological heritage. Parts of this area, a large alluvial floodplain, had been farmed from 500 to 1,500 years earlier by Native Americans from the Woodland and Mississippian cultures. Additionally, this land had been the site of foraging Native Americans dating back 11,500 years, and included the Dalton through the Archaic era cultures.[4] There is also evidence to support the claim that Hernando de Soto's expedition of 1541–1542 traversed parts of the Petit Jean River and that French explorers in the area used physical features to assign names.[5]

A group of Cherokees, known as the "Western Settlers," traveled into present-day northwest and north-central Arkansas beginning in the 1790s.[6] By the early 1800s, several Native American tribes hunted in or inhabited the area along the Arkansas River including the Osage, Caddo, and Cherokee. The Osage vacated their lands in northern Arkansas in 1808, and in 1812 Chief Tahlonteskee led 300 Cherokees to settle in the Arkansas River Valley. In 1817, based on a treaty to exchange their Tennessee lands for Arkansas lands, additional Cherokees arrived. In 1818, 331 natives led by Ooluntuskee (John Jolly), brother of Chief Tahlonteskee, moved to Arkansas. The Jolly group settled on the north bank of the Arkansas River, slightly west of Galley Creek. This settlement was known as Galley and later as Galley Rock.[7] Chief Tahlonteskee died in 1819, and John Jolly became one of the primary chiefs of the Western Cherokees. In 1819 naturalist Thomas Nuttall made his famous trip along the Arkansas River replete with journal entries of his observations. By this time, according to these entries, the Cherokees were living in log cabins along the Arkansas River south of Dardanelle Rock surrounded by cotton fields and peach and plum orchards.[8]

Even though the Western Cherokees, or Western Settlers, had been granted land in Arkansas by treaty, by the early 1820s white encroachment created additional problems for the Cherokees, who were also faced with bickering and brawling with the Caddo people in the area. These problems resulted in a council meeting between acting Arkansas territorial governor Robert Crittenden, representing United States interests, and Chief Black Fox, representing the Western Cherokees, near Dardanelle Rock in late 1822. The meeting was contentious as the Cherokees noted that white settlers were undermining their treaty boundaries. United States Government Indian factor Colonel David Brearley persuaded the Cherokees by majority vote of those present to resettle their people north of the Arkansas River. This Council Oaks Treaty, as it came to be called, guaranteed the Cherokees 3,285,710 acres of Arkansas land north of the Arkansas River in accordance with the boundaries established by the earlier 1817 treaty.[9] Certainly some of the Cherokees remained on their farms south of the Arkansas River, and this group identified itself as "Black Dutch." The Black Dutch intermarried with the white population over time and simply blended into the area's American population.[10] Aside from this group, the Western Cherokees were officially removed from Arkansas to Indian Territory by the Indian Removal Act of 1830 although movement of local Native Americans began in the late 1820s.

# Dardanelle

The town of Dardanelle began as an Indian Agency created by the United States Government in 1813 and under the direction of agency factors. The government factors included Major William L. Lovely (1813–1817), Reuben Lewis (1817–1822), Colonel David Brearley (1822–1823), and Major Edward M. Duvall (1823–1828).[11] The small settlement of a few businesses and homes scattered along the riverbank slowly began to transform into a town. In 1847, Colonel Brearley's son, Joseph Brearley, officially laid out the original streets of the town, and Dardanelle was incorporated on January 17, 1855.[12]

Recollections of an 1857 settler to the area offer a glimpse of the town just prior to the Civil War. Dardanelle was a small village that "did not exceed much a hundred souls" and containing approximately four merchandising establishments, one saloon, one hotel, one lawyer, one established church (the Presbyterian) and two circuit-riding church routes (Methodist and Baptist), one schoolhouse, and a ferry connecting Dardanelle north across the Arkansas River to the settlement of Norristown. The unidentified author of this memoir was moving his "white family and my families of negroes" from Georgia in order to establish himself as a planter in the area.[13] One can gather from this that the town of Dardanelle prior to the Civil War was an appendage of the planter/farming activities in the surrounding rural area.

The area was still very much a part of the frontier during the antebellum era. While Yell County was created from parts of Scott and Pope Counties and formed as a separate entity on December 5, 1840, the area remained fairly remote and untamed. Dardanelle was a "brawling frontier town" sprawled out adjacent to the Arkansas River and filled with saloons, riverboat men, and all sorts of rough characters.[14] The presence of the Arkansas River had everything to do with the town's reasons for existing, as well as its general character and morals, or more precisely, the lack thereof. The river's presence was also an integral reason for the growth of the Dardanelle Bottoms with its emphasis on agriculture.

## The Arkansas River as Transportation

Prior to 1819 and until approximately 1840, the only regular method of transportation on the Arkansas River was the flatboat and the keelboat. These types of boats continued in use to a lesser extent through the Civil War.[15] The earliest steamboats on the Arkansas River were the *Comet* in 1820 and the *Eagle* in 1822. These were western steamboats designed to displace less water while producing great power, and thus they could maneuver the occasionally shallow and shifting waters of the Arkansas River from Little Rock up the river to Fort Smith and beyond. Low water levels during the summer months precluded the rapid expansion of Arkansas River steamers, as only ten steamboats worked the Arkansas River during the period from 1820 to 1830. From the late 1830s to the 1850s, steamboat companies began to combine their earnings while operating a fleet of individually owned and operated steamers, which carried passengers and freight. During the late 1850s, fleets of steamers operating according to set schedules appeared on the Arkansas River and reaped good profits from what was quickly becoming their monopolistic hold over certain shippers and ports.[16]

Between 1834 and 1840, large steamers made nine successive trips from Little Rock up the Arkansas River to Fort Gibson, Indian Territory. In 1841, the *Arkansas*, a side wheeler drawing not less than six feet, successfully made six successive trips to Fort Gibson. In 1853 a total of 28,000 tons of freight and 2,380 passengers were brought to Little Rock by steamboat and 17,000 bales of cotton were shipped from up river to Little Rock. From 1864 until 1871 steamers operated as a general rule for about six months each year. The largest cargo ever carried by steamer on the Arkansas River was recorded in 1873 by the *Exporter,* which departed Fort Smith carrying 600 bales of cotton, passed Little Rock carrying 4,803 bales, and completed the trip to New Orleans with 5,301 bales on board. Steamers from St. Louis usually made six round trips annually to Little Rock while New Orleans steamers made one to four trips annually to meet the demand for the transport of cotton. When river levels on the Arkansas were too low to allow for steamers, keelboats were used. Under favorable conditions, a keelboat made a round trip between Little Rock and Fort Smith in approximately twenty days.[17]

During the nineteenth century as Dardanelle increasingly grew in importance as a port town and then as the major port between Little Rock and Fort Smith by the mid-nineteenth century, improvements in the frequency of travel and the cargo potential of steamers directly affected the development and prosperity of the town and of the planters and farmers in the outlying rural areas (see Appendix, fig. 3). Although steamboats operating on the Arkansas River prior to the Civil War had an average life of between three and four years as accidents were common and frequently deadly, by the 1850s steamers had become the most desirable, comfortable, and efficient mode of transportation available. This only increased during the twenty years following the Civil War.[18] Steamers were the business lifeline for port towns like Dardanelle as they efficiently transported freight into town, shipped farm goods from town, and engaged in a busy passenger business. The importance and necessity of the steamer was only modified and ultimately replaced by the arrival of the railroads beginning in the 1870s to the early 1900s.

For important port towns like Dardanelle, the busiest port between Little Rock and Fort Smith from the 1840s to the early 1920s, the steamer was essential. The town operated two wharfs, the Upper Wharf, named the Quay, situated at the end of what is now Quay Street; and the Lower Wharf, located at the end of what is now called Market Street but was known as South Main Street until the early twentieth century. As farm goods rolled into town from the Dardanelle Bottoms via mule, oxen, or horse-drawn wagons, goods were offloaded at the wharfs and shipped out. Middlemen—such as cotton factors—and farmers were paid and money flowed into local businesses. The economic lifeblood of Dardanelle and the Bottoms was regenerated. These same busy wharfs unloaded goods destined for local Dardanelle merchants' shelves and customers' homes. Thus the Arkansas River and its steamers were essential. The agricultural activities of the Dardanelle Bottoms and the business activity of the town of Dardanelle would not have been possible without the Arkansas River, the primary means of transportation.

During the antebellum period many of the steamboat crews ("roustabouts" or men doing any required work) were composed of Irish or German immigrants. Once the steamer docked and the men were free of their duties, most went directly to the local saloons. The presence of these "tough men" and much free-flowing liquor added to Dardanelle's colorful reputation. After the Civil War, many African Americans found employment as steamer crew members. As their patronage of the white saloons was not welcomed, several African American drinking establishments began to appear in Dardanelle.[19]

If steamers were essential for traversing rivers, the ferry boat was equally crucial for crossing directly from one side of the river to the other, given the fact that very few bridges existed on the Arkansas River and none at Dardanelle. There was a ferry boat operation between Dardanelle and Norristown operating as early as 1841. Three ferry crossings operated in the Dardanelle Bottoms: Reed's Ferry operating from Fowler, a Carden Bottom community, which crossed the Arkansas River, and Lacy's Ferry, which crossed the Petit Jean River near the community of Pontoon as did Crain's Ferry during the late nineteenth century. Until permanent roads and bridges were constructed, ferry boats were an essential link in the transportation network allowing for the passage of people and goods.

## Frontier Agriculture

During the antebellum period Dardanelle and the Dardanelle Bottoms, like much of Arkansas, can best be characterized as a frontier area with definite southern roots. As such, slavery was certainly present.[20] In 1840, the typical slaveholders in Yell County owned no more than a family of slaves. Thus most slaves lived among a white majority within the setting of a family farm. There were only 82 slaves out of a total population of 1,247 in Yell County in 1840.[21] During the late 1830s, farmers had begun to grow cotton, and by 1850, Yell County ranked twenty-third in cotton production among the state's fifty-one counties. At this time, cotton was the only cash crop being produced in Yell County.[22]

In 1850 the farmers in Yell County were split with approximately 50 percent growing cotton exclusively and 50 percent growing a variety of crops including some cotton on subsistence-oriented farms. In fact, these subsistence farmers produced 60 percent of the county's 1850 cotton crop as well as a fairly impressive record of other crops: 13,202 bushels of oats, 5,208 bushels of wheat, 3,828 bushels of Irish potatoes, and 8,984 bushels of sweet potatoes. Most of these subsistence farmers lived in the uplands or mountain valleys of Yell County since these areas provided a healthier climate, resulting in less malaria or yellow fever. On a typical upland Yell County farm in 1850, an average of one-half bale of cotton and approximately thirty bushels of corn was produced per acre.[23]

An example of an early pioneer family was the Hart family from Tennessee, who homesteaded in the Mount George area of Yell County during the 1840s (see Appendix, fig. 6). They also farmed land in the Upper Dardanelle Bottoms and eventually moved to that location although the mosquitoes posed a constant irritant. The mother died and an aunt, Elizabeth Gayle Hart, raised the Hart children. Several years later when the father came to reclaim his children, the children refused to leave their "auntie." Elizabeth Gayle Hart along with her sister continued to work the land in the Upper Bottoms, and she continued to add to her holdings, eventually employing laborers to work her land in Carden Bottom and the Upper Bottoms. She never married and became the family matriarch. When one of the children she raised reached adulthood and was asked to marry a young man from Fort Smith, Howard Hunt, "Auntie" Hart announced her acceptance of the marriage only if Hunt would come to the Dardanelle Bottoms and farm. Thus, Rebecca Jane "Bessie" and Howard Hunt began their farming career in the Bottoms and over the decades added more land as did their son, Charles. By the 1950s the Hunt family owned and farmed approximately 900 acres in the Dardanelle Bottoms.[24]

In contrast to the uplands, the Bottoms of Yell County yielded about one bale of cotton and up to seventy bushels of corn per acre, twice the yields of the county's uplands. The floodplains of the Bottoms with its rich soil produced large yields but posed challenging problems. Bottom lands were difficult to clear of the huge stands of hardwoods, and their swampy nature was a breeding ground for a variety of deadly diseases and health problems. Thus, in 1850 Dardanelle and the Dardanelle Bottoms (then the Dardanelle Township and the Galley Rock Township, respectively) contained less than 25 percent of Yell County's slave population and produced less than 17 percent of the county's cotton.[25]

## Slavery

By 1860 Yell County contained 998 slaves. Whereas in 1850 the largest single category of slave owners (32 percent) held only one slave, by 1860 the largest slave owner category held two to four slaves (31 percent). In 1860 only 15 percent of all Yell County farmers owned slaves, and yet these farmers produced 60 percent of the cotton produced. The top cotton producers were all slave owners, and eight Yell County slave owners were classified as planters owning twenty or more slaves. Six of these eight planters (Samuel Dickens, B. J. Jacoway, R. E. Waters, Thomas Waters, William Nunnelley, and Alexander Williams) came from Dardanelle or the Dardanelle Bottoms. Indeed, in 1860 Dardanelle and the Dardanelle Bottoms accounted for 46 percent of the county's slave owners who owned 59 percent of the county's slaves and produced 39 percent of the county's cotton.[26] Thus by 1860 Dardanelle and the Bottoms, while still frontier like in many ways, had become highly involved in the southern cotton economy and were therefore quite similar to their Arkansas Delta cohorts in the eastern portion of the state.

Still the majority of the county's farmers and a sizable percentage of its slaves lived in the uplands, not in the Bottoms. Only two of the county's total of eight planters (individuals who owned twenty or more slaves) were from the uplands, Samuel Cole and John Howell. In 1860 the uplands of Yell County were dominated by small slaveholders and non-slaveholding farmers. These groups produced, on average, approximately one bale of cotton annually. Cotton sales allowed for the payment of property taxes and the purchase of a year's supply of salt, coffee, and ammunition. The rest of what was needed for the survival of an upland family and its livestock was grown, trapped, or shot. In these mountainous areas of the county, a small slaveholding farmer usually worked alongside his slaves in the field and fished and hunted with them. Owners and slaves generally lived in adjoining and similar log cabins. Other than the obvious, the distinction between slave and slave owner in the uplands of Yell County was not pronounced in that both engaged in similar hard work in order to survive.[27]

One is able to discern distinct differences by 1860 in the lives of Yell County's upland farms and those in the Dardanelle Bottoms. Whereas in the Dardanelle Bottoms planters and slave owners worked for profits and production of cash crops (cotton), the upland farmers were either non-slave owners or small slave owners using sales to ease their workload as they produced food and fodder for their primarily subsistence farms.

## Civil War

The population of Dardanelle in 1860 included 239 white residents and 74 slaves. The town had acquired a "boomtown" reputation as an important river port and emerging trade center for the surrounding farming area (see Appendix, fig. 1). Dardanelle was a weekly port stop for steamboats from New Orleans, Memphis, and Little Rock, and enjoyed a trade in whiskey, gin, and cotton. The town sported three taverns, several mercantile businesses and cotton gins, three churches (Baptist, Methodist, and Presbyterian), one weekly newspaper, a Masonic Lodge, several attorneys, one doctor, and a school. Most of the town's residents had migrated from Tennessee or North Carolina. Dardanelle was on the 1823 military road linking Little Rock and Fort Smith, and in 1860 it was linked by telegraph to both those towns.[28] Thus, when the Civil War began in 1861, Dardanelle's future and that of the Bottoms looked promising, even progressive.

This promise would be denied, however, as the Civil War brought destruction and chaos. Dardanelle was caught in the battles and skirmishes that raged over control of the Arkansas River, and Jayhawkers (Union supporters) and Bushwhackers (Confederate supporters) unleashed terror and violence on the civilian population. Union forces took control of Dardanelle in October 1862, and military actions in Dardanelle and the Bottoms occurred on four additional occasions between September 1863 and January 1865.[29]

Between January 14 and January 17, 1865, a Confederate force of more than 1,500 men and one artillery piece attempted to wrest control of the Arkansas River at Dardanelle from the Union forces who were dug in with two artillery pieces in stockades guarding the roads into town. Shells exploded in and around Dardanelle, and two Union steamers, the *New Chippewa* and the *Annie Jacob,* were struck and destroyed while the Union steamer *Lotus* was severely damaged. On January 22, 1865, Union forces in Dardanelle were reinforced by the arrival of the First Kansas Colored Infantry and the Fifty-Fourth US Colored Infantry Regiment. Dardanelle remained in Union hands as did that section of the Arkansas River. This and an accompanying action at Ivey's Ford eighteen miles upriver from Clarksville, Arkansas, marked the last serious Confederate attempts to challenge Union control over the Arkansas River.[30]

These military engagements and the Union occupation of Dardanelle resulted in much destruction and intense hardship for civilians. The original Presbyterian Church, erected in approximately 1855, "was taken to pieces and used for Army purposes when Col. Brooks was trying to take Dardanelle in the winter of 1864–65. Col. A. J. Bryan, U.S. Army, gave the order to tear it down."[31] The Dardanelle Baptist Church was also destroyed by Union forces, and many local residents left Dardanelle in order to avoid the perils of the fighting and destruction as well as the near-starvation conditions.

While the residents of Dardanelle suffered greatly during the Civil War, those in the Bottoms also experienced trauma and hardship. As mentioned earlier, Elizabeth Gayle Hart was a young woman living approximately three miles south of Dardanelle in the Upper Dardanelle Bottoms. She and her younger sister were attempting by themselves to make a go of their family's homestead when the Civil War began. "Lizzie" Hart suffered at the hands of passing Union forces. Despite her pleas, the Union commanding officer ordered the destruction of the Hart property. The soldiers took her only horse, which she needed for plowing, stole all the meat from the smokehouse, plundered the root cellar taking all its stored provisions, and even dug out a foot or so of earth from the smokehouse floor so the Hart sisters would not be able to boil the dirt in order to retrieve any salt residue for future use. Lizzie Hart and her younger sister were left with almost nothing to eat and no way to plant a future crop. It is not surprising that as Confederate troops scattered from Dardanelle during the 1863–1865 skirmishes, Lizzie and other Confederate women took wounded soldiers to Moore's Hill to escape from the Union forces and seek a safe haven for the wounded soldiers. Moore's Hill is five miles south of Dardanelle and its elevation of some 400 feet above the surrounding land afforded a commanding 360-degree view for several miles as well as additional safety due to its steep terrain and sudden rise in elevation. Young Lizzie Hart's Civil War experiences colored her lifelong view of the United States Government, understandably a highly negative view, which was passed on to future generations of her family.[32]

Hart distrusted paper money, trusting gold instead as she would frequently remark to her family that "gold talks." She kept her wealth in the form of gold, which she kept in a velvet purse because she also distrusted banks. Decades later, during the Great Depression, Hart told her nephew by marriage, Howard Hunt, to immediately withdraw all his money from the banks. He did, and two days later the Farmers' Bank in Dardanelle closed. The Hunt family survived the Depression without selling or losing any property and actually purchased some land paid for with gold from the velvet purse. When the government ordered citizens to turn in all their gold reserves, "Auntie" Hart turned in only half of hers, remarking to her family, "I'll give the lying bastards half of it." This was the only time anyone ever remembered Ms. Hart using profanity. Decades later, in the 1990s, when the estate of Elizabeth Gayle Hart's great-nephew (Charles Hunt) was settled among his four children, the contents of the velvet purse were divided among Ms. Hart's great-grand nieces and nephews, who then deposited their shares in safety deposit boxes.[33]

In addition to the desperation of a harassed civilian population, local soldiers also suffered during the Civil War enduring wartime fears, wounds, loneliness, and depression. A letter dated June 1, 1862, written by Confederate soldier J. T. McGuire to his mother, Elizabeth McGuire, who lived near Dardanelle, reveals the writer's despondency. McGuire wrote that he "has nothing important to write" but wishes to see all the members of his family, although he does not know when he will be home but certainly not in time to attend to the wheat harvest. He closes with "my pen is bad, my ink is pale, my love for you shall never fail." J. T. McGuire never returned from the war.[34]

If the wartime destruction and loss of life were not sufficiently abhorrent, then the danger and woe brought on by Jayhawk activities made the tragedy of war seem almost interminable. Numerous bands of thugs, "primarily freebooters [who] terrorized the area with their killing and robbing," operated throughout Yell County. One of the most notorious of these was William J. "Wild Bill" Heffington, a Confederate deserter, Union sympathizer, and native of Yell County. Wild Bill led 125 men, mostly Confederate army deserters, who occasionally aided Union forces and more generally played havoc on the civilian population. Between 1863 and 1865, this band of Jayhawkers caused a panic in Dardanelle as it boldly conducted raids within three miles of the town.[35] Bushwhackers, Confederate sympathizing thugs, engaged in similar terror activities in the southern and western sections of Yell County.[36]

In 1863 W. R. Knight, a proprietor of a small store located at Dutch Creek near Danville in western Yell County, was making his way to Dardanelle accompanied by a neighbor named Pledger in order to take the oath of allegiance to the Union, a requirement if Knight was to continue operating his business. One mile west of Chickalah, a small village a few miles west of Dardanelle, Knight and Pledger were detained by Union troops who, not wanting to be troubled with the two men, handed them over to the Putman gang, Bushwhackers, who immediately shot and killed both men. The Putman gang did not want Knight and Pledger, former Confederate supporters, to take the Union oath and thus be able to resume their daily lives. Their murders were simply war-related revenge killings. Their bodies were left near the road where they fell. Later, after hearing of the murders, members of Knight's family retrieved his body and buried his remains at Dutch Creek. Pledger was buried some fifteen feet away from the roadside spot where he was killed.[37] This incident illustrates how confusing and difficult the Civil War years were.

Knight, Pledger, and all those harmed by Jayhawkers and Bushwhackers were just as surely Civil War casualties as were those who died on the battlefield. Certainly the civilians of Yell County, like Elizabeth Gayle Hart and her sister, suffered grievously and in numerous, diverse ways from the Civil War in all of its incarnations.

## Reconstruction

When the hostilities officially ended in April 1865 and the Reconstruction era unfolded, the residents of Dardanelle and the

Bottoms began to recreate some degree of normal daily life. The massive amount of dislocation caused by the war, coupled with new migration into the area during Reconstruction, resulted in a new wave of local residents. Many of these new postwar transplants arrived in Dardanelle and the Bottoms from South Carolina, Mississippi, Alabama, Georgia, and Texas. A letter dated March 16, 1866, postmarked from Dardanelle and written by Captain J. E. Lindsay, formerly of Jonesville, South Carolina, to his friend James Reed Eison, who lived in South Carolina, offers insight into the minds and motives of these new migrants. Lindsay notes that prior to the Civil War "these people here were living in clover. They had everything necessary. They lived easy." Now in 1866, Lindsay continued, labor was scarce and expensive and most of the Negroes are sharecropping. Bottom land, consisting of black sandy loam soil, was renting for $6 an acre and could be purchased for $255 an acre. This land was expensive not only because it could produce wonderful yields, but also because its accessibility to the navigable river made it doubly desirable. Lindsay estimated that the Bottoms could produce 2,000 pounds of cotton per acre (four 500-pound bales). He noted that some of the Bottom fields have been in cultivation for thirty years and are still producing 1,500 pounds of cotton and 100 bushels of corn per acre annually. He also told Eison that wild game of all kinds was plentiful and that the land was deemed good for stock. In reference to the war, Lindsay noted that the people of the Dardanelle area were "divided" with about 25 percent supporting the Union. These folks were called "mountain Boomers" by their neighbors and now "a good many of the Boomers have been killed since the war, some have left and now this is as peaceful country as any." The frontier nature of the area also garnered Lindsay's interest. He noted that a buggy or carriage in the country "would be a curiosity" and that most people ride horses or families are loaded into farm wagons to go to church. The inhabitants are "generally rough looking" and the "wimen [women] are not pretty, but they are clever." He found the people to be "honorable and generous." The Bottoms, he concluded, was a good place "for a young man who will take hole [hold]." There was good land to rent and good houses were available. However, Lindsay advised any young man moving to Yell County "to bring his wife with him" as the women here are not particularly attractive.[38]

During Arkansas's Reconstruction era (1865–1874) Dardanelle and the Bottoms began to recover. A visitor to Dardanelle from Texas in 1869 offers a glimpse of the condition of the town. Dardanelle had one newspaper, the *Arkansas Transcript*, a weekly paper with a yearly subscription rate of $2.50 and the only newspaper operating in Yell, Pope, Johnson, Pike, Conway, Scott, and Perry Counties. This Texas visitor also noted the town's six attorneys, three teachers, one tuition-based private academy, and seven retail mercantile establishments specializing in various goods from whiskey and drugs to harnesses and groceries. County government was operating with the offices of sheriff, county clerk, tax assessor, treasurer, and probate and circuit judges elected and all were performing their duties.[39]

By 1872 obvious growth had occurred. Town government had been reestablished as Dardanelle had a mayor and a city recorder. The Masonic Lodge, Bright Star Lodge 213, was operating. Mail was being received three times a week on Tuesdays, Thursdays, and Saturdays, and Dardanelle again had weekly steamboat service. The United States Land Office, located on the corner of Front and Locust Streets, was manned by a registrar and a receiver. The town still had one private tuition-based school and one operating newspaper. Dardanelle had one medical doctor, five attorneys, fourteen retail mercantile businesses with two also operating a wholesale division, a jeweler, barber, hardware store, drugstore, skating rink, blacksmith, hotel, boot/shoe store, house/sign painting business, auctioneer, private boarding-house, livery stable, building contractor and milling plant operation, photographer/picture gallery, and two competing river wharf operations.[40] It appears that by 1872, Dardanelle was beginning to emerge from the devastation of the war years.

Despite this obvious upswing in business investment and activity, crime continued to be a major problem until near the end of the Reconstruction era or just beyond. This criminal activity persisted in some areas of the state, such as Conway County, well into the early twentieth century as residents settled old Civil War grudges with arson, assault, and murder.[41] In Yell County much of the activity that had been fueled by Civil War hostilities ended by approximately 1880.

Charles H. McGuire first arrived in Dardanelle as a boy with his family in 1869. He saw the town as "nothing but a straggling village with some 300 to 400 inhabitants, and most of them about as poor as my father was." Dardanelle and the countryside were, McGuire noted, "not yet recovered from the ravages of the Civil War ... and Reconstruction ... and was at the hands of outlaws, bandits and thieves who hesitated at nothing, but outraged, murdered, robbed and burned at will."[42]

McGuire specifically remembered how violent life was in the Dardanelle downtown business district.

> From South Main Street north to Pine Street, between Front Street and the river, was an open square, called a "quay" and in it a number of horse-racks. Many times have I seen bands of outlaws, composed of both white and negroes, all armed with at least two six-shooters and a bowie knife, ride into town, hitch their horses at those racks and start out for a season of drunkenness and debauchery. . . . I pray God that I may never again witness such sights as were enacted on the streets of Dardanelle at that time. These acts of lawlessness continued, though in a diminishing degree, until 1874, when the State was wrested from the hands of this lawless element and peace, law and order began to be restored.[43]

The growth of Dardanelle and the Bottoms during this transitional period of Reconstruction was fairly dramatic. In mid-1865 Dardanelle only had approximately 200 people as many residents had left the town and the surrounding area due to battles that included Union cannonballs shot down Quay Street toward Dardanelle's main river wharf, wide-scale destruction of property including the Union troops' dismantling of the Baptist Church for firewood and the total razing of the Presbyterian Church, and near starvation for the remaining trapped townspeople. By 1870 Dardanelle's population had increased to 926 with new residents arriving from Georgia, Mississippi, Alabama, and South Carolina.[44] In 1872 the Presbyterians built a new church on Pecan Street, a brick structure referred to by many as "the little red brick church."[45] Three years later, a new local newspaper, the *Dardanelle Independent,* went into operation. Although it would have a questionable early record due to its first editor/owner's acquittal on second-degree murder charges, the paper featured early Populist style editorials calling for equal treatment for and the joint alliance of small farmers and working men. The newspaper survived for several years and was purchased by more conservative owners ultimately renaming it the *Independent Arkansian*. It continued to develop a readership while providing much-needed information to its subscribers as well as advertising space for Dardanelle businesses.[46] Slowly the people of Dardanelle and the Bottoms were pulling themselves out of the morass created by the Civil War and Reconstruction.

## Conclusion

The first six decades of Dardanelle and the Bottoms featured a frontier environment, untamed and opportunistic. Its residents were "men on the make"—farmers, planters, businessmen, river roustabouts, and slaves. They settled here for the land and the river, seeking profits and hoping for a better future. In many ways they could be characterized as Jacksonians. The dislocation, death, and destruction caused by the Civil War and Reconstruction severely challenged them. By the late 1870s, economic distress and racial inequality remained as old problems yet unaddressed. During the next three decades, 1880 to 1910, Dardanelle and the Bottoms would continue to grow and develop as the unfinished business of their beginnings remained to cloud their possibilities and shape the contours of their lives.

## CHAPTER 2

# Reestablishment, 1880–1910

*Numerous reports come to us of destitution, on the bread question. While a few have surplus of corn and many are already out and cannot get for love or money. Money is exceedingly scarce.... The merchants have scarcely any cash trade, and are taking mortgages by the wholesale every day from the farmers, who come in and ask for assistance in making the coming crop.*

INDEPENDENT ARKANSIAN,
*February 1882*

*The cotton crop in Carden's Bottom is better than it has been since 1875 ... waist high to man head high ... too high for a coon to climb.*

INDEPENDENT ARKANSIAN,
*July 1882*

*[D]own at the Stump last Saturday night there was a smashing of bottles and a chawing of ears. Several of the 'boys' were right in the middle of the fracas but they checked out all right Sunday morning, condition excepted.*

DARDANELLE POST,
*May 1883*

*The Arkansas River is on a rampage . . . the Bottoms all under water while Dardanelle lost 1200 feet of telephone and telegraph wires . . . bad caving of the riverbank at Neely . . . post office, stores, gin mill, church, schoolhouse and numerous residences are lost.*

DARDANELLE POST-DISPATCH,
*January 1909*

## Introduction

In 1880 Dardanelle's population of 748 and the Bottoms' population of 363 (66 African Americans, 75 mulattos, and 222 whites) faced the future with determined optimism. The challenges to be addressed during the next thirty years would be formidable. So also would be the opportunities. New rural communities were created by a determined, hard-driven people, and their relationship to the town of Dardanelle would be of paramount importance to both (see Appendix, fig. 6).

## Bohemians

During 1877 and 1878 and into the early 1880s, new foreign immigrants settled near Dardanelle. These Moravian, Slovakian, and Bohemian families settled just west of Dardanelle, and while a few were coal miners initially finding work in Johnson and later in Pope Counties, most were farmers, quite good farmers. These newcomers were primarily Roman Catholic and brought new cultural habits, languages, and fashions to Dardanelle. Hard working and law abiding, the "Bohemians" of Dardanelle were quickly accepted by others. They formed and participated in their own fraternal and social organizations, which continued to function for some fifty years. One of these organizations was a community brass band that provided musical entertainment for numerous local political and community gatherings in and around Dardanelle.[1] While there were only 17 foreign-born people residing in Yell County in 1870, by 1880 and 1890 these numbers had increased to 117 and 133, respectively.[2] By 1880 Arkansas's entire foreign-born population was only 10,350, a very small percentage of the state's total population of 802,525. Efforts to encourage foreign immigration to Arkansas generally proved unsuccessful while white and African American migration to Arkansas was recorded at 367,075 between 1860 and 1880.[3]

Dardanelle's local newspaper, the *Independent Arkansian*, was busy promoting the area. The town was described as "a lovely town of 2,000 inhabitants . . . the principal town between Little Rock and Fort Smith . . . doing a heavy inland trade," having "good honest people from Kentucky, Tennessee, Alabama, Georgia, Mississippi, North and South Carolina, Missouri, Indiana, and Virginia," and having schools running from three to ten months yearly in every country village as well as religious denominations established with regular services of "Baptists, Methodists, Presbyterians, Episcopalians, Catholics, and Lutherans."[4] This public relations promotional exaggerated the population and probably other features as well, and also touted rural Yell County: "backcountry and bottoms which are fine and very productive" with homestead lands to be purchased "for $1.25 an acre or $2.50 if on the railroad line property."[5] This was a reference to the Little Rock and Fort Smith Railroad Company, which ran within approximately five miles of Dardanelle on the north side of the Arkansas River. The article concluded that Dardanelle, as well as the rest of Yell County, offered desirable inducements to the "immigrant, farmer and mechanic."[6]

## Transportation

Given this sense of optimism based primarily on hope for a better future, some new blood settling in the area, and a strong self-promotional effort, the residents of Dardanelle and the Bottoms faced their future. One major challenge to their success, however, was their need for improved transportation. Dardanelle and the Bottoms had always relied on the Arkansas River, which was passable during most of the year by steamboat or flatboat, and on the Petit Jean River, which was generally navigable by flatboat. During the railroad-building craze promoted by Republican Reconstruction administrations, the Little Rock and Fort Smith Railroad began construction in 1869 and was completed in 1879. The rail ran five miles north of Dardanelle on the north side of the Arkansas River, opposite from Dardanelle and the Bottoms.[7] During the last decades of the nineteenth century as the Bottoms and Dardanelle grew in population and agricultural production, improved transportation needs required decisive action.

Since no bridge spanned the Arkansas River at Dardanelle, a particular transportation challenge was connecting the trade and freight of Dardanelle and the Bottoms to the railroad across the river. Until 1891, ferry service or steamers carried passengers and freight over river to and from Dardanelle. On the north side, travel then proceeded on a poor and frequently impassable road that continued on to the Little Rock and Fort Smith Railroad Depot. As noted in 1882, "the roads between Dardanelle and Russellville are in a most wretched condition . . . the vast amount of travel has cut the road into gullies until they are almost impassible [sic]. We certainly need a railroad!"[8] The idea of a rail linking North Dardanelle (the area on the north side of and immediately adjacent to the Arkansas River and directly across the river from Dardanelle) to the Little Rock and Fort Smith Railroad at Russellville began to develop traction with continued appeals for a rail link "for keeping up the freight hauling, when it has been so killing on stock, destructive to wagons, and fatiguing on teamsters, and expenses are high and receipts light."[9]

Between September 1, 1882, and June 1, 1883, 15,000 bales of cotton were shipped from Dardanelle. These bales had to be ferried across the Arkansas River, hauled by wagon from North Dardanelle to Russellville, and then loaded onto freight cars of the Little Rock and Fort Smith Railroad.[10] A rail line from North Dardanelle to Russellville, it was determined, would better facilitate the economic growth of Dardanelle. Profit was the motivation for improved transportation.

On September 30, 1882, a meeting of Dardanelle townspeople was held at the Yell County Courthouse in Dardanelle to develop plans to connect the town to the railroad depot in Russellville. This link would give both the freight and people from Dardanelle and the Bottoms access to Fort Smith to the west and Little Rock and Memphis to the east. The Dardanelle businessmen who called and chaired the meeting established a three-man committee to raise financial support for a railway line and to "confer with the Fort Smith Railroad Company to secure the co-operation of that company in building this road."[11] In order to maintain the "bustling appearance on our streets with goods coming in," Dardanelle businessmen knew that they had to devise an adequate and improved transportation link to ship agricultural goods (see Appendix, fig. 7).[12]

The agricultural goods produced in the Bottoms had traditionally been shipped by steamboat or flatboats if the river levels allowed, and river traffic would not cease if a new railroad connected Dardanelle to the greater markets. In fact, steamer trade continued well into the twentieth century.[13] A rail connection would enhance trade and travel opportunities and, therefore, profits for local businesses. With cotton selling at between 9.0 to 9.5 cents a pound and corn at 15 cents a bushel by the end of September 1882, any means of increasing profitability were worth pursuing.

On February 13, 1883, stock in the new Dardanelle and Russellville Railway Corporation (D&R) began to be issued at $100 a share. Dardanelle businessmen purchased the majority of the stock, and the new railway was initially capitalized with a $45,000 investment.[14] The Dardanelle and Russellville Railroad, a short-line railway five miles in length, began operations on August 15, 1883, as a crowd of approximately 4,000 to 5,000 people celebrated with 2,600 pounds of barbecue, parades, brass bands, a baseball game and, of course, speeches.[15] By 1885 a total of 273 shares of D&R stock had been issued.

After 1891 when the Dardanelle Pontoon Bridge was constructed, the Dardanelle Transfer and Storage Company, located on Front Street in Dardanelle, shipped freight and carried passengers by hack (either wagon or carriage) across the bridge to the D&R Depot in North Dardanelle. Prior to the installation of the Pontoon Bridge, all freight, passengers, and other goods such as the US mail had to be ferried across the Arkansas River to the D&R Depot.[16]

By January 1885 the D&R made two trips daily to Russellville connecting with both the east- and west-bound trains of the Little Rock and Fort Smith line. Trains departed Russellville for Dardanelle at 11:30 a.m. and 4:30 p.m., and trains left Dardanelle for Russellville at 9:00 a.m. and 2:30 p.m. daily.[17] The D&R continued to be controlled and managed by Dardanelle businessmen until January 13, 1900, when a group of northeastern financiers purchased the operation and changed the name from the Dardanelle and Russellville Railway to the Dardanelle and Russellville Railroad. Local residents continued to simply call it the D&R. Operations continued smoothly during and after this change in management/ownership.[18] The D&R is in operation today as it has been continuously since it opened in August 1883.

A momentous transportation improvement for the region was the construction of the Pontoon Bridge at Dardanelle that opened in 1891. The ferry boats used prior to this to transfer goods and people over the Arkansas River could not operate during exceedingly low or high water levels. As such, without some sort of bridge connection, Dardanelle, its citizens, and its agricultural goods became isolated when river levels were extreme. The D&R Company welcomed the Pontoon Bridge as it would also greatly facilitate their trade.

Work on the Pontoon Bridge began in October 1890. Consisting of seventy-two wooden pontoons—or enclosed boats floating on the river—supporting an 18-foot wide wooden roadway, the bridge spanned 2,208 feet across the river. The pontoons were grouped into twelve sections of six boats each with each section fastened to the floating bridge. Anchoring all of this were wooden poles placed in three large groups at intervals across the river and driven into the riverbed, thus serving as pilings. Richard Joseph Keilch, born in Dublin, Ireland, in 1858, had railroad bridge-building experience and served as the foreman for the pile-driving crews. He then became the operations manager for the Pontoon Bridge, a position he held until the structure was replaced in 1929, and which he took very seriously during the thirty-eight years of operation of the Pontoon Bridge.

When the Pontoon Bridge opened in 1891, it was the longest pontoon bridge over running water in the world, and its construction cost was approximately $25,000. A toll bridge, the initial rates were 5 cents for a person walking, 5 cents for a cow or a horse, 15 cents for a person on horseback, 25 cents for a single buggy, and 35 cents for a double buggy. With the arrival of automobiles, the rates were 10 cents for a person walking, 25 cents for a person on horseback, 50 cents for a coupe, and 75 cents for a touring car. The Pontoon Bridge was frequently "out" due to high river flows, rising waters, and floods. Nonetheless, it served as a vital link between Dardanelle northward for thirty-eight years and played an important role in the operations of the D&R with its Dardanelle freight and passenger transfer service located on the northeast corner of Front and Locust Streets.[19]

Another transportation improvement became a reality in 1907 with the opening of the Dardanelle, Ola, and Southern Railway (DO&S) that linked Dardanelle to the Choctaw Railroad, which ran through Ola some twelve miles south of Dardanelle. The DO&S was soon acquired by the Rock Island Railroad, which continued to provide a connection to Little Rock and Fort Smith on the south side of the Arkansas River (see Appendix, fig. 7).

## Agriculture

While Dardanelle businessmen were actively creating an improved transportation network in order to assure their continued prosperity, the inhabitants of the Bottoms were struggling with economic uncertainties. Their reality during the 1880s was far different from that of their town peers. By 1883 farmers in the Bottoms, and indeed throughout Arkansas, were organizing themselves in order to demand the means to control cotton prices given rollercoaster price fluctuations: 15 cents a pound in the 1870s to 9 cents a pound in the 1880s to 5 cents a pound in the 1890s.[20] Business interests, mainly "cotton buyers, the railroad men, merchants, and the lawyers" prospered from the 1880s through 1900, while southern farmers were paying the highest freight rates in the country and were frequently charged outrageous prices by monopolistic ginners and competing furnishing merchants.[21] Worldwide overproduction of cotton kept prices depressed for the farmer, while simultaneously with every cotton wagon prosperity flowed into the towns as furnishing merchants, business houses, cotton factors, and shippers profited.

In early 1882 the condition of farmers in the Bottoms was becoming quite alarming. While they cleared and fenced more land so as to increase their production in the hopes of improving their situation, the realities of daily life for the farmers were trying as "money was scarce, bread stuff short, and the people are hard run."[22] During the last two decades of the nineteenth century, the optimistic belief that "there will always be a better tomorrow for those who work hard" was altered in many farmers' minds, and many began to organize in an effort to protect themselves from unscrupulous capitalists.

Traditionally, farmers had sought commercial opportunities but had relied primarily on self-sufficiency, family labor, and the support and assistance of neighbors and kin. Thus, they had frequently not engaged in the most aggressive commercial actions. Their world was dominated by weather, seasons, and naturally occurring events like floods and illnesses. Farmers were accustomed to functioning as individuals, glorying in their independence from corporate and governmental rules, in loyalty to family, and close farm community networks. Consequently, the activities of the town were generally foreign to the people of the farms.[23]

The farmers of the Dardanelle Bottoms generally fit this description. Life was governed by the season, and weather dictated one's activities. The planting, weeding, and harvesting of different crops; the slaughtering of hogs and maintaining of the smokehouse; the winter clearing of land; tree and stump removal; fence and tool repairs; and caring for the livestock all posed the rhythms of the farmer's life and all were dictated by seasons and weather. Likewise, the farmwife's work was also controlled by the same factors. Seasonal work included preserving foods, tending the garden, caring for livestock, and overseeing the orchard. The woman's seasonal work was in addition to her "everyday jobs" of child rearing, food preparation, and housekeeping duties as well as any community activities, both church and social, in which she participated.[24]

Thus, while the farmer and his family were not totally ignorant of the profit-minded motives and activities of the townspeople, the farm life was attuned to a seasonal rhythm that tended to somewhat alter the goals and forces governing the daily lives of rural people as compared to town people. Both sought to prosper economically, but how to achieve that end was altered by the nature of farming versus business.

Regardless of the cultural differences created by the context of rural versus town life, it is clear that the town and the country lived in total interdependence. The town was dependent on the country for the production of agricultural goods, and the country was dependent on the town's businessmen for financing and marketing. Without the farm commodities, the town would have little reason to exist with fewer goods to market and fewer customers to serve. This relationship is evident in a study of the prosperity of Dardanelle and the prosperity of the Bottoms, as every local newspaper edition well into the 1940s quoted the going prices of cotton and other agricultural commodities ranging from wheat to corn to turnips to strawberries to peaches. The people of Dardanelle understood that their livelihoods and prosperity were directly related to, and resulted from, the agricultural production of the Dardanelle Bottoms: "Cotton has begun coming in and our streets show more life. Business will boom up in a week or two."[25] In August 1883 prospects for a fine cotton crop were high, and Dardanelle businessmen had great "expectations for a lively season" as merchants quickly laid in additional inventories of groceries, boots, shoes, and household goods. In addition, the livery stable and the machine shop prepared for an anticipated onslaught of rural customers, with all such activities indicating "a confidence in the future of the town."[26] This essential town/country interdependency sometimes resulted in a harmonious relationship and sometimes it was more conflicted, but it was always clearly a reciprocal relationship critical to both Dardanelle and the Bottoms.

A thorny issue but significant element of the town/country relationship revolved about credit. Farm credit in part was responsible for the development of the sharecropping system during the Reconstruction era as well as the pivotal role played by the furnishing merchants. For the farmer, high interest rates for farm loans could put a family in the poorhouse or turn a small farmer and his family into a tenant farmer or worse, a sharecropper.

Even as late as 1882, the nearest bank to Yell County was 150 miles away. With so many towns devoid of banks, many local merchants filled the credit/lending vacuum. These merchants became known as furnishing merchants, and there were numerous furnishing merchants operating in Dardanelle. They extended credit to the farmer allowing him to plant and harvest the crop and in doing so the furnishing merchant placed a lien on the prospective crop. When the crop was harvested, furnishing merchants profited by repayment of his loan plus interest, and some furnishing merchants also collected fees if they marketed the crop. If the crop did not make, then the farmer was in debt to the furnishing merchant who could carry the debt forward with additional interest charges being accrued or foreclose on the farm in order to resolve the debt and/or convert the farmer into a tenant or a sharecropper.[27] While this system allowed credit to flow to farmers, the interest rates could be extraordinarily high. Also, if the two contracting parties had difficulties getting along or the harvest did not materialize or it was a poor harvest, then the farmer would be in some degree of jeopardy. Thus, the farm credit system placed farmers at risk.

C. M. Freed, a major Dardanelle merchant for some twenty years and a furnishing merchant, ran a standard advertisement in every local weekly newspaper that included the sentence, "Special attention given to the buying and selling of Cotton and all products of the Farm."[28] By late 1883 some Dardanelle furnishing merchants were marketing cotton in Little Rock using the steamer *Maumelle* for transportation of their shipments rather than shipping it to New Orleans.[29] A shorter distance would result in smaller freight charges for the merchant shipping the goods. Thus the furnishing merchant collected good interest payments on his well-collateralized loans to the farmers plus, if he acted as the buyer of the crop, he then made a profit on its resale. Wealth was flowing from the producer (the rural farmer) to the financing agent (town merchant). This financing system did not involve the exchange of money but was based instead on contracts involving payments/debts for the exchange of goods and secured by a lien on the future crop.

Another problem that resulted from the crop lien system was the pressure for farmers to produce cash crops preferred by the furnishing merchant to the exclusion of engaging in diversified agriculture. In the South this meant cotton production over other more-viable crops. As such, the crop lien system exacerbated the nondiversification of southern agriculture, which in turn put the farmer at a greater financial risk given his inability to sustain the shock of market price fluctuations as well as his inability to produce the most essential crops needed for his family's survival. An illustration of this problem is evident in a report on hunger in the Dardanelle Bottoms due to the lack of corn.

> Numerous reports come to us of destitution, on the bread question. While a few have surplus of corn and many are already out and cannot get for love or money. Money is exceedingly scarce

and by the time the people get their taxes paid, money will be almost entirely layed out. The merchants have scarcely any cash trade, and are taking mortgages by the wholesale every day from the farmers, who come in and ask for assistance in making the coming crop. We regret to report such a state of affairs, we regret that such a state of affairs exists and hope for the best.[30]

The same edition of the *Independent Arkansian* reported that corn and wheat shortages in the Bottoms were causing anguish, and that the possibility of hunger and want was very real.[31]

Regardless of recurring reports on the condition of the fruit crop (mainly peaches and strawberries in Yell County) and concern over rust in the wheat crop, the true locus of the agricultural effort and interest was cotton.[32] Even if crop diversification was in their best long-term interest, farmers were always excited by the possibility of a great cotton crop. One can almost feel the farmers' excitement when reading farm reports, such as the cotton "crop in Carden Bottom is better than it has been since 1875 . . . waist high to man head high . . . too high for a coon to climb."[33] Enraptured by the glorious possibility of a return to the days of King Cotton, it was frequently too sobering to accept the reality of the cotton trap. Besides, the furnishing merchants usually demanded cotton be grown given that it was nonperishable and easily marketed.

If the lack of crop diversification was not a sufficient problem given its resulting surplus of cotton production and declining market price coupled with its cause of a lack of foodstuff production, then the distillation of corn into whiskey simply compounded the problem. Rather than grinding corn into cornmeal for food use, many farmers turned to whiskey production and its quick cash return. The *Independent Arkansian* complained as follows:

> Toomer and Cotton, Distillery No. 54 distilled 621 wine gallons of corn whiskey during the month of January . . . when the fact is considered that there is not sufficient corn in this county to bread the people, and many poor families are already destitute, is it not time to stop converting the little corn we have on hand into whiskey when it is needed so badly for bread. . . . Let the poor men of the country have the corn to feed their starving wives and children.[34]

The combined effect of nondiversified agriculture, an undue reliance on cotton, and the crop credit system frequently resulted in rural poverty and sometimes in near starvation.

The crop lien system elevated the status of the merchant as he became the primary and frequently only lender and broker/marketer of the region's primary crop. This significantly altered the dynamics of the rural to the town. The wealth flowed from the countryside into the town, *but* the origination of that wealth depended on the credit advanced by the town merchants. The crops were from the country; the credit was from the town. This is the heart, the core, of the rural/town dichotomy and its reciprocity. This relationship encapsulated an almost mercantilist dynamic with the town providing the finance/marketing needs and functioning in the dominant "mother country" role and the rural area serving as the source of raw materials and functioning in the inferior "colony" role. The relationship was dichotomous, but it was not necessarily equal.

A review of the statement of property taxes in Yell County for 1883 quickly reveals the location of property and taxable wealth. Some 308,825 acres of land were assessed at a value of $1,318,720 while the 1,239 town lots recorded were assessed at $195,720. The assessed value of cattle (12,599 total head), horses (3,342), mules (1,361), sheep (2,881), hogs (23,189), and wagons and carriages (1,742) amounted to a total of $405,643.[35] Certainly some of the livestock, wagons, and carriages belonged to town's people, but the bulk of these items were located in and used by rural people in the production of agricultural crops and foodstuffs, the creation of wealth. Regardless of the origin of agricultural wealth, if the debtor farmer could not satisfy his financial obligation to the creditor merchant, then the farmer stood to lose his land, equipment, livestock, and way of life. The reciprocal, dichotomous relationship of rural to town could dramatically alter an individual's life and fortunes. This relationship was dynamic.

Debt created a shifting balance resulting in a steady increase in the number of sharecroppers and tenant farmers. By the early twentieth century, the sharecropping system, initially used to employ African Americans and maintain the traditional African American farm labor system following the Civil War, included increasing numbers of poor white farmers. During the period following the Civil War until the

1920s, most landless white farmers were tenant farmers who worked a designated plot of land in exchange for a house. The furnishing merchant and crop lien system resulted in an increase in the number of new landless farmers, tenant farmers. The furnishing merchants' demands for farmers to produce specific cash crops (cotton primarily, along with some corn or wheat) resulted in the farmer's inability to adjust his crop selection regardless of market price fluctuations. Thus, as wheat fell from $1.37 a bushel in 1870 to $1.06 in 1880 to 89 cents in 1890 to 60 cents in 1895, and as corn prices declined from 40.9 cents during 1878 to 1881 to 39.8 cents in 1882 to 1885 to 29.7 cents during 1896 to 1899, an increasing number of debtor farmers lost their mortgaged land to furnishing merchants and sank into the ranks of tenant farmers, frequently working the land that they previously owned. During the period from 1880 to 1900, the percentage of tenant farmers in Arkansas increased from 30.9 percent to 45.5 percent. Racial barriers to farm ownership are also revealed in these tenancy numbers, as 74 percent of all Arkansas tenant farmers in 1900 were African Americans. At the same time, however, within Yell County only 49 percent of tenant farmers were black.[36]

## Farmers' Organizations

Farmers in the Dardanelle Bottoms responded to these challenges, as did many of their peers throughout the nation, by organizing themselves, outlining their goals, and attempting to achieve their mutual success through solidarity. The Southern Farmers' Alliance—organized in Texas between 1874 and 1877—sought to form cooperative enterprises that would assist farmer members in marketing their own crops and buying supplies on more advantageous terms. Efforts like those of the Southern Farmers' Alliance spread into Arkansas during the 1880s.[37] One earlier group, the Greenback Party, considered by some historians as representing "one aspect of the nineteenth century's 'Agrarian Revolt,'" was extremely active in Pope and Yell Counties. William Barry, a Greenback Party member who became a Republican in 1882, had been instrumental in the 1870s in organizing the Farmers' Alliance in Yell County.[38] On February 15, 1882, near Des Arc another farmers' group known as the Agricultural Wheel was organized, and in April 1883 was incorporated statewide. The Agricultural Wheel had many of the same self-help goals as the Farmers' Alliance, including using cash for purchases, crop diversification, and creating joint-stock exchanges with merchants.[39] By November 1883 the Agricultural Wheel was "growing in number and influence throughout Yell County … and had over forty lodges organized in neighboring Pope County where contracts had been secured with four merchants."[40] Yet another farmers' organization, the Brothers of Freedom, originated in 1882 in Johnson County and grew rapidly to 40,000 members including some Yell County farmers who joined the organization in September 1883. The Brothers of Freedom, which advocated the use of cooperative enterprises and cited railroads, financiers, and corporations as the exploiters of farmers, merged with the Agricultural Wheel on October 15, 1885.[41] At the time of their merger, the Agricultural Wheel had 10,000 members, 5,000 of whom were Arkansans primarily in the eastern Delta of Arkansas and the Brothers of Freedom had 40,000 members, 30,000 of which were from western Arkansas, including Yell County.

Between 1884 and 1890 the Brothers of Freedom and the Arkansas Agricultural Wheel launched a third-party political effort following their conclusion that the Democratic Party was self-serving and was ignoring the producing classes. The Union Labor Party was a powerful challenger to Democratic Party control, even though it had a short-lived existence. The efforts of the Brothers of Freedom, the Agricultural Wheel, and the Union Labor Party effectively united Arkansas farmers and laborers behind a platform that addressed the interests of each group while simultaneously securing the cooperation of the state Republican Party and securing significant support from African Americans from 1884 to 1892.[42]

Any alliance that would serve to strengthen the Republican Party while cementing the loyalty and votes of farmers, workers, and African Americans was the proverbial "worst storm" imaginable for the Democratic Party. The Democratic Party responded to this political threat by creating an atmosphere of hysteria and lawlessness that included harping on the evils of Republican and African American rule in order to scare independent voters. In addition, they actively engaged in election fraud in order to maintain Democratic Party rule.[43] By 1892, just as Populism was on the rise elsewhere, efforts of this nature declined in Arkansas as the Union Labor Party collapsed due primarily to its opponent's masterful use of racism, fear tactics, demagoguery, and election fraud.[44]

The similarities and mutual appeal of these various groups is illustrated in the life of W. B. W. Heartsill, who lived near Greenwood in far-western Arkansas. In 1884 Heartsill joined the Brothers of Freedom, the Agricultural Wheel in 1885, and then the Knights of Labor in 1892. At the end of 1887 Heartsill and other members of the Farmers' Alliance from Sebastian, Scott, Logan, and Montgomery Counties formed a new agricultural association, the "Farmers, Mechanics, and Working Men" otherwise known as the Farmers' Co-operative Alliance of Arkansas. In 1890 a single Farmers' State Alliance, generally referred to as the Farmers' Union, was organized with a membership from twenty primarily northwestern Arkansas counties including Yell.[45]

Farmers in Yell County were active members in most of these agrarian groups, but the Farmers' Union proved to have the greatest lasting presence. According to an article in the *Independent Arkansian*, eighty-five Yell County farmers met on May 26, 1882, to organize a "farmers union for the purpose of advancing the agricultural interest of its members to cooperate together in protecting all their interest."[46] In the same edition, a separate brief article noted the increased acreage of food crops saying this was a "first step in the abolition of the wholesale credit system that holds the soil tiller's nose to the grindstone with a tight grip."[47] The Farmers' Union Resolutions approved by the members in August 1882 excluded from membership all lawyers, merchants, doctors, and ministers (unless also farmers), and called for reduced taxes, regulation of railway rates, opposition to monopolies of all kinds, and support for women's rights and immigration.[48]

The formation of the Farmers' Union in Yell County underscores the dire conditions present in the 1880s. Record harvest amounts were resulting in overproduction of cotton, and this was pushing down the price per pound. On February 24, 1882, cotton was selling for 7 to 10 cents a pound as opposed to just six weeks earlier when it was selling from 8 to 10.5 cents a pound. In June 1882 the annual cotton shipment from Dardanelle exceeded 15,000 bales with three months remaining in the harvest season. This 15,000 figure was 2,000 bales

above the entire 1881 local cotton shipment total.[49] Another side of this
was the number of property tax delinquencies in 1882 irrespective of
high production and, at least, in large part because of high levels of
production. In May 1882 there were 618 tracts of land in Yell County
listed as having delinquent property taxes. Of these, 23 sections were
located in Galla Rock Township, a part of the Dardanelle Bottoms.[50]
Farmers were suffering.

Regardless of depressed prices and increased production, the hold
of cotton remained strong. By the late spring of 1883, projected corn
and cotton yields looked good with more cotton being planted than
in the previous year. The same report anticipated that the wheat crop
would yield six to seven bushels per acre.[51] Records of cotton bales
purchased and shipped by Dardanelle merchants from September 1,
1882, through June 1, 1883 (with three months still to be reported for
the 1883 prime harvest) showed 15,010 total bales with four Dardanelle
merchants buying 1,000 or more bales each and a total of nineteen
Dardanelle merchants engaged in that period's cotton purchasing and
selling trade.[52]

By late September 1883 local farmers' organizations were working to spread their message. A small local farmers' group, the Sons of
Liberty, urged every member to plant at least two acres of wheat "to
prevent suffering and want next year."[53] The group was soliciting new
members explaining that they sought to create cooperatives in order
to gain special rates from railroads as well as merchants, save money
on marketing wheat and cotton, stop the ridiculing of the country
farmer and laborer, and inform farmers of ways to improve their lot.[54]
The larger Farmers' Union distributed a more specific Resolutions of
Purpose, noting that they were "not organized as a political party"
but rather as "a particular class of citizens upon whom a certain
kind of wrongs is inflicted," and intended to use peaceful methods to
relieve these wrongs in the "material, political, and social interest of
the farmer and laborer."[55] On December 20, 1883, the local *Dardanelle
Post* advertised fourteen separate land/farm auctions being executed
by the sheriff.[56] The farmers' organizations had much work yet to do.

By 1888 the Farmers' Union was the primary farmers' organization in Yell County. Also referred to as the Trade Union or Farmers'
Alliance, the group was forming joint stock corporations and coop-

eratives to sell its members' products and buy their supplies. Despite limited financial resources, the organization was proving successful.[57]

By January 1905 Yell County cotton farmers were calling for the storage of surplus cotton—currently selling at 5 cents a pound—and the following year they urged farmers to reduce cotton acreage and increase corn acreage in an effort to hold prices high.[58] The local newspaper urged both farmers and merchants, "two classes . . . whose interests overlap," to put aside the "hurtful prejudices . . . that are traced to early organization" and work together.[59] Meanwhile farmers had developed a pledge system to reduce cotton acreage, and five Dardanelle merchants were supporting and advertising this as a method for holding prices higher.[60] The Farmers' Union opened its cotton warehouse in Dardanelle in October 1907, with plans to market its members' cotton at not less than 15 cents per pound.[61] On January 30, 1908, the Farmers' Union announced that it had secured a $6,070 cash advance from Memphis cotton buyers and was holding cotton off the market until prices increased.[62] Four months later, it was announced that the Farmers' Union warehouse would be open every Saturday to accept cotton to be sold to "our home buyers" (local cotton factors and merchants) and to attract outside cotton buyers.[63] While the local Farmers' Union operated primarily as a cooperative marketing tool for its members, it also worked to forge somewhat successful links with local Dardanelle merchants. In addition, the Farmers' Union spoke against tenant farming, arguing that the farmer's ability to "price his own labor" would ultimately bring about the end of tenancy.[64]

In addition to farmers' organizations, other voices also began to speak on behalf of farmers. In early 1908 the director of the Arkansas Agricultural Experimental Stations conducted a well-attended Farmers' Institute meeting in Dardanelle, featuring educational lectures on soil fertility, crop and cultivation methods designed to double productivity, orchard management, insect protection, and poultry diversification.[65] In July 1908 the Farmers' Union launched its own educational lecture series including those held in Yell County that were designed to create more equitable farm prices through individual production of meat, bread, and foodstuffs, and the farmer's avoidance of debt.[66] This approach, while in opposition to the established farm finance method of the crop lien system and the furnishing merchant, was a direct attempt at improving the farmer's economic autonomy.

By late 1910 the Farmers' Union warehouse appeared to be a smoothly running operation as it advertised regularly for local cotton and produce and advised farmers it would hold or sell their crops as they directed with the new local bank advancing the farmer "money to pay your debts and hold your receipts." The warehouse charged a fee of 50 cents for the first month and 25 cents every month thereafter for holding a farmer's crops with the funds paying for the warehouse's insurance and its fee for marketing the crops.[67]

The Bank of Dardanelle had opened in 1895, and a second bank, the Yell County First Bank and Trust Company, opened in 1909. The latter bank expressly stated that it was to "make a specialty of the business of farmers, wage earners, women and children."[68] While the presence of area banks did not immediately or completely undercut the power of the furnishing merchant as a credit agent for farmers, the banks' presence did offer alternatives, and in time banks would become key players in the agricultural credit system in Dardanelle and the Bottoms. Although the ingredients for change were beginning to form, established, traditional patterns of behavior would not be quickly replaced.

## Threats of Violence

The potency of low cotton prices was indeed great, capable of producing all manner of misery and difficulty. During the early 1900s as cotton prices declined, episodes of radicalism increased. In October 1908 a warning notice was illegally posted on the door of the Arkansas Valley Cotton Oil Company's gin in Dardanelle. This notice warned farmers to withhold their cotton from merchants until the merchants paid 15 cents a pound or more for the cotton, and it warned gin operators to cease all operations until 15 cents a pound for cotton was a reality. The notice, written "in a steady, school-boy hand, the spelling and punctuation being incorrect," was signed with a skull and crossbones emblem apparently taken from a medicine bottle. The notice contained a direct warning: "You are notified to close your gin until further orders. We are your friends, and to keep us so head [sic] this warning. Head [sic] it not and your business might suffer. Look out if

your gin runs."[69] This "night rider" scare definitely frightened all parties and resulted in a $250 reward being immediately offered for the
perpetrator's identification and arrest. A meeting was scheduled for
the following day, October 8, 1908, between farmers and townspeople.
Approximately three hundred people packed into the Dardanelle
courthouse, and county judge G. L. Wirt was elected to chair the
meeting. Judge Wirt wasted little time in denouncing the night rider's
directive, which he said would result in gin closures, unpicked cotton
left in the fields to rot, and an economic catastrophe for the people of
Dardanelle and the farmers of the Bottoms. R. R. Jones, county vice
president of the Farmers' Union, then spoke emphatically disavow-
ing the Union's involvement in the incident and disapproving of all
illegal actions. The meeting adopted a joint resolution, which in part
read, "we, the businessmen of the town of Dardanelle, the farmers and
members of the Farmers' Union are in favor of all gins being operated
that we may save our cotton."[70]

One day prior to this October 8 Dardanelle courthouse meeting, the Union had adopted a resolution asking the merchants of Yell
County to refrain from buying any cotton for a period of thirty days
in order to control the cotton market supply and thus increase cotton prices. The people attending the October 8 meeting wanted to
know if the previous day's resolution and the night-riding incident
were related. Night riding—also known as "whitecapping" or "bald
knobbing"—denotes "extralegal acts of violence targeting select groups
and carried out by vigilantes under cover of night or disguise."[71] Those
attending the October 8 meeting in Dardanelle after a lengthy discussion adopted a second resolution, which read as follows:

> We the merchants and businesses of Dardanelle agree to not buy
> any cotton for the next thirty days, provided the farmers or pro-
> ducers sell enough cotton to pay their actual expenses of picking
> and ginning their cotton, and provided further that this action is
> to be general throughout the entire cotton producing section of
> the United States; and request the merchants and their buyers to
> adopt this course of action.[72]

This second resolution was signed by six of the major Dardanelle
merchants and was exceedingly well received by the more than
one hundred Farmers' Union members present at the October 8

Dardanelle courthouse meeting. "The readiness of the merchants to cooperate with the farmers in their efforts to secure a better price for their cotton met with hearty approval."[73] The meeting ended with those members of the Farmers' Union who were present clearly stating that they opposed violence and intimidation tactics and that the infamous night-riding incident must not be repeated.[74]

Several additional newspaper condemnations of this incident were also printed. One said, "the citizens of Yell County, irrespective of avocation, will not countenance acts of intimidation, arson or assassination, and their vehement denunciation of the cowardly deed in question will probably prevent a repetition of the crime." Another simply stated that the businessmen of Dardanelle were in "hearty sympathy with the farmers in their efforts to secure a better price for their cotton" and the businessmen can be relied upon for "cooperation."[75] Night-riding incidents were fairly common beginning in the early 1900s as cotton farmers not only in Arkansas but in Mississippi, Tennessee, and Missouri were targeted for selling their cotton to large agricultural firms at lower prices than many poor farmers desired. As the twentieth century progressed, violence resulting from night riding increased, taking various forms to include the burning of cotton warehouses, assaults, the killing of livestock, and the destruction of cotton still standing in the fields.[76]

Examples of this increased violence were present as the night-riding incident in Dardanelle in early October 1908 and the actions taken in its immediate aftermath, which were not the end of the story. On October 28, 1908, two fires occurred in Dardanelle within one and one-half hours of each other. The first fire was at J. J. Boyce's grocery store, which caused roof damage primarily. Boyce was one of the six merchants signing the second resolution on October 8 pledging not to buy cotton for thirty days. The second fire occurred at the Arkansas Valley Cottonseed Oil Mill and resulted in the destruction of "a small quantity of cotton."[77] Were these fires the result of vengeance taken by the night riders? While unproven, it certainly seems highly plausible that this was the case.

Another fire that may have been linked to this night-riding incident occurred on October 5, 1909 (almost one year to the day of the original incident) at the Arkansas Valley Cotton Oil Company's gin at

Fowler in Carden Bottoms. This gin was owned and operated by the same company that received the night riders' notice in Dardanelle in 1908. The gin at Fowler was totally destroyed and the fire was reported to be "a complete mystery." This gin, just completed and opened on September 1, 1909, was one of the best-equipped and most modern gins in Arkansas and the fire loses were high: $18,000 for the facility, $10,000 for equipment, and $8,000 for the eighty tons of cottonseed and the eighty bales of cotton stored in the gin at the time of the fire.[78] Again, the evidence linking the night riders and this fire is inconclusive, but it is highly plausible that there was a direct connection between these events. No one was ever charged or prosecuted for the threatening night-riding incident or the probable arsons that followed.

## Reciprocity

The conflict between the Dardanelle Bottoms and Dardanelle's businessmen was real, but it was not monolithic given two undeniable conditions. First, many of the Dardanelle businessmen clearly understood the absolute importance of the Bottoms farmers for their success. Second, many Bottoms farmers understood their need for the products and marketing services available in Dardanelle. This dance of reciprocity, sometimes conflicted and sometimes harmonious, would continue during the twentieth century, but never did the rhythm become so syncopated and disjointed that it could not again be made reciprocally rhythmic and regular. "Towns belong to the country . . . the country can't succeed with all the people farmers, nor a town with its whole population merchants. Diversity of calling is essential."[79] And so it was.

Between 1880 and 1910, both Dardanelle and the Bottoms developed. Prosperity was still a hard thing to capture and hold, but the farmers' lot had generally improved during these three decades and the townspeople were definitely more secure. The bleak survivor-oriented existence that so characterized the 1880s, in which both people of Dardanelle and the Bottoms forged a hardscrabble struggle for improvement, gave way to a more hopeful future and endurable present.

By 1910 the Farmers' Union, now officially known as the National

Farmers' Co-operative and Educational Union of America and head-quartered in Texarkana, Arkansas, had successfully sidestepped direct political action and concentrated on three issues having significant potential benefit for farmers and their families: "scientific agriculture, good roads, and reclamation of swamps and wet lands."[80] Likewise, a coalition composed of Arkansas's director of agriculture, United States Department of Agriculture (USDA) agents, the Arkansas superintendent of education, and Arkansas's university agricultural department heads was sponsoring the Boys Corn Clubs. These were county organizations for boys designed to further agricultural knowledge and development whose purpose was not to "dethrone King Cotton but to encourage scientific corn production" given corn's ready markets and its lack of insect problems as compared to cotton. The Boys Corn Club in the Bottoms enjoyed the support of the Farmers' Union, local school districts, and teachers, as well as Dardanelle merchants who "readily contribute money and commodity prizes for the county contests."[81] These agricultural clubs were forerunners for agricultural training courses in secondary education.

By the end of 1910 the desperation of farmers and their farm problems generally seem to have lessened. The Yell County field agent for the USDA reported that four hundred Bottoms farmers were following the government's scientific agricultural instructions and were developing model farms. Cotton prospects looked good throughout the county, especially in the Dardanelle Bottoms; wheat was being more generally planted; and hay, which would serve as feed for mules, horses, and cattle, increased production in the Bottoms yielding three cuts per field.[82] The future looked hopeful and the present, as the colloquial saying goes, had become "more tolerable."

## African Americans

The status of African Americans during the period from 1880 to 1910 was not a story of continually improved possibilities. The window of opportunity for improved living conditions following the Civil War soon became narrowed during the 1880s and was ultimately slammed shut in the late 1890s by the neglect of the federal government to enforce constitutional guarantees and federal laws and by the determined racism exhibited in southern state laws, traditional practices, and court decisions.

Whether one accepts C. Vann Woodward's thesis that southern segregation was not the result of old folkways but rather developed during the racial chaos of the late nineteenth century or whether one is more inclined to agree with Joel Williamson's thesis that it was custom, not law, that created the Jim Crow system, it appears that in Arkansas Jim Crowism cannot be solely explained by either.

During Arkansas's Reconstruction era (1865–1874), African Americans in the state created their separate churches as well as established segregated school systems.[83] African Americans created their own separate "Negro businesses" from the Reconstruction era forward. Near the end of Arkansas's Reconstruction period a law was passed in 1873 dealing with public accommodations—which extended to public carriers, hotels, saloons, restaurants, and public amusements—requiring that all persons have equal services at equal costs regardless of race. This law remained for thirty-four years, not being repealed until 1907.[84] Toward the end of the nineteenth century tremendous pressure for racial separation was shaping the new social landscape. Understanding why and how this happened is essential to understanding racial inequality well into the twentieth century.

The essence of racial segregation in Arkansas had more to do with economics and socioeconomic class concerns, and the 1880s proved a pivotal time. The political order of the 1870s, which used the so-called fusion principle, began to crumble during the 1880s and was defunct by the early 1890s. The "fusion principle" involved African American leaders and conservative white Democratic Party leaders quietly working together to map legislative agendas and pass laws that maintained a voice for the African American population in exchange for their votes and support for the Democratic Party.[85] The reasons for the demise of the fusion principle centered on the economic depression of the 1880s and the resulting hardening of socioeconomic class distinctions.

Poor white farmers had always been prone to have highly prejudiced racial biases. In the 1880s they were debt-ridden, down-trodden, and fearful of anyone they believed posed an economic threat to their survival. As a consequence, they became ardently opposed to extending complete political rights and economic power to African Americans. In 1881 cotton was selling at 10 cents a pound; by 1888 the price had dropped to 8.5 cents a pound. Falling cotton prices, the crop lien system, high interest rates, and the constant terror of impending economic collapse, coupled with real human misery based on want all culminated in increased racial tension. As these white farmers organized and joined farm organizations, they also began to increase their "hostility, suspicion and fear" of African Americans.[86] Thus, the African Americans' window of opportunity was quickly closing.

Meanwhile, many upper-class Arkansans, the planters and the merchant business classes, exhibited a more paternalistic spirit of *noblesse oblige* toward African Americans, especially those whom they employed and particularly those who lived in towns and thus were in close proximity to these white folks. This relationship exhibited a fair amount of white aristocratic superiority and condescension toward African Americans mixed with sincere elements of friendship and affection.[87] Thus, one can better understand the frequently used phase "our good Negroes." It should also be noted that many of these upper-class whites also exhibited a suspicious, negative attitude toward the "white trash" from the rural areas: the poorest, landless, struggling farmer, and the hired laborers.

In the 1888 election, African Americans, Republicans, and members of the Agricultural Wheel and the Union Labor Party joined forces to make a respectable political showing while advocating the class interests of poor farmers. A concerned Democratic Party launched a major push back in 1890 and 1891, successfully destroying this coalition.[88] In the 1890 gubernatorial election, 70 percent of adult male African Americans in Arkansas voted and the vast majority voted for the Republican candidate, as they had done in 1888.[89] The farmers' organizations and African Americans had used a "second fusion model" and applied it for a Republican victory. This was a direct threat to the mastery of the Democratic Party, which feared for its political life; this simply could not be allowed to continue. After 1890 the "fusion model" was dead and a new chapter of racism and segregation was ushered into Arkansas by the Democratic Party.

In 1891 Arkansas enacted the Separate Coach Law for railroads and a new Arkansas election law that systematically disenfranchised

African Americans. The following year a poll tax amendment was rat-
ified and added to the state constitution. In 1906 Governor Jeff Davis
ordered the statewide use of the "white primary" system, thus by the
early twentieth century, Jim Crow was fully present in Arkansas and
the possibility for racial equality and opportunity was not to return
for at least another half century.[90]

So what accounts for the complete closure of the window of opportunity for African Americans? The ingredients for this included (1) two
very different racial perspectives based on socioeconomic class; (2)
the economic distress of the 1880s and 1890s; (3) the increased agrarian unrest that resulted as farmers began to organize themselves; and,
(4) the challenge to continued Democratic Party political domination
given the prospect of a political alliance between the Republicans,
African Americans, and farm protesters. These combined elements
forced the planter/merchant/business socioeconomic class into a more
segregationist position in order to elevate the standing of the white
farmer and maintain Democratic Party control over Arkansas. Based
on class and economic concerns, African American equality and a
cooperative, integrated society had to be sacrificed. The mandate was
simple: put the Negro in his place and everything else could go well.

The very foundation for Jim Crow was the overpowering significance of economic considerations and the need to maintain town/
rural reciprocity. The business class of the town had to have the loyalty
and economic support of the white rural class in order to continue and
prosper. By 1894 in Arkansas, African Americans were abandoned and
the Republican Party was crippled. Jim Crow had been seized upon
by the Democratic Party and the business classes as the instrument
to guarantee the continuation of the economic success of the town.
The role of economics in Arkansas's town/rural reciprocity was the
motivation for the institutionalization by law of racial discrimination.

The work of Willard B. Gatewood Jr. supports this view. Prior to
1890, Arkansas's racial atmosphere for African Americans was supe-
rior to that of other southern states. Then between 1888 and 1891 and
forward well into the twentieth century, Arkansas experienced "a substantial increase in anti-Negro prejudice and the hardening of the
color line," and there was an abrupt end to the vision of Arkansas as
a "Negro's paradise."[91]

As a result of the 1891 Separate Coach Law, some Arkansas African Americans emigrated to northern cities, others went to Oklahoma, and a few left bound for Africa.[92] While the intensity of Jim Crowism in Arkansas varied greatly, it was present everywhere. By the early 1890s African Americans, like whites involved in the various farmers' organizations, saw their future fortune impacted more by economic issues than by political activities. Social and economic prowess was emphasized by African American ministers, educators, and business-men as the surest, and perhaps safest, way to improve their overall quality of life.[93] Even here, there was not consensus on the method to attain social and economic success.

The downward spiral in the prospect of racial equality was only worsened by the philosophical schism that occurred within the leader-ship of the African American community. William Edward Burghardt (W. E. B.) DuBois would soon develop his "talented tenth" philosophy while Booker Taliaferro Washington's "accommodation approach" was already being articulated and widely accepted. Washington's approach advocated industrial education for young African Americans and the need for a patient approach to racial betterment via hard work, pro-priety, and law-abiding service. Most whites embraced Washington's approach as reasonable and even educated whites spoke of the "good Negroes," meaning hard-working people who took care of their finan-cial obligations and their families and were polite, sober, law abid-ing, and deferential to whites.[94] In essence, this was the Negro in his proper place in society, an idea embraced and understood by most whites. It is an interesting fact that Kirkbride Potts, father of G. L. Potts (Carden Bottom plantation owner and highly respected mem-ber of that Lakeside community), was a personal friend of Booker T. Washington.[95]

As historian William Holmes noted, African American organiza-tions of this period—such as the Colored Alliance—urged their mem-bers to uplift themselves via hard work and sacrifice, a message that fit nicely with Booker T. Washington's approach and was amiable to whites. When, however, African Americans attempted to implement policies that conflicted with the interests of whites, as did the Colored Alliance beginning in the early 1890s, violent opposition developed in order to maintain the economic and racial class policies of the white South.[96]

Some African Americans also accepted, or at least offered lip service to, Washington's accommodation approach as was evidenced in the sermon given by a visiting African American minister in Dardanelle. He urged parishioners to "pray for a special benediction upon the white friends of Dardanelle and vicinity who have so generously aided in the erection of a house of worship." An even more obvious "accommodation" call was heard by the African American and white attendees at an African American–sponsored barbeque dinner held at Bata's Mill (later known as New Neely) for the residents of the Galla Rock and Wilson Townships (the Bottoms). Reverend M. A. F. Easton, minister of the Dardanelle African Methodist Episcopal (AME) Church, urged African Americans to remember that southern whites were their friends and that African Americans' advancements were predicated on the success of the white man. He called for friendship between the races, noting that this is possible "if the colored man will only keep his place and learn to wait." He concluded with "colored men should be grateful, be patient, learn to labor and to wait."[97]

Other African Americans issued a more strident call for action urging people to throw off the shadowy chains of slavery, assume responsibility for one's self, demand liberty and good treatment for self and family, and be "free men."[98] The shaping of the place occupied by African Americans in American society was just as much a product of the debates in Dardanelle and the Bottoms as it was in the varied views of Washington and DuBois. Differences regarding race and the proper place for African Americans existed both within the white and the African American communities, as people struggled to create a new southern society that functioned.

One obvious feature of race relations during the period from the 1880s until the early twentieth century was the almost universal lack of respect shown African Americans, whether in Dardanelle or in the Bottoms. African Americans were generally referred to only by their first name and more generally as "colored," "negro," or "nigger." The accepted level of discriminatory practices and beliefs was evident in the language used as well as in the message it conveyed.

An 1882 newspaper advertisement unabashedly called for a "first-class white barber" for the town of Atkins, an adjacent Pope County community just six miles across the river from Carden Bottom.[99] In 1910, Bill Lyttle, a white customer at Ward's Restaurant on Front Street in Dardanelle, became angry over the quality of his food and began berating John Walker, the African American cook. Lyttle began shooting at Walker, and the local newspaper stated that Walker ran from the restaurant into the back alley to avoid being wounded so fast that he "clipped seconds from the record made by Uhlan [a contemporary track star] at the track meet in New Jersey last week."[100] Although this is a report of an assault with a deadly weapon and probably with the intent to murder, the tone of the report was not serious, but rather light hearted. In fact, Lyttle was not arrested or charged with any crime. Through this single incident, one sees that the prevailing racial views in Dardanelle and the Bottoms mirrored the national views of the time: a begrudging acceptance of African Americans while simultaneously creating conditions that dehumanized them while limiting their place in society.

Between 1874 and 1892, forty-nine African Americans served in the Arkansas General Assembly: forty-seven in the House and two in the Senate. None of these were from Yell County. Working within the Democratic Party majority, these legislators coordinated closely with their white leadership in the fusion model or "clientage politics." In return for gaining patronage from the white politicians on issues such as basic security and protection for African American citizens, African American legislators were responsible for delivering the African American vote to the Democratic candidates. However, by the early 1880s African American politicians had concluded that their race lacked educational opportunities, were not receiving justice from the legal authorities, and were being excluded from economic opportunities, primarily landownership. Therefore, increasingly during the 1880s, many African American politicians began to turn away from the Democratic Party.[101] In Yell County, however, African Americans continued to be a part of the Democratic Party, and Republicans were told that the county held only "bad soil" in which they would not flourish.

As late as 1882, African Americans were still voting in Dardanelle and running candidates, albeit unsuccessfully, for local, county, and state offices. In 1882 two African American candidates ran for Dardanelle constable positions, one for justice of the peace, and one for state land commissioner. All lost their races, with the local comment that "the colored troops are very well for voters, but not fancied much by their political associates for office-holders" and they will receive "no help from their white allies" at the ballot box.[102] Throughout the 1880s a common way to refer to the African American voters in Dardanelle, as elsewhere in the South, was "the Nigger Vote."

Rumors of race riots in the nearby Pope County communities of Dover and Atkins in the fall of 1882 prompted the Dardanelle newspaper, the *Independent Arkansian*, to comment that "the negroes certainly have sense enough to know that such a step would recoil on their own heads, and not one engaged in such proceedings would escape alive."[103] While strong verbal intimidation of African Americans was a factor, so was physical intimidation. John Cole, a "colored living seven or eight miles below town [the Dardanelle Bottoms] was assaulted by armed masked men."[104]

Physical intimidation and murder also continued into 1883 in nearby Faulkner County near Pinnacle Springs on the Van Buren County line, as whites tried to remove African Americans from their homes. Following a series of threats, twenty-five masked men appeared at an African American home and fired into the front door as the residents fired back as they ran and scattered. One young African American was killed and several other individuals, both white and black, were wounded.[105]

Another incident in the Dardanelle Bottoms probably resulted from night-riding (whitecapping) actions and ended in murder. Samuel Sutterfield, "a colored man living on the Carter place [was] found face down in a puddle of water and mud where he was drowned. The supposition is that he had a fit, and the coroner's jury returned a verdict accordingly."[106] The message to African Americans, not so subtly stated, was know your place and stay in it. Clientage politics aside, racial equality was not a concept to be tolerated.

Even successful African American business ventures were not well tolerated. Wiley Johnson, the Dardanelle High School janitor and owner of Johnson's Café in Dardanelle, received threatening messages against himself, his business, and his family for months that had been signed "the Good White Citizens" of Dardanelle. These messages referred to his café as "a dive" in which young people were allowed to dance. Courageously, Johnson wrote an open letter addressed to the "Good White Citizens of Dardanelle" stating that his café was not associated with any criminal activities, that he and his family were living a crime-free life, and that, having lived in Dardanelle, he was astonished that the good white citizens of the town were concerned with his work.[107] This seems to have worked, as no additional reports regarding Johnson were noted.

The place of African American women was also delineated, both by race and gender, and significantly limited their degree of maneuverability and advancement within the male, white dominated world. In Dardanelle, as in tens of thousands of American communities, African American women were employed as maids, cooks, laundresses, and nannies. In the South especially, but also in the North, the ability of an African American woman to escape domestic service and advance into employment in business was highly limited. Professionally, a scant few African American women became nurses and teachers. The "aristocrats of color," a small group of educated, affluent, and influential African Americans who lived in major American cities between 1880 and 1920 of which Willard B. Gatewood Jr. wrote, certainly did not exist in Dardanelle.[108] The African American women of Dardanelle remained confined primarily to domestic service for employment until the 1970s. Their leisure activities were primarily centered around the African American churches and church groups and their activities. In Dardanelle African American women and men loyally supported the efforts of the town's African American elementary school and its school functions. Beyond these avenues for work, leisure, and shared community involvement, little else other than family activities existed for the African American women of Dardanelle until the 1970s. At that time, the larger racial changes occurring within the nation—political participation, educational opportunities, improved economic potential, and a degree of decline in racial hatred—also began to have an impact on life for African American women in and around Dardanelle.

The African American women in the Bottoms, as in other rural areas throughout the South, primarily worked the farms with their husbands and children as the entire family's labor was required in order to survive. In some ways the life of the rural African American woman was similar to that of her white counterpart. She cooked, canned, cleaned, kept a garden, birthed and raised the children, attended church meetings and singings as she could, and tried to maintain the health and well-being of her spouse, children, and self. However, unlike her white counterpart, some of whom given their "middle-class" economic standing did not work in the cotton fields, almost every African American woman did. Another difference involved the effects of extreme poverty that most rural African Americans endured, usually being poorer than the poor whites of the rural countryside. These effects limited health and options for medical care; increased the negative effects of poor diet, little or no education, and highly limited horizons of opportunity; and reinforced and strengthened racist hatred, violence/abuse, and stereotyping. Yes, African American rural women's lives were like the lives of rural white women except, except, and except.

The contemptuous attitude of whites toward African Americans is also evident. While reporting on a Sunday outdoor baptism service held by the "colored Baptists" of Dardanelle, a local reporter seemed amazed that the "assemblage was quiet and orderly, each one seeming to be duly impressed with the solemnity of the occasion."[109] One doubts that a report about a white baptismal service would have contained these remarks. When the "colored Masonic Lodge" was organized in Dardanelle in early October 1883, the reporting was highly racist: "judging from the unearthly sounds that came from the hall after midnight it is evident that 'de [the] visiting 'bredren' [brethren] had fun 'nisltriatin' [initiating] the new members."[110] Twenty-six years later, the Negro Masonic Lodge Hall was destroyed by fire, and never rebuilt.[111] Humor, of course, is also capable of carrying a racist message. In 1910 a group of young ladies from the finest Dardanelle families who had summer residences on nearby Mount Nebo offered an afternoon entertainment, a satire entitled, "A Negro Wedding." Blackface and elaborate, satirical costumes guaranteed a fun social event, which was, indeed, well received, enjoyed, and complimented by the guests.[112]

The racial views of most white citizens of Dardanelle can perhaps best be encapsulated by a lovely, yet highly racist 1909 editorial regarding the death of Joe Bagby, known generally as "Uncle Joe Bagby." The writing noted that it was so sad to see the passing of one of "those loyal souls who served ofttime [often time] for love alone, and faithfully and well: who made their master's cause their own, his grief their grief— the old time Southern slave." Following a three-sentence summary of the decedent's life with the basic facts only, the tribute nears its end with "All honor to the negro of the old South."[113]

A constant flow of racist stories appeared in the Dardanelle local newspaper throughout the period from 1880 until the early twentieth century. These included reports of a drowning with the victim only identified as a colored boy, a colored man shot and killed, and a colored man from Carden Bottom on trial for murder. One begins to wonder if every citizen from the Bottoms and Dardanelle was encoded with racism. Then one finds a brief notice entitled simply "To the Public" written by Mrs. J. J. George, which read as follows:

> Having received several letters threatening to burn my houses if I did not move the old negroes that have been on my land for the last 25 or 30 years, and the attempt last week by the party or parties, to burn my barn, I will pay $50.00 reward for any infor- mation that will lead to the arrest and conviction of said party or parties.[114]

No additional reports of threats or damage to Mrs. George's property were reported.

Nonetheless, the contrast and inequality in the application of jus- tice based on race is starkly evident in an 1895 special report from Dardanelle published in the *Arkansas Freeman*, an African American newspaper published in Little Rock. In June 1895, an African American father using a club removed his daughter from the clutches of a white man who was attempting to rape the child. An African American posse organized, caught the man, and turned him over to law officers in Morrilton, Arkansas. The court fined the defendant $50 and sen- tenced him to three months in the county jail and then fined the girl's father $14 for his use of a deadly weapon (i.e., the club). At approxi- mately the same time (April 1895), an African American male accused of the attempted rape of a white girl in Morrilton was tried, sentenced to death, and hanged on June 7, 1895, after the governor denied his appeal for a new trial.[115] Justice was meted out in both cases, but the nature of that justice was based on race and informed by racism.

Race relations in Dardanelle and the Bottoms mirrored that of the rest of the country during the period from 1880 to 1910. There is evidence of racial violence as well as a callous disregard for morality, the law, and human rights. Justice was etched with a certain matter-of-fact mean-spiritedness that is the essence of racism. During the 1920s, racial violence would become more pronounced as the racial practices of the period become more ingrained both individually and societally.

## Floods and High Water

Just as human interactions based on race posed challenges for the people of Dardanelle and the Bottoms, so too did natural forces. The Petit Jean and Arkansas Rivers, the initial life force for Dardanelle and the Bottoms, were both a pathway to prosperity and a means of misery. Since 1874, major floods occurred in 1874, 1892, 1898, 1904, 1908, 1916, 1927, 1935, 1943, 1945, and 1957; with less severe, but still costly, high waters posing problems in numerous other years.[116] Dardanelle was located just above the floodplain and usually, with the exception of 1927, escaped inundation by floodwaters. The Bottoms, however, were frequently flooded with several feet of water, mud/silt, and in some areas river sand. Rising waters could bring economic devastation; loss of property, livestock, and life; increased health risks; and tremendous inconvenience. Plainly stated, "floods were bad!"[117]

For good reason, the people of Dardanelle and the Bottoms exhibited a strong preoccupation with river levels and rainfall amounts. Floods could not only destroy crops and the potential for a decent harvest, they could also bring about economic catastrophe for Dardanelle merchants. In addition, floods washed out roads and bridges, thus creating financial predicaments for county and local governments. Often times, floods left several feet of mud behind in the houses of the Bottoms, as well as an assortment of unwelcomed house guests: snakes, fish, frogs, and various insects. Even if property damage and loss of life were limited—and this was not always the case—a flood's disruption to the normal daily patterns of life and the conditions it created for fostering disease and illness long after the waters had receded were major problems. Thus, for all of these reasons, people paid close attention to the weather and the levels of the rivers and major creeks. Reports of a "big boom" on the Arkansas River generally brought about anxiety, whereas news of receding water levels brought on relief, even celebration. While the focus was usually on the Arkansas and Petit Jean Rivers, the levels of the Mississippi River were also closely followed as indicators of potentially locally rising waters.

The February 10, 1882, edition of the *Independent Arkansian* was filled with news of rising waters and flooding, all of which gripped the attention of its readers. "Petit Jean rose four feet on Tuesday night. . . . Old Arkansaw [*sic*] is on a big boom, rose four feet on Wednesday and was rapidly climbing up the banks on yesterday. . . . Heavy rains continued to fall Wednesday night, creeks all up from recent rains, and the roads in a bad condition. . . . Petit Jean is up in a high old way and out all over the Bottoms."[118] Two weeks later, reports of river levels and flooding were still being published: "The Petit Jean has been on a high old boom the past week, and overflowed the bottoms considerably . . . cattle lost in overflow."[119]

While receding river levels often brought about emotional relief, low river levels also threatened Dardanelle and the Bottoms with potential devastation. During the 1880s—and to a lesser degree thereafter—much of the area's cotton and farm commodities was shipped via steamboat. Reports of falling river levels and the appearance of sandbars in the spring of 1882 and again in the fall of 1883 caused the steamers to be "laid up" and a return to flatboat traffic was temporarily necessitated.[120] While inordinate river levels, either too high or too low, posed problems for merchants as well as residents of the Bottoms, high waters especially inconvenienced other Dardanelle businesses, including the local newspaper, which occasionally missed an edition or issued it late as the river's waters crept closer to its offices.[121]

The floods of the Arkansas River in 1908 resulted in several major problems, with waters covering the Bottoms in both the spring and fall. In early June farmers were hurriedly replanting flooded-out crops both with corn and cotton in the hopes of favorable fall weather and the possibility of achieving an adequate harvest.[122] Then, in late November, the waters rose again as the Arkansas River was "on a rampage" and "the Bottoms all under water while Dardanelle lost 1200 feet of telephone and telegraph wires."[123] The telephone and telegraph wires were laid at the bottom of the Arkansas River, destroyed by extreme water levels and rapid currents. This loss left Dardanelle without communication systems for several weeks, as the downed lines connected Dardanelle to those services in Russellville, and thus on to the wider world. As a result of the 1908 floods, farmers—who had previously suffered from several years of adverse crop conditions—posted unusually high numbers of delinquent property taxes. Consequently, the 1908 floods did serious damage to both the land in the Bottoms and its people.

In addition to the high waters, it was common for the Arkansas River's current to undercut and carry away the banks of the river during floods. Referred to locally as "caving," it presented a frightening reality to those living near the river's banks. The community of Neely, located in the Upper Dardanelle Bottoms seven miles south of Dardanelle, became another victim of the 1908 floods when most of the community was completely taken out by the caving of the riverbank. Lost to the waters were Neely's "post office, stores, gin, mill, church, schoolhouse, and numerous residences."[124] While a few residences and some citizens remained, Neely basically ceased to be a separate community after the 1908 floods.

The 1908 floods had closely duplicated the river's flow during the smaller 1892 and 1898 floods, which if not corrected, could permanently and drastically redirect the channel of the Arkansas River during future floods. All three of these flooding events saw the Arkansas River flowing in such a way as to create a new channel through the lowland or slough of the Gibson Lake area (sometimes referred to as the Beaver Ditches) and then westward from Gibson Lake into Bata's Creek (later known as Mill Creek), at which point the river would return to its original channel. (see Appendix, fig. 6). Should this Gibson Lake route become the new channel for the Arkansas River, several thousand acres of farmland would be taken away and the river channel would become unnavigable in this section given its newer and more shallow depth. If these prospects were not sufficient cause for alarm, then one must also consider that during the 1908 floods the Arkansas River in Carden Bottom cut to within one-half mile of the mouth of the Petit Jean River. If this were to continue in future floods, then the intersection of the Arkansas and the Petit Jean would move westward and thousands of acres of farmland, homes, and livestock would be lost as the river's banks caved and created new channels. The Lower Bottoms was in serious jeopardy.[125] In short, the 1908 floods exposed a threat to the communities and lands of the Bottoms.

These floods also posed an immediate threat to the downtown business district of Dardanelle. The churning waters of the floods had carried away and "caved off" large amounts of the riverbank adjacent to Front Street, the town's primary business district and the location of its two riverboat wharfs. These "cavings" resulted from the floods redirecting the river's channel closer to the south bank on the Dardanelle side of the Arkansas River.[126] If this were to continue, the business district area located on Front Street could be lost to the river. This was a threat requiring immediate attention.

Plans quickly developed for building levees to protect Dardanelle and the Bottoms from future ruinous floods and to enlist the assistance of the federal government in studying and financing these protective measures. A committee of Dardanelle businessmen contacted the Arkansas congressional delegation to gain governmental financial assistance.[127] As a result of these efforts, two levees were constructed.

Levee District No. 1 called for 35,000 cubic yards of level embankment to be constructed with one large reinforced concrete lock and dam and ten reinforced concrete culverts varying in length from 50 to 100 feet. Bids were announced in mid-July 1908.[128] This levee, located at the south end of Dardanelle, ran along the Arkansas River and separated the Arkansas River from River Road, a dirt road that traversed the area from south Dardanelle west of the Arkansas River to Fields Chapel, Neely, and New Neely (see Appendix, fig. 4).[129]

Levee District No. 2 began construction in late August 1909 and consisted of $5,000 worth of concrete pavement at the mouth of the Petit Jean River and was fitted with locks in order to control the overflow and backwater as the Petit Jean River intersects with the Arkansas River. Approximately one mile back from and south of the Arkansas River, the principal levee ran one mile in length and consisted of a series of smaller levees constructed along the Petit Jean River at its lower points. Materials began to arrive in Dardanelle and on site in August 1909, and Levee No. 2 was completed later that same year. The primary purpose of Levee No. 2 was to protect Carden Bottom and nearby areas in the Lower Bottoms such as Pontoon, Cotton Town,

New Neely, and Slaty Crossing from Petit Jean River flooding. Noting the fertile tracts of Carden Bottom lands and its propensity to varying degrees of annual flooding, Levee District No. 2 was expected to double land values in Carden Bottom (see Appendix, fig. 5).[130]

Thus, rising waters terrorized the residents of the Bottoms, inflicted financial hardship for both the people of the Bottoms and the business interests in Dardanelle, and literally redefined the physical landscape given the changing of the river channel. The 1908 floods prompted quick action to avert future problems, although future floods would occur and create new dangers and problems.

A year after the devastating flood of late 1908, most Arkansas locations were experiencing a drought. While lasting from three to eight weeks—depending on location—the drought put the cotton crop at high risk. According to reports in the *Dardanelle Post-Dispatch*, the Arkansas River at Dardanelle recorded a level of "7 feet and falling possibly to 3 feet," the lowest river level ever recorded at Dardanelle.[131]

The Arkansas and the Petit Jean Rivers, with all of their nuances, alternating river levels, bank cavings, and changing river channels, posed an omnipresent threat to the people of Dardanelle and the Bottoms. These rivers truly were a source of both misery and prosperity, of desolation as well as hope.

## Crime

Given the chaos and disorder in Arkansas during the late 1860s and 1870s, most people during the 1880s possessed a keen desire for immediate law and order, even if this meant that the finite elements of the law were not fully observed. Typical circuit court cases included horse and mule stealing, burglary, assault, rape, as well as murder and less serious offenses. These were violent times, and of the approximately six hundred convicts serving sentences in the Arkansas State Penitentiary in 1882, one hundred or so had been found guilty of murder.[132]

Arrest, trial, and conviction did not necessarily mean that justice would prevail. Reports of jailbreaks during the late nineteenth century in and around Yell County were very common. If prisoners had been allegedly involved in somewhat lesser crimes, the attitude toward their escape and the need for their recapture was rather relaxed. This seems to have been the case in 1882, when three prisoners escaped from the Dardanelle Jail. One was quickly recaptured in Dardanelle, but the posse search for the other two escapees ended "on account of the dark rainy night." One of the two African American escapees had been indicted for murder and the other for larceny and burglary; however, the circumstances surrounding the convictions did not particularly raise the ire of the population. Thus, the sheriff simply offered a $50 reward for the capture of each man.[133] Just two weeks prior to this event, an attempted jailbreak at Dardanelle had failed, to which the *Independent Arkansian* satirically commented that "no prisoners escape from the Dardanelle jail, much."[134]

While jail escapes were fairly common and generally did not raise much of a fuss, some crimes incensed the public and the demand for swift justice, by whatever means, was loud. For example, during 1881 fifteen murderers were executed by hanging in Arkansas and "several others with the assistance of the mob" were lynched.[135] The people of Dardanelle and the Bottoms were certainly in favor of quick and certain punishment. A local newspaper editorial noted that "it is pretty well known throughout the country that the people of Dardanelle are not very patient with murderers and that during the past few months tightrope performances have not been very rare."[136] People also wanted punishment to be expeditiously applied. An example of nondeadly, citizen-inflicted justice took place on April 16, 1882, at Danville, in western Yell County. A dozen citizens took control of Tab Rains, who had been convicted of stealing a small amount of bacon. Rains had pleaded guilty and was assessed a $25 fine, which he could not pay and, thus, he was placed in the Danville Jail. The townspeople took Rains from his cell and "gave him a sound flogging and turned him loose, and told him to 'get' and he got."[137] Strictly observing the law was a nicety, not a necessity.

What perhaps is most shocking about crime during the period from 1880 to 1910 is the apparent casualness with which murder and brutal crimes were committed. For example, in July 1880, W. E. DeLong, owner/operator of the Dardanelle Machine Shop in Dardanelle, shot and killed Charles Burch, his employee, during the day on Front Street, even firing at Burch as he tried to escape by running down the street. This murder, which was officially charged as manslaughter, was apparently precipitated by a dispute over wages.[138]

Another incident offers additional insight into the apparent cav-
alier approach to certain crimes. Tom White, a deputized law officer,
was shot in Carden Bottom in May 1881 while attempting to arrest
John Taylor on a misdemeanor charge. The shooter, John Taylor, was
interviewed in his Dardanelle jail cell the following day. When asked
what had prompted him to shoot White, Taylor simply answered:
"They [a supposed reference to the law] got me scared up" that they
were going to "get me in trouble and it would cost me $500 to get
out."[139] Taylor admitted shooting White, saying eight to ten shots
were fired. Was Taylor a hardened criminal, a danger to society? No.
Taylor, a young tenant farmer, had lived in Carden Bottom for over a
year. He was married and had a young family. Following the shooting
of White, Taylor was arrested on the original misdemeanor charge
and was fined $11. Since White had not been seriously wounded, the
charges for the assault were later dismissed, and Taylor's name did
not appear on any future court dockets.[140] Here was a case of a young,
poor, hard-working tenant farmer who became so frightened by the
prospect of owing $500 that, in a panic, he shot a law enforcement
officer. White posed an economic danger to Taylor, which resulted in
the shooting. Since most of the people in Dardanelle and the Bottoms
could understand this reaction, some even identifying with Taylor's
response, there was no public outcry for the absolute application of
strict legal punishment.

In Yell County it seems that the law was the law, but one must
consider the circumstances of the crime as seriously as the crime itself
when applying the law. Only then will Yell County justice prevail. As
such, when is a serious crime in Yell County truly a serious crime? The
answer seems to have been when the majority of the people believe the
crime is sufficiently serious to warrant punishment rather than being
justified by the events and circumstances leading to the commission
of the crime. Some would deem this a sophisticated application of the
law. Some would call this a callous disregard for justice. Some would
simply say this is common sense since sometimes the crime is justified. Some would also say justice in Yell County is uniquely defined
and the law is open to the public's interpretation.

An illustration of this Yell County interpretation of justice can
be seen in a knife fight that occurred between William Wright and
John Brooks at Brooks's logging camp in Carden Bottom. Following

the knife fight, guns were drawn, but Wright retreated from the scene before any blood was shed. Brooks had a unfavorable reputation with most local folks, which prompted the local newspaper report on the incident to question whether the area was "ready yet to lose John Brooks" and rid it of a continued source of mayhem.[141] In another case heard in the 1882 Yell County Circuit Court, the defendant was assessed a fine of $50 after his guilty plea for assault with intent to kill. Since, however, no lasting harm occurred, the court reduced the punishment to a $5 fine.[142] These examples illustrate that justice in Yell County was not finite, and frequently lacked a consistent definition and application.

Carden Bottom gained a reputation for violence that would exist well into the twentieth century. Many people believed that the inhabitants of Carden Bottom had a general disregard for basic law and order. Beginning in the 1880s and continuing increasingly until the 1970s, many Carden Bottom families would travel to Dardanelle on Saturday, much to the delight of Dardanelle businessmen, swelling the town's population and its level of minor crimes. One report noted that on a single Saturday, there were "17,984 fights in town."[143] While this number was most likely highly exaggerated, it does underscore the violence that seemed to accompany the inhabitants of Carden Bottom. As late as the 1940s, one woman recalled her father telling her she could date and marry anyone she chose, except any boy from Carden Bottom.[144]

Carden Bottom's reputation for violence was based on numerous celebrated criminal acts, one of the grisliest of which occurred in 1879. William Casey and Jim Holland approached Charles G. Helphrey, a day laborer and drifter from Mississippi employed to pick cotton, with a scheme to murder Burgess James, a Carden Bottom planter who purportedly carried $1,500, mostly in gold, on his person. After several days of drinking and planning the crime, Helphrey met James on River Road about four miles south of Dardanelle. It was late at night and the two men, while walking back to Carden Bottom, engaged in conversation and then sat down to rest on a log near the river's edge. Helphrey pulled out the pistol given him by his accomplices, and James ran down the riverbank as five shots were fired, with one striking him. A hand-to-hand struggle ensued at the river's edge, during which Helphrey struck James several times in the head with the butt of the pistol and ultimately strangled him. He took James's cash, a total of $130, and returned to Carden Bottom, where the three accomplices met and split the money. Within several hours, a posse rode into Carden Bottom. Helphrey fled to Missouri, was arrested approximately two weeks later, returned to the Dardanelle Jail, and, while awaiting trial, escaped. He would later be recaptured, found guilty, and hanged.[145] Holland was arrested, escaped from the Dardanelle Jail, and fled to Tennessee. He was recaptured approximately two years later and returned to the Dardanelle Jail arriving there at about 6:00 p.m. on Saturday, November 27, 1881. Six and one-half hours later, approximately 125 to 130 masked men broke into the Dardanelle Jail, removed Holland, and lynched him.[146] It appears that Casey left Carden Bottom and evaded capture.

An aside to this case also attests to the general acceptance of violence. Holland's mother-in-law, identified only as Mrs. Tackett, was prepared to be interviewed by law officers on Monday (November 29) regarding her knowledge of Holland's involvement in the James murder. On the evening prior to this scheduled interview, she was described by neighbors as being "well and hearty" and then "took supper at James Holland's house, died a few hours afterwards, and was very hurriedly buried."[147] Was Mrs. Tackett poisoned in order to seal her silence or was her sudden, unexpected death within hours of giving a statement to law officers just a coincidence?

Another brutal murder took place in May 1882 involving Lazarus Brooks and James K. P. McGhee, both of whom lived on the southeastern edge of Carden Bottom near the Yell and Perry County line. In the spring of 1882 McGhee signed a second one-year farm contract with Brooks but, soon thereafter, discovered that the farmland for which he contracted did not legally belong to Brooks. On May 24, 1882, McGhee confronted Brooks, who was accompanied by his sixteen-year-old brother-in-law, William Stewart. After a brief, heated conversation, McGhee shot Brooks in the chest as the shotgun blast first ripped apart Brooks's left hand. McGhee then emptied his shotgun at Stewart, who was "running as hard as he could go."[148] Stewart was injured—although not fatally—while Brooks was not as fortunate. Although he did not die instantly after being shot in the chest, he was unable to live up to the promise of his given name. Before the sheriff and his posse arrived on the scene, McGhee had returned to Brooks and, at close range, fired into his head blowing it into many pieces. McGhee was soon apprehended with a week's worth of provisions, a knife, and his shotgun as he had planned to hide in the woods in order to escape the posse. He was taken to the Dardanelle Jail, offered a full confession, stood trial, was convicted of murder in the first degree, and sentenced to hang. There were serious questions, however, as to McGhee's mental soundness. An appeal was filed, and as he languished in the Dardanelle Jail, a humble, always polite, and frequently tearful and shaking McGhee begged to see his wife and children.[149] His demeanor was not that of a cold-blooded killer, but rather that of a poor farmer perhaps lacking strong reasoning abilities who had been caught up in an oppressive economic web and who was accustomed to settling disputes in a confrontational, violent manner. Ultimately, the governor commuted McGhee's death sentence to a term of life in prison.[150]

Violence was not confined to only Carden Bottom. In late August 1883, the people of Dardanelle and the Upper Bottoms were shocked by the murder of a respected farmer and longtime area resident, Robert J. Pendergrass. Described as a "good old man," Pendergrass was driving his wagon to his farm some five miles south of Dardanelle on August 31, when he was shot and immediately killed by a double blast from a heavy-load shotgun discharge only four hundred yards from his house. The shooter was his hired hand, James Munroe Underwood, who had become intimate with Mrs. Pendergrass, both of whom were in their early thirties. According to Underwood, Mrs. Pendergrass had encouraged him to murder her husband saying she would then inherit his money and, that if Underwood refused to murder Pendergrass, she would explain their relationship to everyone, and Underwood would be a ruined man.[151] Mrs. Pendergrass was indicted for complicity in the murder, granted a change of venue to Conway County, and was acquitted in October 1883.[152]

Underwood was tried for first-degree murder, convicted, and executed by hanging one mile west of Dardanelle on December 7, 1883. Some 3,000 to 4,000 people witnessed the execution with great interest. The local newspaper noted that "Yell County had never before had a judicial hanging." Underwood's final words included: "I shot Mr.

Pendergrass on account of that woman. . . . I warn all young men to beware of bad women."[153]

The Pendergrass murder included all the elements of an absorbing modern crime story: sex, money, remorse, and pathos. The people of Dardanelle and the Bottoms were riveted by the details, offended by the immorality of adultery, and staunchly called for justice. This was a crime that they could not justify and therefore it deserved prosecution and punishment. In the end Underwood, convicted and soon to be executed, seemed the most earnest of all the players in this very ugly, very human drama.

## Lynchings and Race

Lynching was not uncommon in the early 1880s, and even less uncommon in the coming decades. The national lynching statistics for 1882 totaled 57 reported cases, including 34 white persons, 21 African Americans, and 1 Native American. Of course, these numbers were probably underreported. Of the total events reported, two took place in Arkansas.[154] At the February 1882 opening of the Yell County Circuit Court, grand jury members were encouraged to give "special attention to the 'hangings' and 'hair trimmings' done without regular process and contrary to the peace and dignity of the community."[155] Indeed, few things are more indignant than a lynching, especially if one is the victim.

The first reported lynching in Yell County occurred in Danville, western Yell County, on September 9, 1883. Dr. John Flood and John Coker had been arrested in connection with the murder of William Potter. Dr. Flood and Coker, while not directly involved in the murder, had rendered assistance, medical and otherwise, to Jack Daniels (Potter's killer) and members of his group. Flood and Coker were jailed at Danville while awaiting trial. Fifteen masked men used an ax to break down the jail door, took the two prisoners to the new three-year-old iron bridge over the Petit Jean River, and lynched them. The mob left their bodies hanging from the top iron railing and dangling over the roadway below. It was suggested that the men who performed this lynching should be indicted for "obstructing the public highways for surely no horse would cross the bridge with those men hanging there" and for being under the influence of "John Barleycorn, as an empty flask was found on the bridge."[156] These editorial comments clearly illustrate that the lynching of Flood and Coker did not prompt public outrage, and thus they provide further evidence of a general acceptance of violence if such acts were justified in the public's mind.

Race, of course, also played a role in the public's reaction to criminal acts. Again, however, the seriousness of the offense, coupled with the degree to which the public justified the act, played a key role in determining the magnitude of racist backlash. Selected crime reports illustrate this fact. First is the case of Jeff Perry, characterized as "(col.)," charged with stealing a cow. Perry waived his right to a trial and was fined $300 as punishment; unable to pay the fine, he was sent to jail.[157] In examining the reporting of Perry's offense there is a total lack of racist rhetoric, with the noting of his racial identity being the only reference to race. When compared to the following case, one notices a much more negative, inflammatory presentation of the facts coupled with a highly racist reaction: "Some drunken negroes fired into a tent . . . frightening a lady so badly as to cause the premature birth of a child, from the effects of which she died." This was followed by the editorial racist comment: "The miscreants lived in the bottom below Dardanelle. . . . No punishment is too severe for such barbarians."[158] The difference in reaction to these two criminal acts seem to be predicated not so much on race as on the nature, severity, and consequences of the offenses. Again, one has evidence of the extreme significance of the role played by the public's justification or nonjustification of a crime.

A third case goes even further in making this point. In a report about a white man arrested for raping an eleven-year-old "colored girl," the assailant was described as a "white brute" and the editorial comment was direct: "Let him swing."[159] Therefore, in the early 1880s race was a given fact to be duly recorded and noted in crime reports, but harsh language was accorded primarily to violent acts that deeply offended the public's moral sensibilities, and thus punitive recommendations were not necessarily solely based on race, at least, not in all cases.

A fourth case, while not officially classified as a crime, also affords insights. In October 1883 a death notice for Babe Cravens, "a young colored woman, very well-known in Dardanelle," noted that many of "the colored people" thought her death the result of domestic abuse.

Dardanelle's medical examiner denied that this was the case and thus further investigation was not pursued.[160] Was this a straightforward piece of reporting or, by reading between the lines, can one detect a racist inference? Was Babe Cravens a prostitute? Did Dr. Wilson, the medical examiner, dismiss the possible domestic violence in Cravens's death because he believed that such violence was common in African American households? Did he reason that a wife is the property of the husband and therefore abuse cannot technically occur and certainly cannot be criminally prosecuted? While there are numerous questions surrounding Babe Cravens's death, there are no definitive answers.

Serious crime did not end as the twentieth century began, but there seemed to be a greater preponderance of cases involving moonshining, bootlegging, gambling, and numerous lesser offenses. Conversely, therefore, the serious crimes that did occur seemed even more sensational. Among these lesser infractions, liquor played a major precipitating role in criminal activity and violence. Such was the case in Carden Bottom on April 22, 1900, when Constable Jeff Hunter attempted to arrest three men, the brothers John and Sam Scisson and Rufus Mims, for being drunk and disorderly. As Constable Hunter approached the Scisson home, John Scisson and Rufus Mims walked onto the front porch and began cursing at Hunter. John Scisson shouted, "there are not enough men in Carden Bottom to arrest me," and then he picked up a brick and a knife. Hunter backed out into the yard and drew his pistol. Hunter discharged the pistol several times just as Sam Scisson emerged onto the front porch. The third bullet struck Sam in the heart, killing him instantly. The medical examiner's inquest ruled Sam Scisson's death a justifiable homicide. John Scisson and Rufus Mims were charged with disturbing the peace, but were released in order to attend Sam's funeral. The combination of liquor, weapons, and young men with quick tempers created dangerous Saturday nights in Carden Bottom.[161]

## Liquor

During the 1880s liquor increasingly became a political and moral issue for the people of Yell County and indeed for most Americans, although at the beginning of this decade some Dardanelle merchants advertised that they kept "the finest grades of bourbon whiskies always on hand."[162] While running these advertisements, the same newspaper (the *Independent Arkansian*) would, within months, begin editorializing against alcohol consumption.[163]

In the early 1880s a majority of Dardanelle voters endorsed the presence of saloons, distilleries, and the selling of liquors. Results of the 1880 local option vote (wet versus dry) reveal that fifteen of the nineteen townships in Yell County (including Dardanelle and the townships in the Bottoms) voted to allow liquor sales.[164] Soon thereafter (on October 8, 1880), Distillery No. 54, owned by Joshua Toomer and Thomas Cotton, began business in Dardanelle.[165] The Yell County court was responsible for issuing liquor licenses, and by 1881 two licenses for the sale of liquor in quarts had been issued to two merchants (Cravens and Freeman), two licenses for the sale of liquor in quarts and drams had been issued to two merchants (Blackwell & Boyce and Cotton Brothers), and one license had been issued for the operation of a tavern to its owner (Looney). The same court issued two liquor licenses for two ferries operating on the Arkansas River (one operating at Dardanelle and one operating below Dardanelle north of Fowler in Carden Bottom) and one license to a ferry operating on the Petit Jean River in the Bottoms.[166] Thus, liquor was legal and abundantly available as the decade of the 1880s began.

During late 1881 and early 1882 the temperance movement took hold in Dardanelle, and a reversal of attitudes toward liquor occurred that transformed the views of most townspeople. Since many druggists sold alcohol-laced products—such as cough syrups—as medicine, the legality of this practice was of concern. Subsequently, the Arkansas Supreme Court handed down a decision that clarified unequivocally that "druggists are not allowed to sell liquor without a license from the county court, not even as a medicine upon the prescription of a physician."[167] In addition, Arkansas enacted a so-called Three-Mile Law (common in several southern and midwestern states) on March 2, 1881, which declared that any business with a license to sell liquor could not do so within three miles of a church or a school.[168]

On April 11, 1881, the Dardanelle chapter of the Good Templars Lodge was organized with an initial membership of eighty-one individuals who pledged total abstinence and planned for weekly meetings.[169] As the temperance/prohibition movement captured the interest of most Dardanelle citizens, local lectures were presented, an occasional symbolic burial of "King Alcohol" was held, and the local newspaper announced with pride that "not a licensed Saloon or whiskey shop of any kind is in Yell County."[170] This bit of hyperbole may have been based primarily on the *Independent Arkansian's* advocacy of temperance rather than on facts. Just one week later, two Dardanelle physicians, Dr. Jones and Dr. Harris, were each fined $200 for selling liquor, "believing they had a full and perfect right to prescribe and furnish ardent spirits in the practice to their patients."[171] The liquor question was divisive as reflected in Yell County Circuit Court cases, 25 percent of which dealt with "selling liquor without a license." The standard $200 fine did not appear to be a major deterrent to a continuation of this practice.[172]

While the liquor question may have posed some difficult moments for the citizens of Dardanelle, such was not the case for the people of the Bottoms who firmly held the conviction that people should be able to make, obtain, sell, and consume alcohol. The townships of Wilson and Galley Rock continually voted "wet" from 1880 until 1900.[173] Even after the 1900 "Bone Dry" Law was enacted in Arkansas and the 1919 ratification of the Eighteenth Amendment to the United States Constitution, many people in the Bottoms continued to make, obtain, sell, and consume alcohol. The law was one thing, but the freedom to enjoy liquor was quite another.

As Dardanelle and most of America were becoming increasingly anti-liquor, the Bottoms were "wet." Lacy's Ferry, operating on the Petit Jean River thirteen miles south of Dardanelle and three miles east of Bata's Mill (soon to be named New Neely), advertised in the Dardanelle newspaper that they were "now selling whiskey by the quart . . . prices 80 cents and a dollar per quart."[174] One of the more notorious of the "liquor stands" in the Bottoms was located in Carden Bottom (Wilson Township), a saloon associated with Cowger's Gin, generally referred to as "the Stump." Known for its unbridled enthusiasm, ready liquor, card games, horse racing, gambling, and fairly frequent knife fights among its patrons, the Stump had developed a well-earned unsavory reputation. The "boys" who enjoyed a little fun at the Stump could engage in some rough "play."[175] Saturday nights at the Stump were aptly described in the following manner: "down at the Stump last Saturday night there was smashing of bottles and a chawing of ears. Several of the 'boys' were right in the middle of the fracas but they checked out all right Sunday morning, condition excepted."[176]

Violence at the Stump was almost always expected and usually occurred. In the fall of 1883 a tenant farmer, Ruben Owens, was enjoying an afternoon at the Stump. After having reportedly consumed a large amount of liquor, he engaged in a wager with "the boys," claiming that his mare, "the fastest little mare in Yell County," could beat anyone's horse. Wagers were taken and a race ensued wherein Owens fell from his horse and was trampled to death.[177] In the end, Owens lost the race, his bet, and his life. Incidents at the Stump involving drunkenness, fist and knife fights, and general mayhem continued well into the twentieth century. Doris Hundley Hickey, who was born in nearby Bryant's Cove in 1929, later remarked, "you damned right it was wild there—a race track, honkytonk, drinking, gambling, carousing. Good people didn't go there."[178]

Regardless of the law, liquor was generally available upon demand throughout the Bottoms, and over time, the major recurring "liquor problem" became moonshining and bootlegging. Although cases were prosecuted from the early twentieth century forward, when arrests could be made, as early as the 1880s it became increasingly clear that the people of Dardanelle and the Bottoms had distinctly different positions on the liquor question.[179]

In 1908 Dardanelle began to license pool halls in an effort to curtail the liquor trade and general public disorderly conduct.[180] This was a contentious issue sometimes pitting the mayor, Al Clinton (an ancestor of Bill Clinton), who favored continued pool hall licensing, against the city council. As late as the 1950s, a section of Quay Street in Dardanelle (between Front and Second Streets), which contained several pool halls, was popularly referred to as *El Dorado* or *Tuff* (Tough) Street. "Tuff Street was where you could get a drink or a cold beer, enjoy a game of pool and quite possibly get into a fight of some sort."[181]

Of course, most people from the 1880s onward simply desired safety for themselves and their families, security for their possessions and interests, and generally predictable calm. While a rightful execution or a lynching that followed a terrible crime might make the blood pump faster and vindicate one's sense of right over wrong, nothing is quite as comforting and reassuring as a peaceful, uneventful day. An example of this was the post-holiday demand that "a stop should be put to promiscuous shooting on the streets at night. Christmas is over. Let it go."[182] Citizens called for, and happily generally enjoyed, calm as noted by an *Independent Arkansian* comment: "quiet and good order prevailed in Dardanelle as a rule during the holiday season."[183] One can almost hear the collective sigh of relief. The frontier days of the wild river town were fading, but just a little.

## Education

One indicator of a maturing town is an educational system that functions smoothly. Private and church-sponsored schooling existed in Dardanelle prior to the Civil War, with the first "subscription" school opening in 1848 and operating in conjunction with the Methodist Church. A private academy, the Dardanelle Institute, opened in 1859; the first public school opened in 1873 and included grades one through twelve.[184] During the 1881 school term 194 students were enrolled.[185] By the early 1900s the school had hired certified teachers and was accredited by the Arkansas Board of Education, which meant that its graduates could be accepted into Arkansas state colleges without having to pass qualifying exams. The Dardanelle Colored School, the Douglas School, began operations during the 1870s and operated with a minimum teaching staff offering instruction to students in grades one through eight.

As communities developed in the Bottoms, each little hamlet created its own school, usually a one-room/one-teacher school that included grades one through eight. These rural schools generally had small enrollments and were located such that students had to walk only several miles at most in order to attend. All schools, whether town or rural, operated on a split-term system in order to accommodate the demands for labor during harvesting and planting seasons. The fall term generally ran from September or October to January; the spring term ran from March to June.

The need for an education was great. An 1882 survey revealed that 23.8 percent of white Arkansans could not read, compared to 17 percent nationally; and that 38 percent of white Arkansans could not write. Among Arkansas's African Americans, 75 percent could not write, compared to 70 percent nationally.[186]

By 1910 the Dardanelle Public Schools had the most rigorous academic standards and academic curriculum in Yell County. The school district annually employed approximately ten teachers and two administrators; occupied a large, two-story brick structure; and had an enrollment of three hundred students.[187] The Parents' Improvement Society had been formed and met regularly to discuss educational topics and needs.[188] Among the graduates of Dardanelle High School were students who later attended Ouachita Baptist College, the University of Arkansas, Galloway College, Arkansas College, and several out-of-state institutions.[189]

By 1910 the Douglas School was increasingly stressing vocational/industrial education for its 130 students. Still operating in a one-room building with only one or two teachers, the Douglas School aggressively sought and usually received excellent parental support as well as general support from the local white population. Thus by 1910 some progress, especially for the white Dardanelle Public Schools, had been achieved. If educational pursuits were in fairly good shape (comparatively speaking for the time), the general state of health in the area was not.

## Health and Disease

The period from 1880 to 1910 did not enjoy contemporary general standards of health. Although seven doctors resided in Dardanelle, and several more practiced primarily in the Bottoms, there were many diseases and deaths that, according to current standards, probably were avoidable. Communicable diseases were fairly common and many times deadly. Malaria, consumption (tuberculosis), typhoid fever, influenza, diphtheria, whooping cough (pertussis), measles, mumps, and pneumonia were fairly common maladies especially in the Bottoms. To this list of potential killers one can also add scarlet fever, pellagra, and smallpox, the latter of which rarely was diagnosed in Yell County during this era but was frequently reported as being present in other river ports and thus created great anxiety. Other health concerns that frequently resulted in death included heart attacks, kidney aliments (referred to as Bright's disease), and strokes. In addition, accidents were also numerous and often deadly.

What is perhaps most shocking to the contemporary reader is the large number of infant and child deaths, a trend that continued into the twentieth century. These child deaths were usually announced in beautifully written, short obituaries that offered heartfelt condolences to the family and friends of the deceased. Not as common as these frequent infant and child deaths, but certainly noticeably present, were reports of entire families perishing due to disease. Most of these deaths occurred in the Bottoms to what the *Independent Arkansian* usually described as "a poor family" or "a destitute family" who probably had little or no money to obtain medical help. The disease germs would pass from one family member to another until the entire family was dead, often within a brief period of time.[190]

The Arkansas State Board of Health published directives advising citizens how to avoid and deal with these deadly diseases. These directives included vaccinations for school-age children, isolation of the afflicted, disinfecting all clothing and sick room materials, and getting prompt medical attention.[191] The lack of high literacy rates, however, meant that these precautions did not always reach the poorest and most vulnerable people. Class and race and their corresponding economic resource implications also played a role in health or its lack. Given these reasons, killer diseases and conditions were less common in Dardanelle (although not completely absent) than in the Bottoms. Dardanelle also began to discuss the need for the creation of a sewerage system and a clean street/alley improvement campaign in order to improve health and entice new businesses and visitors to the town.[192]

As mentioned above, accidents were also quite numerous and often deadly during this period. Accidental deaths were associated with hunting, train accidents, drowning, fire, farm animals, farm machinery, and the ingestion of poisons. Some of the most horrible deaths resulted from cotton gin accidents. If these accidents did not cause death, then they almost always resulted in the loss of a limb.[193]

Great turmoil and general anxiety also resulted from a mad animal threat. The local newspaper reported the following disturbing report from Carden Bottom in the fall of 1882:

The cows and hogs are all running mad and are quite dangerous.
Women and children are kept indoors, and the men are . . . out
with their guns shooting the rabid animals. Five or six cows and
as many hogs have been killed, while others are expected to go
mad. People have quit using milk. Considerable excitement is
said to be prevailing.[194]

The threat of rabies would send a shudder through a neighborhood or community as quickly as would a gunshot blast. Rabies was
a threat to townspeople as well as those in the rural areas. In late 1882,
Colonel H. C. Gibson's hired man was "treed" on top of the woodpile
in the colonel's backyard by a mad dog, "frothing at the mouth and
'going for' everything in sight." Colonel Gibson shot three times and
killed the dog, much to the relief of his hired man. All of this transpired in Dardanelle at the corner of Third and Oak Streets, and the
anxiety and general panic that accompanied the threat or rumor of a
"mad dog" roaming the town would continue in Dardanelle into the
1960s.[195]

# Religion

The Baptist and Presbyterian churches had been damaged or destroyed
respectively by Union forces in the Battle of Dardanelle in early 1865.
Rebuilt during the 1870s and 1880s, these churches by the early twentieth century had large, devoted congregations. In early 1880, four
churches existed in Dardanelle: Presbyterian, Methodist, Baptist, and
Episcopal. By 1910 the Cumberland Presbyterians had established a
congregation in Dardanelle, and the Baptists had built and dedicated
a handsome new building, larger than any that they had previously
occupied, in 1909. Each of the Dardanelle churches had highly active
women's auxiliary groups that held afternoon meetings at various
members' homes and mixed their religious agendas with the social.
Whether these women's auxiliary groups were missionary societies,
Sunday school groups, or Women's Aid Societies, the women of the
Dardanelle churches were a force within their respective congregations and the community, devoting countless hours toward achieving
their church and community improvement goals.[196]

Rural churches were frequently ecumenical rather than denominational, regularly met in a dual-purpose community building such as a school, and functioned primarily with lay leaders and circuit-riding ministers as none had fulltime pastors. These congregations would hold brush arbor baptismal services in the spring or summer followed by large "dinners on the ground," a community potluck with the food supplied by each female church member. The rural churches provided spiritual guidance as well as opportunities for social interaction.

## Women

In addition to women's church-related activities, in Dardanelle women also participated in several civic efforts and organized clubs. Literary groups, educational and school support groups, charitable aid societies, the Women's Christian Temperance Union (WCTU), and the local Joe Wheeler Chapter of the United Daughters of the Confederacy (UDC) were all active in Dardanelle at various times between the 1880s and 1910. During the early 1880s Dardanelle women, as well as men, became increasingly involved in temperance efforts.[197]

The efforts of the United Daughters of the Confederacy in part was a subtle means to maintain the earlier southern class stratification with the "better sorts"—the planters, attorneys, physicians, and merchants—in a dominant position over the "lesser" whites and the African Americans.[198] By venerating the glories of the Confederacy's Lost Cause, the ladies of the UDC were upholding the traditional "proper" class roles for different groups within southern society. Furthermore, the UDC affirmed and upheld the values of the Old South, honoring Confederate veterans and preserving their memories.

Certainly women's groups and clubs in the decades from 1880 to 1910 groomed women for a greater public role, but economics also played a key role. As historian Anne Firor Scott notes, it was primarily economic imperatives that caused the erosion of the status quo and the appearance of new social mores for southern women.[199] This, however, does not appear to have occurred in Dardanelle until the 1930s.

The upper-class women of Dardanelle became the social leaders of the town. Included within this elite group were the wives of several prominent and prosperous Dardanelle Jewish merchant families such as the Kaufman, Bondi, Hetch, Hess, and Garu families.

The first recorded Jew to settle in Arkansas was Abraham Block, who in 1825 established a retail business in Washington (Hempstead County). Several decades later (1880s), Jewish settlers arrived in Dardanelle. Typical of the Jewish migration to Arkansas following the Civil War, these settlers were mainly merchants who had close ties to Jewish wholesalers in larger out-of-state locations such as Memphis, Tennessee; St. Louis, Missouri; and Louisville, Kentucky. An example of this was the Kaufman family who arrived in Dardanelle in approximately 1883 and established a large retail business on Front Street named the J. D. Goldman and Company. Goldman, Mr. Kaufman's brother-in-law, owned a wholesale operation in St. Louis. These Jewish businessmen such as Kaufman who came to the South sought to derive economic profits from Arkansas's developing economy following the Civil War, which increasingly had ties to larger national markets. In 1878 Arkansas's population included 1,466 Jews who were mostly of German and French heritage. By 1937 this population had increased to 6,510 Jews living in seventy-two Arkansas counties. This increase resulted primarily from the massive influx of eastern European immigrants prior to implementation of immigration restrictions based on ethnic origin quotas during the early 1920s. Beginning in the late 1870s small but significant Jewish enclaves developed in Fort Smith, Pine Bluff, DeValls Bluff, Jonesboro, Batesville, and Van Buren as well as in Little Rock and Dardanelle.[200] While the Jewish population of Arkansas was—and currently is—a tiny portion of the whole, these individuals contributed greatly to the economic and civic vibrancy of the towns in which they settled. This was certainly true of the Jews in Dardanelle who arrived in the early 1880s and exited during the 1920s.

As the end of the nineteenth century neared, the local newspapers published numerous reports of various social gatherings. Elaborate parties were staged as well as recital performances by the children of the town's leading families. Lawn parties, recitals, dramatic presentations, and holiday celebrations were the common fare. The social scene in Dardanelle was dominated by this elite group composed of select individuals from wealthier families, who were often guests in one another's homes. They sometimes traveled together on vacation trips to Little Rock, New Orleans, Memphis, or New York. Their children grew up as playmates, friends, and classmates and as young adults frequently married one another. Thus, the economic power of Dardanelle continued to be dominated by the same families for decades. Therefore, social class was a significant element in understanding the life of Dardanelle from the 1880s well into the mid-twentieth century.

A social life also existed in the Bottoms, but it was notably different from that of Dardanelle. Social gatherings in the Bottoms centered about picnics, barbeques, singings, children's day celebrations, and community church services with accompanying social functions. While simple affairs when compared to the elaborated town functions, these rural gatherings were just as anticipated and enjoyed, although much less elegant and splendidly appointed.

Wealthier Dardanelle inhabitants enjoyed the summer season (April to October) atop Mount Nebo, located four miles west of town and rising 1,829 feet above sea level. The cooler summer weather attracted families and visitors to Mount Nebo, and those who could afford to do so built summer cottages including several noteworthy people from Little Rock such as Uriah Rose, whose law firm would become renown. The opening of the Summit Park Hotel on Mount Nebo in 1889 was a major attraction for both in- and out-of-state visitors. An elaborate hotel, the Summit Park offered guests a variety of entertainments from horseback riding, hiking, tennis, and lawn croquet coupled with the activities of the large hotel ballroom for dancing and parties, a bowling alley, and a restaurant. The Summit Park Hotel was a Victorian-styled, three-story wooden building featuring piped-in water in every room from the mountain's system of fresh springs. It could host 450 guests and was advertised as a luxurious resort in a beautiful and healthy, outdoor setting. In 1889 one could rent a room and enjoy all of the hotel's amenities for $35 to $40 per month with special rates for entire families. Visitors would travel by rail to North Dardanelle, cross the Pontoon Bridge to Dardanelle, load onto wagons drawn by oxen, and ascend the winding dirt road strewn with boulders to the Bench (a mile below the top of the mountain) before riding the remaining distance to the apex. Mount Nebo became a vacation destination replete with cool mountain breezes, beautiful panoramic views of the Arkansas River Valley below, and a variety of social activities. For the social elite from Dardanelle who built cottages on the mountain, this summer rendezvous strengthened their social and economic ties to one another as well as to other leading affluent families throughout Arkansas and in other parts of the country.[201]

## Conclusion

Great change occurred in Dardanelle and the Bottoms during the thirty years from 1880 to 1910. The areas experienced growth, development, and general improvement. The bleak, survival mode so characteristic of the post–Civil War era gave way to better days. People still spoke resentfully against the "carpetbag oppressors and their corruption for temporary gain" as they recalled the "desponding hearts of a down trodden people . . . bound and shackled" by Reconstruction Republicans.[202] Many challenges were faced: a rich farmland had to be brought back to life and production; Dardanelle needed better transportation and communication systems, as well as a financing system for farms and business growth; and residents desired to again feel hope and engage in frivolous, light-hearted activities. The simple pronouncement of an 1883 farmer laconically captured the spirit of the 1880s: "Yell County is a might good country, but too backwoodsy."[203]

Given thirty years of effort, sweat, investment, and dreaming, the despondent mood of the early 1880s was partially superseded by a new reality by 1910, more optimistic and buoyant. The Dardanelle business community was larger and more diversified; an expanded transportation system had been established; the farmers of the Bottoms were a little less desperate and more unified; and the area enjoyed more social life, church picnics, improved water and sewerage systems, expanded schools, electric lights and telephones in Dardanelle, rural free mail delivery, and a movie house. Levees were built to protect from the terror and destruction of rising waters. Farmers had successfully engaged in self-help unionization and were avidly practicing improved farming methods. By 1910, improvements had indeed been made, although some problems remained such as gross racial inequities, disease, and economic hardship.

The period from 1880 to 1910 saw greater improvement for the people of Dardanelle than for the residents of the Bottoms. Declining farm prices throughout the 1880s and the crippling impact of the

Panic of 1893 resulted in near-starvation conditions for many rural people. The lack of adequate roads and bridges compounded daily difficulties for rural residents. The crop lien system and the power of the furnishing merchant posed a boot heel to their necks. While many people in Dardanelle enjoyed improved overall conditions, simultaneously many people in the Bottoms, while working diligently and producing huge crops, still faced grinding debt and poverty.

The concept of the New South to which the economically powerful of Dardanelle and the Bottoms adhered was not the typical New South interpretation. Instead, the Dardanelle definition of the New South was based on the notion of economic might, with prosperity resulting from the reciprocal nature of the farm to business. This had little to do with industrialization, and thus this was not a true New South model.[204] The Dardanelle business and Bottoms agricultural interests were devoted to an earlier model for economic success, an antebellum model, which they adjusted to fit the realities of the post–Reconstruction era and to which they adhered well beyond 1910. Given this model, the people of the Bottoms, while a little better off, remained perpetually trapped in an antebellum time warp controlled by forces over which they had little, sometimes no, power. They were continually beaten down by declining prices, hunger, poverty, and the demoralizing pain of always losing the opportunity to progress and advance. Between 1880 and 1910 the town/rural reciprocity had produced dynamic, powerful driving forces that resulted in the reestablishment of Dardanelle and the Bottoms and that primarily benefited the former at the expense of the latter.

## CHAPTER 3

# Growth, 1911–1919

*Cotton brings a higher price in Dardanelle than in any other market in this section of the State . . . local merchants are selling goods at a lower margin of profit than the merchants of other places drawing trade from a radius of forty miles. . . . long cotton-laden wagon trains can be seen on our streets almost every day.*

DARDANELLE POST-DISPATCH,
*Editorial, November 1913*

*Robberies of every nature have been reported in this vicinity except holdups and there is no inducement whatever for these as only cotton farmers reside in this section.*

CENTERVILLE RESIDENT,
*February 1915*

*There ain't any one of us bottom folks going to stand for you taking niggers into your house and making them so free-like. Soon we'll have to make another drive to clear 'em all out. We ain't got but a few families of the colored folks left here. They jest ain't welcome.*

HETTIE WOOD,
*Lower Dardanelle Bottoms resident, circa 1922*

# Introduction

As the second decade of the twentieth century began, growth was the hallmark of Arkansas agriculture. Based on comparative data from 1900 to 1910, Arkansas appeared poised for continued development during the second decade of the century. The population had increased 20 percent and the total value of farm property had increased 120.4 percent to $400,089,000. Agricultural growth included a 134 percent increase in the value of farmland, a 97 percent increase in the value of livestock, a 110 percent increase in the value of buildings, and a 92 percent increase in the value of farm implements and machinery. By 1910 the average value of one acre of Arkansas farmland stood at $14.13 as compared to $6.32 in 1890. While the average size of an Arkansas farm declined to 81.1 acres in 1910 as compared to 93.1 acres in 1900, the number of farms increased from 1900 to 1910 by 20.1 percent to a total of 35,984. Total farm acreage increased from 16,637,000 in 1900 to 17,377,000 in 1910 and improved farm acreage jumped from 6,954,000 to 8,062,000 during the same decade. Arkansas in 1910 had 151,085 white farmers (70 percent) and 63,593 African American farmers (30 percent). Although African Americans constituted 30 percent of all Arkansas farmers, they comprised 76.9 percent of Arkansas tenant farmers in 1910. Finally, 1.6 percent (2,458) of white farmers were foreign born.[1]

# Agriculture

While an undercurrent of change rippled through agriculture, Arkansas as well as the Dardanelle Bottoms remained tied to the plantation agricultural model. The call for crop diversity, which had been present prior to 1910, became a clarion call during World War I. New technologies were beginning to alter life on some farms, mainly larger operations. Science and new technologies were in vogue with an emphasis on new training for farmers and placing a greater reliance on the expertise of county farm agents and other experts. While more farmers were buying automobiles, especially Fords, and some began replacing their beloved mules with tractors, the poorer subsistence farmers, tenant farmers, and sharecroppers continued generally to rely on nonmechanized power. While the daily rhythms of farm life remained somewhat constant, the older methods and the fundamental reliance on cotton were challenged by 1920, although the plantation model, traditional farming methods, and cotton remained the norm.

Given the effects of World War I from 1914 through early 1920, Arkansas farmers enjoyed the greatest degree of prosperity they had experienced since before the Civil War. One only needs to look at the selling price of cotton to see this economic change. On November 27, 1912, cotton was selling at 12¾ cents a pound in Dardanelle, and by November 6, 1919, the selling price had increased to 47½ cents a pound.[2] Of course, what this example does not reflect are the lean years in between, such as when the price for cotton in Dardanelle was only 11½ cents in late February 1913, Nonetheless, growth and improved prosperity were fleeting and uneven.

Agricultural dislocation following the prosperous times of World War I created dire conditions for Arkansas farmers. By 1920 Arkansas's two primary crops were cotton and rice and, although agricultural total production figures were impressive, $345,606,000 (including both crop and livestock production), this figure represented a decline of 29.8 percent ($147,000,000) from the previous year.[3] The standard message, preached for two decades, of crop diversification and self-sufficiency would not remedy the farmers' troubles, which included the need for bigger markets, lower interest rates, increased credit availability, and the end of exorbitant freight rates.[4] Some sought economic salvation through cooperative marketing via farm organizations while others relied on more diversification and improved scientific farming methods. During the 1930s, all would ultimately turn to the revolutionary new agricultural policies of the federal government in hopes of saving themselves from economic extinction. Meanwhile, Dardanelle area farmers increased their dairy herds, marketed more cream, began to plant some soybeans, and continued their Elberta peach, strawberry, and Irish and sweet potato production. Irrespective of these efforts, farmers in the Bottoms continued to struggle as cotton prices declined during the 1920s causing increased poverty, deprivation, and economic ruin. The 1920s were full of gloom and want for the farmers of the Dardanelle Bottoms. From 1911 through 1919, Dardanelle and the Bottoms experienced growth, economic promise, and high hopes. During the next decade this would be followed by devastating declines, economic woes, and depression. This was a period of uncomfortable transition from growth to hard times.

This economic rollercoaster was at one of its high points in the late summer of 1911 as cotton gins were gearing up for what was expected to be "a record breaking ginning business" and Dardanelle merchants "expected a bumper crop."[5] Economic optimism is also evidenced by a 1912 local editorial remark: "when the next crop is harvested this country will again be in a prosperous condition."[6] Hopes for the 1913 crop were also high as many observers looked forward to "the finest crop we have ever seen" with gleeful predictions of "an average of more than a bale per acre."[7] While everyone wanted to believe that the worm had finally turned for the hardscrabble farmers and plantation owners of the Bottoms, by the end of 1913 cotton season, the average price per pound of cotton was only 13½ cents.[8] By late 1913 the price of cotton created the gap between high hopes and hard realities.

While the rural standard of living was marginally improved during the early part of the second decade of the twentieth century, small farmers were still poor and deprived of what is currently considered to be basic necessities such as indoor plumbing, electricity, food refrigeration, and sanitary living conditions. Luther Kent spent the first twenty-eight years of his life (1899–1927) in Carden Bottom and recalled it as a "tough place . . . no motor transportation, only mule-drawn vehicles, no radios, telephones. . . . It was not uncommon for one to be killed. . . . and election day ballot boxes were taken by parties on a 'drunken spree.'"[9] In 1911 Fred Phillips, born and raised in Dardanelle and the director of the Arkansas Agricultural Department, advised small farmers that "supplies should be raised at home" and to stop buying on credit what could be produced on the farm.[10] Prosperity prompted by World War I era demands improved cotton prices and many farmers turned away from Phillips's sage advice even as Herbert Hoover, Federal Food Administration director, echoed Phillips's message and stressed self-sufficiency as a patriotic war measure. For most farmers, however, the desire to cash in on high cotton prices during the war was too great a temptation to pass up. No self-respecting cotton farmer wanted to plant feedstuffs when he could earn 25 to 30 cents per pound for his cotton.

In 1911 a female farmer told Clay Sloan, the Arkansas commissioner of agriculture, that she was trying to diversity her crops and stop being primarily a cotton farmer, but that high freight and commission rates plus an occasional market glut for the non-cotton crops left her little profit while her cotton farming neighbors were earning a profit. Sloan responded by arguing that nondiversified cotton farming yielded an increasingly smaller profit margin in each successive harvest while the proper management of fruit, vegetable, and livestock farming was the real solution for the farmers' financial problems. He advocated home canning of surplus fruits and vegetables, suggesting that a home canner costs from $5 to $20 and the canned product could be sold for cash or used to supplement the family diet during the winter months.[11]

Many farm women accepted and acted on the call for greater self-sufficiency even though canning meant that farm women, usually the wives and daughters of farmers, would have to take on an additional duty. However, canning resulted in better family health via an improved diet while also benefiting family finances by the sale of their products. Dardanelle merchants, it appears, understood the importance of canning and preserving farm foodstuffs as evidenced by a three-column front-page advertisement in the local newspaper promoting an available supply of fruit jars of "all kinds and sizes and our prices will interest you."[12]

Canning coincided with another of the farm women's typical tasks: growing and maintaining a garden. Women planted beans, tomatoes, cabbages, and various fruits in order to augment their families' winter diet. As finances became tighter and/or as the government pushed for greater self-sufficiency, farm women enlarged their gardens to include peas, turnips, kale, and collards for early planting in August and then lettuce, radishes, mustard, and spinach for a later planting. A farm woman's garden became a major source for the family's food supply and a major part of her daily workload.[13] State agricultural officials advised farmers to "be careful and do not plant a bigger garden than your wife can cultivate . . . and in the spring buy a home canning outfit. . . . Let the women and children attend to milk and butter and chickens and perhaps the garden. Do the field work yourself or hire a hand to help."[14]

Farmers were also encouraged to get their wives and children involved in raising poultry and thereby profit from selling eggs while also providing the family a source of cheap food.[15] Additional information about raising poultry and designs for building a poultry house appeared in local newspapers from time to time.[16] Sugar rationing during World War I stimulated the stripping of sorghum cane by some farmers as a means to provide a sugar substitute for one's family and a source of additional income. While sorghum meant another task for farm women and children, it was also another "way to beat the high cost of living by raising a living at home."[17] Obviously, farmwives and their children played an integral role in the daily operations and economic success of the family farm whether manifested in poultry and egg production, gardening and canning, or sorghum extraction.

Most people during the early twentieth century, especially in rural areas, accepted the basic premise that "the prosperity of the country is based upon the successful operations of the farmers [and] that as the farmers succeed the country prospers, and that when they fail to make good crops the country suffers."[18] This argument embraced scientific farming as a means to upgrade production levels, which included improved farming methods, seeds, and fertilizers. For example, state agricultural commissioners urged farmers to plant clover to replace the lost nitrogen in the soil.[19] Farmers also took note of new farm machinery, especially reports in 1912 of a horse-drawn cotton picking machine.[20] The argument for scientific farming methods promised that farmers would realize "a great reward for their years of toil and privation if they will take advantage of the opportunity to furnish their country with needed food stuff, as consumption is increasing at a much faster rate than production and prices will remain remunerative for an indefinite length of time."[21] Cotton was still predominant in the fields and the hearts of the farmers, but the undercurrent of change was creating a noticeable ripple.

The Farmers' Union, which had successfully struggled in previous decades to establish itself in Yell County, was now storing and insuring cotton for 25 cents a bale monthly in its cooperative warehouse in Dardanelle.[22] By 1912 there were four hundred Farmers' Union locals in Arkansas, proof that they had created a place for themselves and posed a legitimate presence in Arkansas agriculture.[23] As an established entity no longer seen as radical Populism, the Farmers' Union, by the second decade of the twentieth century, had been largely accepted as demonstrated by its 1911 Little Rock meeting attended by farmers, bankers, businessmen, and Governor George Donaghey. By 1910 the Farmers' Union was the most powerful farm organization in Arkansas.[24] Farmers, while urged to avoid as much debt as possible, were advised to hold their cotton for a 15-cents-per-pound price as bankers would make low-interest agricultural loans.[25] The faint outlines of the agribusiness juggernaut were beginning to become visible.

As small farmers were developing various plans for their advancement so, too, were large landowners who began cultivating increasingly larger tracts of land. One such landowner was C. B. Cotton, who in June 1912 placed a notice in the *Dardanelle Post-Dispatch* calling for one hundred men and fifty mule teams to clear new ground on what would become the Cotton Plantation and later be known simply as Cotton Town. Located in the Lower Dardanelle Bottoms, Cotton Town was east of New Neely and southwest of Carden Bottom (see Appendix, fig. 6).[26] Several months later, Cotton advertised for tenant farmers: "Wanted 50 men and good mule teams to break 600 acres of new ground—$1.00 to $1.15 per acre—good houses and pastures furnished—New Neely."[27]

Dardanelle business owners were also aggressively seeking customers, and merchants promoted their businesses as they promoted the town. Advertisements noting "immense stocks of goods . . . and rare bargains" were designed to bring rural money into Dardanelle. "Local cotton buyers are paying more for cotton and our merchants are selling more goods for a dollar than can be obtained elsewhere." Dardanelle businessmen sought to attract not only trade from the Dardanelle Bottoms (their normal trade area), but trade from western Yell County as well. Western Yell County farmers shopping at J. D. Goldman & Company received $5.00 a bale more than they were offered elsewhere. The distance hauled was about thirty miles.[28] Most of the business advertisements and newspaper editorials that promoted Dardanelle as the trade center for the surrounding rural area were keyed to cotton. Dr. Ed Aikin, a Dardanelle veterinarian, lapsed into hyperbole when describing his 1914 trip into the Bottoms: "the only reason there was not more cotton in the bottom was because there wasn't room on the stalk for it . . . many of the cotton fields resemble great patches of snow."[29] Few things could make the heart of a Dardanelle businessman and a Bottoms farmer race faster than the prospect of a great cotton crop. Indeed, Dardanelle business was tied directly to cotton.

> Cotton brings a higher price in Dardanelle than in any other market in this section of the State, and this, together with the fact that local merchants are selling goods at a lower margin of profit than the merchants of other places, is drawing trade from a radius of forty miles. The long cotton-laden wagon trains which can be seen on our streets almost every day call to mind the days prior to the building of the Rock Island Railroad, when Dardanelle was the cotton market for several surrounding counties.[30]

The frequently heard adage that in Dardanelle a customer's dollar purchases more seems to have its beginnings in the merchants' aggressive retail practices during the early twentieth century. One example was the advertising campaign by Dardanelle Feed and Grain Company offering a new steel range in exchange for a 500-pound bale of cotton.[31] While such advertising may have gotten the customers into the store, the down side was the merchant's low profit margins, which meant businessmen had to be cautious not to price themselves into bankruptcy as they discounted and offered inducements to attract customers.

Beginning in 1911, landowners began to experience labor shortages, a condition that only grew worse over time. In late May 1913, J. A. Rainey, a prosperous landowner from Pontoon, came to Dardanelle looking for workers to hoe cotton and offered to pay for the work done at the end of each day and to provide transportation to and from his farm, both highly unusual. Generally, laborers were paid only at noon on Saturday at the end of the workweek. Even with his generous terms, Rainey failed to find any workers.[32]

From 1911 through 1914, the local newspaper contained numerous advertisements for farm laborers: "100 peach pickers and packers needed" and "Everybody is wanting cotton pickers."[33] Bottoms landowner Howard Hunt ran the following advertisement in 1913: "Wanted: Several families to [pick] 300 acres of big boll Cotton. Easy to pick, any ordinary picker can pick from 300 to 400 pounds per day. Good houses, wood handy, 3½ miles below town."[34] C. B. Cotton was so in need of laborers to pick his cotton that he considered having a cotton picking contest with the winner getting $25.00. Cotton also advertised that twenty-three tenant houses were ready for pickers and that he was constructing four more. He intended to employ one hundred pickers and harvest twenty bales of cotton per day. In order to get the needed pickers, Cotton sent one of his laborers "to the Mountains to bring some cotton pickers down."[35] The "Mountains" is a reference to the Boston Mountains beginning just north of Russellville and Atkins and extending northward into the Ozarks, an area that sent whole families to the Dardanelle Bottoms to pick cotton yearly. Cornelia Daniels, who grew up in Riverside in the Upper Bottoms, recalled that her grandparents came from "the mountains" in the late 1800s, and due to a death in the family and a lack of money, were unable to return and thus became permanent Bottoms residents.[36] There was also a need for seasonal laborers as strawberry and peach pickers. In 1916, T. A. Johnston placed the following advertisement: "Throughout the strawberry season, which lasts two weeks or more, we will want from one to two hundred pickers. Picking will begin between May 1 and 5."[37]

During World War I, many African Americans extracted themselves from the South and farm tenancy and moved north for factory jobs. As some African Americans departed, the Bottoms saw more migrant farm laborers who drifted in during peak labor demands and then left. Meanwhile, the poorest of the poor, both African American and white, remained as tenant farmers or sharecroppers seemingly tied to the land, living in peonage and unable to uproot themselves.

The economic rollercoaster that was the early twentieth century caused many farmers to suffer from 1911 to 1917. In early 1913 cotton was selling in Dardanelle for 13 cents a pound.[38] Lower prices caused J. W. Dunlap, a Carden Bottom cotton farmer, to organize a farmers' meeting in October 1914. Citing low crop prices and cotton market speculation, Dunlap made a strong plea to landowners and merchants for leniency for tenant farmers. J. F. Judkins, a farmer attending the meeting, said that he believed "the local merchants were honest and paid all they could for cotton, but that they, too, were largely at the mercy of the cotton speculator."[39] Judkins urged farmers to plant ten to thirty acres of wheat and reduce their cotton acreage. The extent of the cotton crisis was further discussed as W. D. Cotton, cashier of the Dardanelle Bank and Trust Company, noted that local merchants and bankers were assisting farmers by buying cotton, of which only 150 bales of the 1914 crop had been resold and the businessmen were still holding 3,000 warehoused bales from the 1913 crop, while Dardanelle cotton buyers had marketed 4,000 bales. The problem was an over-abundance of cotton. Cotton said his bank was developing $100,000 for agricultural loans so that farmers "might hold their cotton off the market," and he urged the farmers to produce a 1915 crop that contained less cotton and more foodstuffs and feed.[40]

These sentiments echoed the distress call issued by United States senator James P. Clarke (D-Arkansas) just a month earlier. Noting that simply withholding cotton from the market would do little good given the huge level of cotton production, Senator Clarke said the only remedy for cotton farmers was a set of legal restrictions on the amount of cotton that could be grown. "If we carry over 6,000,000 bales this year, and raise a normal crop next year, it will take three to four years to absorb the surplus. This would mean a period of poverty in the cotton growing states."[41]

A cotton crisis meant trouble for all parties: Bottoms farmers and landowners, Dardanelle merchants and businesses, Arkansas, the South, and the country. A farmer from the Bottoms used humor to express the meaning of the cotton crisis. "Robberies of every nature have been reported in this vicinity except holdups and there is no inducement whatever for these as only cotton farmers reside in this section."[42]

While farmers and businessmen attempted to grasp at ways to solve the agricultural economic woes, some hinted at a noncapitalist solution. The primary inequities of the capitalist system, especially as it affected agriculture, were highlighted in the local newspaper's reprint of an editorial from the *Sheridan Headlight*. The writing warned that the current economic system was producing paupers living in the world's richest country, their children begging in vain for bread in the shadows of the town's magnificent churches, toiling men and women who never wasted a penny remained desperately poor while rich men drove automobiles and had servants lace their shoes. All of this occurred, the writing continued, while the producers of wealth toil for little or nothing and the children of the poor go naked. "There would be no such thing as overproduction if hoarding unearned wealth were prohibited."[43] While this was not the predominant view, nonetheless even in the Arkansas River Valley in 1915 some were thinking and reading about the economic inequities caused by capitalism and the possibilities of a socialist alternative.

Prior to 1916, farmers did generally practice great frugality. Given the prospects for "splendid crops of all kinds" in 1915, it was disturbing that farmers' accounts at local supply businesses were much smaller than usual, a fact that underscored farmers' increasing reliance on self-sufficiency and homegrown supplies.[44] Milk, cheese, butter, wheat for flour, berries both grown and picked from the countryside, peach, pear, and/or apple orchards, pork, vegetables, and even fish caught in the rivers were all examples of "homegrown" supplies. Given these homegrown assets a savvy farmer and his wife through great personal effort could avoid buying many food items. As cotton prices declined, "homegrown" efforts were a means to economic survival. Small land-owning farmers, the agricultural middle class of this time, were able to ensure their economic survival through this greater self-sufficiency.

"Fancy Groceries," the type of items generally only stocked in retail stores in town, were not usually purchased by farm families. A poignant exception to this fact involved the actions of an unnamed tenant farmer on a hot July afternoon at the Gleason and Cravens Store in New Neely in 1917. The tall, thin farmer, dressed in dirty over-alls and a sweat-stained straw hat, had charged to his account some coffee, a bag of flour, and a figure eight of chewing tobacco. As he turned to leave, his eye caught the orange label of a peach can on the shelf behind the counter. The farmer told the young boy behind the counter to hand him one of those large tins of canned peaches. The boy hesitated and told him those peaches were expensive. The farmer defiantly answered, "just add it to my account." The farmer went to the front steps of the store, sat down, and reached in his front over-alls pocket to retrieve his pocketknife. The young store clerk watched as the farmer opened his knife, cleaned both sides of the blade with a quick swipe over his dirty pants leg, and carefully opened the tin of peaches. The farmer speared each piece of peach with his knife and slowly chewed and swallowed. It seemed a serene moment of defiance and ecstasy. Sometime during this process, the young store clerk stepped out onto the store porch and sat down near the farmer.

When all the peaches had been eaten, the farmer carefully drank the peach juice from the tin can, wiped both blade sides of his pocket-knife, folded it, and returned it to his overalls pocket before tossing the empty peach can over to the side of the store's yard. The two sat silent for a few minutes and then the farmer said as if talking to the breeze but loud enough so the boy could hear: "sometimes you just have to have something special." Quietly the farmer lifted himself to his feet and went on his way.[45] Regardless of how frugal and self-sufficient the rural people were, even they on occasion gave in to the desire for a costly treat—this time, a tin of peaches.

In 1915, C. B. Cotton invented, patented, and installed a new gradual ginning system at Cotton Town. This ginning system promised an increase in the amount of cotton (lint) ginned by approximately 20 to 25 pounds per 500-pound bale and cleaner cottonseed, which would result in a higher price paid by cottonseed oil mills. Both results would increase farmers' cash flow. The new ginning system created great excitement throughout the Bottoms.[46] There were 20,000 bales of cotton produced in Yell County in 1915. If one assumes a price of 10 cents per pound for cotton and 20 additional pounds per bale for 20,000 bales, then the new ginning system purported to put an additional $40,000 into the hands of the farmers. Given these claims and highly positive testimonials by farmers, cottonseed oil men, and cotton buyers, it was not surprising that C. B. Cotton's gin in Cotton Town was pulling in new business from throughout Yell County. Farmers were willing to transport their cotton farther and pay about $1.00 more per bale for ginning in order to gain additional revenue.[47] As landowner Rush Cornwell noted in December 1915, although the long haul to the Cotton Town Gin was an obstacle, still he "was more than pleased . . . receiving as I did a little better than 6 lbs. per hundred more than I received on the old process gins."[48] As older gins purchased and installed the gradual gin system, additional testimonials of support were publicized, including those from the new gradual system installed at the Farmers' Co-Operative Gin in Carden Bottom.[49] The inexhaustible search for cotton profits therefore also included the application of new technologies.

As World War I began in Europe in August 1914, American cotton farmers quickly discovered that much of their market had been closed.

On August 24, 1914, a young Fields Chapel farmer, R. A. Horton, produced the first annual bale of Bottoms' cotton, a traditional honor to be celebrated, but he was offered only 8 cents a pound "on account of the demoralized condition of the cotton market occasioned by the European war."[50] Only farming thirty acres and in need of cash, Horton did not think he could afford to place his bale in storage to wait for a higher price. He sold his cotton and before leaving Dardanelle collected his prize for bringing in the season's first bale: a forty-pound sack of flour, a one-year subscription to the local newspaper, and $1.00 funded by twelve Dardanelle businessmen.[51]

As World War I continued to disrupt the cotton market, farmers in the Dardanelle Bottoms increasingly felt the sting of lower prices. A 1914 resolution passed by a meeting of farmers, businessmen, and local and state officials called for holding cotton for a price of 12 cents a pound, a more lenient credit system from bankers for farm loans, and a reduction of farm debt plus a 50 percent reduction in cotton acreage for 1915. "[E]very farmer [must] sow sufficient wheat to supply his family with bread."[52] This resolution also asked the county quorum court to continue to provide funding for the county demonstration agent's work, which had been initiated in 1909. With the call for reduced cotton acreage, the 1915 production figures in Yell County were dramatic. Whereas between January 1 and October 18, 1915, the county ginned 4,152 bales of cotton, during the same time period in 1916 the total was 16,382 bales.[53] Obviously, the 1915 call for reduced cotton production did not carry over to 1916.

During the first three years of World War I (1914–1917), without a market for cotton the farmers of the Dardanelle Bottoms and the businesses of Dardanelle faced immediate and dire circumstances. The prospect of starvation in the Bottoms, especially for the poorest (the tenant farmers and sharecroppers) and, to a somewhat lesser extent, for the small landowning farmers, was stark. With little to no money from the sale of cotton and with limited to no food sources, the need to diversify immediately became very real. The effect of a "cottonless" agriculture was no less dramatic and terrifying to the economically cotton-dependent citizens of Dardanelle. While cotton was still grown, most farmers in the Bottoms, especially small landowning farmers, planted less cotton, diversified their crops, and concentrated on growing what they needed to feed their families and stock. The message so eloquently delivered by the late Fred Phillips, which had been initially followed by only a few, was now the accepted order of the day.

After America entered World War I in February 1917, United States director of the Food Administration, Herbert Hoover, wisely made the case to the American people regarding the need for increased food production for the Allies, the starving populations of Europe, the American soldier fighting overseas, the large number of workers employed in the war industries in American cities, and the American public.[54] With production and population statistics wrapped in patriotic war rhetoric, most Americans accepted Hoover's argument for greater foodstuff production, careful use of all foodstuffs, and a commitment to nonwasteful practices. Since the production portion of the Hoover plan directly rested on farmers, they faced tremendous pressure to alter their crop selections. Most Bottoms farmers—in staunch patriotic fashion—responded positively and planted more food crops, even though they were cotton farmers to the very core of their marrow.

Hoover's message was reinforced by numerous national and state agricultural officials from 1914 through 1919 as they urged farmers to "produce food and feed stuffs at home" as well as the "profitable raising of livestock—horses, mules, cattle, hogs and sheep in Yell County as well as more forage crops and cover crops."[55] Whether a "scientific farmer" or not, the US Department of Agriculture and the Arkansas Commission on Agriculture promoted this diversification agenda and urged farmers' wives to attend demonstration meetings and lectures. All this was an effort to improve the possibilities of a farmer long devoted to primarily raising cotton to realize a new or additional path for his family's livelihood. Yet, while farmers might embrace these plans for the short run given the uncertainty in the cotton market, a cotton farmer was primarily still a cotton farmer.

In March 1918, an article in the *Dardanelle Post-Dispatch* on the early success of truck farming in and around Centerville underscored the economic viability of farm diversification. It reported that in October 1917, ten railway cars of sweet potatoes were shipped and two additional railway cars were about to be shipped. These twelve railway cars held 6,720 bushels of sweet potatoes, which were sold at $1.50 a bushel and thus netted farmers $10,080. "That is a good showing for a small start ... and does not include the bountiful supplies that have been kept for home and local use and that have been retained for seed. ... Farmers now have money and their wants for the near future are supplied."[56] Fruit production was also spurred during World War I. In 1916 three local farmers were considering growing blackberries, while 350 local people were "making a good wage picking strawberries."[57] Peaches continued to be gown in the area, especially in Elberta approximately two miles south of Dardanelle. In 1916, forty-eight railway cars of peaches were shipped from Elberta, although the next year these shipments declined by more than 50 percent to twenty-two railway cars due to the cold and rainy spring. Regardless, the 1917 peach shipments sold for $1.70 a bushel in northern markets, an increase over the 1916 price.[58] Fruit farmers in the Dardanelle area and elsewhere in Arkansas would soon be negatively affected and more closely regulated by new state laws designed to inspect produce entering the state in an effort to create barriers against the importation of harmful insects and fruit crop diseases.[59]

The threat of starvation continued to pose fears as no one was certain just how the flour rationing system would be allocated during 1919. The only sure way to avoid this threat was to plant and harvest one's own food and not rely on an uncertain rationing system.[60] During 1917 and 1918, the US Government promoted the development of Girls and Boys Agricultural Clubs to foster the production of various types of foodstuffs including corn, wheat, and poultry. One such effort was centered in and around Centerville as young children were encouraged to raise poultry both for home use and for profit.

For merchants selling feed and grains, crop diversification and increased foodstuff production during World War I was just what their businesses needed. In late 1917 Dardanelle Feed and Grain Company offered its customers a sincere wish for continued prosperity and a grateful thank-you for their patronage, noting that 1917 had been "the best year in the history of our business."[61] Thus, while cotton ginners and cotton factors may have suffered some loss of business, especially during the early war years, other Dardanelle merchants reaped profits from farm diversification. What happened to the American farmer during World War I did nothing to substantially alter the fundamentally reciprocal economic dynamic that existed between the rural and

the town. This relationship was palatable as evidenced by the formation of the Yell County Business Men and Farmers' Association in
Dardanelle, "an organization whose purpose it is to promote a closer
relationship between the people of the County, irrespective of their
avocations, and to promote by every means possible the progress and
prosperity of the entire County."[62] This relationship, notwithstanding a
revision of crop selection, was just as strong a year after the conclusion
of the war as it was in May 1914, when the association was formed.

Cotton prices steadily increased during 1917 as the war in
Europe continued. On January 17, 1917, middling cotton was selling
in Dardanelle at 17 cents a pound, and by February 1, the price had
increased to 17¼ cents. By mid-December, the price had jumped to
29 cents a pound, and over the next month prices rose three times in
Dardanelle: from 29.15 cents (December 27) to 29¾ cents (January 3,
1918) to 30 cents (January 10, 1918).[63] Despite what casually appeared to
be the return of a good cotton market, the USDA advised caution. Its
Profitable Farmer Campaign met in Dardanelle in February 1917 with
lecturers warning farmers that even though cotton was nearing 20
cents a pound, recent escalation in the price of consumer goods meant
that farm families still had less money to spend on "dry goods, clothing, meat and other goods than in recent years." A representative of the
Dardanelle Bank and Trust Company also noted that the Dardanelle
cotton market generally ran $2.50 to $5.00 less per bale because farmers did not use pure seed and thus produced a bale that was more "half
and half" cotton than 100 percent cotton. He stressed that bank loans
would be made to farmers who invested extra money to purchase pure
cottonseed in order to improve the quality and purity of their crop.
Even with rising prices, the familiar themes of self-sufficiency, diversification, and caution were being advocated by the USDA.[64]

A new marketing and ginning law enacted by the Arkansas
General Assembly went into effect in 1917. Under this law, cotton bales
were to be deposited in a cotton warehouse from which the farmer
could then take his warehouse receipt to a local bank and obtain a
loan against the anticipated price of the cotton and then have his cotton graded by USDA inspectors. Once graded, the farmer could then
take his paperwork to the local cotton buyer and either sell his cotton
for the going price or opt to leave his cotton in the warehouse until

the price increased.[65] The law's purpose was the creation of a more systematized cotton market through the creation of a more uniform pricing system based on uniform cotton grading. Most gin owners supported the law and hoped it would work as intended.[66] The Cotton Futures Act of 1916, a federal law designed to allow the USDA to keep track of what was being grown, required the type and grade of cotton to be determined upon its sale at a cotton exchange. The overarching goal of this law was to control and track the amount and quality of the cotton crop in the United States.[67] Arkansas's cotton warehouse law employed the same basic principles used in the Federal Warehouse Law enacted in 1917 for the regulation of grain farming, a law which had resulted from some twenty years of lobbying by midwestern grain farmers dating back to the Populists of the 1890s.

By the spring of 1918, just a little more than a year since the United States' entry into World War I, the agricultural production of the Bottoms had undergone a notable transition. Farmers were producing notable amounts of corn, oats, hay, Irish and sweet potatoes, sorghum, turnips, vegetables, strawberries, and peaches in addition to cotton. In early 1919, I. C. Jones, a farmer from the Bottoms, sold fifty-nine chickens in Dardanelle in a single day for the sum of $50.00. Mr. Jones commented that poultry was "the most profitable crop" he knew and that he still had "a large flock of hens [and that] he expects to place a fine line of broilers on the market later. More attention is being paid to beef and pork production and poultry raising."[68] While still a local, perhaps small regional enterprise, farmers were beginning to quietly realize the possibilities of raising poultry. Later, as the market broadened, so would their production.

Regardless of diversity, the call of cotton remained a siren call for many. On September 16, 1918, eight cotton farmers from the far reaches of western Yell County, forty-five miles west of Dardanelle, drove into town at 6:30 p.m. in a flatbed Ford truck loaded with ten bales of cotton having driven past Danville—where cotton was selling at 32 cents a pound—and proceeding to Dardanelle for its price of 34 cents a pound. The round trip cost the group $30 and they calculated that driving the extra distance still netted $4.50 more per bale. The cotton buyer paid for the men's supper at Horn's Café before they began the long trip home. Here is proof that, in spite of every effort at

crop diversification, cotton was still *the* crop. "The fact that local buyers are paying top price for cotton, and the further fact that Dardanelle
merchants have complete and up-to-date lines of merchandise which
they sell at the lowest prices possible, are bringing cotton to town from
a radius of fifty miles and the wagon trains now frequently seen on
Front Street recall the good old days before the building of the Rock
Island Railroad."[69] An established way of life and traditional patterns
of living were not easily altered. Cotton was in the soul of far too many
for its quick displacement.

Transition was occurring, however, as farmers adopted new methods and approaches. In 1914 Congress had passed the Smith-Lever Act
that established the agricultural extension service, a cooperative effort
between the USDA and land-grant colleges. The act also provided funds
for farm and home demonstration agents in states and counties that
appropriated matching financial support. In 1917 the Smith-Hughes
Act became law, providing high school training in agriculture and
home economics.[70] These new federal programs, which were fully initiated in Dardanelle and the Bottoms during the 1920s, began to appear
after World War I. In July 1919 the University of Arkansas offered a five-
day agricultural extension course, which several Yell County farmers
attended and which included training in soil conservation, livestock
management, the use of legumes and other crops, as well as marketing.[71] The new county extension agent worked with farmers to cooperatively ship Irish potatoes and hogs to the St. Louis market where
they frequently brought a higher price than in the local markets.[72] In
early 1920 some Yell County farmers attended a training session held
in Little Rock featuring new farm machinery, especially tractors.[73] The
emphasis on better farming methods focused on training farmers to
use modern scientific applications for planting and marketing. World
War I rationing of foodstuffs, the constant demand for self-sufficiency,
temporary blockage to world cotton markets, and the rising cost of
producing a crop motivated farmers to seek and use improved and
modern farming methods. The ripple of change was felt.

## Transportation

During the period from 1911 to 1919, Dardanelle and the Bottoms continued their struggles to develop an efficient system of transportation.

As the previous decades' development of area railroads ended, the
need for better roads and highways and improved bridges was accentuated. By 1919 the transportation system was improved, but was not
yet thoroughly modern.

On December 9, 1910, the Dardanelle, Ola, and Southern Railway
(DO&S) filed for bankruptcy. First opened on May 1, 1906, and primarily financed by Dardanelle businessman John B. Crownover, the
eighteen-mile short line had linked the Dardanelle and Russellville
Railroad (D&R) in North Dardanelle with the Rock Island line in
Ola.[74] The DO&S began with a large debt encumbrance, suffered
from a lack of paying customers, and was ultimately destroyed by
"the gumbo," the black, sticky rich mud of the western edge of the
Upper Dardanelle Bottoms. During wet weather periods, the rails and
the caboose-smoker work car would sink in the mud. A farmer from
the Lower Bottoms would later sarcastically note: "If you stick with
the gumbo during dry weather, it will stick to you in wet weather."[75]
Original bondholders received 10 cents on the dollar of their original
investments as the DO&S literally sank into oblivion. On October 6,
1911, the new Rock Island and Dardanelle Railroad Company (RI&D)
was granted a charter, and the job of repairing and reestablishing a
new eighteen-mile rail from Dardanelle to Ola began.[76] In subsequent
years, this section of rail would become part of the Fort Smith, Subiaco
and Rock Island Railroad (see Appendix, fig. 7).

Meanwhile, despite handling large numbers of passengers and
freight, the D&R line was operating with small deficits. Its 1911 reports
revealed 17,142 passengers and 43,874 tons of freight were hauled, but
a deficit of $188 was the net result. Despite the D&R handling 22,361
passengers and 53,227 tons of freight in 1912, the line had a deficit of
$1,802. The increases, especially in passengers, were due largely to the
increased activities of the Russellville coal mines, but interest payments on indebtedness and taxes were the financial culprits.[77] While
never profitable, the D&R remained highly patronized locally, but its
investors, mainly northeastern financiers, would not continue to support an unprofitable operation. The D&R line was sold on April 21,
1913, to J. G. Puterbaughtm, president of McAlester Fuel Company and
recent purchaser of the Southern Anthracite Coal Mining Company
in Russellville.[78]

While coal and the mining of it were not present in Yell County, it was in nearby Pope County. In fact Arkansas's number-one mineral/ fuel source of production from 1880 to 1920 was coal as it was present in a narrow thirty-three-mile-wide and sixty-mile-long strip running from Sebastian County eastward into Pope County. Pope County mining nearest to Dardanelle occurred in the Bernice Mine located south of Russellville and north of North Dardanelle, an area traversed by the Dardanelle and Russellville Railroad. Between 1880 and 1976 only 3 percent of Arkansas total coal production was mined in Pope County. Peak coal production in Arkansas occurred in 1907 as 2.6 million tons were extracted, with most of it used for home heating and as fuel for industry and the railroads. For a time, beginning in 1903, coal mines in Arkansas were closed shops, and every Arkansas coal miner was a member of the United Mine Workers of America. As the gasoline combustible engine began to become commercialized, the demand for coal declined and economic woes for miners resulted. Increased labor unrest followed. Examples of this were seen at the Bernice Mine, which impacted the D&R primarily because of its coal-related ownership. Ultimately, legal decisions in *Coronado Coal Company v. United Mine Workers of America* (1922) resulted in the end of the closed shop in 1927 in Arkansas coal fields.[79] Thus, while coal was not produced in Yell County, its close proximity in Pope County affected Dardanelle citizens and particularly the D&R and its operations.

Highway and road construction were "hot" topics from 1911 to 1920. The roads into the Dardanelle Bottoms were very poor as noted in the following newspaper editorial:

> In the winter and early spring the river road to Carden Bottom is often almost impassible [*sic*] by an empty wagon being a heavy load for a large team of mules. Is there an acre of land, improved or unimproved, between the city limits and the mouth of Petit Jean that wouldn't be enhanced in value at least $1.20 by reason of the construction of a permanent macadam highway from Dardanelle to Fowler? As a matter of fact such an improvement would increase the value of these lands many times this sum, yet $1.20 per acre will be the approximate average TOTAL cost.[80]

Rural residents had long suffered the inconvenience caused by impassable, muddy roads, and Dardanelle businessmen wanted easy access to and from the wealth of the Bottoms and the town's goods and services available for purchase. Within a week of the above editorial being printed, interested citizens from Ola, Centerville, Fowler, Neely, and Dardanelle met and drafted a plan for the construction of a forty-mile macadam road under the new Alexander Road Improvement Law.[81]

Act 338 of 1915—commonly referred to as the Alexander Road Improvement Law—passed the Arkansas General Assembly with the stated goal of providing for "the creation and establishment of Road Improvement Districts for the purpose of building, constructing and maintaining the highways of the State of Arkansas."[82] Designed to address problems associated with using bonds to finance road improvement districts, this law was one of several legislative attempts since the early 1900s to create a viable mechanism for road development. Between 1915 and 1927, as a result of the Alexander Road Improvement Law, 527 road improvement districts formed a patchwork of locally developed roads. While laudable, this endeavor incurred substantial debt and lacked a financing mechanism for road maintenance and repair. As such, while most of these roads crumbled in time, their debt remained. Finally in 1921 a series of federal road aid bills were enacted that ended local road building, replacing these efforts with state control and state/local building and maintenance programs.[83]

The pitfalls of local road improvement districts were not well known in 1917, and plans moved forward. With great enthusiasm Yell County judge Robert T. Compton gave his support to a road plan and requested the Arkansas Highway Department send engineers and survey teams to prepare for construction. This plan proposed four new roads and preliminary engineering reports were filed on April 1, 1917, noting definite road locations and anticipated costs.[84] The Arkansas General Assembly approved the creation of Dardanelle Improvement District No. 1, and in July highway engineers said the increased assessment would run from $0.57 to $1.00 per acre.[85] Then in September, attorney W. C. Hunt voiced opposition based on assessment and tax concerns.[86] Early muted opposition over the estimated costs of these roads soon became organized and loud, as some cost estimates reached $792,578.20 for 31.57 miles. On May 8, 1920, a meeting at the Dardanelle courthouse attended by one thousand people—primarily property owners fearful of increased assessments and higher taxes—adopted a resolution demanding the resignation of the local road commissioners as "an overwhelming majority of the district . . . are earnestly and urgently and bitterly opposed to the building of the road."[87] As two road commissioners resigned and citizens were circulating a petition for their replacement, all roadwork was stopped. On May 29, 1920, Judge Compton received the citizen petition and appointed new road commissioners (Dr. M. L. Kirkscey, Dr. S. E. Miller, and Joe H. Gleason) who met and issued a board resolution that advised that "the proposed improvement be abandoned" due to the fact that the "benefits from . . . said construction are not commensurate with the cost [and] the Board is unwilling to impose a hardship upon the landowners of the District."[88] It was clear that while most wanted and supported improved roads, they also opposed higher assessment valuations and additional taxes.

While the transportation needs of the Bottoms was of paramount importance both economically and as a general convenience, Dardanelle street repairs were also a concern. In August 1913, 25 Dardanelle merchants closed their businesses for a day and physically worked with 125 town volunteers and those from the Bottoms and their 38 teams of mules to convert Second Street into a "clay dirt" street, a sand-clay road mixture that shed rainwater and reduced dust.[89] Two additional workdays—involving the efforts of 45 town merchants and laborers plus volunteers and their mules from the Bottoms—resulted in the completion of a roadway resurfacing project on a one-mile stretch of Second Street, seven blocks of Front Street, and five blocks of South Main Street at an estimated value of $1,200.[90] In 1917 businessmen and residents of Front and South Main Streets were encouraged to finance, via a small assessment per building and automobile, the layering of crushed shale, "jack" from the coal fields north of Dardanelle, on the streets in order to facilitate water runoff and a smoother driving surface.[91]

Still, by 1922 road conditions were so poor that the *Dardanelle Post-Dispatch* editor called Front Street "the worst public thoroughfare in Arkansas" and called for street widening and paving of the business district with business owners paying for the project.[92] Three years later the chamber of commerce unveiled a residential and business district paving plan for thirty-five blocks with costs to be subsidized by the city but mainly borne by the property owners. This resulted in a lawsuit in which the chancery court ruled on March 15, 1926, in favor of the paving petition and against the citizens who signed the nonpaving petition. The final section covered under this plan, the paving of Second Street, was completed on September 19, 1928.[93] After ten years of intermittent but strenuous efforts, the major streets in Dardanelle had finally become paved roadways.

By far the most dramatic single transportation-related event during the first few decades of the twentieth century was the building of Dardanelle's new toll-free, steel bridge across the Arkansas River, the so-called Free Bridge. Long dreamed of by numerous citizens of Yell and Pope Counties, but particularly by Dardanelle citizens, the realization of a modern steel bridge to replace the Pontoon Bridge was a major achievement involving both economic concerns and emotional trials and tribulations. Dardanelle merchants had sought the construction of this bridge as a means to increase their business activity as early as 1912. Legislative efforts in both 1913 and 1917 had unsuccessfully attempted to create the bridge, with the 1917 failure causing animosity, suspicion, and scorn between the residents of Dardanelle and Russellville as Pope County state representatives fought vigorously and successfully to defeat the legislative measure.[94] The new bridge would ultimately be constructed and opened on January 17, 1929.

## World War I

World War I profoundly affected Dardanelle and the Bottoms, with its accelerated sense of patriotism, military enlistments, increased racial intolerance, local Red Cross chapter efforts and, of course, its agricultural impetus, especially in terms of cotton production. Efforts during the war were unprecedented given the effectiveness and scope in their successful attempts to "foster a sense of national unity" and to organize the nation on three fronts: the military front, the economic front, and the civilian propaganda front.[95] The scope of these efforts during World War I introduced additional elements of modernity to Dardanelle and the Bottoms.

Government films produced by the Committee on Public Information—such as *The Kaiser* and *The Beast of Berlin*—blurred the line between entertainment and propaganda. These propaganda films played well in Dardanelle, attracting large and appreciative

audiences at the local movie house.[96] Local leaders became the face of
American propaganda through the federal government's Four Minute
Men project, as local citizens participated—some more thoroughly
than others—in food conservation efforts and Liberty Loan drives.
Schoolchildren collected goods and donated pennies, young men
went off to fight, local church congregations prayed for victory, and
ministers extolled the virtuous nature of the war.[97] Dardanelle businesses ran advertisements entirely devoted to patriotic propaganda
and activities such as the purchase of Liberty Bonds.[98] Evidence that
these propaganda efforts were effective can be found in the following quip by an unidentified resident from the Bottoms: "the disloyal
Germans in this country [should] be turned over to the tick eradication experts of the U.S. Department of Agriculture."[99]

In November 1917 the Dardanelle chapter of the American Red
Cross was formed. Organized nationally on May 21, 1881, in Washington,
DC, the first Arkansas Red Cross chapters originated during World
War I and raised supplies for the war effort.[100] Organizers of the
Dardanelle chapter sought to enlist five hundred members and were
able to get four hundred people to sign on as members. Leaders were
elected (two men and one woman), each member paid one dollar and
agreed to volunteer in the production (sewing and knitting) of goods
for the troops. The chapter's second meeting developed specific committees and collected donation pledges, and leaders gave reports from
their visit to the Little Rock chapter's workroom. While the town's
leading male citizens were involved, it was the Dardanelle women who
proved to be the workers.[101] Branches quickly were formed in Carden
Bottom (the Wilson Township branch), Centerville, and in Plainview
(western Yell County). Less than three weeks after its formation, the
Dardanelle chapter had a permanent location: Dr. S. E. Miller's former
office. The new headquarters would be "used as a work room, fitted up
with lights, cutting tables, and other needs tables, sewing machines,
chairs and settees for the use of the workers [and] fitted with a commodious rest room with toilet and retiring room facilities, for the use
of all the ladies, either from the town or country."[102] Members collected donations and produced an impressive quantity of assembled
clothes, socks, and bandages, with their first shipment in February 1918
consisting of 107 garments.[103]

Within four months of its establishment, the Red Cross in Yell County had 1,420 members. In Carden Bottom, active fund-raising efforts at Fowler had raised $110.15 from a single box-supper event and White Hall residents were also contributing monetarily. The Dardanelle chapter sent its third shipment of goods in April 1918, which included 155 garments that had been completed in just one week. Additional sewing machines and coal contributions for the heating of the workroom had been received, assisting the efforts to increase production. In addition, plans were announced for the establishment of a Colored Red Cross Branch in Dardanelle. It is important to note that participation in the Red Cross "transcended racial barriers," which included African American males contributing financially as African American women volunteered their time and efforts in the preparation of garments and bandages although this work was performed in racially segregated quarters.[104] By late March 1918 there were six official branches countywide including new chapters in Danville and Ola, and members had raised $1,941.28 in cash, in addition to the production of tangible goods.[105] By April 1918, White Hall in Carden Bottom was planning for hundreds to participant in a giant Red Cross rally and fund-raiser as the Dardanelle workroom continued to produce impressive results as noted below.[106]

| DATE | NUMBER OF "LADIES" WORKING | TIME WORKED |
|---|---|---|
| April 1, 1918 | 18 | 55 hours, 50 minutes |
| April 2, 1918 | 20 | 68 hours, 10 minutes |
| April 3, 1918 | 14 | 34 hours, 10 minutes |
| April 4, 1918 | 22 | 65 hours, 55 minutes |
| April 5, 1918 | 10 | 36 hours, 25 minutes |
| April 8, 1918 | 17 | 53 hours, 15 minutes |
| April 9, 1918 | 15 | 47 hours, 45 minutes |

In May 1918, the Centerville Red Cross branch was primarily creating hospital supplies, basically the rolling of bandages.[107] Thus, within approximately six months of operation the six branches of the Red Cross in Yell County were actively supporting the war effort and the various Bottoms communities were engaged in fund-raising efforts. Dardanelle set the pace for these efforts both in fund-raising and in production of goods. Dardanelle merchants and businessmen continued to collect and contribute financial donations as did rural residents, who additionally donated a rick of wood for auction, which netted the Red Cross $223, an exorbitant amount in part given people's memory of the terrible cold of the previous winter, which created the need for coal.[108] Various benefits and fund-raising events, including ice cream suppers, picnics, and pie suppers, were sponsored by the Dardanelle Bohemian community and at Centerville, New Neely, and in Carden Bottom.[109] The residents of Yell County were actively participating in every way they could to support the war effort. Patriotism was apparent and tangible as divisions by race, class, and gender seemed to be temporarily blurred.

These efforts, whether fund-raising, volunteering work hours, or personally donating funds, can be summarized as having three basic purposes: to allow civilians to care for military members by offering medical aid, clothing, and a touch of home; to maintain strong civilian patriotic support by providing a means of participation in the war effort; and to increase the material comfort of military personnel with millions of woolen sweaters, mufflers, socks, and other handmade items. The Red Cross aggressively advertised that "every dollar received . . . goes for war relief."[110] Certainly, the efforts by the Red Cross resulted in a beneficial production of goods and the promotion of the war's patriotic propaganda message by affording a means for direct participation of the civilian population. It also temporarily created a sense of joint community among citizens with everyone, regardless of socioeconomic standing, race, or gender, engaged in a mutual support of the military. While this war experience did not erase the deep divisions of class, race, and gender, for a short time the lines of demarcation between various divisions of people were blurred and somewhat dimmed. World War I was everyone's war; a study in— if not total, at least substantial—national unity, the result of carefully scripted government direction and propaganda.

These wartime experiences had a lasting effect on American society as historian Robert Murray notes the inability of the American

people to quickly return to a prewar world minus the directed wartime hostility toward all things "un-American." This resulted in the
First Red Scare, increased racial violence, hostilities toward immigrants, and a strong opposition to labor unions.[111] President Warren
G. Harding may have longed to return the nation to "normalcy," a
pre–World War I world, but this could not happen. The war had deeply
affected the American psyche, and thus the 1920s would be a highly
reactionary period nationally and in Arkansas.[112]

Following World War I, the Red Cross redefined its mission as
it began to administer social welfare assistance as a charity outreach
program to deal with the needs of the feeble minded, insane, or delinquent. This refocusing of its message was intended to avoid duplica-
tion of the mission of other more established charitable groups, as the
Red Cross directed these efforts primarily toward the "little country
town" with women trained to carry out this work in their local communities.[113] Certainly, it appears that the American Red Cross had
realized the positive value and power that women volunteers could
have by working within their communities to address local needs.
Nonetheless, this Red Cross effort at a refocused mission did not take
hold in Yell County following World War I. When the Second World
War began, area women immediately used their World War I experiences to again organize, volunteer, and serve.

Government control over the economy during World War I
took various forms, many of which affected the daily lives of people
in Dardanelle and the Bottoms. Dr. S. E. Miller of Dardanelle was
appointed food administrator for Yell County, and he in turn appointed
members representing the various area communities to an executive
committee whose primary purpose was to avoid food hoarding. Miller
took this responsibility seriously as did those working with him. By
April 1918, it was reported that Yell County was one of only two of
Arkansas's seventy-five counties that "had thoroughly perfected its
organization" under the federally mandated Food Administration
Guidelines.[114] Given the great need for foodstuffs for shipment to
European allies, as well as foodstuffs needed for the US military and
civilian population, the hoarding of food in the United States had
been made a crime and local food administrators were charged with
enforcement of these regulations. Under these rules, it was unlawful

for a retail merchant to have more than a thirty-day supply of flour and sugar in his inventory and he "must regulate his sales of sugar to from 3 to 5 pounds to city trade and [from] 10 to 20 pounds to country trade."[115] Fines for hoarding, both for businesses and individuals, were increased to $5,000 plus a minimum penalty of two years to a maximum penalty of five years of imprisonment. Citizens also generally accepted meatless Tuesdays, wheatless Wednesdays, and porkless Saturdays as part of their patriotic contribution to the war effort. For those who did complain about the abrupt upset of their dietary habits, printed articles were quick to remind these complainers of the "horrors of modern warfare . . . with its liquid fire, poison gas, and other creations of the modern Hunkultur."[116] Such patriotic peer pressure usually instilled a quiet obedience to rationing and dietary restrictions. After all, what is giving up pork on Saturday compared to suffering a gas attack?

In late November 1918, restrictions were also placed on business operation hours as issued by the Federal Fuel Administration. "All retail establishments, except drugstores, may remain open only from 9 o'clock a.m. to 5 o'clock p.m. on all week days except Saturdays and Mondays, on which days they may remain open from 9 o'clock a.m. to 9 o'clock p.m."[117] These regulations were designed to primarily reduce coal consumption. Despite the negative impact on their business activity, especially during the holiday season of 1918, supposedly most merchants "cheerfully complied."[118]

World War I also affected citizens in numerous small ways. A first-class postage stamp cost 3 cents rather than the prewar 2 cents, and due to the new war tax, the price of a movie ticket in Dardanelle increased from 10 cents to 15 cents for an adult and from 5 cents to 10 cents for a child.[119] Farmers were asked to plant between one-half to one acre of Irish potatoes primarily for export to Europe.[120] A Centerville farmer noted that the high cotton prices (middling cotton sold for 28 cents a pound on November 1, 1917, in Dardanelle) were a necessity given the inflated prices for everything else. "High prices are now a necessity in order that what we produce will compare in value equally with what we have to buy."[121] It was impossible to escape the effects of World War I, and even in the most remote areas, the war changed, at least temporarily, one's daily routines.

While many ordinary citizens endured shortages and rationing and businessmen dealt with inventory rationing regulations, many American industries were making hefty profits during World War I. This was especially true of foodstuff industries, which saw their profits from 1916 to 1917 far exceed their normal 100 percent markup. Meat and dairy industries all greatly profited by the increased demand for products. The fruit and vegetable industries recorded a 255 percent increase in profits during the same one-year period, and the same profit bonanza was recorded in the molasses and syrup industries primarily due to sugar rationing. The canning industries saw more than a 100 percent increase in profits. While flour, barley, and corn-based industries were increasingly profitable, they were not as profitable as were other foodstuff producers and processors.[122]

Sugar sales continued to tighten as the war continued. In May 1918 it was announced that anyone needing sugar for canning or preserving could buy whatever amount was needed, but they had to sign a card with the retail merchant certifying that the product would only be used for canning or preserving foods plus they had to pledge to return any unused sugar to the merchant. At the same time, the Food Administration announced a monthly per capita sugar allowance limit of two pounds.[123] By July 1918 anyone buying sugar for wholesale, retail, or manufacturing use was required to complete forms with the local food administrator's office. Failure to do so would result in the complete denial of sugar for the remainder of 1918.[124] As more Americans reduced or eliminated their sugar use, molasses prices and sales dramatically increased, eventually reaching a price of 70 cents per gallon by mid-July 1918.[125] Since rural families were typically larger than those living in town and since rural families did more of their own canning and preserving of foodstuffs than did many townspeople, the effects of food rationing for rural people were particularly severe. Inflated prices also added to this misery. Whereas food rationing created an inconvenience for almost everyone, in some cases it resulted in real hunger. Centerville's ordinance requiring that hogs be penned became more significant as some people could no longer afford to buy meat and thus a free-roaming hog could easily become a target for one's smokehouse and dinner table.[126] These World War I dietary restrictions also produced extensive, long-term effects. For several decades following the Great War, Americans consumed less sugar and included more vegetables and less meat in their diets. In addition, the trend toward a leaner silhouette, especially for women, became the cultural norm.

Given the government acquisition of the railroads in order to facilitate efficient transport of military supplies and troops, by early 1918 it became increasingly difficult for civilians to ship goods. These circumstances, coupled with Food Administration regulations, led the government to emphasize self-sufficiency. An example of this was the government's 1917 campaign entitled "Let the South Feed Itself." Assistant Secretary of Agriculture Clarence Ousley encouraged farmers to "raise all you can at home for life's necessities" and avoid depending on cotton because "you cannot depend on getting your necessary supplies shipped from other parts of the country." Producing food, as opposed to cotton, was stressed as Ousley said, "480,000,000 of the world's population are withdrawn from productive industries and . . . it is not humanly possible to produce to exceed demands."[127]

J. C. Barnett, the district agent for the US Department of Agriculture, appointed twelve chairmen in Yell County—each representing an agricultural growing area or a community—to promote increased production of food and feedstuffs. Using the phrase "Food Will Win the War," these twelve men worked directly with farmers to promote the planting and harvesting of more food crops and livestock feed crops.[128] The message was clear: grow as much food as your family and livestock use, depend on yourself, and frequent local suppliers. Self-sufficiency was king.

Patriotism and profits, however, were at odds, and the farmer was caught in the middle of a no-win situation. By late December 1917, cotton was selling at 29 cents a pound, and the price would increase during 1918 to 31 cents a pound. At the same time, cotton farmers were also growing corn, sorghum, potatoes, and wheat.[129] In order to further encourage agricultural self-sufficiency, the government began requiring cotton gin operations to have a license issued by the food administrator.[130] This was a "back door" method to limit cotton production via the limitation of the number of available cotton processors. Thus, despite their reluctance, cotton farmers were forcibly enticed to grow food and feed crops, undoubtedly wincing due to the high cotton prices that they could not completely grasp. The call for patriotic action won out over the desire for profit.

Five Liberty Loan Drives were staged in Yell County during 1918 and 1919, with each exceeding its stated goals.[131] During the third Liberty Loan Drive, which began on April 6, 1918, Yell County's goal was $134,350 and the achieved results were $181,400. During this drive the Dardanelle Bottoms (Wilson and Galla Rock Townships) exceeded its $10,000 goal as did Dardanelle Township with its $30,000 goal.[132] The bonds sold were tax-exempt US Government bonds, offering a 4.5 percent rate of interest.

Much hoopla was associated with the Liberty Loan Drives. Newspaper promotions; support from town businessmen, leading families, and rural leaders; elaborate parades; visits and speeches from the governor, the state attorney general, and various local officials; picnics and ice cream socials were all elements of the Yell County Liberty Loan Drives. Together, these activities built public support and participation, fanned the patriotic flame, created a sense of local/ national cohesiveness, and generated sufficient interest to motivate people to buy bonds—a tangible sign of one's patriotism and support for the military and its men. In Yell County, this all worked beautifully.

If one could not afford to purchase a Liberty Bond, there were less-expensive ways one could financially support the war effort and participate in the great hoopla generated by World War I patriotic fervor. First, for only 25 cents, a Thrift Stamp—a noninterest-bearing device—could be purchased and displayed on a sixteen-stamp tray, which had to be purchased separately from the government. Second, War Stamps or War Savings Stamps—which yielded 4 percent interest compounded quarterly and redeemable with the US Government after January 1, 1923—could be purchased for slightly more than $4.00 each (ranging from $4.12 to $4.23), depending on the month they were purchased.[133] Governor Charles Brough proclaimed Saturday, March 22, 1918, War Stamp Day in Arkansas and urged all citizens to participate. On that one day, Dardanelle citizens purchased $4,000 worth of War Stamps, Danville citizens purchased $7,000 worth, and schoolchildren in various rural hamlets—including those in the Bottoms—had funds to purchase $1,798 worth of War Stamps. On March 22, 1918, total Yell County purchases of War Stamps was reported at $20,000.[134]

While socioeconomic status generally determined whether one could purchase a Liberty Bond, a War Stamp, or a Thrift Stamp, the government created a mechanism that allowed every citizen—regardless of economic status—to participate in financing the war effort. From the fairly affluent and middle-class Front Street merchants of Dardanelle to the average poor farmer in Fowler to millionaires like J. P. Morgan of Wall Street, the country seemed almost united—almost—in support of the war effort. Perhaps such near unity of purpose helped to soothe the misery, fear, and inconvenience created by rationing, intense new government regulations, and young men being sent to war.

Amid this outpouring of patriotic support during World War I, the members of the Joe Wheeler Chapter (Dardanelle, Arkansas) of the United Daughters of the Confederacy never forgot or neglected their mission to venerate, celebrate, and remember the sacrifices of the Confederate veterans of the Civil War. From 1917 and into the 1920s, the members of the UDC held their regular monthly meetings and raised funds for the erection of a Confederate Civil War memorial on the grounds of the Dardanelle courthouse.[135] Plans were announced for the monument, and the public was invited to attend meetings and assist with raising the needed funds. These efforts were successfully completed and the statue was dedicated in June 1921. Veneration of the Confederacy had long been a part of Dardanelle culture as many veterans and their descendants lived in the area. Even as World War I raged in Europe—and the United States was drawing ever closer to its entry into the war—in January 1917, members of the Dardanelle First Presbyterian Church produced an elaborate public celebration of the life of General Robert E. Lee on the occasion of his birth 110 years earlier. The festivities were replete with invocation and scriptural readings, three musical selections, a biographical review of Lee and General Stonewall Jackson, a formal address, a special reading, and the closing with a presentation by the seventh graders of Dardanelle.[136] The citizens of Dardanelle, as in all truly southern places, were capable of loyalty to the national government and its causes without forgetting their personal allegiance to their ancestors and their efforts. Southern loyalty is rarely divided, although it is frequently multifaceted. Southern history is complex and is composed of many layers of historical experiences and loyalties, none of which is forgotten. Thus, as World War I raged and citizens bought war bonds, it is perfectly understandable that the UDC would be promoting a Confederate monument and the First Presbyterian Church youth would be respectfully paying homage to Confederate generals Lee and Jackson. It is also worth remembering that the old Presbyterian Church was destroyed by Union artillery shells in 1864.

A Centerville resident noted in a letter to the *Dardanelle Post-Dispatch* that all eighty-seven members of Company C, Second Arkansas Infantry Regiment (the local Arkansas National Guard unit that had been called into active duty on March 19, 1916, spending fifteen months patrolling along the Mexican border and later deployed to France, as the 142nd Field Artillery Regiment) were descendants of Confederate veterans. The writer argued that both the warriors of 1917 and those of 1861 were fighting for "the love of Liberty and Democracy. The boys of today have responded to the call of their State and Country. The boys of '61 answered the call of their State and Country." Whether wearing khaki or gray, the boys of 1917 and their ancestors served "for the same pure and patriotic motives."[137] Certainly, this comparison between the soldiers of 1861 and 1917 did away with all the contradictions construed by the uninformed, and allowed soldiers from both eras to be simultaneously cherished and honored. In the complex layering that is southern history, there was no contradiction.

After the United States entered the war in April 1917, the Yell County Draft Board—whose total quota was 116—called 232 men in for physical exams. Of the total, 25 percent failed the physical exam, and several others were exempted based on their dependents' needs. In this initial group, 45 men were drafted and 61 others volunteered for duty.[138] By early September, 106 Yell County men were preparing to undergo basic training at Camp Pike in North Little Rock, and as they departed Dardanelle by train (September 9, 1917), the *Dardanelle Post-Dispatch* noted "a feeling of most intense emotion swept over our community." A large crowd of family, friends, and well-wishers gathered at the Pontoon Bridge to shout their goodbyes and well-wishes. Each soldier was given a boxed lunch to carry on the train.[139] By October 1917, 400 Yell County men were serving in the military,

and on June 23, 1918, another 129 men departed Dardanelle for training at Camp Pike.[140] Some soldiers, after completing basic training at
Camp Pike, went on to Camp Beauregard in Louisiana for additional
training prior to being shipped out to France in the spring of 1918.[141]

Military service in any era involves hardships for everyone
affected. For some, simply being drafted necessitated the liquidation of their livelihoods, especially for farmers who did not have a
family member who could "fill-in" for them. This was the case for Cal
West, a Bottoms farmer on the Petit Jean River near Slaty Crossing,
who advertised a public auction of his livestock "on account of being
called to the war."[142] Dr. D. W. Pritchett of Dardanelle in similar fashion advertised his house for sale "due to the fact that I expect shortly
to enter military service."[143] Of the approximately 500 men from Yell
County who served in World War I, some drafted and some enlisted,
16 died from battle, accident, or disease. Of these 16 dead, 12 were from
Dardanelle.[144]

When news that the war had ended reached Dardanelle on
Monday morning November 11, 1918, enthusiasm, relief, and joy swept
the town.

> Like wild-fire the news spread over the city, and within a few
> minutes bells were ringing, whistles blowing and anvils being
> fired. All business was suspended and practically the entire
> population of the city gathered on Front Street where a joyful
> demonstration was held. . . . Local orators made speeches . . .
> and automobiles draped in National Colors . . . joined with local
> citizens and school children in a very pretty parade.[145]

Similar spontaneous celebrations occurred in towns and hamlets
through Yell County.

Slowly, throughout 1919 and into 1920, "the boys" returned
home as demobilization occurred haphazardly. People attempted to
pick up the rhythms of their prewar lives and dance again to the music
of peace. Severely wounded soldiers returned for visits with families
and then returned to military hospitals. The Jewish Relief Fund, organized to send supplies to the dislocated and suffering Jews of Europe,
was active in Dardanelle with a goal of raising $1,000 to $2,250 in Yell
County. Many Dardanelle Jewish merchants led by Arthur Garu were

active in this effort, and by May 1919, $600 had been pledged and contributed within Dardanelle.[146] Postwar trauma—the Paris Peace Conference, the Senate battle over ratification of the Versailles Treaty, and President Wilson's illness—served to jumble the rhythms of the music of peace, but the relief of having the Great War finished created an undeniable mellifluous joy.

Most apparent was the continued appreciation of families who had the wondrous good fortune to have their loved ones return home. On May 16, 1919, Mr. and Mrs. John Johnston hosted a party at their home a mile south of Dardanelle in honor of their son, Vernon, back from France and the war. Despite terrible rains and stormy spring weather, two hundred guests showed up and joined in welcoming "the boy home and each ... enjoyed a royal good time."[147]

World War I affected everyone somehow. Some were affected directly, some permanently, others indirectly or only for a short time, but everyone somehow felt the impact. For Dardanelle and the Bottoms, World War I's impact was great. While the war did not destroy the power of cotton in the Bottoms and Dardanelle, it did alter and change the position of cotton in the overall economic structure. The wealth that had flowed into Dardanelle in the years just before the war was greatly diminished after the conflict. Dardanelle, its businesses, and people—especially the socioeconomic elite—felt this most acutely. For the rural citizens of the Bottoms, the fall of the cotton market following World War I brought on extreme suffering and deprivation. As the war ended, another element of modernity with its numerous changes was beginning to appear.

## Rivers and High Water

Constant for the residents of Dardanelle and the Bottoms were the advantages and problems posed by the Arkansas and Petit Jean Rivers. Numerous suggested plans were outlined during the decade ending in 1919 that, had they been implemented, might have averted much future flooding.

One such plan was suggested in 1911 by Fred H. Phillips, a Dardanelle citizen and Arkansas's commissioner of mines, manufactures and agriculture. Phillips proposed the straightening of the

Petit Jean River by forming drainage and ditching areas, which was estimated to cost landowners 25 to 50 cents per acre for a ten-year period. Phillips argued that this would allow for the clearing of additional Bottom land: "some of the most valuable we have in this county," which would have cost $15 an acre and created adjusted land value returns to the landowner of $75 an acre. By creating a drainage ditch that would have straightened the Petit Jean River, the drift of water flowing down the river during high-water periods would "not lodge on the banks and dam up the stream as at present and navigation by small boats" would be enhanced. Phillips's proposal would have reclaimed "large acres of land that for years have been covered by 6 inches to 6 feet of water the year round . . . acres that are some of the finest agricultural lands to be found in the South."[148]

The Petit Jean River overflow area included some 33,000 acres and the Phillips plan for straightening the river would have created a cutoff that would have increased the available agricultural acreage, greatly reduced the damage of overflows, improved the navigability of the river, and increased the overall economic profitability for landowners and farmers. Unfortunately, little came of this plan. Today the acreage that the Phillips plan would have converted into agricultural land is largely the area included in the Petit Jean Wildlife Management Area. It remains a marshland surrounding the crooked Petit Jean River and is sparsely populated and includes a number of alligators contemporarily in residence.

United States congressman Henderson M. Jacoway (D-Arkansas), a Dardanelle citizen who represented Arkansas's Third Congressional District from 1911 to 1923, secured an Army Engineers' survey of the Petit Jean River as part of the 1912 Rivers and Harbors bill. This survey could have led to river channel work to improve the navigability of the Petit Jean and thereby ensure more "competitive freight rates" for people shipping goods on the river.[149] This effort, however, did not receive funding. Congressman Jacoway also introduced legislation proposing a survey of the Arkansas River near Neely, with the long-term goal of building a wing dam on the Arkansas River six miles south of Dardanelle in order to prevent continued caving of the river-banks during high water, by dramatically altering the river's southward flow to a mostly eastward flow.[150] Rather than a conventional dam, a wing dam is basically a jetty, frequently composed of tons of rock, that juts into the river from the bank and serves to slightly divert the impact of the river's flow away from the bank, thus protecting it from caving into the river. Wing dams also maintain a more open river channel given the fact that a larger amount of water remains in the main channel rather than being dissipated into shallow waters along the constantly receding banks. Thus, wing dams reduce the amount of dredging work needed to continue navigation. Today, wing dams are a familiar sight along the Arkansas and Mississippi Rivers, having been built largely during the 1930s and 1940s.[151]

In 1913 Congressman Jacoway outlined a forward-looking plan for the further development of the Arkansas River. This plan called for the creation of an Oklahoma/Arkansas trade association to lobby for improvements in the Arkansas River as a navigation highway, and Jacoway called upon Congress to appropriate $25 million for the river's improvements. This proposed trade association was to be composed of an equal number of Arkansans and Oklahomans to raise $50,000 annually through subscriptions of towns, cities, and trade groups in order to establish a permanent lobbying presence in Washington, DC. The lobbyist would press Congress to invest in the Arkansas River as a navigation highway from Tulsa, Oklahoma, through Arkansas to the Mississippi River. Jacoway envisioned that the shipment of cotton, coal, and timber via the Arkansas River would make it the "the busiest inland waterway in the country." He noted that as railroads replaced river haulers the freight rates had "tripled in the last 30 years" from 23 cents a pound (in late 1879) to 69 cents a pound (in 1913). In addition, sweet potatoes could be shipped by water for 28 cents a pound cheaper than by rail. Furthermore, coal from Spadra and Coal Hill in Johnson County, the Logan County mines near Centerville, and the Pope County mines near North Dardanelle could be cheaply shipped north, the greatest coal customer base, given improved navigation on the Arkansas River.[152] In the end, Jacoway's plan died due to powerful railroad lobbyists' efforts.

In 1946 the Arkansas Basin Development Association was formed, and later that year the Rivers and Harbors Act authorized the building of the McClellan-Kerr Arkansas River Navigation System. This system encompassed all of the old Jacoway plan provisions, plus hydroelectric

power generation. Funding was finally approved in 1956 and construction of the first of seventeen dams—the Dardanelle Lock and Dam—
began in 1957 (with completion in 1966).[153] Fifty-three years after
Congressman Jacoway envisioned the Arkansas River as a great internal water highway, it began to take shape but with others receiving the
accolades for its achievement. The new project cost significantly more
and represented fifty years of lost opportunities and flood damage to
many thousands of people, their property, and business enterprises.
The Jacoway plan and the Phillips plan were lost opportunities.

In the spring of 1912, the Arkansas River presented a challenge
to the new levee system. On May 1, the Arkansas rose to 24.5 feet, its
highest level since 1905. The levees held against a 9-foot rise along their
sides, thus saving 2,500 to 3,000 acres of the Bottoms from flooding.
At New Neely, the river's flow had caved into the lowland immediately
along its bank and came within eighteen inches of topping the levee.
Residents maintained a careful, nervous vigilance and were prepared
to throw up a temporary embankment within a few hours if the waters
rose any higher. Fortunately, only about 60 to 75 acres in the Bottoms
not protected by the levees were flooded.[154]

Prior to the completion of the Dardanelle Lock and Dam (1966),
the Levee Districts and their boards were of great significance. Election
by the landowners within a particular Levee District to a position on
its board—and the decisions and services that such election entailed—
was not simply a sign of deep respect and trust, but a privilege that
also carried the heavy burden of making crucially important decisions. Not only was the board responsible for the maintenance of the
levee, but it also had to make critical judgments during dramatic times
of high and rising waters. For landowners, tenant farmers, sharecroppers, and businessmen, the Levee District Board members and their
actions could easily determine the difference between profits or losses
and even between life or death.[155]

These facts were underscored by the flood of 1916. On February 1,
the Arkansas River at Dardanelle measured 29.8 feet, the highest
mark recorded during the forty years of federal government river
gauge recordkeeping. During the flood of 1898, the Arkansas River at
Dardanelle reached 29.4 feet and older residents recalled that during
the flood of 1878, for which records were privately kept, the river

gauges at Dardanelle had been at or near 31 feet. None of these com-
parisons mattered much in 1916 as the flooding was a major disaster,
with thousands of acres of Bottom land flooded under 6 to 18 feet of
water. Six miles south of Dardanelle the private Bryson Levee—which
formed part of Levee District No. 1—failed on January 30, 1916. As the
rising water moved southward, the levee in Carden Bottom failed on
February 1, 1916, leaving 6,000 acres inundated. Reports that most
of the livestock had been driven to safety on higher ground prior to
the levee break were good news, but still hundreds of families barely
escaped the floodwaters and many were rescued from second-story
windows and rooftops by fellow citizens in boats. The Smiley Bayou
Bridge some 5¾ miles south of Dardanelle was lifted off its piers and
destroyed by rampaging waters. Hundreds of acres of alfalfa, corn,
and hay were destroyed; barns, fencing, and outbuildings were carried
away by the rushing waters. In addition, fertile land was damaged
and washed away and the flooding deposited several feet of worthless
sand on the top of the fields. Farmers' homes were covered in several
feet of river mud, sand, and sludge as families escaped with few or
no possessions into the frigid winter cold. It took days for the waters
to ultimately recede to the point that farm families could return and
begin the arduous, dirty, spirit-breaking task of salvaging and rebuilding or simply determining how to "make do." In Dardanelle, the flood
of 1916 left 17 inches of water standing in the toolhouse of the Pontoon
Bridge ruining most of its contents. This toolhouse was located on the
incline between the bridge itself and the riverbank and housed most
of the tools and supplies used to maintain and service the bridge.
Small bridges near Ola were 3 feet under water because the Arkansas
River floodwaters had backed up into the Petit Jean River. Throughout
large sections of Yell County there was massive damage, especially in
the Dardanelle Bottoms.[156]

A large, devastating flood, such as that of 1916, does not simply create a few days or weeks of inconvenience and damage; they have ripple
effects. In 1916, schools were closed for several weeks until residents
and teachers could return and cleanup efforts could be completed.
Businesses suffered terrible losses, and consumers were nonexistent.
Farmers and landowners lost their crops, and thus their ability to buy
goods would be highly limited until a new crop could be planted and

harvested. Even with all these problems, as the waters receded following flooding, time and money had to be refocused on the rebuilding of levees, bridges, and roads. A flood's lingering economic impact was lengthy and highly negative. The worse the flood, the greater its negative economic and human toll.

The toll that such events took on people who were its victims would not be easily measured or transcended. Memories of high water made people in Dardanelle and the Bottoms keen weather watchers and cautiously aware of large rainstorms and continual wet periods. One young girl from Fields Chapel, Marie Shepherd, was so nervous over the caving of the riverbanks in her area that she was often tense about any coming major rains, which resulted in tears and increased concerns. "Growing up I always kept an eye on the weather, and I was always frightened when it began to rain."[157]

## Weather Problems

This, however, was only part of the weather-related problems. Excessive weather phenomena of various sorts created difficulties. The winter of 1917–1918 was bitter and posed many hardships. Unusual cold descended upon Arkansas in early December 1917 and remained in place through January 1918. Snow began falling in and around Dardanelle during the early morning hours of December 7, 1917, and by nightfall had turned to sleet. By the next day, seven inches of snow encrusted with ice could be found everywhere, with the temperature dropping to 0°F that evening. Given war rationing, local merchants ran out of coal for heating by December 11, which was further compounded by the fact that their resupply would not arrive until December 17 at the earliest. The people's suffering was real and extensive, and then it intensified.[158] On January 19, 1918, two more inches of snow fell, followed by seven additional inches of snowfall two days later. By January 22, Dardanelle was buried under approximately eighteen inches of snow and ice. In total, between December 7, 1917, and January 24, 1918, the area endured thirty-two inches of frozen precipitation, a record few wanted and even fewer enjoyed.[159]

"The bitter weather and snow blocked roads the past week and have prevented people entering to town . . . business has been practically at a standstill."[160] These conditions were not only highly unpleasant and detrimental to businesses; they were also extremely dangerous. The accumulated weight of the ice and snow caused roofs to collapse and metal awnings to fall onto sidewalks. In addition, even exterior walls were severely damaged. For example, the entire north wall of the Dardanelle Bank and Trust Company—a brick building—cracked and collapsed, which then caused damage to an adjoining wall, rendering the entire structure unsafe. Throughout Dardanelle, it was difficult, and frequently impossible, to find laborers to shovel the snow and ice in order to reduce the weight loads on roofs and awnings.[161]

Frigid weather posed additional hardship on those living in rural areas, as illustrated by a report in the *Dardanelle Post-Dispatch* in January 1918. Jim Shepherd, a farmer living near Mickel's Switch in far-western Yell County, rode on horseback for ten miles through deep drifts of "snow and ice to Centerville in order to obtain medicine from Dr. McCarty for one of Shepard's neighbors who was suffering from pneumonia [in] an act of pure neighborly charity, as the sick man was no kin and a new comer."[162]

## Health

Health-related issues continually hounded the people of Dardanelle and the Bottoms. Dangers—many typical of the time—lurked in the form of rabid animals, hunting and work accidents, and encounters with numerous, sometimes fatal, diseases, such as tuberculosis, pneumonia, measles, whopping cough, typhoid fever, scarlet fever, cholera, and smallpox. While certainly not a frequent occurrence, reported attacks by rabid or "mad" dogs, a particular threat for children, spread quickly as men reached for shotguns, mothers grabbed their children and fled indoors, and a sort of hysteria seized the population. Rabid dog attacks occurred in Dardanelle in 1911 and twice in 1913 involving a total of five children. In each case, the victims survived, the animal was killed, and its skull was sent to the medical examiner's office in Little Rock to determine if it was rabid. Following each of these events local officials warned citizens as a matter of public safety to keep their dogs muzzled or they would be shot by a law enforcement officer or enjoy "a liberal application of beef steak and arsenic administered by some irate citizen."[163] In 1913 the Dardanelle City Council passed a new ordinance requiring a dog tax be paid and dog tags issued in an effort to control the canine population. City officials then intentionally killed dogs that remained untagged. By early June 1913, one hundred dog tags had been issued and seven animals had been killed.[164] Rabid dogs continued to be a sporadic threat in Dardanelle through the 1960s.

Childhood diseases were common and frequently fatal, with the usual cases involving measles, whooping cough (pertussis), pneumonia, and tuberculosis. Almost every edition of the *Dardanelle Post-Dispatch* during the decade included death notices of children. Adults were also vulnerable to these diseases as evidenced by the death of T. J. Bullock, a Dardanelle citizen and area teacher, who died in 1914 of typhoid fever following an eighteen-day illness.[165] In early 1914 an eleven-year-old Dardanelle girl was confirmed to have smallpox, causing a quarantine in both Dardanelle and nearby Russellville (Pope County) that lasted for several weeks. The child survived, and the smallpox scare ended.[166] Goiter was also a fairly common condition in both children and adults and underscored the lack of proper nutrition (in this case, a lack of iodine in the diet), and in 1919 two young Centerville sisters underwent successful treatment in Little Rock for the condition.[167] As late as 1919, a case of malaria was reported in Centerville as a farmer, Julius Jones, was stricken but survived.[168]

For several years Dr. S. E. Miller wrote local newspaper articles regarding various health issues and disease prevention measures. Written in layman's language, the articles attempted to educate and inform the public and thus improve the general state of health in the area. In 1915 one such article highlighted the recommendations of the United States Public Health Service to avoid pellagra, which Dr. Miller noted was "prevalent in certain sections of Yell County." He also noted that pellagra results from a lack of niacin (Vitamin $B_3$), sufficient vegetables, and a generally unhealthy diet, thus afflicting the very poor, such as tenant farmers, sharecroppers, and day laborers in the Bottoms.[169]

Dr. Miller's newspaper articles also informed the reader as to the causes of infectious diseases. In June 1915, a long, detailed article described the causes of typhoid, dysentery, and tuberculosis, as well as conditions caused by hookworms, roundworms, pinworms, and tape-worms. He urged readers to be aware of the health dangers posed by animal and human excreta and urged the support of a sewage system in Dardanelle and the proper disposal of all animal and human waste. He noted the role played by flies, fleas, and other insects in spreading germs and microbes found in excreta, and suggested precautions for establishing a germ-free home, especially in kitchens. In a June 1915 article, Dr. Miller chastised the Dardanelle City Council's decision to allow hogs to be kept within the city limits, and in protest resigned his position as city health officer.[170]

Other local medical doctors also continued to press for improved preventive disease measures. Dr. D. W. Pritchett offered his support for the creation of a city sewerage system, stating that private privies, cesspools, and septic tanks were most unsanitary and led to diphtheria and typhoid fever. He continued: "why is it we haven't so many elderly people? Why do we have so many early deaths? Because we ignore hygiene. . . . We need a sewer system as a safeguard to public health."[171]

In May 1916, Dardanelle citizens presented a petition to the city council for the creation of two improvement districts, one to construct concrete sidewalks and one to build a new sewerage system. Both were approved by Dardanelle property owners; the $24,200 project creating seven miles of sidewalks was completed in late 1916 while a modern sewerage system costing $38,000 was completed in March 1918.[172]

One of the biggest problems with which Dardanelle had to grapple and which had major health and safety implications centered about the town's water system. In 1892 small pipes supplied Dardanelle's water from Varnell Springs on Mount Nebo, which produced plenty of water at low rates and allowed the town an average 30 percent surplus of funds annually. Then in 1910, the pipes partially collapsed. The town immediately had two major problems: less money and less water. To make matters more difficult, a $15,000 bond—issued in 1900 on the municipal water system at 5 percent interest yield—was scheduled to mature in 1915.[173] Citizens petitioned the city council in November 1912 to repair the pipes from Varnell Springs at an estimated cost of $8,000. In 1915, by a vote of 188 to 14, Dardanelle citizens approved floating a new $25,000 bond issue to retire the old indebtedness and to pay for the repair of the water system. With what appears to be a racial swipe at African Americans, the local newspaper reported that "a feature of the election was that only 14 negroes voted."[174] Problems persisted for the city as operating expenses exceeded receipts and the new pump, which had been part of the water system repairs, did not work properly. Finally, in 1919, the pump manufacturer agreed to install a replacement pump, but in the meantime, the old pump, which generated insufficient power to supply an adequate water supply for the town, had to be used. The second "new pump" arrived in April 1919 with "a 40 horsepower Westinghouse motor . . . and a capacity of 250 gallons per minute . . . sufficient to furnish water for all purposes, including the sewer operations."[175] Additional problems were caused by cost repair overruns, and operating costs continued to outpace revenues.

The newly created Dardanelle Chamber of Commerce developed a plan whereby the town would sell $3,000 of city warrants to get the water plant in peak operating form and the city's finances back in the positive. In October 1919, $500 of these warrants were purchased by members of the chamber of commerce.[176] Now invested in the town's water problems, the chamber urged the water commissioners to hire an expert well man in order to guarantee a reliable water supply and pledged that their organization would pay for his work. On December 10, 1919, a contract was signed with National Pump and Well Company of Stuttgart, Arkansas, for a "well with a guaranteed capacity of 215 gallons per minute . . . and to install the big Cook pump now owned by the Water District and connect and line-up the new 45 horsepower electric motor." The total cost for this work was $8,000 and it was endorsed by businessmen and 25 percent of the town's property owners.[177]

With these updates and repairs anticipated to be completed within thirty days, on January 26, 1920, the city council voted to raise all water rates, almost twofold, set drastic penalties for illegal water usage, and created a strict new payment date system for users. Everyone hoped that after almost ten years of water problems, Dardanelle would have a solvent, functioning water system sufficient for safe use, sewage plant operations, and firefighting. But, of course, problems developed. Part of the new pump materials and two 30-foot sections of iron castings used in installation were lost in transit, although in late February these were found in Fort Smith and within days were installed in Dardanelle.

During the system's initial test run, sand intake caused valve damage, leaks occurred in the water mains due to the increase in pumping pressure, and some 80,000 gallons of water were lost.[178] Several days later, the pump's foundation collapsed. The town was completely without water for ten days while pump company workers rushed to reset the concrete foundation and regrind the valves. By March 25, 1920, the system was working and Dardanelle had 5,000 gallons stored, filled to capacity, in its water tower located on Dardanelle Rock.[179] Now, after almost ten years, a sigh of relief was heard as life, perhaps, could go on without water problems. The previously canceled chamber of commerce banquet was happily rescheduled and firefighters and property owners felt more secure.[180]

As Dardanelle grappled with local health concerns, national and state organizations were also studying these problems. In 1913 the Rockefeller Sanitary Commission published results of a three-year study of eleven southern states that concluded that 329,578 children, mostly in rural areas, were infected with hookworms and that private physicians during the time of the study had treated another 162,572 infected persons. The report noted that in some rural schools 100 percent of the children were infected and that most infected children made 50 percent less educational progress than an uninfected child.[181] Act 96 of the 1913 Arkansas General Assembly created the Arkansas Department of Health, which quickly announced it would examine specimens to confirm cases of malaria, typhoid fever, meningitis, hookworm, diphtheria, tuberculosis, and rabies.[182] In 1916, Arkansas accounted for 5 percent of all reported typhoid fever cases in the United States, prompting the new state health department and local physicians to engage in an educational campaign. People were urged to use only clean drinking water, thus not contaminated by soil pollution or seepage of fertilizers or by animal or human waste materials. People were asked to safeguard their wells from contamination and to aggressively assist their neighbors in similar efforts. Typhoid, while preventable, could be fatal and once contracted, usually resulted in sixty days of painful suffering and discomfort.[183] In 1922 several typhoid fever cases were reported in the Upper Bottoms, which prompted Dr. F. R. Sweet, Dardanelle city health officer, to urge everyone to boil their water; sanitize all premises, including hog pens;

and get the anti-typhoid vaccine immediately. Subsequently, no additional cases were reported.[184]

Disease prevention and general health improvement measures were apparently common concerns. In January 1918, the Dardanelle Public Schools announced that all teachers and children, beginning in February, would be required to have had a smallpox vaccination. In the same edition of the *Dardanelle Post-Dispatch,* a report from Fields Chapel casually noted: "we have a little sickness yet, a few cases of smallpox and two cases of scarlet fever. Some of the school pupils are being vaccinated to prevent the spread of this disease."[185] It appears that Dardanelle was more involved in preventive health-care efforts than were the areas of the Bottoms. In early 1924, several smallpox cases were reported in Pope County, but none was present in Dardanelle. Even so, several months later, Dardanelle residents were urged to get the smallpox vaccination.[186] In May 1926, several cases of smallpox were reported in Pottsville (Pope County), approximately six miles north of Carden Bottom and across the Arkansas River.[187]

During World War I, health became a patriotic duty and this advanced the development and enforcement of new measures. When Company C, Second Arkansas Infantry Regiment, was allowed to stay at home for three additional months prior to deployment, the army's surgeon general and city officials urged citizens to voluntarily adopt health-conscious habits in order to keep the troops well. A fairly lengthy set of health suggestions was published and Dardanelle citizens were urged to comply. These suggestions included draining all standing water or oiling these if draining is impossible; cutting all grass and weeds, especially within eight feet of sidewalks; refraining from throwing garbage, slop, tin cans, or any type of filth into the streets; cleaning horse stables, hog pens, and other animal enclosures, and keeping them sanitary; burning tin cans or drill holes in them so they cannot hold liquid; screening and keeping lids on surface outdoor toilets; liming outdoor toilets and placing ashes over toilet contents daily; and cleaning all outdoor toilets every two weeks.[188] Healthy habits were now a civic, patriotic virtue. Obviously Kaiser Wilhelm's actions had some positive results on Yell County health.

The most sinister and high-profile health problem of this era was Spanish influenza and the Influenza Pandemic of 1918–1920. As the pandemic resulted in an estimated 20 million deaths worldwide, some estimates even doubling this figure to 40 million, Dardanelle and the Bottoms did not escape it. The flu first arrived in the area in late September 1918, a result of relatives visiting their loved ones at military bases, especially Camp Pike in North Little Rock, and carrying the virus home as well as any number of travelers to the area who also acted as carriers. Schools were closed, churches canceled services, public gatherings were generally curtailed, and a general quarantine of Dardanelle was implemented. In October 1918, the city health officer, Dr. F. R. Sweet, urged parents to continue to keep their children not just off the streets, but in their homes as there were still "many cases in Dardanelle and continued vigilance is necessary to prevent its further spread."[189]

In early October, a twenty-seven-year-old Dardanelle physician, Dr. F. A. Outlaw, died after attending to patients.[190] By the second week of October, multiple flu cases were reported in Centerville and Carden Bottom, and one flu-related death, Mrs. Jessie Rogers, was reported in Plainview, in the western section of Yell County.[191] In late October, although additional deaths were being reported, Dr. Sweet, acting as an agent of the state and federal Public Health Services, announced the lifting of the quarantine and restrictions against public gatherings, effective November 2, 1918. These restrictions had been in place for one month, during which time Dardanelle had reported two hundred cases of influenza. Surgeon General Rupert Blue, head of the United States Public Health Services, also offered ten specific guidelines for citizens to follow regarding the flu.[192] After the quarantine was lifted, flu cases and deaths continued to be reported in the Dardanelle area.

On February 6, 1920, Dr. Sweet reinstated a restriction in Dardanelle on the activities of all schools, churches, and public amusements to include movie theaters and pool halls. This restriction resulted in the postponement of the spring term of the Dardanelle Circuit Court. Dr. Sweet issued the order after twenty new flu cases had been confirmed and in conference with state public health officials.[193] While no record seems to exist as to when this health restriction was lifted, the last notices of reported flu cases appeared on February 19, 1920, from a stricken family in Fields Chapel.[194] The Spanish flu continued in various locations around the globe until the end of 1920. In the United States, 675,000 deaths were attributed to the Spanish flu pandemic.[195]

## Fires

Fires also posed a danger to life and health, especially since the Dardanelle water system was erratic and had numerous problems, including, at times, being totally out of commission. Added to this was the fact that no safety building codes existed and many older structures were wooden. As such, it is no wonder that so many fires occurred. During the early morning of December 6, 1910, twelve Dardanelle businesses suffered significant losses to merchandise, equipment, and property, including the total destruction of three brick buildings. The $35,000 in damages was only partially covered by insurance, and had it not been for a light rain during the night and the city's night watchmen sounding an alarm, the damage could have been much worse.[196]

The story was much the same when on December 11, 1912, a late-night fire destroyed one brick building and damaged another with a total of five businesses affected by the flames.[197] Then, in June 1913, seven businesses suffered losses and ten additional business operations suffered shattered plate-glass windows in yet another downtown Dardanelle fire. In this inferno, the last of the original wood-frame buildings on Front Street were reduced to rubble.[198] Another fire in January 1915 caused a downtown business to suffer $2,600 in losses with only $300 of insurance coverage being held by the owner.[199] On March 7, 1918, a fire destroyed the Rock Island Railroad Depot and its contents due to a faulty heater/chimney connection. Following the destruction, a boxcar was used as the depot until a new building was constructed.[200]

One of the most dramatic and destructive fires occurred in March 1919, as two separate fire events occurred within fifty-four hours of each other. The first, on Sunday, March 9, began around 5:00 p.m. and resulted in the destruction of eight businesses and most of their contents with a total damage estimate of $25,000. Then, two days later, another fire supposedly caused by faulty wiring was discovered at 10:00 p.m. and significantly damaged seven businesses/offices causing $13,000 in damages. Several of the local fire department's hoses burst during the fire and became unusable. This fire would probably have caused even more extensive damage had it not been for the assistance rendered by the Russellville Fire Department, which arrived on the scene within only fifteen minutes of notification.[201] Within two days of the second 1919 fire, the citizens of Dardanelle presented the city council a petition calling for greater fire protection, including measures aimed at increasing the town's water pressure and inspection of all electrical wiring for both fire prevention and reduced insurance costs. There was good reason for the people to sense terror at the sound of a fire alarm, causing people to run to the fire site in order to assist, and to demand action from the town's leaders.

Residential fires, sometimes deadly, were also common. While too numerous to be individually chronicled, examples include a 1916 Centerville house fire (arson related) and two 1918 Dardanelle house fires, one of which resulted in two deaths.[202]

Two additional examples help illustrate the destructive power of fire: April 1913 and May 1919. At approximately 6:00 p.m. on Monday, April 21, 1913, the original Yell County Courthouse in Dardanelle was consumed by flames, as townspeople looked on in awe. The two-story brick building, originally constructed in 1873 as the lodge for the local International Order of Odd Fellows, a fraternal organization, stood at the corner of Front and Oak Streets facing east. It was adjacent to a large frame livery stable where the fire began in the feed room and spread rapidly. Workers and bystanders rushed in to carry the furniture from the burning courthouse. The county records were in a fireproof vault and, thus, were preserved. The fire destroyed the courthouse, the livery stable, another business, and a nearby house. Five other nearby houses and the old Presbyterian Church were damaged but were not destroyed.[203]

Six days later, on April 27, a large number of Dardanelle citizens met at Cunningham Hall to discuss rebuilding the courthouse. The Dardanelle District of the Yell County Circuit Court had been established in 1875 and the people of Dardanelle did not want to lose the dual county-seat arrangement. County judge J. N. George was convinced that he had the authority to order the construction of a new Dardanelle courthouse and—given the enthusiastic support at the meeting—announced that a new structure would be built. The replacement courthouse would be constructed in the northern part of town on land that had been previously donated to the town by the late Colonel David Brearley, one of Dardanelle's founders and its greatest early benefactor. The citizens of Dardanelle financially guaranteed the scrip payments for the project in annual installments of $3,000 and in less than half a day, the first of these installments had been pledged through the leadership of Judge R. C. Bullock, Colonel Marcellus Davis, merchant Max Kaufman, and Mayor Frank E. (Al) Clinton.[204] Construction bids were let in September 1913 and R. L. Wright & Company of Dallas, Texas, was named as contractor. Meanwhile, the sessions of the Dardanelle District of the Yell County Circuit Court were held in the Electric Theatre on Front Street, perhaps adding to the sessions' courtroom theatrics. The new Dardanelle courthouse was completed on August 12, 1914, at a final cost of $21,800, with the first session of the Dardanelle District of the Yell County Circuit Court convened in the new facility held in September 1914. Judge George had said that he wanted to erect a "neat, commodious building, one that would meet all requirements." This structure still serves as the Dardanelle courthouse.[205]

The second spectacular fire of this era did not end as well. A fire of unknown origin began shortly after noon on Sunday, May 18, 1919, at the Summit Park Hotel on Mount Nebo and quickly consumed the three-story wooden structure. Its new owners had recently completed several thousand dollars' worth of repairs and upgrades to the original 1889 resort hotel and were anticipating a highly successful summer season. The Summit Park Hotel was a grand old Victorian-style facility originally built by Captain Joseph Evins of Dardanelle and several Little Rock investors for $50,000. The hotel contained sixty-five guest rooms, a large ballroom, a dining room, and ample verandas; as well as a bowling alley, stables replete with horses, carriages, and complete riding equipment, and a large croquet field. Different areas of the resort were connected together by a wooden boardwalk and walking paths, and were serviced by a white-clad African American staff of approximately thirty maids, kitchen personnel, and maintenance workers. Guaranteeing guests a pleasant experience graced with the elegance of old southern traditions, the Summit Park Hotel hosted a flourishing seasonal social scene from early spring until early fall as its frequent guests hailed from Tennessee, Louisiana, various Arkansas locations, and even several foreign countries.[206] The mountain's cool breezes, fresh spring waters, and beautiful scenery had assisted the hotel in its successful self-promotion as a health resort. For the upper middle class and wealthy residents of Dardanelle, withdrawing to Mount Nebo was a summer tradition. While locals continue this tradition currently and Mount Nebo has enjoyed a recent resurgence in year-round residents and interest, the 1919 fire at the Summit Park Hotel destroyed the rest of what once had existed there since 1889. The grand ballroom, the concerts and orchestras, the lavish meals, and the mystique of southern elegance were gone as the Summit Park Hotel smoldered and was never rebuilt.

## Accidents

Accidents posed yet another obstacle to good health and life. As was the case nationwide, railroad accidents were not uncommon. One fatality occurred on the Rock Island line just one-quarter mile north of Centerville in late December 1910. Absolom Burkett, "a kindly 65 year old man who was extremely deaf," who had just months earlier moved to Centerville, was walking along the rails and playing his French harp. He apparently did not hear the warning whistle on the train as it approached behind him. Unable to stop, the train struck Burkett resulting in his immediate death.[207] Another accident in 1910 involved the Dardanelle and Russellville Railroad brakeman Paul Hilton, whose foot was caught between the coupling cars and was so badly crushed it had to be amputated.[208] In another accident, rotten rail ties—coupled with a steep grade—caused a derailment on the Rock Island line one-half mile south of Centerville on November 17, 1913, resulting in the death of a passenger, Mrs. R. L. (Annie) Baker, and injuring fifteen others, including the train's conductor and a brakeman.[209]

The Arkansas River also posed the danger of accidental fatalities. On July 27, 1914, seventeen-year-old Benjamin Duke Brown was enjoying a hot summer day with his friends swimming in the shallow water. The boys decided to swim across the river, but, on their return, young Benjamin became exhausted and was swallowed by the current. His friends were unable to retrieve him and he drowned.[210] On April 7, 1916, five-year-old Jimmy Beasley disappeared while playing in his backyard, which was adjacent to the Arkansas River. As his mother frantically searched the neighborhood, search teams assembled. The next day the river was dragged and dynamite was used, believing that the body was submerged and that the blast concussions would cause the body to flow to the surface for recovery. Nothing was found. Nothing was ever found. It was presumed that Jimmy Beasley drowned, as it was not uncommon for a drowning victim's body not be found.[211] Such was almost the case with Horace Rollans, a thirty-four-year-old man whose boat capsized on the Arkansas River several miles northwest of Dardanelle in March 1919. Despite his father's and neighbor's search for more than a week, his remains were not recovered until three months and five days later when fishermen found his body snagged in brush along the river's edge eight miles west of Little Rock. He was identified by his clothing and by the personal articles in his pants pocket.[212] For all of its attributes and benefits, the Arkansas River could be deceitfully deadly. A Carden Bottom resident described the Arkansas River as "that vile and vicious river," and so it frequently was.[213]

The automobile was first seen in Dardanelle in 1908, and by 1917 the city council was enacting speed limit and illegal parking ordinances in an effort to curtail the potential dangers posed by this newest mode of transportation.[214] For young people, however, the automobile represented a source of fun, entertainment, and temporary escape from parental control. Reports of groups of young boys and girls "going car riding on Sunday afternoon" were a frequent newspaper item during the early decades of the twentieth century.[215] A humorous anecdote—which could have been quite deadly—involved a rebellious young woman, Lyle Boyce, who ignored her father's stern warning not to drive the T-Model Ford down Mount Nebo. Naturally, as soon as her father had left for work, young Lyle started driving the car down the twisting, unpaved, steep mountain road and the brakes failed. She stopped the Model T by banking it into a large boulder on the side of a steep mountain switchback and contemplated how to escape her dilemma. She developed an ingenious solution. She placed the car in reverse, backed up the narrow, twisting road, and parked it in the exact spot where her father had forbidden her to drive the car.[216] The narrative does not reveal what happened when Lyle's father determined that the brakes were no longer working. Thus, the advent of the automobile produced some humorous turns of events, an increase in freedom of travel, and, occasionally, some unfortunate accidents.

## Crime

Between late 1910 and the end of 1919, criminal activity was sporadic and usually exceedingly violent. Frequently, the combination
of guns and liquor exacerbated the level of violence and too often
resulted in deadly outcomes. A case in point occurred in New Neely
in October 1910 when J. T. Pickens shot and killed Harden George.
Both men had spent the previous evening and much of the following day drinking heavily. On his way home, George realized he was
missing a considerable amount of money, and reported this to the
Galla Rock Township constable, his cousin Frank George. Soon thereafter, the George cousins and E. O. Hewitt located Pickens on the road
between New Neely and Centerville one-fifth mile west of New Neely.
Pickens told the constable that he would kill him if he tried to search
or arrest him. Constable George handed his gun to Hardin George
and then attempted to arrest Pickens. As Pickens "went for his gun,"
Harden George fired in order to protect his cousin. The bullet struck
Pickens in one of his eyes, exited the roof of his skull, and killed him
instantly. The "considerable sum of money" in question, $45, was found
on Pickens, but no weapon. Harden George was arrested and posted
a $500 bond while awaiting grand jury action.[217] In the end, Harden
George was not indicted for the killing.

## Race

The belief in white supremacy also prompted incidents of violence.
As historian Glenda Gilmore argues, the generation of southern white
men who came of age during the 1890s—and replaced their fathers,
the Civil War generation, as the region's political, economic, and social
elite—deeply resented and empathically opposed any coordination
with or accommodation of African Americans. Instead, these white
men relished the enforcement of strict segregation and subsequent
inequality for African Americans. Political fear caused "conservative
Democrats in Arkansas . . . to assault what interracial compromise
and toleration existed."[218] Fearful of the possibility of real political
power being amassed based on a coalition of poor white farmers,
Republicans, and African American voters, this generation of white

men preached race hatred using propaganda rhetoric that claimed the potential, unthinkable results of racial equality: the mongrelization of the races, the despoilment and rape of white women, and the death of southern traditions and the Democratic Party. Thus, beginning in the 1890s, the ugly message of white supremacy was often articulated. As with any message of hate, its underlying motivation was to maintain the messenger's power position. In this case, the power of white southern males over African Americans intensified as did white males' patriarchal control over white females. This philosophy of self-righteous hatred toward African Americans was highly effective. The South relished in the resulting broken Republican Party, its highly gender-prescribed role for the proper southern woman, and its racial retrenchment policies reinforced by segregation, antimiscegenation laws, and traditions.[219]

Guy Lancaster, in *Racial Cleansing in Arkansas, 1883–1924*, chronicles some of these inimically wicked events, several of which were near Dardanelle and the Bottoms. In 1885 whites terrorized local African Americans along the Conway-Pope County line, encouraging them to leave en masse.[220] On January 26, 1885, a "number of men" rode to the farm of a Mr. Alewine, four miles north of Atkins in Pope County (approximately six miles across the Arkansas River from Carden Bottom) and warned the African Americans at the residence to leave that part of the county. No one left and on February 11, vigilantes returned and shot into the house, but no one was injured. J. P. Strickling and Walter Cole were arrested as leaders of the vigilantes, although the case was dismissed. The Dardanelle newspaper regarding this incident and in response to an *Arkansas Gazette* report of an impending race war in Pope County, reprinted the following editorial:

> That nothing has been heard of this "impending war" ten miles away is satisfactory evidence that the story is a pack of lies. That the negro house was fired into may be true, that Alewine came out and was shot at may also be true, that the negroes were ordered away may be true, but that the body of citizens of that section undertook to drive peaceable negroes away from where they had a right to stay, "on general principles" is an outrageous slander.[221]

Attempts by area whites to intimidate and drive out African Americans were documented. On April 6, 1910, night riders scattered notices to African Americans throughout Lee Township (near Atkins in Pope County) to leave or "we will proceed to move you ourselves in a very rough way."[222] This was supposedly a response to an alleged attempted rape on April 2, 1910, of a white child by a fifty-year-old African American farm laborer on the Potts farm, three miles southeast of Atkins, approximately three miles north of Carden Bottom across the Arkansas River.

Robert Crow—who lived in the Lower Bottoms his entire life—related to his son Bobby, born in 1945, that several African American men were lynched from a large cottonwood tree in Lakeview in Carden Bottom sometime just before or during the early 1920s. Those doing the lynching told the African Americans to leave Carden Bottom and never be there again after dark.[223] Lonnie Dickens was born in 1934 and was an African American who grew up in Riverside in the Upper Bottoms. As a child, he worked on the McClure farm and then worked as a tenant farmer on the Hunt farm in the Upper Bottoms from 1952 to 1960. He said that "African Americans did not go to Carden Bottom after dark. We didn't have any business being there. Everybody knew that."[224] So Carden Bottom and its various hamlets became a "sundown town" at some time around the 1920s.

Sometime between 1910 and the early 1920s, all African Americans living in Carden Bottom left with most resettling at Liberty Hall near Centerville or on farms in the Upper Bottoms. Carden Bottom was a "sundown town" from that point forward. While the details surrounding the African Americans' exit from Carden Bottom are sketchy at best, two references offer some insight. Isodore Thompson, an African American who, as a child, lived and worked with his tenant farming parents (Elton and Nancy Thompson) at Liberty Hall, said that "all the blacks got run out of Carden Bottom sometime around 1920 because the blacks were too friendly with some of the whites down there, so the whites ran all the blacks out and Carden Bottom became a big sundown place."[225] Another account by Mr. Whitey Robinson stated that his father told him that a black man was lynched from the Pontoon Bridge over the Petit Jean River in Carden Bottom in the late 1910s because he was intimately involved with a white woman. According to this account, the lynch mob improperly prepared the hanging rope and, as a result, the victim's neck was stretched, but the man was still alive. So he was cut down, the rope adjusted, and then the victim was hanged a second time, this time successfully.[226] Unfortunately, there are no corroborating reports of this in either state or local newspapers, although the interviews noted previously do generally provide confirmation. Additional evidence of the racial tensions and violence in Carden Bottom during this period appears in Genevieve Grant Sadler's *Muzzled Oxen: Reaping Cotton and Sowing Hope in 1920s Arkansas*. The Sadler family lived approximately one-half mile south of Carden Bottom on a bend in the Petit Jean River. The following is advice given to Genevieve Sadler by a white neighbor in approximately 1922.

> I feel I just have to let you know this. There ain't any one of us bottom folks going to stand for you taking niggers into your house and making them so free-like. Soon we'll have to make another drive to clear 'em all out. We ain't got but a few families of the colored folks left here. They jest ain't welcome. Can't stop Meek from hirin' em, it's all the help he keeps. Parker is his straw-boss. But they all stay back by the bayou. It's a cryin' shame, I says, and him with all that rich land, a-pilin' the niggers in.[227]

Thus, while African Americans were forced out of Carden Bottom making it a "sundown town" sometime between approximately 1915 and 1920, African Americans continued to live and work primarily as sharecroppers, tenant farmers, and farm laborers in other areas in the Upper Bottoms with the greatest concentration of African Americans in and around Liberty Hall on the eastern edge of the Lower Bottoms approximately two miles south of Centerville.

Guy Lancaster stated that the attempts to drive off African American competition "would certainly seem to be related to the emergence of sundown towns, which occurred during a period when whitecapping was particularly widespread."[228] Therefore, it seems highly probable that the violence during the late nineteenth/early twentieth century in the areas adjacent to the Bottoms, the interracial sexual liaison based violence in Carden Bottom during the early twentieth century, and a 1924 night-riding episode, to be discussed later, were all prompted by perceived infractions of community racial norms and economic concerns followed by vigilante violence.

## Women

While gender roles remained highly prescribed and traditional from 1911 through 1929, women did have a more prominent role in public affairs, especially during the 1911 to 1920 period. Still, far from being equal participants in elective offices and business management, women actively volunteered their skills, time, and work in numerous public efforts sometimes even sharing management/oversight responsibilities in these efforts with men. Certainly, this was the case with Red Cross work during World War I. Women were also highly involved in church organizations, women's clubs, and in suffrage and prohibition efforts. Many historians have described this as women's use of domestic ideology acting as municipal housekeeper.[229] Historian Anne Firor Scott argues that while women retained the qualities expected of them, such as maintaining their femininity and reproductive role, they were, during the early twentieth century, becoming a force in public life.[230] Historian Nancy Woloch interpreted this surge in women reform activities during the early decades of the twentieth century as the integration of Victorian domestic values and social activism, resulting in the "New Woman."[231] However one wishes to explain it, women in Dardanelle and the Bottoms were more active in public events during this period than during any previous periods.

For example, the women of the Dardanelle Presbyterian Church were actively involved in raising funds to pay for the new church building including selling 15-cent ham sandwiches and coffee on Front Street on election night in 1912, and hosting 25-cent pie suppers and elaborate presentations such as a Tom Thumb Wedding.[232] Some events presented by the Presbyterian women illustrate both Scott's and Woloch's theses. For example, in 1913 a colonial tea was held at the home of Judge and Mrs. L. C. Hall during which costumes from different eras in American history were worn, each room featured the furnishing styles of various historical eras, and the program included lengthy musical selections and readings. This event was described as

"one of the most unique, artistically gotten up and altogether pleasing social events enjoyed by Dardanelle folk in many years."[233] The
Methodist Church women were also busy raising funds for extensive
building renovations including the sale of their 100-page cookbook
for 35 cents a copy and hosting elaborate social functions such as the
1916 Valentine Tea and the 1919 Silver Tea.[234]

Improvements to the Presbyterian and Methodist Church properties were greatly assisted by the efforts of their women members. Plans
for a new First Presbyterian Church at the corner of South Second
and Quay Streets in Dardanelle were finalized in April 1912. First organized on April 9, 1843, at Norristown just across the Arkansas River
from Dardanelle and composed of both Norristown and Dardanelle
members, the separate Dardanelle congregation was established on
May 25, 1856, with seventeen members. Reverend Cephas Washburn,
famed Dwight Mission director, served as its pastor until his death in
1860. After the Union army destroyed the church building, a new brick
building was built in 1872 on Pecan Street, between Second and Third
Streets, and was sold in 1912. The church received $1,700 from the US
Government for the Civil War destruction of its property and "the
ladies of the church began working on a church fund" as they spearheaded the building fund efforts, which included asking for donations,
selling food at public venues, and picking cotton. Picking cotton was
certainly not a normal activity for the white, upper-class women of the
Dardanelle Presbyterian Church. Thus, when they announced their
plan to work for one day in a cotton field donated for their use, with
the proceeds going toward the church rebuilding fund, everyone took
notice. Some businesses closed on the appointed day and several hundred people, mostly men, gathered to watch these elite women engage
in such a provocative act. A photograph of their cotton picking foray
appeared in the *Christian Observer*, a Presbyterian magazine, and
attracted the attention of New York philanthropist F. T. Hopkins, who
then donated $2,000. By 1912 the women had amassed $6,000.[235] In
early 1912, a building committee comprised of three women and three
men was appointed, and they decided on a building design, continued
to raise funds for the new building's total cost ($10,000), and acted as
overseers for the project.[236]

In 1917 the First Methodist Church also undertook a major property improvement project for the renovation and addition of their 1891 church building. Originally established in 1848 with twelve members, the first of its structures was a small, white frame building near Brearley Cemetery followed by an 1858 frame building costing $900 on the northeast corner of Second and Locust Streets. In 1891 this structure was replaced with a brick building costing $6,000. In 1917, with a membership of 361 persons, the Methodists designed an addition that included fourteen Sunday school rooms on the north, west, and south of the existing building, and a pastor's study and choir room on the east of the existing building, which formed the central sanctuary. An arcade gallery was added on the west front of the building. Additional improvements included a pipe organ, oak pews, basement, steam heating and ventilation system, and an oak dressed sanctuary with galleries on three sides. The renovation cost $10,000 and the women of the church worked diligently to raise the funds to retire the mortgage note.[237]

In similar fashion, the First Baptist Church completed a handsome new structure on October 1, 1909, which measured 72 by 68 feet, seated six hundred, and cost $10,000. Donations from church members and Dardanelle citizens paid for the building and the women of the church assisted in these efforts.[238]

Numerous women's clubs flourished in Dardanelle, including the United Daughters of the Confederacy, the Anti-Tuberculosis League, various school support and improvement groups, the Cemetery Association, and the Women's Civic League. The Women's Civic League, formed in 1914 with two representatives from each local women's club, studied community needs and developed plans to address them. As with many women's organizations, its primary focus was children and safety needs. In 1914 they created a children's summertime playground and reading sessions using school facilities and overseen by volunteers.[239] In November 1919, the league established a free health examination of all Dardanelle schoolchildren, which coordinated the services of the local dentist, doctors, and eye specialists and sent notices to parents when concerns were identified. These activities foreshadowed future public health laws requiring health screenings and vaccinations for children enrolled in public schools.[240]

One of the most efficient and respected women's clubs in

Dardanelle was the Ladies Cemetery Association founded in May 1899 after city officials found Brearley Cemetery neglected, the records in disarray, and great confusion and inconvenience caused to families using the cemetery. The men turned the management of the cemetery over to the Ladies Association and by 1915 "the present splendid condition and carefully kept records of the cemetery attest to the wisdom of the action." Between 1899 and 1915, the Ladies Cemetery Association exhibited diligence and reverence for their mission as they managed the records, improved the ornamental iron entry gates, built a gazebo, and arranged for continual lawn maintenance. During its first sixteen years, this group had forty-two loyal members, such as Mrs. M. E. Walker, who missed only three regular monthly meetings during the entire sixteen years.[241]

As discussed previously when the United States went to war in 1917, so did the women of Dardanelle. In addition to their impressive work in the local American Red Cross chapter, women learned and followed the rationing rules, conserved resources, and held their families together as men were called into military service. In July 1917, the Yell County Women's Committee of the National Council of Defense was organized, and Dardanelle women joined in order to "do their bit" in the war effort.[242]

In February 1917, Arkansas governor Charles Brough signed into law the so-called Riggs Primary Bill. Named after its sponsor, John A. Riggs of Hot Springs, the new law allowed Arkansas women the right to vote in primary elections if, of course, they paid the $1 poll tax.[243] The Yell County Equal Suffrage League and the Dardanelle group held meetings and ran newspaper advertisements urging men to pay the poll tax for women, as well as attend suffrage meetings and support the cause of women's suffrage.[244] In the May 1918 primary election, two hundred women voted in the Dardanelle Township.[245] Arkansas became the twelfth state to ratify the Nineteenth Amendment to the United States Constitution on July 28, 1919, and on August 26, 1920, the proposed amendment received the requisite three-fourths vote, making women's suffrage the law of the land.[246]

During the early decades of the twentieth century, women's lives were beginning to change. Some women continued to live traditional lives within the tightly scripted gender roles of previous decades.

Some women began to work outside the home for a salary in clerical jobs, while others utilized their skills as hostesses and organizers to engage successfully in politics. Some rural farm women used their housewife skills to engage in retailing their food products in exchange for cash and a degree of independence. In short, gender roles were in transition.

## Entertainment and Leisure

During this period, one can also see a transition occurring in the forms of entertainment. Leisure time, given the fact that some people now had some, was becoming more important, and how one chose to use that time provides insights into people's class, race, and gender. The ways in which the citizens of the Bottoms and Dardanelle entertained themselves underscored both what leisure they could afford in time and money and what they considered entertainment based on their socioeconomic class.

In Dardanelle prior to World War I the social elite enjoyed frequent, lavish social gatherings, some of which were related to women's organizations while others were strictly personal social gatherings. One of the most glittering social functions of this period was sponsored by the Ladies Aid Society of the Presbyterian Church at the home of Judge and Mrs. L. C. Hall in June 1911. The ladies charged a 25-cent admission fee and produced an evening emphasizing their exhibition of sophisticated culture. The New Orleans vocalist Hope Bidez Reid was the featured solo performer, and nine additional local female musicians also performed offering vocal, violin, and piano presentations coupled with several literary readings.[247] In April 1912 Mrs. Max Kaufman, wife of one of Dardanelle's leading merchants and sister of J. D. Goldman from St. Louis who had extensive mercantile operations in Dardanelle, hosted "one of the most elegant social functions of the season," at her home on the corner of Third and South Main Street, a surprise party in honor of Mrs. J. T. Miller, the retiring president of the Presbyterian Ladies Aid Society who was leaving Dardanelle. Guests were welcomed at the front door of the Kaufmans' home and escorted into the parlor where they enjoyed a selection of bonbons shipped directly from Holland for the party. A group photograph of the honoree's party, the hostess and her assistants, and guests was taken on the veranda followed by an elaborate four-course luncheon served in the dining room. This room was decorated with white and purple live wisteria and lilacs and featured a horseshoe table centerpiece encircling a miniature train. During the luncheon a mechanical dove of peace carrying in its beak an engraved message of good luck slowly descended to the honoree. Between the various courses Mrs. Kaufman read messages expressing love and admiration of numerous Dardanelle citizens for Mrs. Miller. At the conclusion of the luncheon the Ladies Aid Society presented the honoree with a silver card case and Mrs. Kaufman presented a silver tea ball and engraved spoon. The ladies then retired to the parlor where musical entertainment was provided.[248] For the women of the elite social class in Dardanelle entertainment was an art, an expression of one's refinement and social station, and to be taken seriously and executed well. Their social events were far removed from the ordinary of this place and time.

While the white, upper-class ladies of Dardanelle enjoyed imported bonbons, the poor farm laborers in the Bottoms occasionally also gathered, but for much less pretentious entertainment. Genevieve Sadler chronicled one such event, a singing in the Lower Bottoms at a private home, where "the walls were covered with old, dirty, snuff-spitted paper, the floor bare and rags stuffed in the holes in the broken window." The hostess, Mrs. Randall, "was dressed in a long, dirty, dark-colored calico dress, with dirty bare feet and snuff stains around her mouth" and guests leaned against the walls or stood in the tiny tenant farming house. Two "coiloil" (kerosene) lamps provided light and much black smoke as people gathered around one hymn book written in the shape note, four-part harmony style and those gathered "faithfully . . . feelingly sung."[249]

## Education

The Dardanelle Public School District also encountered its own rollercoaster ride of transitional growth from 1911 through 1919, including changes in its funding, major facility renovations, and near financial collapse. On the first day of school, however, in 1911 all "started off under most favorable circumstances" with an enrollment of "about 300," believed to be a record high. This was the first year in which designated secondary schools could receive state aid, which allowed any Yell County student to attend Dardanelle High School without paying tuition. The previously used tuition system meant that out-of-town students had to make boarding arrangements in Dardanelle, and many hosting student boarders would allow them to work off their payments with tasks completed before and after school hours and which, of course, were in addition to their required tuition payments to the school.[250] By the beginning of the 1912–1913 school term, Dardanelle Public School opened with 285 students enrolled. As a four-year high school approved by the State Department of Education, a graduate of Dardanelle could be admitted directly into any state university without passing entrance exams. Dardanelle High was not a "normal high school," which was a two-year high school program whose graduates had signed a pledge to immediately serve as teachers. Danville hosted the county's Normal High School.[251]

By 1913 the Arkansas State Board of Education had $50,000 to distribute with allocation amounts based on the length of a high school's program of study: two-year schools (such as Danville) were allocated $200 annually, three-year schools (such as Ola and Plainview) were allocated $300 annually as were four-year schools (such as Dardanelle).[252] Dardanelle's support for education was evident in its May 1914 approval of a new 7-mill property tax, the highest level then allowed by law, with only five votes opposing the millage increase.[253] Several months later the State Board of Education apportioned $1,302,697.10 among the schools in the state's seventy-five counties with a student per capita apportionment of $2.05. Yell County's apportionment of $19,595.95 was divided among its 9,559 school enrollees.[254]

Given Dardanelle's high enrollment numbers, the lack of adequate state funding, and its policy of free tuition for students, a financial imbalance occurred in November 1915. In order to save funds the local school board ordered that several elementary grades be combined into one class of between sixty to seventy students with one teacher. Four elementary school teachers refused this class consolidation assignment and walked off the job. A number of high school male students then walked out in protest supposedly showing sympathy for the teachers or perhaps simply noting a good excuse to take the day off. New teachers were employed, but a crisis point had been reached, and the stopgap solution of fewer teachers and larger classes was only an immediate remedy.[255] During the next three years, no long-term solution was formulated and frequent teacher turnover continued.[256]

In June 1916 the school board initiated a renovation of the old 1885 building that had originally been built at a cost of $15,000 and paid for largely by private donations led by Dardanelle businessmen.[257] The 1916 renovation plans called for the addition of a two-room, two-story annex on both the north and south side of the existing structure, and the entire original upstairs to be converted into a large 800-seat auditorium with stage, new steam heating plant, new plumbing system, and additional ventilation and lighting.[258] Each of the north and south new annexes contained four classrooms, two on the first floor and two on the second floor, measuring 24 by 32 feet with a hall bisecting each floor running north and south and the entire renovated structure having metal ceilings installed.[259]

Regardless of the fifteen-to-twenty-man work crews, the building renovations were not completed in time for the start of classes in the fall of 1916. Different grades were housed in churches and other public facilities around Dardanelle at the beginning of the school term with few complaints. Despite "various grades . . . temporarily scattered about over town like a charge of shot from a sawed-off smooth bore fowling piece . . . citizens were so excited about the beautiful new building taking shape that little criticism was heard."[260] The "new" school was completed in late February 1917 and classes resumed at that location on Monday, March 5, 1917.[261]

Financial woes soon replaced the town's pride over its stately new school building. In June 1918 during an emergency school board meeting it was announced that the district was deeply in debt with $21,000 in outstanding warrants and an additional $26,000 in bonded indebtedness that had been slowly increasing during the past ten to twelve years. In order to complete the 1918–1919 school term, approximately $2,000 had to be quickly raised. Citizens and school patrons raised sufficient funds for the school district to scrape by and complete the current term, but the debt problem remained.[262] The school board developed a plan calling for the passage of a voluntary additional 5-mill tax, which was endorsed by the local newspaper as well as the town's two largest businesses and which on average would have resulted in an annual tax increase of approximately $5.00.[263] By early June 1918, 90 percent of the property owners, a total of 316 people, had signed a petition imposing upon themselves and/or their businesses the additional millage for the next five years.[264] This secured the continuation of the Dardanelle School District No. 15 with a standard annual eight-month split term. According to the *Dardanelle Post-Dispatch*, this commitment was supported by men and women, African Americans and whites, wealthy and poor, all of whom placed "a high value on boys and girls of this vicinity than on a few paltry dollars."[265] Disaster had been averted, at least temporarily.

In the Dardanelle Bottoms several rural districts were also improving their schools. In 1917 at New Neely, the voters of the Galla Rock Township approved a 12-mill school tax with 5 mills earmarked for a new modern school building designed to seat 125 children in grades one through six.[266] Centerville schools were increasing their teaching staff and citizens raised $1,000 to support their school.[267] Rural schools were more than simply educational institutions: they were the anchors of the rural community. Most major events took place at the school: basketball games, pie suppers, and community fund-raisers, meetings of the boys' and girls' agricultural clubs, programs featuring the county extension agent or the home demonstration agent, and all sorts of community social gatherings. In some small hamlets, the school was used by the traveling circuit-riding preacher for religious purposes. In bad times, families would take refuge there, and in good times, a school could be turned into a makeshift community theater by using a white sheet for a screen and a projector to show the movie. The school was the center of rural community life. As a Centerville resident noted, there were several elements that made a good community: "good farming, good roads, good schools and good general conditions."[268]

# Conclusion

Thus, the second decade of the twentieth century was a time of unevenly applied growth and transition. One can detect the elusive beginning of new gender prescriptions, while the tragedy of racism intensified and persisted. Both extreme poverty and wealth were present and starkly contrasted the period's limitations and opportunities. The want for bread coexisted with the importation of party bonbons. Patriotic World War I service was dutifully performed while the veneration of Civil War heroism continued. Additionally, in Dardanelle and the Bottoms, the multidimensional facets of southern town/rural reciprocity and dichotomy were still fully present.

## CHAPTER 4

# Hard Times and High Water, 1920–1929

*[T]he farming class, which is the one that all of us must depend on for prosperity . . . can recover more quickly from a bad economic condition than any other class.*

DARDANELLE POST-DISPATCH,
*Editorial, September 1921*

*We are unimportant people going about our everyday tasks, but our ladies have a greater view of life than to spend it idly at cards . . . we study and learn something that will be of value to others.*

FARMER'S WIFE AND HOME
DEMONSTRATION CLUB MEMBER,
*Dardanelle Bottoms, June 1924*

*A farmer who can't farm without someone to tell him how, doesn't need a county agent, he needs a guardian.*

FARMER,
*Dardanelle Bottoms, October 1926*

# Introduction

When the Great War ended in 1918, cotton prices, which had steadily been increasing since 1917, peaked in mid-1920 and then completely collapsed. During the second decade of the twentieth century farmers borrowed money and bought more land at high prices to increase the yield of cotton. In 1920 the "good times" bubble burst, although even prior to the market collapse, all was not well. In 1918 the production cost for one pound of cotton was 35.5 cents while the market price was 28.75 cents a pound; by 1919 the production cost had increased to 44 cents but the market price had only increased to 31.2 cents a pound. In late 1919, the *Dardanelle Post-Dispatch* gleefully reported "middling cotton brought 47½ cents a pound on the streets here yesterday, the highest price paid in more than half a century."[1] The report failed to note the high production costs for that pound of cotton. Others were speaking out about cotton's troubles. United States congressman James Aswell (D-Louisiana) noted that the "cotton producer received a smaller share of the profits from his work than any other farmer in the world." While cotton mills were highly profitable, Aswell said the abused southern cotton farmer and "his family have been 'slaves,' his children toiling in the fields when they should have been in school."[2]

Cotton, of course, did not disappear from the Bottoms, nor did its profitability problem and its effects of grinding poverty on growing numbers of tenant farmers and sharecroppers. The diminishing profitability of cotton also adversely affected the degree of wealth that flowed into Dardanelle from the Bottoms. The town, its businesses and its citizens, especially the socioeconomic elite, felt this downturn slide most acutely.

# Agriculture

The 1920s posed hard times for both Dardanelle and the Bottoms. The Farmers' Union was still present and still enunciating its old message of fighting against the grafters and the rascals. The western portion of Yell County was more unionized with twenty-three local farmers forming District No. 1 of the Farmers' Union, while the eastern portion of the county witnessed thirteen locals forming District No. 2 with it greatest apparent synergy in Centerville and Ola.[3] In reality, however, the days of the Farmers' Union posing a potent instrument for change for the Yell County farmer were long gone. In late 1924 the Co-Operative Store at Ola was placed into receivership and its contents and accounts sold at auction.[4] Aside from periodic meetings featuring talks about the evil acts of the tricksters, gangsters, and parasites, supposedly the capitalists and railroads, it appears that by the 1920s the Farmers' Union had become more of a social organization for the like-minded than a finely tuned mechanism of reform and change.

Agricultural reform during the 1920s was not the result of Populist-styled unions and cooperative schemes; it was prompted by applied science and new vocational education. As American society became infatuated with science and technology and the wondrous results they might produce, so did the farmer. The Smith-Hughes National Vocational Education Act of 1917 was revolutionary as it provided secondary classes regarding current crop information, disease and pest control methods, livestock and poultry training, as well as agricultural education for adult farmers and agricultural clubs for youth. Life down on the farm was becoming information driven.

The embodiment of the Smith-Hughes Act in Dardanelle and the Bottoms was Fred A. Smith, a 1925 graduate of the University of Arkansas, employed on July 1, 1925, as the Smith-Hughes vocational agriculture teacher at Dardanelle High School. Smith was one of fifty-eight Smith-Hughes teachers employed in Arkansas, of which two were in Yell County (Dardanelle and Danville). A tall, burley young dynamo full of energy and information, Fred Smith was soon named Dardanelle's football coach and produced unbeaten teams for three consecutive years (1925, 1926, and 1927). In addition to his teaching and coaching jobs, he participated in civic fund-raisers, worked with the Dardanelle Chamber of Commerce, married into the Cotton family, conducted night classes for adult farmers, traveled out of state with farm committees to purchase new breeding stock for farmers, wrote extensively on a variety of agriculture topics in his weekly column in the *Dardanelle Post-Dispatch*, and built a new brick home on North Second Street in Dardanelle. From dairy cattle, to poultry, to grapes, to soybeans, Smith presented sage, scientific-based advice given freely to anyone who would listen or read. He quickly became the most respected and easily recognized agricultural expert in Dardanelle and the Bottoms. At six feet tall, having a muscular two-hundred-plus-pound body topped by a shock of thick black hair, displaying high energy and always on the move, Smith educated, informed, and inspired many a young farm boy. In 1929 he was named master teacher for the twelve states in the Smith-Hughes Southern Regional Conference.[5]

During Fred Smith's first three and a half years as the Smith-Hughes vocational agriculture teacher at Dardanelle, significant progress was made: area farmers imported 756 purebred livestock, including 15 bulls; the number of dairy farmers engaged in shipping cream increased from 26 to 400, which during 1928 alone produced an income for farmers of $73,500; 268 acres of pasture land was improved; 13,200 baby chicks were distributed; poultry profits had increased to $18,550 in 1928; and 125 local farmers enjoyed educational tours through the dairy farms of northwest Arkansas and southern Missouri.[6] These facts were impressive and agriculturally significant. Add his winning football record and his civic work, and one understands why Fred Smith became highly respected by the citizens of Dardanelle and the Bottoms.

Such would not be the case for the positions of county agent and home demonstration agents in Yell County. The primary problem was the county's lack of funds to pay their salaries coupled with a growing public sentiment against their hiring. In 1920, Yell County employed E. B. Randle as county agent and his wife as canning agent, the forerunner of a home demonstration agent. Unfortunately, Mr. Randle died soon after taking the job. The next year, Yell County judge T. E. Wilson declined to fill the vacancy due to a lack of funds and public support for doing so.[7] In 1922 the quorum court also refused to allocate the required funds.[8] By 1923, forty-nine of Arkansas's seventy-five counties had a county agent and a home demonstration agent, but Yell County was not one of these.[9] Although the quorum court funded both positions in 1924, by the next year Yell County was grappling with a county debt of $150,000 and a federal lawsuit of $85,000, and by a margin of three votes, funding was removed.[10] By 1926 public sentiment both for and against the funding of these positions was extremely strong. One Ola resident concluded that "a farmer who can't farm without someone to tell him how, doesn't need a county agent, he needs a guardian."[11] A supporter responded that the nation produced 16,000,000 bales of cotton in 1925, and 1926 predictions were on schedule to produce 17,000,000 bales. He concluded that the farmer "needs something, perhaps a guardian, but he's more likely to get a receiver."[12] In 1926 the Yell County Quorum Court voted 38 to 7 to appropriate funds for a county agent and a home demonstration agent.[13]

By 1927 the county agent and the home demonstration agent were tirelessly working and developing extensive programs including boys' and girls' 4-H Clubs involving one thousand Yell County youth, erosion prevention using land terracing, planting home orchards, cooperatively purchasing fertilizers, home preparation of dairy products, vegetable and fruit canning programs, teaching winter gardening, control of flies and mosquitoes, clothing construction and reuse of older garments, improved home poultry production, and establishing dress-making/sewing contests.[14]

The work of the home demonstration agent also involved social change by inculcating in rural women new skills and attitudes that would lead to significant changes in their lives. Through the efforts of the Home Demonstration program, farm women improved daily life for themselves and their families by learning how to prepare healthier foods; improved sewing, canning, and sealing techniques; cleaner homes and yards; and improved health care for themselves and their families. As one farmwife put it: "our ladies have a greater view of life than to spend it idly at cards . . . we study and learn something that will be of value to others."[15] Most rural women remained fairly traditional in their views of gender roles, believing that women should be able to vote and take a more active role in public affairs but not hold public office. While rural women spoke of themselves as "we unimportant people going about our everyday tasks," the efforts of the home demonstration agents allowed them to perform those tasks more efficiently and yield numerous tangible benefits for themselves and their families.[16]

County judge Earl E. Ladd was highly supportive of the work of the county agent and the home demonstration agent, but county finances were lacking. In early 1928 Judge Ladd called a meeting of businessmen, farmers, and anyone interested in the welfare of farm families to meet and brainstorm regarding a financial means to continue the agents' efforts.[17] Since federal funds had been completely exhausted by other counties, it would be up to the citizens of Yell County to subscribe and pay for the services of the agents if their employment was to continue. Temporary financing was secured, but by mid-1929 the sources were depleted and the county could no longer raise the needed funds.[18] As such, on August 1, 1929, Yell County dismissed its county agent and home demonstration agent.[19] Certainly the assistance and information from Smith-Hughes vocational agriculture teacher Fred Smith and other USDA sources helped, but the farmers and their wives sorely missed the aid of a county agent and a home demonstration agent.

Whether with or without the services of a county agent, cotton farmers endured continued problems with armyworms and boll weevils.[20] Another insect problem over which intense disagreement developed from 1915 and into the 1920s was the Texas tick, which, if untreated, could produce Texas tick fever and lead to a host of problems in cattle: weight loss, infertility, reduced milk production, and death. The Arkansas Tick Eradication Law went into effect on May 1, 1915, but actual compliance did not begin until 1916. Under this law every head of Arkansas cattle had to undergo chemical dipping twice a year for three years in order to eradicate all the Texas ticks in Arkansas.[21] In addition to the state-run efforts, Arkansas participated in the federal tick eradication program from 1907 to 1943 in order to prevent Texas tick fever.

In February 1916 Dalton Stubbs lost three of his two hundred cattle that were pastured west of Centerville due to Texas tick fever. Demonstrations were conducted by representatives of the US Department of Agriculture and the county agent, and dipping vats were built in Yell County and opened in late June 1916.[22] Some cattle owners objected to the program, especially small farmers who owned only a few cattle or a milk cow, but by 1920 the debate had principally become a verbal battle.

Then in 1921 Yell County was placed under a federal quarantine that prohibited bringing new cattle into or selling Yell County cattle outside the county. An existing tax of 5 cents a head had been collected by the county that normally could be used to cover the cost of the dipping materials. However, because of the county's quarantine status, the state refused to sell the dipping supplies to the county. Thus, some cattle owners purchased their own tick dipping supplies, and county judge T. E. Wilson ordered county reimbursement to those individuals.[23] In 1922 a group of livestock owners who opposed the mandatory dipping filed a restraining order against the county judge, clerk, and treasurer in order to cease all dipping activities and the payment of county monies for dipping supplies.[24] In late 1922 the quorum court refused to authorize fund allocations for tick eradication.[25] While local and state officials and numerous citizens took sides and voiced opinions, cattle owners were left in economic limbo. They could not sell their cattle or easily ship them by rail, nor could they bring in new healthy stock to replenish their herds. This was an immediate obstacle to the development of a thriving livestock operation. Judge Wilson, working with state representative W. C. Blackwell and state veterinarian Joe H. Bux, found a way out of the predicament. Cattle owners were allowed to perform their own eradication program with an affidavit to the railroad, which would allow shipment of cattle to Little Rock for dipping inspection approval and then the stock could be sent to market.[26]

By late 1925 the federal quarantine had been lifted for all counties north of the Arkansas River, while cattle owners in Yell, Logan, Scott, and Perry Counties were told that beginning on March 1, 1926, cattle would be dipped every two weeks and that representatives of the federal government (namely federal government employees H. H. Little and a crew from the Federal Bureau of Animal Husbandry) would be in charge of this systematic dipping program.[27]

This federal/state mandate was bound to bring a response. Rumblings began in early March as citizens questioned under what authority the dipping was mandated and unconfirmed reports circulated of a dynamited dipping vat in western Yell County.[28] While some citizens acknowledged the federal government's power to mandate cattle dipping, others wildly claimed that 95 percent of people were opposed to it and that dipping was an intrusion on property rights and thus posed "an undue molestation on a law-abiding citizen for the sake of few cattle profiteers."[29] Another opposition statement argued that dipping only benefited about 10 percent of the people while it created a hardship on farmers by interrupting their work every two weeks. This writer ended by saying that dipping was nonsense and just "another nail in the farmer's coffin" supplied by uninformed, uncaring lawmakers.[30] Cattle dipping did pose real hardships on the small farmer whose cattle were generally left to roam, and thus they had to be rounded up and driven to the dipping vat location. This took time away from other farm tasks and for many small farmers who lacked adequate farm labor, this was a real imposition. Additionally, the 5 cents a head Arkansas dipping tax created a financial burden for struggling small farmers. These concerns that so aggravated and hurt the small farmer did not create the same problems and degree of hardship on the larger cattle rancher. In fact, tick eradication was "designed to benefit more prosperous cattlemen and an 'improved'-breed cattle industry."[31] The small farmer really did have a beef regarding the tick eradication program.

The cattle dipping controversy touched an old Populist nerve in many Yell County residents, resulting in a Jeffersonian-like verbal salute to the small farmer: "everyone knows that when the farmer is successful and prosperous that all the world prospers too, but when he is pressed down and under bondage all the world cries hard times."[32] Furthermore, this line of reasoning asked, "has the time come when 5 or 10 percent of the people rule the other 90 percent? This doesn't sound like the Monroe Doctrine, freedom of the old U.S.A., Yell County."[33] While some dipping protests were based on freedom of choice and a perceived intrusion of governmental authority over the small farmer, others concentrated on the economic cost of dipping, an example articulated by the following from a farmer in the Bottoms:

> Crippled cows nor sick ones don't have any effect on the iron hearted Booger Man's nephews or whatever they be that race around over our country with their high topped boots on and rope on the horn of their saddle trying one scheme and another to get the poor farmers' cows so he can make him take them to that awful dipping vat and charge them fifty cents or a dollar and some a dollar and a half and three dollars a head. Don't know why they charge so many prices unless they just charge whatever they think a man has got or can get. Seems they are determined to rob the farmer every way.[34]

On November 6, 1926, state veterinarian Dr. Joe H. Bux declared the Texas tick fever quarantine in Yell, Scott, Logan, and Perry Counties lifted. While the protracted effort to protect cattle and a growing livestock industry had ended, the animosity it had generated remained.

Historian Robert Wiebe called the 1920s movement to create a variety of professional and business organization "the organizational age." This organizational tendency was seen in Dardanelle and the Bottoms. On March 15, 1921, a group of Dardanelle businessmen formed the Allied Poultry Breeders' Association and T. A. Wright of Centerville, former Yell County school superintendent, was elected its president. Noting that $50,000 of egg and poultry was being marketed annually in Yell County, these men believed that an association to assist growers and marketers would increase production and dollar yields.[35] In August 1926, Yell County farmers joined others from Sebastian, Logan, and Perry Counties and the Rock Island Railroad in forming the Organization of Western Arkansas Development Association, whose mission it was to encourage and assist the growth of small fruit and vegetable farming for greater commercial purposes.[36] Melon growers had previously organized for the same purpose.[37] In 1926 Dardanelle area dairy farmers were also forming an organization in order to improve the marketing of their products.[38]

Dairy cattle, an attractive addition to the family farm, were rigorously promoted by Smith-Hughes teacher Fred Smith, who organized and held dairy fairs in Dardanelle that emphasized the economic possibilities and agricultural methods involved in managing a dairy herd.[39] Twenty-one local farmers operated a local cream station that stored and shipped their dairy products weekly and semiweekly to a Little Rock dairy company. During 1925 this group shipped 9,830 pounds of butter fat resulting in a total net payment of $3,981.40. One of these farmers earned $211.35 for his product, a tidy addition to the family income.[40] Cooperative marketing became an important method for increasing the farmer's profitability and keeping the nation's 6.5 million farmers out of debt and desperation.[41]

Poultry and egg producers were also provided with educational advice ranging from hatching tips, feed selection, insect control, and proper housing.[42] By 1927 the growing of poultry and production of poultry products in Yell County had substantially expanded, but a large marketing plan for poultry had not yet developed. Without a larger market "farmers will find chickens and chicken products like they have found cotton, useless as a money crop."[43] It would be twenty-five years before this marketing capacity developed in Yell County and with it the explosive growth of the poultry industry.

The traditional reliance on cotton, a crop farmers knew and understood, was challenged during the 1920s. Without a strong demand for their product, cotton farmers were bombarded once again with recommendations to reduce their acreage and produce other crops and livestock. The cotton market completely collapsed by mid-1920, and some agriculturalists and bankers were advising farmers to cut cotton production by 59 percent.[44] The Southern Cotton Conference adopted a resolution in December 1920 calling for cotton planting in no more than 33 percent of cultivated land, the "Memphis Plan." Many Arkansas bankers and businessmen pledged not to supply farmers with financing unless they followed this plan. Some even suggested that enforcement be carried out "with shotguns if necessary."[45] This was echoed in certain areas of the Arkansas Delta. It was suggested that night riders be used to enforce reduced cotton planting.[46]

In order to understand what happened to cotton in the Dardanelle Bottoms in the 1920s, one must briefly review cotton as an international commodity and the dramatic changes that occurred in the cotton trade especially from approximately 1900 to 1930. In 1900 the world's top cotton producers were the United States, India, China, Egypt, and Russia while Japan was a major player in cotton manufacturing due to its cheaper production costs. In 1908 the estimated world production of cotton was 19.6 million bales, with the United States producing over 13 million bales—approximately two-thirds of the world's total output.[47] At approximately the same time (1910), the Mississippi River Valley region, of which Arkansas is a part, produced 10.9 million bales. At this time, cotton producers in Arkansas and the rest of the Mississippi River Valley region were 55 percent tenant farmers who primarily used mules, although they were beginning to use limited mechanical equipment. Furthermore, these producers suffered greatly from boll weevil infestations.[48] By 1920 the worldwide cotton production had increased to 26 million bales, of which 13.7 million bales were produced in the Mississippi River Valley plus now Oklahoma and Texas. Although tractors were becoming more common in cotton farming, cotton farms in the region remained small (averaging approximately fifteen acres), and tenant farmers remained the primary cotton producers. In addition to old pests such as boll weevils and financing agents—be they bankers or furnishing merchants—farmers now had to more greatly contend with world price fluctuations after World War I and the growth of foreign cotton production.[49]

A daunting number of challenges faced cotton producers following the Great War. First, from 1918 to 1921 prices for general farm machinery in the United States, not including tractors, had increased 60 percent above prewar prices, tractor fuel costs for the same period had risen 90 percent, feed costs for livestock had increased by 50 percent, and the cost of farm labor had increased 250 percent from 1914 to 1920.[50] Second, during World War I the United States had increased its cotton production in order to meet worldwide demand given that parts of the cotton-producing world were directly involved in armed conflict and thus those areas were not producing cotton. When the war ended and areas in Europe and Russia plus colonial areas under European control reemerged and even expanded as cotton producers, there quickly developed an oversupply of cotton. As supply outstripped demand and as the United States was the world's leading cotton producer, the effects of oversupply proved highly difficult for any American involved in the cotton industry. This oversupply of cotton caused severe price declines as well as a carryover of cotton from one production year to the next, a price-destroying phenomenon that peaked in mid-1921 and again in 1932, 1934, 1935, and 1938. Carryover bales during the 1930s were equal to more than 67 percent of an individual year's newly produced cotton bales, and as late as 1938 that year's carryover bales equaled 110 percent of the entire 1939 production.[51] This market glut kept prices low and cotton farmers in distress. Third, following World War I the introduction of new synthetic fabrics, particularly rayon, became increasingly popular. As the fashion industry generated new styles of women's clothing that were less bulky, shorter in length, with lower necklines, and new thinner fabrics, a decline in the demand for cotton for clothing threatened the preeminence of cotton for women's apparel purposes.[52] Fourth, the rising costs of all associated parts of cotton production, especially labor costs, in the United States led to a slow increase in market share by other countries, particularly Egypt, China, and India.[53]

For all of these reasons, cotton was in trouble following World War I. Whereas in 1920 the United States produced slightly more than 50 percent of the world's cotton, by 1930 that percentage had declined to just over 31 percent (9.4 million US-produced bales compared to 30 million bales worldwide).[54] Thus the era of cotton's greatest economic eminence in the United States, with its production centered in the Mississippi River Valley, which included Arkansas, was during the first two decades of the twentieth century. The effects of the problems in the cotton industry outlined above that became evident following World War I can be studied on an international, national, regional, and individual basis. Certainly their impact on Dardanelle and the Bottoms caused significant pain and difficulty.

In Dardanelle the cotton crisis of the 1920s resulted in a fairly cooperative, studied approach. A January 1921 meeting in Dardanelle of area farmers, bankers, landowners, and businessmen called on farmers to voluntarily reduce their cotton acreage. This initial plan became more precise at a February meeting attended by state, county, and school officials as well as businessmen, landowners, and farmers. In 1920, of 2,000 acres of rich Cardin Bottom land, 1,480 acres were planted in cotton (74 percent) and 520 acres in feed crops (26 percent). Pledges were taken to reduce the 1921 cotton acreage to 1,170 acres (58.5 percent) and plant the remaining 830 acres in feed crops (41.5 percent). Additional county crop census information was called for and additional meetings were scheduled.[55] By March 1921 winter picked cotton (the last of the 1920 crop) was selling in Dardanelle for 3 cents a pound.[56] By May 1921 Yell County's cotton acreage had been reduced by 34 percent over that of 1920 while the statewide reduction in cotton acreage stood at 36.7 percent.[57]

S. C. Alexander, president of the Merchants and Planters Bank of Pine Bluff, probably articulated the view of many southern bankers when he called for both the destruction of surplus cotton currently warehoused, and a reduction of 16 percent in newly produced cotton. He said it was "common sense and good judgment" to make production meet market demand, and thus save the southern cotton farmer and the entire economic structure that had developed around his work.[58] By early April 1921 cotton cost 33 cents a pound to produce and the selling price ran from 12 cents to 15 cents a pound.[59] According to anyone's accounting, this was unsustainable.

In 1920 the United States produced 12,987,000 bales of cotton while cotton consumption fell by 25 percent, in part due to high unemployment and the introduction of new synthetic fabrics. The world's 1920 surplus cotton amount was 5,846,000 bales, and by mid-1921, the American South alone carried over a cotton surplus of 11,000,000 bales. Obviously, the surplus had been accumulating for years, and by 1921 it was estimated that sufficient cotton stockpiles existed to fulfill the worldwide demand for two years.[60] Thus in 1921 it became cheaper to buy cotton than it was to raise cotton and, therefore, cotton was no longer a cash commodity. As such, farmers who were solely dependent upon cotton went bankrupt. The American South had finally reached a crossroads: cotton or prosperity; or perhaps more starkly accurate, cotton or survival. Unless the surplus could be erased, the production reduced, and the market demand increased, profitable cotton farming would be only a memory.[61]

If all of these difficulties were not sufficient to drive a cotton farmer to the nearest moonshine still or church, then there were insect infestations to consider, especially the boll weevil. While not a new problem, by 1921 it was accepted that the hated boll weevil was a permanent fact of life. Farmers were given new advice on seed selection to increase resistance, treatment of stalks following picking, and methods to minimize damage.[62] What damage the boll weevils did not do during the spring and summer, the armyworms did in late summer and into the fall. State agriculturalists predicted a 25 to 50 percent cotton crop reduction due to insect damage alone. Boll weevil and armyworm damage to Yell County cotton was high during 1921.[63] There were also additional difficulties caused by unusually dry conditions and excessive heat during August and September 1921.[64] With all of these issues, cotton was selling at Dardanelle for 16 cents a pound in early September.[65] For comparison, in late 1919, middling cotton brought 47½ cents a pound at Dardanelle.[66]

In 1922 the cotton crop also suffered from intense dry weather and boll weevil infestations, but little damage was done by armyworms.[67] In late August middling cotton was selling in Dardanelle for 23 cents a pound, and at the end of the month a total of only twenty-seven bales had been sold on Front Street to merchants and cotton buyers.[68] By November the price for Dardanelle cotton reached 28.3 cents a pound, the highest price of the entire 1922 season.[69] In 1923 the spring weather was unseasonable and the Arkansas River levels increased causing overflows. The boll weevils and leaf worms arrived with one local observer concluding that "if the cotton farmer isn't the world's premier gambler, then we're an 80 car freight train."[70] In 1924 poor market demand once again forced prices downward, and farmers were advised to warehouse their crop.[71] The following year, President Calvin Coolidge endorsed the cooperative marketing plan, which included a six-step marketing refinement approach that included establishing grades and standards, eliminating poor varieties, and providing a unified product for market.[72] In September 1925 the Cotton States Protective League, noting that from 1920 through 1925 the average bale of cotton sold for $50 less than the cost of production, urged bankers, farmers, and businessmen to demand a floor price of 30 cents a pound.[73] In February 1926 Fred L. Page, sales manager for the Arkansas Cotton Growers Co-operative Association and Dardanelle born, issued a dire warning: "another big cotton crop in 1926 will mean virtual ruin to thousands of farmers and business men in the South."[74] In September 1926 one of the first bales of the season marketed in Dardanelle and grown in the Upper Bottoms sold for 18 cents a pound, approximately $90.00 a bale.[75] By early December 1926 estimates of the crop size stood at 18,618,000 bales, the largest United States crop ever produced.[76] By April 1927 cotton sold in Dardanelle for 11 cents a pound to which the local newspaper quipped: "11 cent cotton; 40 cent meat."[77]

Politicians, bankers, cotton association groups, businessmen, and farmers all seemed equally incapable of slowing the production and, thus, rising prices. Nothing seemed to stop the almost addictive desire to produce cotton: nothing short of financial ruin. By 1929 the cotton interest in Dardanelle and the Bottoms had suffered greatly. Gins were in a general state of disrepair, cotton pickers were scarce, many farms had been foreclosed, and bankruptcies were common. A cloud of gloom and inactivity seemed to hang over the Bottoms and Dardanelle businesses.

Throughout the 1920s farmers suffered from unstable markets, low prices, overproduction, uneven product demand, high shipping costs, a lack of reliable credit, and high debt. While some farmers had survived through diversification, others had succumbed. Farmland sale notices, publication of bank suits for nonpayment of loans, and notices of sheriff courthouse-step auctions for delinquent taxes had all become common. If the farmer was to survive, he had to farm smarter. Agricultural education and training efforts were all welcomed by struggling farmers, whether they were sponsored by farm associations, the University of Arkansas Extension Service, Arkansas Polytechnic College (known as the Fourth District Arkansas Agricultural School prior to 1925), Smith-Hughes vocational agriculture teachers, county agents, or home demonstration agents. Meanwhile, Dardanelle businessmen prayed for better cotton prices soon and waited as they struggled to hold on while their business volume and cash flow dwindled.

## Transportation

Cotton or not, people, freight, and mail still had to travel. By 1926 the Dardanelle and Russellville rail was shipping large quantities of coal from North Dardanelle to Russellville in addition to its usual passenger and freight shipments. On March 5, 1926, its North Dardanelle Freight Depot was set ablaze, doing $5,000 damage. Arson incidents involving D&R property and the Pontoon Bridge (owned by the D&R) were reported during early 1926, probably resulting from labor disputes at the Southern Anthracite Coal Company: "mysterious series of disastrous fires recently . . . deliberately planned and carefully executed by some person or persons with a financial grievance."[78]

The area's final significant rail transportation link was the Fort Smith, Subiaco and Rock Island line (Ft.S.S.&R.I.), which offered passenger coach service from Ola to Centerville, to Dardanelle, across Delaware Creek to Subiaco, and on to Paris (Logan County), all on the south side of the Arkansas River. It began service in 1920 and remained active until the 1950s, offering a vital link between the Rock Island line (which connected at Ola east to Little Rock or west into Oklahoma) and other western Arkansas rail lines for passenger, freight, and mail service. Ft.S.S.&R.I. service was expanded on October 21, 1927, with the introduction of a new eighty-seven-capacity passenger car (see Appendix, fig. 7).[79]

Meanwhile the county and its succession of road overseers gradually improved road equipment used to maintain its large road network, as numerous recurring, cooperative volunteer efforts between townspeople and rural residents using mule teams and shovels occurred to drag, grade, and resurface the well-used dirt roads.[80] In May 1920 some fifty Dardanelle businessmen, professionals, and laborers worked with farmers on four roads leading to Dardanelle as the newly created chamber of commerce provided cars and coordinated efforts with the county road overseer: "the merchants and citizens of Dardanelle ... are willing to work with the farmers on the different roads leading out of Dardanelle with a view of getting better dirt roads."[81]

Nonetheless, throughout the 1920s reports noted the deficiency of rural roads: "it is not reasonable to expect the farmers ... to haul their crops to Dardanelle through 20 odd miles of hub-deep sand" and "the roads are single track, narrow gauge sort, and they must be a source of much dissatisfaction in wet, bad weather."[82] Four new steel bridges were erected in Yell County during 1924, and the Arkansas Highway Department used new heavy equipment to improve existing Yell County roads beginning in 1925. State Highway 7 from Dardanelle to Ola was graveled, and Highway 7 from Dardanelle to Hollis was graveled in 1928 and 1929. Even with these important improvements, the roads generally remained in poor condition throughout the county.[83] Tomela Wright Keenan, who grew up in Centerville, called Highway 7 from Ola to Hot Springs "terrible, just one huge boulder after another," a condition that changed little until finally paved in the early 1950s.[84] By mid-1925 Yell County had more miles of state roads than any other county in Arkansas, a fact that facilitated the state highway department's efforts to maintain and improve these roads, which greatly pleased the citizens of Yell County (see Appendix, fig. 1).[85]

Even with these improvements, the February 1929 session of the Yell County Circuit Court at Dardanelle had to be postponed due to impassable roads in the Bottoms. The judge and court officials reported for court, but "not more than half the Grand and Petit Jurors were able to reach the city."[86] The Great Flood of 1927 had severely damaged most of the roads into and out of the Bottoms. By 1929 the road from Dardanelle to the Bottoms was in such poor condition that the Dardanelle Chamber of Commerce, county road crews, and farmers from the Upper Bottoms joined together to rebuild the road from New Neely to Highway 7 at Centerville. These efforts restored an adequate year-round transportation artery into the Bottoms.[87]

A third attempt for financing a free (i.e., no toll) bridge was introduced into the Arkansas General Assembly in March 1925. A local commission working under the auspices of the Arkansas Highway Department set about acquiring property owners' signatures in support of the bridge by agreeing to property tax increases that would be used to support the issuance of bonds. The cost of the bridge would be supported in half by local increased property taxes and in half from a combination of federal and state funds.[88] Local advocacy was immediate, often citing the inadequacy of the then thirty-five-year-old Pontoon Bridge that was frequently out of commission due to high water and strong river currents. In addition, the $1.50 toll for automobile crossings fueled support for the new "free" bridge. Arguments centered on economics and the potential for increased area tourism.[89] On June 5, 1925, the voters of Yell and Pope Counties voted to support the "Free Bridge," thus agreeing to increased property assessments.[90]

By January 1927 the Arkansas Highway Department decided to locate the new bridge west of the old Pontoon Bridge and in alignment with Union Street in Dardanelle. They approved a design costing $600,000 with a 22-foot-wide roadway and a side footpath of 7 feet on the downstream (east) side of the structure.[91] Throughout 1927 and 1928, the work continued as a 133-man crew worked three 8-hour shifts daily with a huge amount of heavy equipment, concrete pilings, and iron spans rested in North Dardanelle as work progressed south across the river toward Dardanelle.[92] By June 1928 the first of six permanent spans, each 214.5 feet in length and weighing 196 tons, had been set. The design called for a seventh draw span 362 feet in length on the Dardanelle side of the bridge as well as shorter concrete spans entering the bridge roadway on both sides of the river. All total, the bridge was 2,045 feet in length.[93]

The new free bridge was officially opened on January 17, 1929. Although the weather was miserable—windy, cold, foggy, and drizzling rain—a jubilant, celebratory atmosphere prevailed as state, county, and local officials joined several thousand citizens to celebrate this monumental achievement: a sturdy, steel, toll-free bridge—a "free bridge"—across the Arkansas River.[94]

As these opening celebrations ended, the pathos associated with the demise of the old Pontoon Bridge became apparent. Born out of practicality, a way to deliver people, freight, and mail across the river, the Pontoon Bridge was also a product of supreme optimism. Although frequently "out," the old pontoon functioned—well, sort of. By 1929 not a single of its original timbers remained as the bridge had been rebuilt many times following destructive water rises. "Captain" Richard Keilch, with his Irish temper, salty language, and omnipresent pipe, had faithfully served as the Pontoon's supervisor for its entire thirty-eight-year history. He was almost as much of an institution in Dardanelle as was "his" bridge. Now, both would be retired. For much of its life the Pontoon Bridge did not make money. Only during its last fifteen years or so, given the area's increased coal field activity, was there any profit. Its early owners continued its operation primarily as a civic duty for the convenience of the public and the profit for Dardanelle businessmen and Bottoms farmers. In many ways the very existence of the Pontoon Bridge was an act of civic faith by Dardanelle businessmen, as well as a source of Dardanelle pride and an object of citizens' affection.

As the Pontoon Bridge was dismantled, its timbers were sold as salvage, and its standby steamboat, the *City of Dardanelle,* was sold to the W. M. List Company of Kansas City, Missouri, a construction company that would renovate the old vessel and use it as a work crew facility for the company's Missouri River work. The *City of Dardanelle* was the last steamboat to operate in Dardanelle.[95] With its departure, another step toward modernity had descended upon Dardanelle.

## Rising Water, Floods, and Natural Disasters

During the 1920s the power and problems posed by the Arkansas River seemed omnipresent. On May 24, 1923, the river gauge at Dardanelle measured the Arkansas River at 20.4 feet and rising. With continued, intense rainfall in Oklahoma it was expected that the river would rise another 3.5 to 5 feet at Dardanelle within thirty-six hours. People braced themselves for a 25–26-foot river level. Waters began to cover farmland south of Dardanelle in the Upper Bottoms, and it was hoped that the two levees in the Lower Bottoms, the New Neely levee with a topping point of 27 feet and the Carden Bottom levee with a topping point of 31 feet, would provide protection for the crops from rising waters (see Appendix, figs. 4 and 5). A "spirit of abject gloom and discouragement" descended as residents anxiously waited to see how high the water would rise.[96] Fortunately, the levees did hold and, although approximately 1,000 acres of crops were damaged, major flooding was avoided.[97]

In 1926 rising water again caused concerns. In early September and even more so in October, several hundred acres of lowlands in the Bottoms, mainly cotton and corn acreage, were inundated. Lowlands near the Petit Jean River were flooded as the Arkansas River pushed back into the Petit Jean River, thus forcing the high waters onto the lowlands. On October 7, 1926, the river gauge at Dardanelle measured 24.1 feet with the expectation of the rise to reach 24.5 feet within twelve hours.[98]

From January 18 through January 26, 1927, rain fell almost continuously, causing numerous problems. The Pontoon Bridge was out of commission; the streets in Dardanelle were basically impassable in most places; the lowlands in and around the Petit Jean River were all flooded; the Fort Smith, Subiaco and Rock Island Railroad had two to four feet of water covering its tracks near the Petit Jean River and in the Upper Bottoms; and the levee across the Petit Jean Bottoms was entirely under water as of January 25. The river gauge at Dardanelle measured the Arkansas River on late January 25 at 19.06 feet.[99]

The exceedingly wet fall of 1926 and winter of 1927, however, would soon be almost pleasant memories compared to the massive flooding that occurred during the spring of 1927. A succession of weather events culminated in the flood of 1927, which affected not only Dardanelle and the Bottoms but also Arkansas, the entire Mississippi River Valley region, and, ultimately, the entire nation. During the spring of 1927 warm weather caused an early snowmelt in Canada that swelled the Mississippi River. Excessive rains in the Midwest further increased the flow of rivers, and this became magnified by excessive rain in the South.[100] Given these events by late spring, a one-thousand-mile stretch of the Mississippi River Valley—from Cairo, Illinois, to the Gulf of Mexico—began to flood.[101] It was estimated that the Arkansas River was carrying 813,000 cubic feet per second of water, approximately a one-third greater flow than it had carried previously.[102] On April 14, 1927, the Dardanelle River gauge measured the Arkansas at 31.0 feet, 1.4 feet higher than it had ever measured. As a result "the greatest flood that ever devastated the Arkansas River bottoms [was] now ravaging the fertile bottom lands above and below Dardanelle." As the swollen Mississippi River pushed southward toward the Gulf of Mexico, water spilled out of its banks. Numerous tributaries including the Arkansas, St. Francis, and White Rivers experienced a backup of waters at precisely the same time they had increased flows. Waters inundated the land, with some estimates contending that in Arkansas alone 5,104,735 acres were flooded.[103] A yellow torrent of waters spilled out onto the fields as hundreds of Bottoms residents sought higher ground beginning on April 13. Some went to Petit Jean Mountain, while many others fled to Dardanelle, which prompted Mayor W. H. McClure to busily organize immediate aid and relief supplies and places for these "refugees" to stay. Water stood 4 feet deep at the base of Johnson Hill outside Ola, and Highway 22 to Fort Smith was closed as Hayes Creek overflowed. In addition, water at Brearley Cemetery covered the road to Danville. Dardanelle basically was an island surrounded on all sides by rising water. Electric power went out at midday on April 14 as did telephone and telegraph services. While river level reports from Fort Smith were being received at Dardanelle via the Hot Springs radio news broadcast, the water was rising at a rate of 2.4 inches per hour at Dardanelle. Fort Smith already measured the Arkansas River at 32.1 feet.[104]

If conditions were bad in Dardanelle, and they were, conditions were even worse in the Bottoms. Farmers were moving families, livestock, and feed supplies to the safety of high ground. While the levee in the Upper Bottoms was holding, already hundreds of acres had flooded due to the constant, heavy rains. The levee in the Lower Bottoms was also holding, but the smaller levees along the Petit Jean River were expected to have more overflows and breaches. The Petit Jean River had been out of its banks since April 12, causing thousands of acres to be flooded. Farmers and landowners suffered thousands of dollars in destroyed crops, drowned livestock, and property damage to say nothing of the human misery and danger posed by rising water.[105]

One week later, the *Dardanelle Post-Dispatch*'s report on flood conditions began with phrases like "stark tragedy," "grim disaster," and "suffering humanity," language not usually used, even given hyperbole. The reality was that the newspaper offered the primary facts as they were then known for the period from April 14 through April 21, 1927.

On April 15, reports reached Dardanelle that many people were marooned in the Bottoms and in danger of drowning. The chamber of commerce presented this information to the Pontoon Bridge Company, which sent its ferry steamer, *City of Dardanelle*, onto the Arkansas River making a dangerous trip down river into the Bottoms through flood debris and swirling currents. The *City of Dardanelle* went as far as Cotton Town and returned to Dardanelle ten hours later with sixty-seven passengers including men, women, and children. On April 16, the steamer undertook another rescue mission to pick up stranded people at Fowler in the Lower Bottoms. Just below Reed's Ferry, the crew found eighty people and a large number of mules and other livestock crowded onto a narrow strip of dry land. As these people and animals were loaded onto the ferry, the crew was told that more people were stranded one mile southwest of Reed's Ferry at the Fowler Gin (see Appendix, fig. 6). This one-mile distance was covered by 25 feet of fast-moving water flowing over the Carden Bottom Levee and swirling about a large crevasse (see Appendix, fig. 5). It was determined that the *City of Dardanelle* could not safely make this run. Therefore, John Worsham, operator of Reed's Ferry, set out in a small power boat toward the Fowler Gin and found a group of people huddled together and needing assistance. Worsham returned and reported his findings to the crew of the *City of Dardanelle*, who launched two skiffs and made their way to the Fowler Gin to collect the people. The two skiffs made a successful rescue of mainly women and children, returning them to the steamer. The skiff crews also found forty-three people gathered in a house south of the Fowler Gin and offered to carry them out, but given these people's fear over the flood currents, they declined the rescue offer.[106]

Rather than traverse the tricky floodwaters in the dark, the *City of Dardanelle*, its crew, and rescued passengers and cargo tied up for the night and enjoyed a meal from the provisions of hot coffee, flour, bacon, cheese, sugar, canned goods, and molasses. The next morning, April 17, at 5:55, the steamer ferry, its crew, seventy-three refugees, and livestock began their dangerous upriver trip to Dardanelle, a twenty-one-mile journey that took three hours to complete. Upon their arrival at Dardanelle, private cars took the rescued to the homes of relatives or friends or to the homes of citizens who volunteered their residences as rescue centers. The chamber of commerce organized a three-man committee to gather donations and money for these people's needs, and within a few hours $850 had been raised.[107]

A group of people including five unnamed men and the Tedford and Worsham families had elected to stay in the Bottoms to protect their livestock and other property. On April 18 the *City of Dardanelle* again traveled to Reed's Ferry and found John Worhsam using one of his two power boats to check on numerous houses searching for anyone in need of assistance. While doing this, he had also attended to the needs of many mules and livestock and thus averted further disaster for their owners due to the potential loss of their valuable livestock. The ferry steamer then sent its skiffs to rescue people at Riverside and to engage in animal rescues there while en route.[108]

On April 18 the Arkansas River crested at Dardanelle at 33 feet. Approximately forty-eight hours later, it had fallen to 32.2 feet. Dardanelle was "crowded with refugees . . . from the stricken bottom lands . . . [as] . . . sympathetic citizens" attended to their needs.[109] By April 21 Lakeview in the Lower Bottoms was five to six feet above the receding waters, but provisions were running low. The same problem was occurring in Cotton Town to which many Cardin Bottom residents had fled since Cotton Town was the highest point in the Lower Bottoms and stood "high and dry," some ten to twelve feet above the water line.[110]

Not only were the major rivers involved, but the overflow from creeks and lakes also added to the massive amount of unwanted water. In Arkansas the flood of 1927 involved 6,600 square miles in thirty-six of Arkansas's seventy-five counties and covered over five million acres impacting 350,000 Arkansans.[111] A total of twenty-six levee breaks occurred statewide along the Arkansas River and fifty-five thousand

Arkansas homes were flooded. Of all of the states involved in the flood of 1927, Arkansas was the hardest hit.[112] The scenes of devastation witnessed in the Bottoms were played out thousands of times in other Arkansas and Mississippi River Valley locations. From Cairo (IL) to the Gulf of Mexico the Mississippi River and its tributaries flooded 16,570,627 acres in 170 counties in seven states, resulting in crop losses valued at $102,562,395. Records note that 162,017 homes were flooded, 41,487 buildings were destroyed, 5,934 boats were involved in rescues, 325,554 people were cared for by the Red Cross in 154 separate camps and 311,922 others were fed by the Red Cross in private homes. In addition, between 250 to 500 people were killed. This was the "big picture" of the flood of 1927.[113]

In the Bottoms most of the initial rescues were completed within six days of the levee breaks. Lives were saved and refugees cared for, but then people began to determine their losses, which were extensive and proved difficult for many to overcome. Some livestock (mules, cattle, hogs, and poultry) had drowned, and gardens, feedstuffs, and provisions had been destroyed. Houses and outbuildings had been submerged and many washed away. For example, the Henson Gin at Fowler was washed away. Acres of land near Fields Chapel had caved into the river taking away houses and the local church. Other homes were seriously damaged. Damage to the Pontoon Bridge was initially estimated at $6,000 with a lengthy repair period anticipated. Railroad service to Dardanelle and other Yell County towns was discontinued for several days, due to high water over the tracks. Mail service from Little Rock to Dardanelle was out for several days, and service from Dardanelle to other Yell County communities had to be resumed on alternate routes as water still made numerous roads impassable.[114] Significantly, no lives had been lost in Dardanelle or the Bottoms in the flood of 1927; however, the road back would be difficult for those who proved physically and financially able to undertake it.

As the floodwaters continued to recede, a closer inspection of the Bottoms offered a sad and sobering report by April 28. The Dardanelle Bottoms suffered $750,000 in damage to or destruction of levees, land, loss of food, feedstuffs, crops and livestock, dwellings, barns, and other outbuildings. This figure did not include the financial loss due to the washing away of hundreds of acres of land and the ruin of additional

hundreds of acres due to topsoil removal replaced by multiple feet of
sand. Luckily, the Lower Bottoms escaped most of the sand deposits.
In Carden Bottom between Reed's Ferry and Stubbs Town, only five
houses escaped major damage. Housing, therefore, would be an immediate problem, which prompted the American Red Cross to distribute
tents. In addition, all the wells in the Bottoms were contaminated.
While few mules drowned, it was estimated that thousands of hogs,
poultry, and cattle died.[115] In the end, the destruction was widespread,
massive, and crippling for many.

As a consequence of the flood of 1927, the American Red Cross
established 154 refugee camps in the states affected, with 80 of these
being located in Arkansas. They attended to the immediate needs
of 325,000 refugees providing tents, food, and clean drinking water.
As families returned to their homes, the Red Cross assisted in their
rebuilding efforts although their funds were scarce and most families
received only scant assistance.[116] In total, the American Red Cross
spent less than $17 million to rescue, house, feed, and clothe nearly
700,000 people, some for as long as ten months, plus assisted with the
rebuilding and furnishing—at least, to some degree—several thousand homes.[117]

In Dardanelle a closer inspection of damage to the Pontoon
Bridge adjusted the estimated cost of repairs from $6,000 to $15,000,
and despite the plan for a new steel bridge, it was announced that the
old Pontoon Bridge would be repaired.

Approximately one hundred African Americans who sought refuge in Dardanelle in African American homes were allotted $20 each
by the Colored Charity Board. The *Dardanelle Post-Dispatch* noted
that Dardanelle was proud of "her colored citizenship, who are not
only industrious, law-abiding and charitable, but are also ever-ready
to aid in every worthy undertaking."[118] The article did not note to what
extent, if any, the white citizens of Dardanelle assisted its "colored"
citizens. It appears that even a major catastrophe could not erode the
color line.

In early May 1927 Beulah Bussel, a field representative of the
American Red Cross, was in Dardanelle to assess needs and outline
rehabilitation efforts. The Red Cross donated $2,000 added to the
$1,602.25 donated by Dardanelle citizens and businesses to supply

food, bedding, furniture, and stoves for some of the residents of the Bottoms. The Red Cross assessment reported 108 houses in the Bottoms had been totally destroyed, 150 additional houses were badly damaged, and 200 families had been affected by the flooding. Of these, 140 families had already been provided aid and had returned to begin rebuilding their lives.

Bussel noted that housing and sanitation were the two major problems remaining. In an effort to control the spread of diseases, the Red Cross noted that the carcasses of livestock must be burned or deeply buried, including those floating in the rivers. In addition, people needed to get typhoid fever inoculations, boil their drinking water, and drain all standing water in a proactive attempt to avoid future health problems.[119] Unfortunately, it was later noted that some landowners had cheated the Red Cross by applying for and keeping aid rather than distributing it to their tenant farmers and or sharecroppers.[120]

In Arkansas during the flood of 1927, more than 41,000 families sought the rehabilitation measures offered by the American Red Cross. Under this need-based plan, a family would be provided a month's supply of food, seeds for replanting crops, feed for livestock, and, if needed, work animals, farm implements, and temporary shelter.[121]

In the Bottoms farmers began replanting crops within approximately one month of the flood as their families cleaned houses, if they still had one, and landowners advertised for new replacement tenant farmers. In other areas affected by the flood, stagnant pools of deep water remained throughout the summer of 1927, which made it impossible for farmers in those areas, such as in numerous Delta locations in Arkansas, to replant.[122] Luckily for the farmers of the Dardanelle Bottoms, this was not the case. Rural residents attempted to reestablish their normal daily lives. One bit of dark humor came from Fields Chapel. This Upper Bottoms community lost hundreds of acres to the Arkansas River as the river's course cut further southward. "We suppose this community will still retain the name of Fields Chapel, although it has been suggested that 'Wash-Out' would be more appropriate since the overflow."[123] In September the local farmers of Fields Chapel undertook the grim task of dismantling and removing their wrecked community church, while their wives supplied a homemade dinner at noon for all of the workers.[124] Events like this illustrate the reality that neighborliness and hospitality were always a characteristic of the Bottoms, both in good and bad times.

Levee repairs utilizing local labor and some state highway department equipment began in late May 1927 in the area from Dardanelle to New Neely, a section of Levee District No. 1. Levee District No. 2, which involved the area between the Arkansas and the Petit Jean Rivers in the Lower Bottoms, had almost been completely destroyed in the flood. By late May an assessment of the needed repair work had still not been undertaken, and farmers who had already replanted their fields were anxious to get the levee rebuilt as quickly as possible.[125]

Just as essential to the welfare of the residents of the Bottoms was the proper cleaning of their houses and property. Bess Hodges, a University of Arkansas Extension Service specialist, instructed farmers to place lime underneath their houses and porches as both a disinfectant and to improve the foul odors that lingered after the floodwaters receded. She urged the boiling of all drinking water and the use of carbolic acid and whitewash as a germicidal wash for the entire inside and outside of houses.[126] By late June, the local Red Cross announced that it had distributed feed, household goods, food, and seed to 270 area families—approximately 1,600 persons—affected by the flood. The national Red Cross had expended $14,000 for flood relief in Yell County and local donations continued to be raised.[127]

The flood of 1927 claimed approximately one hundred Arkansas lives, although some estimates are much higher. Only Mississippi recorded a higher death total. Monetary costs were also huge as relief and recovery amounts totaled one million dollars. Arkansas incurred the highest amount of monetary losses of any state from the flood. While the flood of 1927 was also felt in Illinois, Kentucky, Louisiana, Mississippi, Missouri, Oklahoma, and Tennessee, the destruction was the greatest in Arkansas. In some places in the eastern Delta of Arkansas the Mississippi was sixty miles wide. More farmland was flooded in Arkansas (2,024,210 acres) than in Mississippi and Louisiana combined.[128] Only through the actions of brave individuals, such as those noted previously in Dardanelle and the Bottoms, was a higher loss of life as well as an even more wide-scale loss of livestock and business/agricultural equipment averted. The flood of 1927 was a major national disaster that was felt on an intensely personal level in Dardanelle and the Bottoms.

Even as relief and rebuilding efforts were underway, continued rainfall caused additional havoc, especially causing the Petit Jean River to overflow again. By late June 1927, the Petit Jean River had over-flowed its banks ten times since January 1, 1927. Misery abounded.[129] Then, on October 5, the Arkansas River at Dardanelle reached 23.1 feet. Backwaters at New Neely inundated a small amount of corn and cot-ton acreage, but the major threat was at Fields Chapel where the levee repairs were incomplete. Local landowner Howard Hunt and a crew of men quickly added height to two temporary levees constructed in the late spring. These levees reached a height of only 22 feet. Hunt and the men working with him raised these levees an additional three feet.[130] Within a week the local Red Cross was again opening its rooms to farmers in need of clothing, stoves, bed clothing, linen, and food in order to survive.[131] By November, the local Red Cross calculated that $30,000 had been expended for relief efforts in Yell County during 1927, some funded from the national organization and some from local donations.[132]

Crop reports for 1927 were indicative of the extensive nature of these disasters. Cotton production prior to October 6 for the Dardanelle Bottoms was recorded at 6,243 bales as compared to the 1926 report for the same period of 9,525 bales.[133] This 34 percent decrease in cotton production clearly illustrates that it had been a difficult and sad year, filled with much misery. Unfortunately, more trouble was on the way.

In early April 1928, torrential rains again caused overflows, espe-cially in the Lower Bottoms around the Petit Jean River. Roads were washed out, several small bridges were destroyed, and crop dam-age occurred.[134] By late April, with continued wet weather and the Arkansas River reaching 21.4 feet, additional crop damage and over-flows occurred in the lowlands outside the levees. Backwater at New Neely inundated "considerable acreage."[135] During the latter half of June, continued heavy rain pushed the river gauge at Dardanelle to 22 feet, causing 3,500 acres of corn in the Lower Bottoms along the Petit Jean River to be flooded.[136]

The following spring witnessed unusually high flows on the

Arkansas River. On May 16, 1929, the Arkansas River gauge at Dardanelle measured 26.2 feet and an additional 8–11-inch rise was anticipated. Such a rise at Dardanelle would result in a river level rise in the Upper and Lower Bottoms from between 1 and 1.5 feet. The threat from high water was exacerbated by the fact that the levee system repair work from the 1927 flood had never been totally completed. Weak spots in the levee above Riverside and at Fields Chapel were strengthened by local farmers in early 1929, but still they did not yet constitute an adequate levee system. On May 17, 1929, the river level at Dardanelle reached 27 feet, but luckily the levees in the Bottoms held. In the Lower Bottoms, the Arkansas River overflowed its banks, but only minor crop losses were incurred. Near Stubbs Town, backflow from the Petit Jean River flooded several hundred acres, destroying the crops. In Pope County, the levee at Holla Bend failed and 2,500 acres of Holla Bend crop land was engulfed, but the Dardanelle Bottoms escaped major damage.[137]

The high waters during the period from 1926 through 1929 accentuated the need for adequate and well-maintained levees. When the levees failed, everyone suffered. Damage resulting from breached and overtopped levees was not quickly ameliorated, and for some the losses were simply too great to sustain continued farm and/or business operations.

## More Bad Weather

In addition to high water, other forms of weather also posed life-threatening conditions. One of these was the extreme cold. A case in point would be the "deep freeze" of 1921. During a 27.5-hour period between February 18 and 19, a record snowfall of twenty-five inches was recorded at Dardanelle. Roads were blocked, rail and mail service halted, thirty-two Pontoon Bridge boats sank under the accumulated weight of the snow and only foot traffic was allowed on the bridge, automobile windows were crushed, awnings on downtown buildings collapsed, and roofs throughout Dardanelle and the Bottoms were damaged and some even collapsed under the weight of the snow and ice. The only means of travel was by horseback as all roads were covered in ice and snowdrifts. Most residents did not have a large reserve of coal on hand for heating. Misery ruled. Near the end of February, conditions began to improve as the temperature climbed to a balmy 13°F.[138]

Especially from 1915 through 1929 a variety of punishing weather incessantly pelted Dardanelle and the Bottoms. Winter storms involving feet of snow, ice, and sleet plus flooding overflows had each taken their toll on a population that was already enduring its typical, ongoing difficulties with economic distress, as well as health and disease threats. These challenges, while endured to varying degrees by everyone, were more severe, of course, for those who were less affluent, which included the African Americans and the working-poor laboring classes. It seemed that the modern world was perplexing and filled with deeply troubling concerns, all of which were made even worse by the perils of bad weather. The *Dardanelle Post-Dispatch* may have summed up the contemporary view of conditions in saying, "bad weather, business depression and other adverse conditions."[139]

## Health

Another of these adverse conditions was health, or the lack thereof. In 1921 President Warren G. Harding requested US surgeon general Hugh S. Cummins to investigate the extent and site locations of pellagra. The resulting report noted that "conservative estimates indicate 5,000 deaths and 100,000 cases of pellagra [occurred] in 1921." Arkansas was one of the five states in which "a definite increase of pellagra" had occurred during the period.[140] This report argued that while no scientifically defined famine existed in the South, the lack of crop diversity resulted in a poor and nutritionally unsound diet, resulting in pellagra. In some locations in the South, "the essential foods required to prevent the development of pellagra were obtainable only with difficulty and in some instances were entirely beyond the reach of the poorer working people . . . a situation brought about largely by the custom of one crop farming."[141] This report termed the food shortage in some southern states to be "acute."

Dr. N. Herbert Jackson, longtime physician in the Lower Bottoms, claimed that 90 percent of the aliments he treated could be cured in three weeks if his patients had a balanced, nutritional diet. He believed this so strongly that he and his wife had a huge garden and a large fruit orchard, and Mrs. Jackson (Olive) spent months annually preserving and canning the bounty from the garden and the orchard. Thus, after Dr. Jackson examined a patient he would usually request his wife to go into their basement cellar and retrieve jars and cans of fruits and vegetables for the patient to take home.[142] The normal diet of a resident of the Bottoms varied greatly depending on his socioeconomic standing. Small landowning farmers and their wives usually maintained gardens, smokehouses, and orchards and produced their own cheese, butter, and other dairy goods because they had several cattle or, at least, a milk cow.[143] Therefore, this "middle class" group of farmers had a fairly nutritional diet. The larger landowners had access to a greater and wider variety of foods. But the tenant farmers, sharecroppers, and itinerant farm laborers frequently did not have access to fresh dairy products, many vegetables, fruit, or lean meats except in extremely limited amounts. These people's diet was exceedingly unhealthful, consisting of much corn in various forms, pinto beans, fried fat salt pork, biscuits or cornbread, and large amounts of grease used for frying foods and then using the leftover grease—called "soppins"—to drizzle over foods as a flavor enhancer.[144] For these people, the lower class of farmer and laborer, developing pellagra was highly probable.

Pellagra again became front-page news following the flood of 1927, which caused the dislocation of massive numbers of people for extensive periods of time. In the months following the initial flood, some 50,000 flood victims reportedly had pellagra.[145] At the instruction of Surgeon General Cummins, the American Red Cross distributed yeast to all pellagra sufferers in the flooded areas. In the absence of a proper diet (milk, fresh lean meat, eggs, fruits, and vegetables), taking two teaspoons of powdered yeast three times a day for a period of six to ten weeks would usually improve one's pellagra condition, at least temporarily. This was only a short-term "fix" but with tens of thousands of displaced people living in tents atop levees, the condition of these poor farmers, the typical pellagra sufferers, was more desperate than ever. A temporary treatment was better than none.

By 1920, the Dardanelle City Council was beginning to pass ordinances to improve the town's health and general appearance. In May 1920, the town issued orders that "it will be unlawful for any citizen of

Dardanelle to keep more than two pigs on his premises" and that citizens must keep weeds and grass cut and that it is unlawful "to dump rubbish and refuse matter on the river bank, or to burn paper or trash on the streets in the business section unless a proper metal receptacle is used."[146] During this time period, keeping livestock within the city limits seems to have been a fairly common practice as well as a source of periodic complaints. One such complaint in 1919 noted that people were using city sidewalks to move their cattle, which resulted in a situation "decidedly unsightly, unsanitary and distressing to pedestrians who are forced to make use of the same sidewalks especially after nightfall."[147] Here the problem was not the presence of cattle inside the city limits, but their use of the sidewalks and the manure they frequently deposited there.

Water problems continued. On February 19, 1921, a vandal removed the bearings from the City Water Works pump. The disappearance of the bearings caused a disappearance of town water.[148] A new pump was installed, and then, in September 1922, the State Board of Health notified Dr. F. R. Sweet, Dardanelle's city health officer, that water samples revealed sewerage was infiltrating the water system and thus *Escherichia coli* (*E. coli*) bacteria was present in Dardanelle's water.[149] By early 1923 upset citizens crowded into a well-attended city council meeting wherein three businessmen (George F. Upton, J. J. Boyce, and C. D. Singer) were appointed as a committee to investigate the possibility of having the Dardanelle Ice Plant supply water to the city.[150] Within a month, it was announced that the town would sell its water works and entered into a franchise with the local ice plant to pump water to the city for $300 monthly. This arrangement went into effect in May 1923 and worked so well that the contract was extended in November 1923.[151] By February 1924, the town's $8,000 note for the failed 1920 water wells had been paid off and Dardanelle's water system was currently operating in the black.[152]

As the pumping problem was apparently solved, the town's wells began to run dry. Two new wells were dug near the Dardanelle Rock and after some battery problems, by July 1929 everyone hoped the sorry saga of water woes was finally over. Then, on August 2, 1929, both pumps ceased to operate and all of Dardanelle was without water for more than twenty-four hours. The problem appeared to be sand from the new wells, which damaged the pumps, but repairs were made and the town's water supply was again secured.[153]

While the influenza pandemic had ended in 1920, sporadic flu cases remained. In February 1923, Arkansas reported 3,000 cases, but none of these cases was reported from Yell County. Nonetheless, local reports from Carden Bottom noted "scores of cases of influenza but ... in a mild form." However, Cotton Town attributed the death of Mrs. Hugh Stout to influenza and pneumonia complications.[154] During the same period, Old Neely, renamed Riverside by its residents, reported influenza cases and New Neely had numerous cases of chicken pox.[155] In early 1929, some 250 cases of influenza were reported "in and around Dardanelle," mostly deemed mild cases, but some were serious given pneumonia complications. This outbreak caused the Dardanelle Public Schools to close for one week.[156]

Measles, first noted in large numbers in Fields Chapel in February and then in Liberty Hall in March, swept through the Bottoms in 1928. By spring, recurring outbreaks of both measles and whooping cough (pertussis) severely interrupted the school term at Liberty Hall in the Lower Bottoms.[157] While none of these disease outbreaks reached epidemic proportions, they do serve to emphasize the vulnerable and generally poor state of the area's health during this period.

Tuberculosis—also popularly known as "consumption"—was a continual major health problem during the early twentieth century. In 1921 it was estimated that one Arkansan died from "the Great White Plague" every 2.5 hours and that a single infected person could spread the disease to eight others. State and local groups focused on preventive health training during the 1920s, particularly health education programs for children via traditional public school programs and among African Americans, a population that was more difficult for preventive efforts to reach.

The Yell County Health Association sponsored health crusades and health contests within local schools, emphasizing tuberculosis prevention. In early 1921, six county schools, including those in Dardanelle and Centerville and both white and African American schools, received twenty-five visits from this group.[158]

It was estimated that approximately 600,000 African Americans would ultimately die of tuberculosis. To forestall this projection, the traditional wisdom for the "Negro problem" called for "Negro doctors working in Negro tuberculosis clinics."[159] No such clinics existed in or near Dardanelle nor in many other lesser populated areas of Arkansas. Somehow health information and prevention/treatment approaches had to include the African American population. This health problem could easily become infused with racist rhetoric, which, whether intended as such or not, would do little to address the health issue while readily stimulating a racist backlash. The following is an example:

> The negro waits on your table, nurses your children, cooks for you—he is a menace to the health of the white person in his present condition. They are not concerned, it is our problem and we must solve it if we are going to try to save the many thousands who die from the dreaded disease every year.[160]

The tuberculosis threat, therefore, served to reinforce the racial stereotype that implied every individual African American was uneducated, impure, untrustworthy, and, as a group, were a subservient, dull, and disobedient class of rightfully underprivileged individuals in need of white supervision. In fact, the McRae Sanatorium, which was established in 1930 for African Americans suffering from tuberculosis, received its impetus for establishment based on the perceived threat that African Americans who were ill posed to the white population.[161]

In 1921 several of the Arkansas women's clubs created the annual Health Ride to raise money for the Arkansas Tuberculosis Association, originally known as the Arkansas Public Health Association, in communities throughout the state. The local Yell County Tuberculosis Association was formed in 1921 with a mission to educate and prevent the disease. In Dardanelle a special *ad hoc* women's committee annually organized the Sunday afternoon Health Ride from Dardanelle to Belleville in western Yell County, charging 25 cents per rider. In 1924, three hundred cars participated in the Dardanelle Health Ride.[162]

While the women participated in organizing fund-raising efforts, the stricken tuberculosis patient faced a lonely future. Most Arkansas tuberculosis patients were sent to the state sanatorium near Booneville (Logan County) where, in strict isolation, they either survived or died. C. W. (Walter) Flater, who had grown up in Dardanelle, was confined to the Oklahoma State Tuberculosis Sanatorium in Talihina, Oklahoma. There he was forbidden to do anything but stay in bed for eighteen months, the last thirteen of which he spent in the death-watch ward. Flater, like other patients, had no visitors, had little to do other than occupy himself with correspondence, and was intensely homesick. He sent a note to the *Dardanelle Post-Dispatch* editor thanking him for continuing his mail delivery of the paper although he could no longer pay his subscription, adding that "reading the local newspaper and eating are my only pleasures."[163] It is unknown in what condition Flater was released from the sanatorium, cured or dead, but in his letter dated July 8, 1923, he stated, "don't know how much longer I will last."[164] The outcome did not look promising.

Tuberculosis had been a major health threat, both nationally and within Arkansas as well as internationally, for the four decades since it was first discovered in 1882. As a potentially fatal, highly contagious bacterial infection primarily affecting the lungs, tuberculosis by 1900 was the second leading cause of death in the United States. In 1908 160,000 Americans died from tuberculosis and Arkansas's deaths accounted for approximately 3,000 annually. In Arkansas it was estimated that the disease affected one in sixty persons and was the cause of death in one of every seven fatalities (almost 14.3 percent). To combat this threat, the National Tuberculosis Association was founded in 1904 and the Arkansas Tuberculosis Association, the first in the South, was established in 1908. The Arkansas State Tuberculosis Sanatorium was established in 1910 near Booneville and originally contained sixty-four beds and was expanded in 1941 to one thousand beds. It served only white patients, while twenty years later in 1930 as noted above, a twenty-five-bed unit, the Thomas C. McRae Sanatorium in Alexander (Pulaski County), was established for African Americans and expanded in 1940 to serve two hundred patients. In 1944 the waiting list to be admitted into the McRae unit was 650.[165]

Tuberculosis remained a stubborn health threat in Arkansas into the 1980s. By the late 1930s the lack of medical X-ray facilities made it difficult to diagnosis the disease. This coupled with limited sanatorium facilities within the state resulted in a continued flourishing of the disease. Even as new diagnostic and treatment methods developed during the 1940s and 1950s, Arkansas still ranked third in the nation in 1957 for tuberculosis deaths, and mortality rates in African Americans were three times that of white Arkansans. Although by 2009 Arkansas's tuberculosis death rate was ranked as one of the lowest in the country, a hundred years of tuberculosis history in the state involved the suffering and deaths of tens of thousands as well as the cascading anguish and fear this threat permeated throughout the state and its people.[166]

The tuberculosis threat did, however, apparently energize health prevention efforts on a broader scale. Prior to the opening of the Dardanelle school term in September 1921, parents were reminded of the new state law requiring vaccination prior to school enrollment.[167] Arkansas was the first state to develop a compulsory school vaccination program, which initially mandated smallpox vaccination.[168] By early 1927, Dardanelle had organized its own Health Club, and with the assistance of local physicians were conducting regular health and disease prevention programs in the schools, including free physicals and dental exams for all elementary school children.[169] Likewise, the county health association also educated citizens as to the need for more sanitary privies (outhouses) by hooking into the local water supply and thus having an indoor toilet. This would greatly reduce the occurrences of hookworm, typhoid fever, and other intestinal diseases while also reducing the number of flies, mosquitoes, foul odors, and the need for weekly outdoor privy cleanouts.[170] "Hooking into city water" was not an option for rural citizens.

Early statewide efforts to improve the general health of citizens had focused on these issues—the control of infectious diseases such as malaria, hookworm, typhoid, and tuberculosis. The Arkansas Department of Health, which had been established in 1913, promoted these efforts as well as increased immunization against critical infectious diseases.[171]

In 1927 Yell County judge Earl Ladd and the quorum court approved the permanent establishment and expanded funding for the county health unit, including a full-time county health officer, nurse, and sanitary inspector (originally Dr. T. J. Pool, Octavia Lowrey, and William Eldridge Upton, respectively). Their mission was to work through the schools, perform physical exams, and notify parents of their findings. The most common health problems reported were dental and eye problems.[172] In 1928 the county sanitary inspector, W. E. Upton, warned of the dangers of disease from flies and the imperative of removing the fly's breeding grounds. Urging cleanliness, frequent cleaning of livestock pens, screens for windows and outdoor toilets, and the removal of standing water, the message was direct: "it is unquestionable that most of these deaths have resulted from germs carried into the homes by flies and mosquitoes. The fly breeds and feeds in the open toilet, from which it flies to the house and contaminates food. Protect your family, especially your baby, from the deadly menace."[173] Upton solicited the help of the Dardanelle Chamber of Commerce, local banks, businessmen, and town officials to launch a major clean-up of the Arkansas River bank, which had become a dumping ground for rubbish and refuse including sewage. This effort also included the installation of two outdoor toilets for the public's use, which greatly assisted rural residents spending long hours in town while conducting business and engaging in trade.[174]

The three-person county health unit in a period of just less than six months conducted ninety-two lectures to 3,188 attendees, distributed 1,849 health alert bulletins, conducted six health exhibits, provided 2,050 private premise inspections and 1,225 public premise inspections, and immunized 1,611 people for typhoid, 412 for smallpox, and 49 for diphtheria. They also had built fifty-nine sanitary privies and restored twenty-eight, supervised twelve sewer connections and eleven water connections, improved four wells and the sanitary conditions in eleven food-handling businesses, screened fourteen structures, and directed fifty-five corrections of physical defects.[175] By January 1929, the county health units activity report included 2,505 smallpox immunizations, 9,083 health lecture attendees, 4,710 school-children examinations, and 350 health defects corrected.[176]

During the 1920s, there was a noticeable increase in the number of surgical procedures performed, primarily tonsillectomies and appendectomies. Not a single appendectomy had ever been reported prior to 1920, while twenty-five were reported in less than nine years. Some were performed in Little Rock hospitals via transport by rail and a few were performed locally. Occasionally, deaths followed surgery, but most patients eventually recovered although some spent weeks in the hospital.[177] It is assumed that the medical community was better at diagnosing the appendicitis or a new procedure was being taught to deal with this condition, which prompted this expansion in the number of reported cases. In May 1920, the first area hospital, St. Mary's, opened in Russellville (Pope County).[178]

Accidents of various sorts also posed a danger to health and life. The arrival of automobiles brought new demands, opportunities, and some danger. One tragic automobile accident in Ola in April 1920 involved Otis Johnson, a traveling salesman and a "drummer" employed by Fone Brothers Hardware Wholesale Company in Little Rock, and his livery man, J. O. Ploughman. Driving between Ola and Danville, Ploughman rounded a curve at six miles an hour and swerved to miss several children playing in the road, but ran over one little girl crushing her legs with his front wheels. Both men jumped from the car, picked up the child, and were in the process of carrying her toward her home when the child's father, Sam Covey, who had just returned home from a hunting trip, fired a single shot striking Ploughman in the face instantly killing him. Covey reloaded with the intent to kill Johnson, but the salesman successfully pleaded for his life and implored Covey to get his daughter to a doctor immediately.[179] Such was the nature of road rage in 1920.

Work-related accidents, especially those related to farming, were also frequent. Cotton gin accidents frequently resulted in serious injuries and fatalities. Getting one's shirt sleeve sucked into the gin arm would often result in one's arm being lacerated by the revolving saws of the gin. Death or amputation was the typical result.[180] Likewise, runaway mule teams, particularly susceptible to being frightened and blotting, sometimes dragged or trampled a farmer as he became entangled in the leather harnesses. Such was the case for twenty-one-year-old Carden Bottom farm laborer Will McMillen, who, on June 10, 1920, was riding a plow mule to a field on the Ward Brothers farm. The mule "became frightened and threw him. He was caught in the harness and dragged a distance of nearly half a mile being repeatedly kicked by the terror crazed animal, and was dead when picked up."[181] A similar accident occurred to Van Novy, a Bohemian farmer living west of Dardanelle, who was dragged by his mule team, and, after several weeks of painful and unsuccessful rehabilitation, was taken to a Little Rock hospital where his leg was amputated.[182]

Children also worked on farms, usually having particular assigned daily or weekly tasks. Sometimes these tasks posed dangers. Ten-year-old George Gleason had the job of watching the irrigation system his father operated on Mill Creek as it flowed into the Arkansas River near New Neely. The boy walked the approximate one mile from his home to Mill Creek and then sat alone along the creek's bank carefully checking the flow of the water. Years later, he recalled the absolute terror this task caused him as packs of feral dogs would occasionally wander along the creek bank, and he felt defenseless against their potential attacks. While these wandering dogs never attacked him, the fear this threat prompted was still tangible half a century later.[183]

Two additional cases underscore the particular danger that accidents posed for the people of the Bottoms. The first is the case of Mrs. Ed Adcock, who lived near Cotton Town and suffered some undisclosed injury to a bone in her arm in late August 1928. Despite doctor care and hospitalization—which included two amputations due to blood poisoning, one below the elbow and the second one below the shoulder—Mrs. Adcock died on September 5, 1928.[184] The second case involved Ruby Elnora Ohler, a six-year-old Carden Bottom child who in January 1927 drank a small amount of concentrated lye, which was used by rural families for general household cleaning and washing of clothes. Ruby's mouth and throat were severely burned, for which she received medical treatment at St. Mary's Hospital in Russellville and at a Little Rock hospital and was returned home. Due to Ruby's continued intense suffering, in early June her father decided to return with her to St. Mary's Hospital, but as they waited for the boat at Reed's Ferry, the young girl died. Neighbors raised $26.50 and gave it to the parents, who had four other children for which to provide.[185]

Poor transportation, poverty, limited readily available medical care, and the dangers of daily work all resulted in great suffering, the loss of life, and otherwise avoidable consequences for residents both in Dardanelle and in the Bottoms. Rural life, especially, was filled with potential dangers. A simple mistake, a careless, inattentive moment, a wild animal, or a "spooked" mule could cause a serious injury or even death. Rural life was particularly imbued with unexpected outcomes and potential tragedies, all of which were often intensified by poverty.

During the early twentieth century, diseases and accidents resulting in injuries, death, and financial woe were not rare occurrences.[186] Although the outcome was frequently profound or even tragic, the people of Dardanelle and the Bottoms seemed to have stoically accepted these unwanted hardships as a part of life to be endured and overcome. Accidents, diseases, and their results were life altering, and sometimes life destroying. These were a resilient people determined to cope with adversity and move forward. What other course of action could they possibly have taken but to persevere?

## Crime and Violence

Violence often resulted in deaths and injuries. For example, in November 1924, a twenty-two-year-old farmer, Lawton Hunt, spent a long night drinking and losing at poker. In frustration, he drew a pistol on fellow poker player Dick Troxwell, who proceeded to hit Hunt several times with an undisclosed blunt object, causing Hunt's death several hours later.[187] Liquor, gambling, and self-defense frequently became a lethal combination.

Domestic violence appeared to be the basis for a tragic murder/ suicide near Dardanelle in 1920. Albert Pigeon, age fifty-nine, of the Bohemian settlement west of town, used a shotgun to murder his wife of forty years, whose body was discovered by one of their six children. Pigeon then entered the attic crawl space of an outbuilding behind his home and, using the same shotgun, took his own life. This crime shocked many people as the Bohemians had arrived in Dardanelle during the late 1870s and early 1880s and were recognized almost universally as "thrifty, honest, law-abiding people." In fact, this tragic event was the first criminal activity associated with the Bohemian citizens that anyone could recall.[188] Other crimes during the second decade of the twentieth century were less violent and included several instances of forgery, hog stealing, and bank robbery.[189]

While the period from 1920 through 1929 saw an increase in the frequency and variety of criminal activity in part due to difficult economic times and enforcement of prohibition, occasionally, more serious crimes were committed.

R. L. Hopkins, a thirty-eight-year-old tenant farmer residing in Cotton Town, was bludgeoned to death as he slept in his bed around

5:00 a.m. on April 5, 1921. The murderer, his wife, had used an unusual weapon, a Ford automobile axle. This event and the circumstances surrounding it were shocking. For two years prior to his demise, Hopkins had repeatedly raped his wife's fifteen-year-old half-sister who also resided in the home. Both Mrs. Hopkins and the victim were threatened with death if they reported the activity, attempted to get assistance, or tried to leave. In the predawn hours of April 5, Hopkins sexually assaulted his sister-in-law and, before returning to his own bed, he demanded his wife prepare his breakfast. Mrs. Hopkins could be intimidated no longer, and she walked outside to the yard, picked up a car axle, and then struck her husband twice in the head as he slept, resulting in his death. She then walked to a neighbor's house, explained what had transpired, and waited for Justice of the Peace J. W. Hundley to arrive. A subsequent inquest deemed the homicide justifiable.[190] Without a funeral or memorial, R. L. Hopkins was buried in a far corner of Harris Cemetery near Cotton Town with the murder weapon as his monument. The murder weapon/headstone remained in place until approximately 2010 when it disappeared, supposedly stolen and taken to the salvage yard in exchange for cash.[191] The reality is that during this time period, justifiable homicide was fairly common in Yell County.

A somewhat similar case involved the second-degree murder indictment of Mrs. Hesper Montgomery, a widowed mother living in the Bottoms, for the 1925 murder of young Joe Starkey, whom she believed was responsible for her daughter's delinquency. Montgomery pleaded guilty to having gone into the cotton field where Starkey was plowing and shooting him to death. A Dardanelle Circuit Court jury found Montgomery guilty of the crime, sentenced her to five years in the state penitentiary, and then suspended the sentence.[192] Again, it seems that murder was deemed appropriate, particularly in those cases involving illicit sexual activity. This dynamic is evidenced again near New Neely in September 1926. Esley Knight, age forty-five, described as a "peaceable, industrious tenant farmer [who had] never before been involved in similar trouble," was arrested for the shooting of Clyde Jones, age twenty-five, following a quarrel over Jones's "attention to Knight's daughter." Even though Knight had severely beaten his daughter, which brought about the chain of events leading to Jones's death, what is most interesting about this case was the report that "the sympathy of the public seems to be largely with Knight."[193] The reality was that challenges to tradition and parental authority, coupled with real or perceived inappropriate sexual activity, apparently justified an otherwise criminal response. Approximately ten additional violent crimes involving murder, assault, and several apparent suicides were reported during the 1920s, especially after 1925.[194]

Crime reports from this era also offer a window of understanding into the generally accepted perceptions of race. Two cases illustrate prevailing views on race. First, in late 1927 Dave Thompson, an African American, was arrested for assault following a financial disagreement with Ess Holland, the proprietor of the Majestic Auditorium, an African American restaurant and dance hall on Fourth Street in Dardanelle. Thompson used a 12-gauge shotgun loaded with bird shot to settle the argument for which he was arrested.[195] Such incidents served to reinforce the general white perception that African Americans, especially men, must be controlled, feminized into obedient passivity, and always kept in their proper place. By doing so, the community avoids sexual violence, vile public misconduct, and general beastly, unacceptable, uncivilized acts.

It seems that every criminal act large or small committed by an African American served as yet another bit of "proof" that racial equality was a fantasy pipedream that would destroy all that was good, decent, holy, and productive. In addition, relationships between law officers and African Americans were strained and illustrated the suspicious attitude of African Americans toward most authority figures as well as the negative attitude of whites toward African Americans as dangerous brutes and criminals. These racist assumptions were simply reinforced by every criminal report involving African Americans.

The second illustration of the racist dynamic occurred in June 1921 as two local law enforcement officers were sent to the Bottoms to find and arrest Henry Spencer for attempted murder and assault. Spencer had a "bad reputation and was said to be a desperate character." So desperate, in fact, that while he was running *away* from the two officers, one bullet was fired that shattered the bone above Spencer's left leg resulting in amputation. When searched, Spencer did not have a weapon, but he did have several shotgun shells in his pocket.[196] This was apparently sufficient enough to justify the officers' actions of shooting Spencer as he ran away from them. No one questioned the propriety of the police shooting, and rules regarding police use of deadly force, especially against African American citizens, were not particularly stringent or even thought to be necessary at this time.

Burglaries were also common during the 1920s, almost none of which resulted in arrests. These crimes in rural areas usually concentrated on small stores, which throughout the Bottoms, represented easy targets for thieves. Stolen items often included dry goods, clothing, groceries, and sometimes cash.[197] Robbers also stole from the United States Post Office. In April 1921 criminals blasted their way into the safe at the Ola Post Office and stole $427, and by late 1921—in reaction to numerous robberies—the United States Post Office Department placed armed guards on mail trains with mail carriers armed with .45-caliber Smith and Wesson handguns.[198] This action prompted the *Dardanelle Post-Dispatch* to run advisements pointing out to mail robbers that their activities would be a good way to commit suicide.[199]

Occasionally the crime reports yielded some humor, such as when the automobile belonging to T. R. Cornwell, Dardanelle's city marshal, was stolen from in front of the local Baptist church while his sons were attending Sunday service in November 1925.[200] The abandoned car was found undamaged the next morning near Ola. Another "funny" crime story occurred on September 13, 1922, when seven prisoners escaped their Dardanelle Jail cell by filing the steel bars of the door. Two of the escapees, one charged with moonshining and the other with gaming, left town. The other five escapees "after visiting the picture show and the pool hall, returned to the jail and spent the night, being on hand when the jailer brought them breakfast the next morning."[201] Perhaps the jail's food was better than was its general entertainment.

Certainly during the 1920s the greatest number of crimes involved the illegal manufacture of liquor, moonshining, and its illegal sales, bootlegging. During 1921, twenty-two stills were destroyed on the Petit Jean and Fourche Rivers, in Carden Bottom, Cotton Town, Holla Bend, and near Danville; arrests and one-year state penitentiary sentences were common for such crimes.[202] In 1923, in an effort to shut down moonshine activity throughout Yell County, Sheriff Joe Gault announced an amnesty program for all moonshiners. In exchange for

admitting to their actions in a court of law and assisting law officers in destroying all stills, all would be given a one-year suspended
sentence in the state penitentiary. Nineteen moonshiners signed the
amnesty plan, but within less than three weeks all had returned to
their whiskey-making ways and were sent to the penitentiary.[203] Even
the Arkansas Supreme Court added its support for strict enforcement of the Volstead Act when, in 1924, it held that flavoring extracts,
given their high alcohol content, were prohibited.[204] There went the
vanilla extract on the grocer's shelf. Despite all efforts, moonshining
and bootlegging activities continued in Yell County, as both generated cash—something poor farmers desperately needed—and cheap
liquor—one of the few available pleasures for the poor man.

Liquor and gaming cases clogged the courts' dockets. The
February 1922 Dardanelle Circuit Court docket had twenty-three
criminal cases, nine of which involved various liquor offenses while
eleven were for illegal gambling (gaming). The court's fall 1922 term
had sixty-six total cases, of which twenty-one involved liquor and
twenty-four were for gambling.[205] Throughout the 1920s, circuit court
judge J. T. Bullock railed against gambling and liquor crimes, saying
that "strict enforcement of morality laws . . . constitute the foundation of society." In fact, nineteen of the twenty-five homicide trials in
four Yell County Circuit Court sessions from 1923 through 1925 also
involved liquor violations.[206] By 1927 Judge Bullock had developed an
even more puritanical tone:

> There is a spirit of unrest among the youth . . . that has resulted in
> a large number of serious offences—murders, stealings, robber-
> ies and crimes against morality . . . there is a general revolt by the
> youth of the land against governmental and parental authority;
> a relaxation of the moral code that bodes ill for the future.[207]

Of course, Judge Bullock was in a unique position as a circuit
court judge to observe highly unruly and destructive human behaviors and their resulting suffering. However, his increasingly forceful
pronouncements from the bench against liquor and gaming and his
linking of these to youthful indiscretions represented his opinion that
a breakdown of the moral code was threatening all of society. This
seems a bit exaggerated, and the judge's views may simply have been

his reaction to the overall cultural changes that were happening across the nation during the 1920s. Traditional society was changing, and modernity had indeed altered some of the old patterns of life. While this was certainly unsettling for many, these changes probably did not represent a complete unhinging of society's foundations.

Nonetheless, many citizens agreed with the judge's interpretation. An understanding of the pivotal role that moral concepts played during the 1920s can be seen in the sentences issued in two separate criminal cases during the fall 1926 Dardanelle Circuit Court session. Dan Beasley of Rose Creek was indicted and convicted of first-degree murder, and Ed Eubanks was indicted and convicted of bootlegging. While the crimes were significantly different, the sentence for each man's crime was one year in the state penitentiary.[208] Another example illustrating the power of morality concepts on criminal sentencing came from the 1922 circuit court session in which an assault conviction netted a $10 fine and a moonshining conviction netted a $100 fine.[209] One can only conclude that the general public and the criminal courts were more concerned with maintaining traditional morality codes than punishing an occasional outburst of violence.

Further proof of this can be seen in the 1922 first-degree murder trial of Charles Jackson. A poor tenant farmer, Jackson had recently arrived in Centerville along with his wife, children, and a brother-in-law who was a moonshiner. Jackson refused to maintain the secrecy of his brother-in-law's activities, which prompted his brother-in-law to beat Jackson, his wife, and their children. As Jackson grabbed his shotgun, the brother-in-law fled into a nearby cotton field and Jackson followed. Jackson fired his shotgun twice, striking the moonshiner with both blasts, thus killing him. At Jackson's trial, his religious beliefs against the use of liquor and illegal distilling were emphasized. Prosecutor Sam Rorex concluded that he "did not believe any jury would find the prisoner guilty under the circumstances and Judge J. L. Davis discharged the prisoner. The large audience showed their approbation by a unanimous clapping of hands . . . all the facts and all the neighborhood knowledge of the occurrence clearly justify the acquittal and the applause."[210] Similar to the previous decades, local justice was more a matter of applying the local concepts of morality than enforcing a strict interpretation of the law.

Throughout the 1920s, law enforcement officials continued to find and destroy stills and arrest moonshiners and bootleggers. Court convictions followed, with the standard punishment of a one-year sentence in the state penitentiary, which, depending on the circumstances, might be suspended. Moonshining and bootlegging, however, were never eradicated. In fact, these practices continued to thrive in the Bottoms well beyond the 1920s. As one Centerville resident wrote in late February 1915: "The drouth we expect this summer will be nothing compared with the 'drouth' we will have to suffer next January the first, and we know a man who says, 'Give us licker, or give us death.'"[211] Given the flow of moonshine in the Bottoms, it appears the gentleman was long lived.

Based on an analysis of area crime from 1920 through 1929, it appears the most crime can be attributed to two things: prohibition and hard times. Liquor flowed in Yell County, both before and after prohibition. In 1912 the voters of Arkansas decisively defeated Proposed Initiated Act No. 2—which would have allowed for a "local option" for liquor in Arkansas—by a vote of 56,806 for and 78,230 against. The Dardanelle Township voted 198 for this act and 260 against.[212] Additional liquor laws were enacted and became effective on January 1, 1916. In keeping with the anti-liquor sentiments in the town, the Dardanelle Methodist Church hosted Dr. Madison Swadener, a nationally renowned Anti-Saloon League lecturer, in November 1920.[213]

Obviously, the split between Dardanelle and the Bottoms regarding the liquor issue was stark. Regarding liquor, Dardanelle was more elitist and moralistic whereas the Bottoms can be characterized as being more democratic and capitalistic. Two factors created this divergence. First, the upper class in Dardanelle, including its more activist women, opposed liquor as a detriment to a healthy and moralistic life, whereas in the Bottoms most residents were not of the upper class and the women, while some may have opposed liquor, were not activist in this regard given their lack of club organizations. To organize in opposition to liquor was a step beyond the organizational focus of these women, whose greatest concern outside their homes and families was education. Second, liquor in Dardanelle was perceived to be a source of various kinds of trouble, whereas in the Bottoms moonshining and bootlegging were seen as a means to preserve the family given the additional cash flow they rendered to families living very close to the edge of financial disaster. The moonshining and bootlegging activities of the area were not unique, as these activities transpired in numerous American locations across the country as a reaction to the Eighteenth Amendment and as a result of poverty. So class and its implications on gender played key roles in the liquor debate and moonshining/bootlegging activities of this period, and produced starkly different positions as manifested in town versus rural residency.[214]

Regarding crime in general, economic want and class were significant determinants. Certainly it appears that the increase in the number of robberies and burglaries can be attributed to human need resulting from deprivation and harsh economic circumstances. Stealing food and warm clothing does not necessarily make one a career criminal. In fact, numerous convictions for gambling—of primarily rural men of the lower class engaging in one of their major forms of entertainment—and judicial attempts to reimpose a more elitist puritanical moral code failed to achieve their aims. Thus, crime in Dardanelle and the Bottoms during this era seems to have resulted from mostly sociological factors as opposed to an increase in pathological conditions.

## Race and the Ku Klux Klan

The second Ku Klux Klan (KKK), founded in 1915 by William J. Simmons in Georgia, had a strong presence in Dardanelle, Centerville, Havana, and Danville during the 1920s. By the fall of 1922, the KKK reported its Yell County membership exceeded 1,400 as 104 locals of the Arkansas Klan existed with a statewide membership of 25,000 men and a national membership in excess of 100,000.[215]

One of the first local public notices of the revised Klan in Dardanelle was a letter dated June 5, 1922, sent to a local bank instructing the bank to send $25 from the organization's bank account to Deputy Sheriff Elmer Warren as a reward for his recent destruction of moonshine stills. The letter stated "we will not be satisfied until the moonshiner and the bootlegger are entirely and permanently banished."[216]

While the KKK nationally was outlining its purposes to "uphold the United States Constitution, all federal and state laws, and to promote American patriotism," it was limiting its membership to "the native born, white Protestant, Gentile Americans" while specifically rendering ineligible "the negro, the Roman Catholic, the Jew and the foreigner." The local Klan was receiving publicity for its "good deeds" such as the issuance of $50 to Mrs. Lee Hammon, a poor widow living in the Bottoms with her eight children.[217] It was easy for many people in Dardanelle and the Bottoms to feel positively toward the Klan and to become members. Many residents believed that prohibition, morality, segregation, nativism, and Protestantism were essentially required for the United States to remain strong and pure. As such, the Ku Klux Klan appealed to fearful people in a time of change and uncertainty as it upheld "100 percent American" traditional values. As such, frightened people were reassured. In other words, the Klan's message resonated well for those who disliked and perceived as un-American the "Catholics, Jews, African Americans, foreigners, radicals, bootleggers, moonshiners, prostitutes, adulterers, wife-beaters, crooked politicians and other 'objectionable' types."[218]

Not everyone was convinced that the KKK was an honorable organization. On August 9, 1923, a bitter verbal confrontation erupted between M. E. Dixon, of Fowler & Dixon Mercantile in Ola, and E. L. Pike, a produce salesman. When Pike denounced the goals and work of the Klan, Dixon voiced his strong opposition to the comments. Ultimately Pike stabbed Dixon, who survived the attack, and Pike was held for trial.[219] Generally, opposition to the Klan was very sparse as most people longed to preserve the nineteenth-century social order with which they identified and which, to a large degree, reflected the position of the era's Fundamentalist and Evangelical Protestant churches, especially in the rural South and its nearby towns.

To add credence to how the Ku Klux Klan reflected, enhanced, and articulated the cultural context of the 1920s in Yell County, one has only to read short newspaper editorials. For example, while not written by or about the KKK, the content and spirit of the *Dardanelle Post-Dispatch* editorial below perfectly reflects the Klan's message. The editorial articulated the thinking behind its opposition to two proposed bills in the Arkansas General Assembly, one to allow Sunday baseball and the other to allow Sunday prizefighting.

Sabbath observance in Arkansas is perhaps more general than in any other State, due to the fact that we are practically free of the curse of foreign population, and for the good of the State, and the Nation, too, the Legislature should sanction nothing that savors of Sabbath desecration. . . . if we start down that road it leads to wrecked civilization and ultimate chaos. . . . The rest of what we once called the civilized world is writhing in the red vortex that may result in a reversion to barbarism. If America falls, if we discard our old-fashioned religion, adopt evolution and deny the Bible—then will civilization be tossed into the discard, and mankind can go back to the caves and jungles for a new start.[220]

To most citizens, the Ku Klux Klan mixed patriotism and southern tradition in forming a comfortable blend of nativism, anti-intellectualism, intolerance, and racism. The Klan advocated those values and practices that were proven to be "right" to most people—familiar, unchallenged, and accepted. In short, the Klan reinforced the comfort provided by long-held traditions. The KKK made the small town and rural citizens feel like change was unnecessary and that their conservative approaches and views were "100% American," pure and correct. Simply put, the Ku Klux Klan offered psychological comfort in the traditional mode—white, Protestant, native-born Gentile.[221]

In 1922 the Ku Klux Klan's political strength was demonstrated in Pulaski County as it helped elect the sheriff, the county and probate judges, the prosecuting attorney, a state senator, three state representatives (one of which was a former Dardanelle boy, Neil Bohlinger), and a US congressman. By 1924 the Klan had reached its peak in Arkansas, and began to decline as the reactionary attitudes of the post–World War I period began to wane and as the national Democratic Party moved slightly to the left.[222] While there were perhaps "nearly five million registered members" of the Klan nationwide in 1925, by 1926, reportedly, "there were less than 10,000 active Klansmen" in Arkansas. While Arkansas Klansmen still held the same views against "Catholics, Jews, African Americans, foreigners and flaunters of orthodox morality and prohibition laws," now they concentrated on charity work, support of patriotic public education, and opposition to all things modern.[223] Additional reasons for the KKK's decline during the 1920s include the general decline in American fraternalism and race-based outbursts, Congress's newly enacted anti-immigration legislation, and the fact that men of greater social standing gradually left the Klan.[224] Only the fervent anti-intellectual white supremacists, hate mongers who adhered to moralistic authoritarianism, the true believers, remained. The Ku Klux Klan would, however, reignite in Arkansas during the late 1940s.

In 1919 Arkansas's population was 1,752,204, which included 472,220 African Americans and 13,975 foreign-born whites.[225] With a highly homogeneous white society, the concern of most Arkansans during the First Red Scare (1919–1920) did not focus on the radical Bolsheviks, except in selected newspaper editorials. Instead African Americans were targeted as a threat to white society. This, in part, was due to the longstanding, lingering fear of African Americans using mass violence against whites and in part due to the fear that poor African Americans were taking jobs from whites, especially tenant farming jobs.

Violence against African Americans was serious and frequently deadly. Between 1889 and 1918, Arkansas ranked sixth in the nation in number of lynchings of African Americans with 214 reported incidents.[226] Violence toward African Americans resulted from ingrained, long-existing racism, although the general hysteria of the First Red Scare helped to sustain and promote this race-based violence. The renewed actions of the Ku Klux Klan—beginning in 1922 in Arkansas—played off this foundational racism and resulted in increased racial tensions and violence directed toward African Americans.

In late 1924, a night-riding episode took place in the Upper Bottoms. As a general term, "night riding" described a range of racist tactics from physical assaults to murder and economic threats designed to intimidate African Americans in order to maintain the racial status quote—Jim Crowism. On December 10, 1924, local law enforcement officials placed seven men (John Adams, Forrest Adams, Avery Trimm, Lawton Smith, James Hefley, John Shannon, and Will Darning) under arrest for violation of the Arkansas statute outlawing night riding. All seven individuals resided in the Upper Bottoms between Dardanelle and New Neely, and several admitted to participating in meetings during which they discussed how to "get rid of the negroes" and have only white farm laborers. With the confessions and statements offered by some of the arrested, three additional individuals were arrested (Zach Upchurch, Bill Dodson, and Roscoe Lyons) with more arrests anticipated.[227] On December 13, two more arrests were made (Yell County deputy clerk L. E. Hill and Ira Taylor, both of whom resided in Dardanelle). The following day, four more men were arrested (Jerry Johnson, Alfred Lipsey, Jody Hefley, and Josh "Bud" Harbert) and by December 18, the total number of arrests had grown to twenty-two. Bud Harbert was bound over to await grand jury action in February 1925 while the others waived examination and were arraigned in circuit court (December 13, 1924) with bonds set at $1,000 per person. These included R. A. (Arthur) Dodson, Lawton Smith, Forrest Adams, John Adams, Jody Hefley, Doll Moore, Luther Hightower, Willie (W. B.) Wells, John Shannon, C. M. Miller, A. L. Pierce, Hez Stracner, Avery Trimm, Zach Upchurch, Wilbourne Apple, and Henry Merritt.[228]

Casa Township (Perry County) justice of the peace A. L. Pierce admitted to writing the threatening notices at the request of Hez Stracner and Doll Moore. These notices were typewritten and were posted on shingles and then attached to African Americans' cabins in conspicuous places during the night of November 24, 1924, by Wilbourne Apple, Jody Hefley, Forrest Adams, and Doll Moore. According to the *Dardanelle Post-Dispatch,* the message was simple: "every negro tenant farmer living between Bata Mill Creek and the district gate just south of Dardanelle [the Upper Bottoms] was warned to leave the bottom by December 20, 1924, or suffer the consequences."[229] Several landowners residing in Dardanelle also received letters demanding removal of African Americans from their employment and threatening violence to these landowners if they did not comply and in the future only employ white tenant farmers and laborers. These letters were sent through the United States mail. Wilbourne Apple had taken these landowners' letters to the Dardanelle courthouse seeking county clerk Earl Page's assistance in addressing the envelopes. Since Page was not present, Yell County deputy clerk L. E. Hill addressed the letters to the landowners, which he admitted doing at a taxpayer's request, but avowed he had no knowledge as to the envelopes' content.[230] Given these facts, Hill was released and was not indicted. Two other men who had been arrested, Will Darning and Roscoe Lyons, were also released and were not indicted. In total, twenty individuals faced charges in the circuit court from this incident.

On February 9, 1925, the grand jury quickly returned indictments against the following eighteen white sharecroppers from the Upper Bottoms and one Dardanelle resident for their night-riding activities: John Adams, Forrest Adams, Avery Trimm, Doll Moore, Luther Hightower, Henry Merritt, Joshua Douglas, Jody Hefley, Ira Taylor, Arthur Dodson, Willie Wells, Hez Stracner, C. M. Miller, John Shannon, Bud Harbert, Wilbourne Apple, A. L. Pierce, Lester Bolin, and Tom Bolin. Judge Bullock delivered a strong statement to the jurors "on the menace of night riding and painted a very fearsome word picture of what would follow if such acts of lawlessness were not promptly and effectively checked" and then recused himself and was replaced by Judge Davis.[231]

On February 13, a Yell County Circuit Court jury found nineteen men guilty "in connection with a threat to drive local negroes away from the plantations here, were assessed costs of $39 and given a suspended sentence of one year in the penitentiary pending future good behavior." Bud Harbert, previously indicted by a grand jury in February—along with the above-mentioned individuals—refused to plead guilty to the charges and was later found guilty by a Yell County Circuit Court jury and given a suspended sentence.

While certainly having racial implications, this incident can best be understood as a class conflict issue having a racial cast. The night riders, almost all sharecroppers, said that they feared that "they would be driven out by competition with colored labor, and that the negro absorption of school facilities was becoming too great."[232] The *Arkansas Gazette* noted that "practically all of the accused were 'share-croppers' who claimed that negro labor on the larger plantations made it difficult for them to obtain a living."[233] Local landowners became so concerned that such incidents would harm their labor resources that they hired private detectives from Little Rock to assist county law enforcement officers in their efforts to break up the night-riding ring.[234] As historian Guy Lancaster notes, the plantation system of this era "brought whites and blacks into economic competition with one another, as both sought employment—and were sought by employers."[235] Anyone might be subjected to this form of vigilante violence, even upper-class elites such as businessmen, cotton merchants, gin owners, and bankers if their actions were deemed to conflict with community norms or threatened citizens' livelihoods.[236] Everyone had his or her "place" in southern society, which, if their actions did not properly maintain and uphold, would suffer consequences. Historian Jeannie Whayne notes that many lower-class whites envisioned tenant farming as the first rung on the ladder to actual landownership and thus the "presence of lower-paid black sharecroppers simply worked against their economic interests."[237] As landowners noted, "the labor question is always acute in the bottom, and any effort to drive out negroes, most of whom are industrious and law-abiding, can but work harm in the community."[238]

Landowners wanted abundant cheap labor (i.e., African American farm laborers and sharecroppers); poor white tenant farmers wanted noncompetition from African Americans; poor African American tenant farmers, sharecroppers, and farm laborers wanted an opportunity to work and live; and Dardanelle businessmen and elected officials wanted a smooth continuation of trade, which required peace in the Bottoms. As lower-class white tenant farmers, sharecroppers, and farm laborers perceived African American farm laborers as an economic threat, night riding and violence erupted. Thus, by the 1920s the old plantation agricultural system had created class stratifications that resulted in severe economic deprivations and concerns, which in turn brought about an increase in racial conflict. This reality also underscored the class divisions that existed between Dardanelle and the Bottoms. Most of the large landowners resided in Dardanelle and were a definite part of the town's upper class, and their decisions regarding who they employed to work their lands directly affected the lower-class residents of the Bottoms from which their wealth and that of the town's was derived. Night riding in the Dardanelle Bottoms in 1924 was most often based first on class economic conflicts and only secondarily on racial divides.

Not only in Dardanelle but throughout the South in the early 1920s, African Americans were making their way to northern cities, leading to a heightened concern over the availability of farm labor. J. S. Wanamaker, president of the American Cotton Association, noted that "labor is being drawn from the agricultural to the industrial centers and from no section to a greater extent than from the South."[239]

Arkansas governor Thomas McRae was also concerned, and canvassed other southern governors as to how to jointly organize to prevent this exodus.[240] Lonnie Dickens, a third-generation African American sharecropper from the Bottoms, noted the departure of many of his relatives during the 1920s and into the 1940s to Detroit and Chicago for jobs in industrial plants.[241] Many southerners believed that the "idle negroes" had fallen prey to advertisements placed by labor agents of the "wonderful jobs" in northern cities, but given the "cold weather . . . an increase in rent . . . and the tightening up by the police the Southern negro will think of the wonderful Southern climate, the comparatively cheap rent and the tolerant police departments and the number of negroes 'flying South' almost will equal the ducks and geese."[242] Thus for most white citizens, racial injustice affecting African American tenant farmers and laborers was perceived to be of little, if any, importance compared to farm labor needs and potential lost profits for landowners and local businesses resulting from labor short-ages. In the plantation-model South of the early twentieth century, as during antebellum days, African Americans were needed in order to produce profits for elites (landowners and business owners), especially if the African American was "industrious and law-abiding." This is the old, only slightly revised model of the African American "in his proper place," serving the needs of the larger society. In fact, James Henry Hammond's Mudsill Theory continued to operate according to plan into the first half of the twentieth century.

African Americans persevered, although inequality was abun-dantly present. By 1925 the Douglas School in Dardanelle was serv-ing grades one through eight and had one teacher and one teacher/principal, Ms. Ella Davis and Mr. D. W. Reddick, respectively. In contrast, the white Dardanelle Public Schools meanwhile were admin-istered by a superintendent while its elementary school, grades one through six, had four teachers and one principal; and the high school, grades seven through twelve, had five teachers and one principal. The African American students, however, were not offered any public schooling within the Dardanelle system beyond grade eight. It was said that the Dardanelle Colored School (the Douglas School) "maintained a high standard . . . and taught the things that will make better and more useful citizens of our colored people."[243] Within the segregated world of Jim Crow, African American education in Dardanelle did what it could, what it was allowed to do, and, therefore, it was riddled by woefully systemic inequality.

The Douglas School also operated the Opportunity School, a twice-weekly night school for adult African Americans. Principal Reddick was its teacher, and instructional materials were obtained through donations such as the one organized by the Methodist Church's Women's Missionary Society, which asked for "readers, spelling books, or arithmetic of the grades One to Eight."[244] The Opportunity School, first organized in 1924, was "well attended by colored men and women who were deprived of educational advantages in their youth." The *Dardanelle Post-Dispatch* noted that two of the Opportunity School's early successes involved teaching two African American women over the age of seventy to read and write.[245]

Churches continued to play a major role in the cultural lives of African Americans. Not only was church a place of racial refuge, but it also served as a safe link between the African American and white communities. This is obvious in a *Dardanelle Post-Dispatch* notice from 1925 "extending a cordial invitation" to the white community from the Jubilee Singers' presentation at the African Methodist Episcopal (AME) Church in Dardanelle. Even this notice, however, contained that exploitative innuendo attesting to racial subservice by ending with the phrase "and we beg your cooperation."[246] The need for African Americans to observe Jim Crowism while advancing themselves was also evidenced by the public thank-you issued by St. John's Baptist Church after raising $140 to help retire the church's debt:

> something happened that only tends to confirm the opinion that
> has long existed among the thinking negroes of Dardanelle, and
> that is that we are living among some of the best white people
> on earth. My! How liberally they donated! Their generous dona-
> tions are proof positive of the fact that we are living among white
> people who are ready at all times to help a negro or an organi-
> zation of negroes who prove first that they are striving to help
> themselves.[247]

St. John's Baptist Church continued and successfully completed its efforts to become debt free in December 1926, having raised $450. Its

pastor, Dr. T. S. Sandefur, exhibited leadership and great public relations expertise by tapping into a Jim Crow message of racial cooperation and African American clean living. His self-sufficiency message
from the pulpit was followed by a call for racial harmony. For example,
in 1928 he urged both African Americans and whites to stop complaining about "hard times and a lack of money and grow something to get
money with."[248] While praising the "amiable relations . . . between the
races" in Dardanelle, Dr. Sandefur noted that "good relations will continue if the leading elements on each side will continue an occasional
contact." Furthermore, he said he hoped the white people "know that
element of our people who are striving for right living, right thinking and right doing."[249] This was an approach, a message, that whites
could comfortably accept. Their ideal African American, the "good
Negro," knew his place in society, obeyed all laws, and worked for
the white man, as opposed to being idle, a criminal, or a drunkard.
One wonders to what extent Dr. Sandefur truly believed his message
or was it the only message he could articulate to illicit white support
while advancing his congregation's needs. The answer is unknown.
What is apparent, however, is that segregation and Jim Crowism were
accepted, accommodation was viewed as enlightened, and vocational
education for African Americans was judged proper. These forms of
racism were all part of the African American experience in Dardanelle
during the early twentieth century.

Nowhere is racist condescension more evident than in reading
obituaries for respected African Americans written by a white person.
For example, a forty-eight-year-old "respected colored citizen," Neal
Parker, was celebrated in death as "an ideal 'house-boy' having been
employed in that capacity for years."[250] Another example is the obituary for eighty-three-year-old "Uncle Dan" Perry described as "upright,
industrious, loyal and faithful" with scores of white friends. His death
"decreases to a small number the old-time antebellum negroes who live
in and around Dardanelle, and is a real loss to the community."[251] Mr.
Handy Woods, deceased sexton at Brearley Cemetery, was described
as an "industrious, law abiding, useful man."[252] There is no comparison, however, for revealing the depth of racism as was evidenced in the
death notice of "Aunt Mahala" Smith. Born into slavery in 1821, Mrs.
Smith moved her family in an ox cart to Dardanelle in the late 1860s.

She was celebrated for her "habit of that respectful demeanor and pol-
ished courtesy absorbed from her intimate if servile relations with the
cultured classes of the old-time South," while it was noted that "she
may not be entitled to any ornate eulogy for her sphere of labour in
this life was of the very humblest."[253] Here is an example of the white
person's articulation of the concept of the "good Negro" and, while
not intended at the time as anything less than a respectful appraisal
of an African American's life within the parameters of accepted racial
relations, it is in today's terms highly racist. Obituaries such as these
offer real insights into the texture of race relations during the early
twentieth century.

One additional *Dardanelle Post-Dispatch* writing, while not an
obituary, sheds additional light on this subject. Mr. Eli Perry and his
wife, P'lina, an elderly African American couple, went blackberry
picking one late afternoon with family members eight miles south of
Dardanelle in the Upper Bottoms. "Uncle Eli" became disoriented and
separated from "Aunt P'lina" and a search began, without success, as
evening turned to night. While lost in the woods, Mr. Perry found his
way to the home of an African American family who gave him shelter
and food and offered to return him to Dardanelle the next morning,
but Mr. Perry fearfully declined because he did not know the family.
Luckily the next day the search party found him tired but safe. While
seemingly a simple story with a happy conclusion, the tone of the newspaper report and its reference to the "good Negro," the "old-time negro,"
offers an opportunity to discern more about the white view of race.

> Dardanelle numbers among its residents some fine specimens
> of the old-time negro, those who were formerly slaves to lead-
> ing families and who remember and cherish the traditions of
> the anti-bellum South, and who are affectionately referred to
> as "uncle" and "aunt" alike by white and black. Such are "Uncle
> Eli" and "Aunt P'lina" Perry, an aged and respected negro couple
> who formerly belonged to the well known pioneer family of that
> name, and whose latest master was Capt. Jas. K. Perry, an ex-Con-
> federate soldier and prominent business man of Dardanelle who
> has been dead for many years.[254]

While obviously intending to offer a respectful and caring view, the
language and tone reveal a lack of racial enlightenment so common
and so representative of this period.

In a 1925 newspaper article, while complimentary of African Americans' demonstration of civic involvement, the undercurrent of Jim Crow racism still prevailed:

> The colored citizens of Dardanelle devoted Wednesday of last week to cleaning and beautifying their cemetery on the Nebo road. The colored folks of Dardanelle take a great pride, not only in their own institutions, but in all civic matters, and can always be depended upon to do their full part in all movements for local improvement.[255]

The limits of white racial enlightenment, or more directly stated the inherent racism of the 1920s, is illustrated by a highly successful black-face minstrel show produced by local Dardanelle performers for the benefit of the local baseball association and staged during a winter storm, which, regardless of the weather, generated $135 and was hailed as wonderfully entertaining.[256] A similar type of entertainment, "Dispelling of Big Jim," A Negro Farce That Never Grows Old was presented at New Neely in 1923 and received rave reviews including "three hours of pure laugh."[257] Racist humor was present in advertising as well as in popular entertainment forms. A full-page Christmas advertisement for Cotton Veazey Grocery Company of Dardanelle in 1922 included a "Sambo" remark presented in black dialect that had nothing to do with the rest of the ad's content and was simply included as humor.[258] A final example of limited racial enlightenment by whites is seen in a brief 1923 *Dardanelle Post-Dispatch* report on the advent of Ground Hog Day. The editor—in reference to the weather—wrote: "it's raining 'pitchforks and nigger babies' and the water laden skies are banked miles high with clouds."[259] Obviously, in 1923 Dardanelle, the limits of white racial enlightenment were quite low.

Several conclusions regarding race during the 1920s can be reached. First, segregation in almost all cases ruled, institutionally, physically, and psychologically, for both African Americans and whites. Second, the concept and practice of accommodation also ruled, especially regarding educational and employment opportunities, which, of course, resulted not only in pervasive economic inequality, but inequality in most phases of human activity and opportunity. Third, racial violence occurred frequently in varying degrees and was primarily used as a means to bolster white supremacy. Fourth, there was little, if any, public sentiment exhibited to alter the status quo of racism in all of its variations.

## Women

While there is no evidence of any public outcry or efforts opposing women's suffrage in Dardanelle—perhaps based on the contributions to civic life and town improvement by the various local women's organizations—securing women's voting rights did not mean that complete gender equality existed. The degree to which highly stratified gender roles and old gender traditions continued to be the status quo is obvious in the local newspaper's editorial entitled "Flappers." The writer creates a story line in which several unescorted young women accept an invitation to join a group of young men. Although the young women are sexually assaulted, the writer defends the young men and casts blame on the women.

> [W]hat were the boys to expect of girls who would accept their escort and treats? No more blame should attach to these boys than would attach to your boy and mine under similar circumstance. Any boys and girls who are given freedom of the streets and the public halls can find themselves in similar circumstances and the mothers and fathers are to blame. Human nature is the same here as elsewhere, and when girls are allowed to accept the attention of hot blooded young men without the proper conventions, shame and disgrace are apt to result.[260]

As America was lunging toward modernity, moral values and gender beliefs were slowly changing, but uniform change was not occurring. The more restricted, highly prescribed female gender roles of premodernity would remain the norm in many minds well into the twentieth century. This sort of cultural morality would be preached in churches, underscored by public schools, expected by most parents, and became entrenched in many communities, especially in the rural South. Dardanelle was no exception, and a double standard for gender behaviors and expectations would remain "premodern" until the late 1960s.

This double standard was visible from 1920 through 1929 even as transitions were underway. In addition to women's normal household/family duties, the organized women's club activities of the past two decades continued, and new women's groups—such as Home Extension Clubs and Farmers' Wives Clubs—were organized. Women became more politically active, both as elected officeholders and as members of juries. While some women embraced these changes, others rejected them and remained highly traditional.

For some, the rejection of the new woman, as idealized by the Flapper, was all but automatic. According to this view, young women who once had been the pinnacle example of conservatism in dress, activities, and speech were now

> parading up and down the thoroughfares and giving exhibitions of their nudeness . . . it is about time to park our cars of progress and take stock . . . if we can adjust where we are headed . . . the moral status of our mothers . . . is a barometer of public sentiment . . . and whether they be loose or stable it's up to the dear women. . . . No man . . . can look on the nakedness of woman and have chaste, refined thoughts. . . . Kindle in him the fires of animal passion, and he is not very far removed from the jungle.[261]

For individuals having this view, the traditional women's clubs and church organizations were the ideal forum for female activism. They desired to "turn back the clock" to an earlier, more traditional concept of gender as the paramount means to save the family, community, and society from the dangers of modernity.

The efforts of the United Daughters of the Confederacy and the Ladies Cemetery Association continued and were lauded. During 1928 a new and fairly traditional women's organization, the Civic Club, was formed to engage in clean-up and beautification efforts in Dardanelle. The Civic Club planted shrubbery and flowers on the new courthouse lawn, the school campus, and vacant town lots while it urged property owners to maintain their yards and plant pink crepe myrtles as Dardanelle's town shrub. By July 1928, the Civic Club had sixty-eight members and within several months twenty-eight more women had joined.[262] These women tenaciously attacked Dardanelle's weeds, wandering chickens, and wayward lawns as rightful targets of opportunity. They skillfully employed the aid of local businessmen, as well as male-dominated civic organizations and companies, for financial donations and the use of equipment, materials, and workers and were highly successful in improving the general appearance of the town.[263] Several years prior to the Civic Club's formation, a *Dardanelle Post-Dispatch* editorial had equated a dirty town with the moral, mental, and material decay of its people: "It is the duty of all men and women to make their homes and their home town just as clean and attractive and beautiful as possible."[264] The members of the Civic Club concurred as they prioritized their efforts and provided the leadership that vastly improved the appearance of Dardanelle and perhaps instilled a greater sense of community pride and cohesiveness. Their improvement and beautification effort was "a man-size job yet the women are shouldering the burden."[265] The Civic Club's agenda was still within the traditional sphere of women's activities, but the scope of their efforts, zeal, and great success represented a more assertive approach by women.

While the women of Dardanelle were pursuing civic improvement via club work, the Dardanelle women who resided for part of each year on Mount Nebo were achieving their goals through the acquisition of political power. In 1924, the eight elected positions, which comprised the entirety of Mount Nebo's municipal government, were won by women with each winning their position by unanimous vote, all fourteen of them.[266] Certainly the only totally female municipal leadership team in Arkansas, it was believed to be the only one in the United States at that time.[267] The new mayor, Mrs. Jessie McCray, despite a deficit of funds, immediately set to work planning for road improvements, mosquito prevention, and repairs/improvements of public facilities. In order to remedy the deficit while also improving the quality of life for Nebo's residents and guests, municipal officers ambitiously arranged for a series of entertainment activities and parties.[268] After all, Mount Nebo was primarily a resort community and having fun was extremely important. A Sunday school was organized; telephone lines were reestablished from the base of the mountain to its summit; and municipal officers hosted benefit breakfasts and coffees, midweek dances for young residents, and weekly community singings at Sunset Point and organized bridge parties and other popular card games in the screened-in Tee-Pee Pavilion on Sunrise Point and Saturday night dances featuring Little Rock jazz bands.[269] Mount

Nebo was hopping! The "Ladies Government," as some called it, netted $336.62 in five months from these events and several improvements were undertaken and paid for: the purchase of a piano and its transportation up the mountain ($37.00), repairs to the pavilion ($29.75), benches placed at Sunset Point ($5.00), clearing underbrush ($25.00), payment to musical performers ($79.00), and various materials for public facilities ($3.50). By the end of the 1924 season, Mount Nebo's municipal government had a surplus of $45.45. Then in an effort to avoid thefts and vandalism to properties closed during the winter months, a $2.50 watchman's fee was assessed on all residents, and if not paid, a sign reading "Not Protected" would be placed on that property. A night watchman was then employed for the period from October through mid-June (the off-season on the mountain) to protect the area's property.[270]

The interests of the property owners on Mount Nebo had been advanced by an energetic group of female elected officials who demonstrated their ability to harness their skills and talents as hostesses in order to organize successful money-raising ventures, perform sound physical improvements and additions to the mountain's assets, and develop Mount Nebo's standing as a summer resort. By 1928 a new store had been established on the mountain, Cornwell Brothers, which replaced the previous retail concern, Croom & McCray, and a post office opened during the summer resort season. The nondenominational Sunday school continued to operate and was well attended.[271] Thus on Mount Nebo in the 1920s, a group of Dardanelle women demonstrated their political skills as municipal leaders.

Transition was also seen among some rural women as they began to organize themselves during the 1920s in order to sell their home-produced goods. The Farmers' Wives Club was formed in the Bottoms in 1924, with the first of its Dardanelle food fairs held on September 27, 1924, offering "poultry, butter, eggs, pickles, preserves, fruits, vegetables, prepared dishes, cakes and pies."[272] Farmers' wives used the approach of the farmer's market, so common today, to emphasize how the woman in town could purchase something fresh and good for Sunday dinner. Rural women were utilizing their normal skills set to make this retailing venture a success. Certainly the members of the Farmers' Wives Club wanted to sell their goods and make

money, but this association and its success, as well as the members'
association with one another, offered something more than money:
a greater sense of self. As Lu Ann Jones argues in *Mama Learned Us
to Work*, rural women's productive efforts during the 1920s and 1930s
such as those of the Farmers' Wives Club gave their families some
margin of economic safety and afforded the rural women some degree
of independence, while also allowing them to function as agents of
economic and cultural change.

## Leisure Time

During the 1920s, entertainment for rural residents centered around
the church and the rural schools. Activities such as singings and children's plays were usually informal and inclusive, involving most of
the community. Segregation reigned, so usually white entertainments
were for whites only with the same segregationist rules for African
Americans. Schools also served as community meeting places, as seen
in Riverside in which the school hosted the Literary Society meetings
on Friday nights, a singing on Saturday nights, and Sunday school on
Sunday mornings.[273] Community singings served to improve most
people's disposition: "the Singing Convention here Sunday, April 18th
was well attended. Several singing classes were present and we fully
believe most everyone went away feeling better after hearing the
beautiful songs which were sunny."[274] Other occasional entertainment forms in the Bottoms included quiltings for the married ladies of
Centerville and Fields Chapel, Easter egg hunts, pie suppers as school
fund-raisers, and simply visiting neighbors and entertaining house
guests.[275] Typically, life for most Bottoms' residents was demanding,
allowing little time, energy, or money for entertainment other than
school or church-related events. Thus, a typical note regarding entertainment would read: "cotton chopping was the order of the day for
most everybody and several people attended the baptizing at Fields
Chapel Sunday afternoon."[276]

Of course, one's economic status played an enormous role in the
frequency and method of one's leisure-time pleasures. Since most of
the big landowners in the Bottoms resided in Dardanelle, they were a
part of the town's social events. However, one Carden Bottom land-

owner, G. L. Potts, lived in the Carden Bottom hamlet of Lakeview. Mr. Potts and his wife, Orra, certainly hosted some of the Bottoms most elaborate social functions. The son of the founder of Pottsville (Pope County) across the Arkansas River from Carden Bottom, G. L. Potts was a respected Bottoms landowner, farmer, and merchant. Mrs. Orra Potts was celebrated in the Lower Bottoms for opening her fine two-story home to area families for holiday parties, especially Christmas parties in which everyone in the Lower Bottoms was welcomed. Each year a few days prior to Christmas, Mr. Potts would visit his wholesale grocer in Little Rock and return with large quantities of fresh fruit and candies, which he distributed to the children who attended the annual children's Christmas party at the Potts's home. Children were encouraged to retrieve several treats from the hanging "banana tree" (a large banana stalk containing several hundred pieces of fresh fruit).[277] Most children in the Lower Bottoms rarely had fresh fruit, certainly not something as exotic as a banana. The Potts's annual Christmas party also included Mrs. Potts, a good pianist, playing the piano and leading the children in Christmas carols as well as providing Christmas cookies and punch for all, and candies to be taken home. For the poor children of sharecroppers and tenant farmers, the Potts's Christmas party was truly ecstasy, a rapturous delight completely beyond their daily lives.

The Potts also hosted lovely family functions over the Christmas and New Year's holidays. A niece, Mary Potts Hall, remembered the beautiful white linen tablecloths, the fine china and crystal, and the sumptuous food that her aunt Orra and uncle Larry always presented to the family, as well as listening to Mrs. Potts at her piano and the wonderful joy of family singings.[278]

In September 1929 Mr. and Mrs. Potts hosted an unusual two-day excursion for forty-five adults and older children to Diamond Cave in Newton County. The trip included a visit through the cave, a long hike into the Ozark countryside, and a dance at a nearby motel. The Pottses provided for the transportation, the camp-out dinner, breakfast and lunch, and all other expenses.[279] This was probably the closest experience of leisure, unscripted fun, and gracious companionship those participating Bottoms residents ever knew.

The Pottses had lost two infant daughters to disease, both dying prior to their first birthdays: Dorothy in 1907 and Grace in

1917. Thus, having no children of their own, they poured out their parental grace to their extended family members and to their fellow Bottoms residents. Later in life, Mrs. Potts was highly involved in the Home Demonstration Club of Lakeview working with other women in the Lower Bottoms to improve their nutrition, the general state of their homes, their lives, and the lives of their families. While not the only glimmer of entertainment in the Bottoms, Mr. and Mrs. G. L. Potts probably were the brightest. As a resident of Cotton Town wrote in early 1922 "this place is dull once more with the exception of church."[280] Indeed, the lives of most rural residents, especially following the economic recession beginning in 1920, were plain and dull and frequently without any bright hope for improvement. A Centerville resident wrote: "a Sabbath-like stillness prevailed in our town on July 4th.... It was the first Fourth that the writer felt like a hermit."[281] During the 1920s the people of the Bottoms, while so in need of something to celebrate, generally found instead the emptiness of quiet and struggle.

During the 1920s a popular form of entertainment in Dardanelle was baseball, which the town promoted with a new ball field featuring fan amenities and continual news coverage. The town's baseball team enjoyed good attendance at its games, and several local players advanced into the college and professional ranks. The game's popularity as a community activity was important throughout Arkansas during the 1920s, as it was also promoted during this decade as America's sport, which somehow intertwined baseball with the rabid "100 percent American" patriotism of the post–World War I period.[282] Country towns and hamlets also developed their own teams and engaged in robust competition with the teams of other small rural hamlets, but these teams generally lacked a dedicated field, fan amenities, and the more developed application of the game that Dardanelle possessed. The rural teams, however, did not lack talent, fan enthusiasm, or a love for the game.

Baseball had long been played and enjoyed in Dardanelle, but by 1921 people were demanding a ball park be built and a local team created.[283] The city council leased one block of property for $75 annually, and within minutes of this action donations poured in and the work to convert the empty block into a field was undertaken.[284] Within one month, Dardanelle had joined with Russellville, Clarksville, Atkins,

Morrilton, and Conway to form the new Western Arkansas League. The by-laws specified that every team player had to reside in the team's county, no salaried players could play, and the schedule would begin in June and include a total of twenty-four games, two a week with one home and one away game weekly. Admission to the games was set at 25 cents for children and 35 cents for adults.[285] Baseball fever enveloped Dardanelle. In August 1921 a rules infraction (playing a person from Logan County) forced Dardanelle to forfeit seven wins and their second-place standing, with the *Dardanelle Post-Dispatch* noting that "gloom over spread Dardanelle Wednesday morning when the tragedy was made known."[286] The sports rollercoaster ride had become a part of the fabric of Dardanelle life. In 1924 Dardanelle beat Russellville by one run in the bottom of the ninth inning, and secured the first game in the five-game "League World Series." The largest crowd ever recorded at any Western Arkansas League game watched and cheered throughout "the greatest ball game ever played in Yell County."[287]

Some citizens, while they believed in the value of the team and its entertainment during the "dullest part of the year," expressed concerns over the approximately $6,000 a year the town was spending to maintain the field and its amenities.[288] Baseball had become an obsession for many residents, such as May Boyce (Mrs. Jack Boyce), who exhibited an almost religious devotion to listening to the radio broadcasts of the games of her favorite team, the St. Louis Cardinals. Baseball, an inexpensive and wholesome American form of entertainment available both locally and via the radio, was something everyone could understand and perhaps in the 1920s really needed as a diversion from so much bad news. Baseball became the elixir for all of life's problems, or so it seemed for many in Dardanelle. In 1926 two Dardanelle youth, Carey Selph and Walter Jacoway, were signed by the St. Louis Cardinals.[289] The 1928 University of Arkansas's fifteen-man baseball team included three Dardanelle boys, Gilroy and Gilbert Cornwell (twins) and J. P. Baker, all infielders.[290] Another Dardanelle boy, Richard Keilch (the son of Captain Keilch of the Pontoon Bridge) spent several decades employed as a scout for the Chicago White Sox. Such successes only intensified Dardanelle's baseball fever.

By 1927 baseball had developed such a devoted fan base that a proposed bill in the Arkansas General Assembly called for Sunday afternoon and evening games in counties having a population of more than 75,000. This meant that Dardanelle citizens could drive to larger towns to take in a Sunday game on the Sabbath. This also meant trouble. Four local churches (the Christian, Methodist, Baptist, and Presbyterian) drafted a joint resolution condemning Sunday baseball as an affront to the celebration of the Sabbath.[291] Sports might be fun for the players and fans, but tradition holds that one cannot have modernity trampling on the sanctity of the Sabbath. In the end, both baseball and the Sabbath managed to continue.

Other popular forms of entertainment were also available. In 1925 plans for a new movie house, the New Theatre, to replace the Electric Theatre were announced. The New Theatre was built, featuring modern amenities and technology, and having a 500-seat capacity on the main floor and a 150-seat capacity in the balcony or "colored section."[292] Just three years later, the number of moviegoers had out distanced the theater's seating capacity and an expansion was undertaken. The new expanded structure was opened on October 15, 1928, with a renovation price tag of $20,000.[293] In July 1929 the New Theatre installed $7,000 worth of equipment to show "talking pictures" and proudly announced that the facility would compare well with any theater in Little Rock, Memphis, or St. Louis.[294] On the night of July 25, 1929, patrons from throughout Yell County as well as those from Russellville, Clarksville, Morrilton, and Atkins attended the screening of the first "talkie" in the area, a seldom-heard-from-again feature entitled *Twin Beds*, a comedy starring Jack Mulhall and Patsy Ruth Miller.[295]

Another popular social group formed in the 1920s was the Dardanelle Gun Club, having an initial membership of twenty-eight. Well-healed gentlemen who could afford the time and weaponry to participate met weekly to hold shooting contests. The results were posted weekly in the local newspaper, usually getting a front-page placement.[296]

After World War I, the upper social class of Dardanelle did not entertain as lavishly as they had previously. It seems that modernity and the economy conspired to deflate the once-buoyant social calendar of the Dardanelle elites. The more traditional parties and teas continued, but in a more curtailed and less frequent manner. More novel approaches to elite social functions appeared—such as the 1923 outdoor picnic luncheon held on the banks of Stinnett Creek west of town—in which many of Dardanelle's most socially well-placed young ladies and gentlemen participated.[297] Occasional dances were held at Cunningham Hall, which allowed these young social elites to have a chaperoned evening event for their enjoyment.[298]

Adult ladies of the upper class began to have afternoon bridge parties and form bridge clubs replete, of course, with refreshments and homes beautifully decorated for their guests.[299] There was also an occasional example of a more elaborate social function once so frequent during earlier years, such as the "silver tea" held in 1926 to benefit the Methodist Church. Held in the handsome new bungalow home of Mr. and Mrs. Jack Duff, the event was reminiscent of the glamour imparted by the over-the-top social events of pre-1920, although definitely a downsized version of that eloquence. The home was decorated with fresh flowers, ferns, and foliage as guests were graciously ushered from room to room. Formal tea was served in the dining room, and the program presented in the parlor included numerous musical offerings.[300] This was traditional entertaining: formal, elegantly managed, and gracious, and during the 1920s and ensuing decades becoming increasingly scarce.

It seems that the elites in Dardanelle had not forgotten how to host lovely functions, but they did not do so very often during the 1920s. Perhaps the poor economy had something to do with the lack of truly beautiful social functions or perhaps the fact that a new generation had come of age and either were not as socially adept as their mothers or simply chose not to entertain or to do so differently. For whatever the reason, the post–World War I world was certainly a step down socially from that of the prewar period.

Another sign of this change in social norms was a new young men's organization, the Boathouse Club, organized in late 1921 in Dardanelle with thirty-two "of the best young men of the city" as members and whose purpose was to help develop its members "spiritual, physical and mental lives."[301] It appears that the organization's model was somewhere between the life of Theodore Roosevelt and Robert E. Lee in that it was attempting to capture the sanguine, the masculine, and the eloquence of a time gone by as if its members realized the modern world was present but they were not quite yet ready to fully join it. The Boathouse Club existed for approximately two years and then disbanded. Obviously, it was very difficult to straddle the line between the traditional and the modern.

If the young gentlemen of Dardanelle were attempting to create a comfortable social niche for themselves during the 1920s, so also were their counterparts. Young women formed the Dardanelle Aesthesian Club, sometimes called the Culture Club, which usually met monthly at a member's home. The program generally contained musical presentations, recitations, and discussions of selected study subjects. This effort was not the full-throated social or cultural gathering of Dardanelle's socially elite women of previous decades. Instead, the Aesthesian Club was more of a study club with an entertainment element included. For instance, their chosen areas of review for 1923 included southern authors, famous American composers, and child care.[302]

Transition and change were the norms during the 1920s as Dardanelle had its connection to the Lost Generation (i.e., people who came of age during World War I). The changes in types of entertainment, their frequency, and their purposes attest to these transitions. Distinct differences according to class, gender, and race are also clearly seen when examining entertainment modes from 1920 through 1929.

## Education

Change and hard times were regular parts of the educational scene. During the 1920s, financial shortfalls again threatened to close the Dardanelle schools and donated funds again forestalled the crisis twice between 1921 and 1923.[303] Finally, a way to overcome school financial woes was found when on May 21, 1927, voters in Dardanelle approved 18 mills in additional taxes (the new maximum allowed by law) with only six votes opposing this millage hike.[304] The approval of the new funds stabilized the school district's finances for the immediate future. In 1928 Dardanelle High School graduated twenty-three students, and the 1928–1929 term began with twelve teachers employed in the white schools (elementary and high school) and two in the Douglas School. In August 1929 it was announced that the Dardanelle School District had earned a Class A status from the state, meaning that all of the district's teachers had four years of college training. Still carrying a now-manageable debt, the district's $20,000 annual budget, excellent facilities, and well-trained staff meant the Dardanelle schools were the best in Yell County.[305] In the Dardanelle Bottoms, rural elementary schools dotted the countryside every few miles with most having one teacher and enjoying great community support as local citizens built the buildings, raised funds for furnishing the school, hired a teacher, and managed the operation year round. The rural schools were imbued by their patrons and communities with their values of self-sufficiency, self-improvement via hard work, and the dignity and pride that quietly comes from a great thing being realized. In many ways, during the early twentieth century the rural schools signified the strongest and best traits of rural life. A rural school was the anchor for its community, a material actualization of its heart and soul. Furthermore, the school was the rural community's badge of honor, and it afforded rural children an opportunity to learn and improve their lives.

This is evident in the New Neely School, which opened its 1922–1923 term in November with 59 students and two teachers and was proud to be "one of the best equipped rural schools in the county."[306] It suffered, however, from a huge fluctuation in enrollment and teachers, a recurring rural school dilemma: children went to school only when they were not needed for farmwork. By mid-November the enrollment had dropped to 47; by late November it had jumped to 117 and a new teacher was hired; by December the number further increased to 124; by January it was 146; and by March enrollment reached 158.[307] These dramatic fluctuations caused many problems and were simply a staple fact of school life in rural areas. The New Neely residents earnestly did all within their power, however, to provide a good school for their children even if they could not attend every day. For example, a 1922 Christmas pie supper raised $93.00 from which $45 was spent on digging a new well on the school yard, two basketballs, parts for a sanitary drinking fountain, an unabridged dictionary, and resurfacing blackboards in one classroom, with the remaining $13 being donated to the school expense fund. Patrons formed a sort of public relations cluster that produced biweekly Friday afternoon school programs, spearheaded money-raising efforts, developed improvement agendas, and invited guests to come and see the school.[308]

These rural schools probably did not offer as good an educational product as did the Dardanelle School District, given the course offerings, attendance rates, and enrollment fluctuations. Furthermore, rural schools were only grades one through six or eight, as compared to grades one through twelve in the Dardanelle School District. Added to these factors would be the crucial issues of Dardanelle's better-qualified teachers and greater resources. However, it is difficult to measure the true value that these rural schools provided, which included accessibility to education, understanding teachers, and the support of their communities. These small rural schools were the centers of their communities, and for many students these schools provided either the foundation for future schooling or the total of their formal education. While one might reasonably question their level of academic rigor, one must conclude that the rural schools were of critical importance.

The most thoughtful critics of rural schools advocated consolidation in order to grant rural children the same advantages as their town counterparts, along with generally improved instruction, curriculum, and facilities. Consolidation advocates emphasized monetary savings for the state as concerned landowners worried about possible increases in their property taxes. Even today, consolidation remains a hot-button issue. In Carden Bottom consolidation held a special meaning, as the area included four local elementary schools: Wasp Nest, Stubbs, Lakeview, and New Hall. On November 11, 1929, Carden Bottom Consolidated High School dedicated its new high school building, which allowed elementary-age children to attend their own centrally located secondary school once they reached the seventh grade. In other words, the new school allowed children from Carden Bottom a high school education in the Bottoms. Dedication of the new high school building was a huge celebration, with eight hundred enthusiastic Carden Bottom patrons and residents and guests from Dardanelle attending a parade, a home-cooked free meal served to all, and numerous speeches.[309]

During the 1920s, Carden Bottom High School had a general student population of approximately three hundred, making it the largest high school in Yell County.[310] The high school operated as School District No. 67 until 1958, when it began consolidation with Dardanelle, School District No. 15.

During the first few decades of the twentieth century, area students pursued higher educational opportunities at several state colleges, including the University of Arkansas, Ouachita Baptist, Hendrix, Galloway, and the Fourth District Agricultural School (later known as Arkansas Polytechnic College and then Arkansas Tech University).[311] Some of these students were the beneficiaries of the power of Yell County judges to make seventeen appointments annually (eighteen after 1918) of county students to the University of Arkansas, free of the $10 annual tuition fee. The *Dardanelle Post-Dispatch* reported that thirty-three Dardanelle residents were attending colleges or universities in September 1928, including numerous state and several out-of-state institutions, some public and some private.[312] Most of these university students were the sons or daughters of Dardanelle's white upper class: landowners, businessmen, and professionals. Women of this class generally studied in the humanities fields or home economics, and rarely ventured into business or professional fields, other than education, which was not highly respected as a profession at this time.

Working-class students, from Dardanelle and the Bottoms, generally completed high school or perhaps ended their schooling at the completion of the eighth grade. The children of farm laborers, sharecroppers, and the poorest of the tenant farmers—simply because they had to work the fields in order to help the family survive—frequently received only the most sporadic education, especially if African American. Thus, who one was generally determined the amount and type of education one could access. In 1921, of the then forty-eight states, Arkansas ranked first in strawberry production, fourth in lumber/timber production, fifth in cotton production, twentieth in apple production, and forty-sixth in educational attainment.[313]

## Conclusion

In all of the above-mentioned ways, the period from 1920 through 1929 posed an adjustment, a period of transition characterized by hard times for Dardanelle and the Bottoms. The pre–World War I world, while still present in some forms, was beginning to fade away. While this past offered little stability and the future was yet unmarked, the social and economic landscape of 1920 through 1929 lacked definition and offered little certainty. Therefore, for many the only sure path forward was a reactionary reliance on the landmarks of traditional conservative religion, politics, race, and gender relationships. As the older generation died or moved away, a new generation of leaders struggled with economic challenges as they attempted to maintain the town/country relationship. The dominance of the social elites was lessened as the new economic realities gradually increased a social class leveling, and thus class stratification, while still present, became slightly more muted.

The decade of the 1920s and its difficulties only strengthened individuals' reliance on Jim Crowism and racial oppression and, thus, outbursts of race hatred became more pronounced and visible. The reemergent Ku Klux Klan was strong in Dardanelle and the Bottoms, and night riding and other forms of violence and intimidation were evidenced as most people feared what racial equality, if ever realized, might mean. African Americans carefully walked the color line, offering deference to racial traditions while striving within their churches and schools for enhanced opportunities. During this period, Dardanelle women entertained less and participated more in community improvement efforts. Organized, vocal, and highly efficient, "the ladies" maintained their traditional standards of feminism while pushing forward community betterment. Women in the Bottoms continued to play their traditional roles as wives, mothers, and homemakers. At the same time, however, they organized Sunday schools, singing conventions, and community fund-raisers, and actively engaged in economic pursuits to uplift themselves and their families through direct economic actions and improved educational opportunities. Even as these subtle, gradual changes occurred, the presence of poverty, deprivation, disease, and near starvation in some cases created the gloom of despondency and a begrudging acceptance of fate among many rural residents. Great economic hardships were endured primarily by the poorest farmers (sharecroppers, day laborers, and tenants), both white and African American.

World War I caused farmers in the Bottoms to have a brief period of prosperity followed by the collapse of the cotton market by mid-1920. In August 1919 the New Orleans price per pound of cotton was 38.2 cents; by August 1920 it had declined to 16.5 cents and although the price fluctuated upward during the 1920s, by August 1929 cotton had fallen again to 16.2 cents per pound.[314] During the 1920s declining prices, shrinking markets, the production of the new synthetic fiber rayon, and changing tastes and fashion styles all combined to sternly challenge many farmers. Some were financially destroyed, and conversely Dardanelle businesses felt the financial pain as well.

By 1929 the New South approach with its emphasis on the creation of a more balanced, diversified economy, containing both agriculture and expanded manufacturing, had basically failed in Arkansas. According to Carl H. Moneyhon, "between 1919 and 1921 the state lost nearly 60 percent of its manufacturing companies in almost every area of industrial effort. This cost some 16,000 jobs, nearly one-third of all manufacturing employment."[315] Agriculture faced formidable problems as new world market demands altered demand for Arkansas crops. Prices tumbled, farm mortgages increased to nearly 38 percent of all holdings by late 1929, and many farmers went bankrupt while tenancy increased statewide from "51 percent in 1920 to 63 percent by 1930."[316] Food processors, a significant component of Arkansas's "New South" manufacturing, suffered as farmers suffered. Even as manufacturing rebounded during the late 1920s, it was not enough to save Arkansas from a severely marred economy.[317] The transition embodied in the New South approach resulted in a fundamental shift away from small farms relying on subsistence agriculture and minor cash crops supported by towns that furnished trade and marketing opportunities for these farmers. In the short term, this transition brought poverty to farmers, stymied the growth of supporting towns and their businesses, and resulted invariably in far-reaching social changes that would not fully materialize until the late 1940s but whose impetus was established during the tumultuous 1920s. Dardanelle and the Bottoms experienced these transitions as well.

Local efforts to introduce the New South approach in order to alter traditional agriculture included the establishment of a steam cotton compress in September 1923, the replacement of old gins with more efficient modern ones, improved roads and streets for more efficient travel and growth, new municipal franchises (water and electric) for better service, fruit and vegetable crops and dairy products for regional markets, a new toll-free steel bridge for expanded trade, and the acquisition of local banks by better managed and more profitable banks.[318] Dardanelle, however, did not attract any lasting manufacturing concerns. As a 1929 editorial in the *Dardanelle Post-Dispatch* noted, "what our town needs is a few new factories employing skilled labor and having large payrolls."[319] The pull of the traditional cotton culture was too great for Dardanelle and the Bottoms to escape its power, and, thus, the New South approach failed.

Throughout the 1920s, small farmers in the Bottoms fell into tenancy, farm bankrupt notices became common newspaper items, and merchants experienced low levels of activity. A retail outlook report in the *Dardanelle Post-Dispatch* noted that farmers "suddenly stopped buying anything except those articles which represented absolute necessities." Merchants stated, however, that "the farming class, which is the one that all of us must depend upon for prosperity . . . can recover more quickly from a bad economic condition than any other class."[320] This wishful, erroneous belief was held by most Dardanelle businessmen throughout the 1920s as they offered sale promotions and credit to entice the farmer to buy, an approach that was only marginally successful. "Merchants generally appreciate the fact that trade is slow because of the depressed conditions incident to the low prices farmers are receiving for their products, and for this reason they are putting on special sales and reducing the prices of their goods to a level that puts merchandise on a basis with ten and twelve cent cotton."[321] Many continued to believe that cooperation between Dardanelle and the Bottoms would solve the problems: "the significant fact is that the business interests of Dardanelle are working in harmonious accord for the development and upbuilding of the city and country and are ready and anxious to extend the hand of friendship and co-operation to every deserving enterprise."[322] The concept of reciprocity upon which the wealth of Dardanelle had been created based on the agricultural production of the Bottoms could not alleviate the source of economic upheaval. Many farmers were broke, and soon most farmers would be broke. The limits of reciprocity were about to be reached.

As the wheels of the traditional Dardanelle/Bottoms relationship were wobbling, children's letters to Santa Claus were printed in the local newspaper. A typical letter from a five-year-old girl read: "I want you to bring me a big doll and some oranges, apples, candy, peanuts, popcorn and all kinds of nuts."[323] Generally the children of the poorest tenant farmers, sharecroppers, and laborers did not write these newspaper-published letters to Santa (most of these people could not read or write and could not afford a subscription to the newspaper). Thus, these requests were written by the more nearly "middle class" farm children who, without exception, requested perishable fruit and nuts or as many wrote, "something good to eat" for Christmas. Poverty and want could be found in Dardanelle among its poorer residents, but this suffering was more readily encountered and concentrated in the Bottoms, especially among the poorest of its residents and even in the slightly better off nearly "middle-class" farmers.

Hard times were the hallmark of the period from 1920 through 1929: a period of both hope and trouble, of muted triumph and massive devastation, and of change and adjustment. In Dardanelle the steam cotton compress opened in 1923, as did the chicken hatchery in 1928; however, cotton prices collapsed in mid-1920 and the flood of 1927 caused major damage. Befitting such a hard and uncertain time, on June 1, 1926, Dardanelle buried Susan A. Kimber Dodd (Mrs. David Washington Dodd) at Brearley Cemetery. Her nephew was the late David O. Dodd, the "boy martyr of the Confederacy." Another link to the past that most believed they understood was gone. An uncertain future approached as a familiar past faded. As the decade ended, hard times and high water had not destroyed Dardanelle and the Bottoms, but many difficult challenges remained unsolved and an even harsher future beckoned.

Pontoon Bridge, circa 1927, looking south toward Dardanelle. Foundation of the new "Free Bridge," which opened in 1929, is seen on the right. *Photo courtesy of the Forest History Society, Durham, NC. Photographer unknown.*

Span of the 1929 Free Bridge over the Arkansas River at Dardanelle being floated into place. Circa 1928. *Photo courtesy of the Forest History Society, Durham, NC. Photographer unknown.*

Span of the 1929 Free Bridge over the Arkansas River being set onto concrete foundation joints. Circa 1928. *Photo courtesy of the Forest History Society, Durham, NC. Photographer unknown.*

A group of Dardanelle Elementary School children and their teachers in front of an entrance to the Dardanelle school. Circa 1920s. *Photo courtesy of Joe Grimes, Dardanelle, AR. Photographer unknown.*

Corner of South Main (Market) and Front Streets in Dardanelle in 1909 looking south on South Main Street and west on Front Street. Notice the horse-drawn wagons, sidewalks, and dirt streets. *Library of Congress Photograph. Sherwood T. Grissom, photographer.*

View of Front Street in Dardanelle in 1909 looking east. Notice the Arkansas River on the left (north), unpaved streets, and electricity poles. *Library of Congress Photograph. Sherwood T. Grissom, photographer.*

Saturday visitors in Dardanelle circa 1940s at the corner of Front and Locust Streets. Arkansas River is seen in the background. *Photo courtesy of Joe Grimes, Dardanelle, AR. Photographer unknown.*

A Dardanelle Saturday Front Street scene circa 1940s. The building in the imme- diate background housed the Dardanelle Transfer and Storage offices of the D&R Railroad. *Photo courtesy of Joe Grimes, Dardanelle, AR. Photographer unknown.*

The entrance and marque of the Joy Theatre on Front Street in Dardanelle circa 1950s. The building adjacent to the theater as seen in the background here housed the offices of the *Dardanelle Post-Dispatch. Photo courtesy of Joe Grimes, Dardanelle, AR. Photographer unknown.*

Jack J. Boyce (1876–1954)—Prominent Dardanelle merchant and businessman circa late 1940s. *Photo courtesy of Lynne Gleason Murphy, Dardanelle, AR. Photographer unknown.*

The ferry on the Petit Jean River near Pontoon, Arkansas, operated in the late 1800s and was later replaced by the swinging bridge in the early twentieth century. Pictured here is Mr. Crain, owner/operator, and his family. Mr. Crain was the grandfather of Gordon and Jack Crain of Stubbs Town, Arkansas. *Photo courtesy of Joe Grimes, Dardanelle, AR. Photographer unknown.*

A group of farmers working as a hay crew in Carden Bottom in the early 1900s, a time when hay was gathered, loaded onto wagons, and taken to the baling location. *Photo courtesy of Joe Grimes, Dardanelle, AR. Photographer unknown.*

A class of Carden Bottom Elementary School children and their teacher taken outside the Carden Bottom school building circa 1930. *Photo courtesy of Joe Grimes, Dardanelle, AR. Photographer unknown.*

Carden Bottom homecoming court circa 1930. Picture shows Carden Bottom High School in the background as well as the homecoming float. *Photo courtesy of Joe Grimes, Dardanelle, AR. Photographer unknown.*

Carden Bottom homecoming queen Opal Moore (Alexander), the four home-coming maids, and their attendants are pictured at the entrance of Carden Bottom High School circa 1930. *Photo courtesy of Joe Grimes, Dardanelle, AR. Photographer unknown.*

The original Carden Bottom school pictured here circa 1937 was destroyed by a tornado in 1938, rebuilt on the same location, and reopened in 1939. *Photo courtesy of Joe Grimes, Dardanelle, AR. Photographer unknown.*

Three unidentified Carden Bottom residents circa 1930s. *Photo courtesy of Joe Grimes, Dardanelle, AR. Photographer unknown.*

Carden Bottom farmer Monroe Parker and his son, Sam, circa late 1930s. The photo was thought to be taken at a photo booth at the Yell County Fair in Danville, Arkansas. *Photo courtesy of Joe Grimes, Dardanelle, AR. Photographer unknown.*

Two Carden Bottom farmers, Tom McGowen (*left*) and Leonard McGowen (*right*), and their families dressed in their Sunday best. Circa 1930s. *Photo courtesy of Joe Grimes, Dardanelle, AR. Photographer unknown.*

Members of the Ard Home Demonstration Club circa late 1930s. Many residents of Ard (five miles south of Dardanelle on State Highway 7) regularly worked as cotton pickers in Carden Bottom. *Photo courtesy of Joe Grimes, Dardanelle, AR. Photographer unknown.*

Members of an unspecified New Deal project work crew in Carden Bottom circa mid-1930s. Front row beginning second from the left are Screw Ragsdale, Ode Underwood, Monroe Parker, and Leonard McGowen. Dogan Vaughn (*first from left, second row*) was the group's crew chief and farmed at Potts (generally known as Lakeview) in an area locals called "Nigger Ridge" in Carden Bottom. *Photo courtesy of Joe Grimes, Dardanelle, AR. Photographer unknown.*

A typical farming scene from the early 1940s on the McGowen's farm in Carden Bottom. *Photo courtesy of Joe Grimes, Dardanelle, AR. Photographer unknown.*

Sunday churchgoers at the Lakeview Assembly of God Church in Carden Bottom circa 1950s. Reverend Finley from Russellville, who frequently preached at this church, is pictured on the far right. *Photo courtesy of Joe Grimes, Dardanelle, AR. Photographer unknown.*

Following the Sunday service, the women of the Lakeview Assembly of God Church hosted a "dinner of the ground" potluck, which actually was staged here on a flatbed trailer. Circa 1950s. *Photo courtesy of Joe Grimes, Dardanelle, AR. Photographer unknown.*

Carden Bottom High School's last graduating class gathered here in the Carden Bottom High School gym before the 1957 commencement. Pictured from left to right are Jerry Ragsdale, Sue Brim, Jerry Wells, Dorothy Booth, Scotty Moore, Lauvone Robinson, and Ronald Gene "Mutt" Parker. *Photo courtesy of Joe Grimes, Dardanelle, AR. Photographer unknown.*

G. L. and Orra Potts's once beautifully appointed and maintained home in Lakeview (Carden Bottom) sits abandoned and dilapidated in March 2009. Once the site of the most lavish and gracious social gatherings in the Bottoms, the structure was bulldozed down and buried in July 2009. *Photo courtesy of Diane Gleason, Dardanelle, AR. Photographer Joe Murphy.*

Carden Bottom High School, the pride of Carden Bottom residents, now sits abandoned and overgrown. The vulture resting atop the nearby tree seems to be an omen of the building's inevitable, complete demise. March 2009.
*Photo courtesy of Diane Gleason, Dardanelle, AR. Photographer Joe Murphy.*

## CHAPTER 5

# Deprivation and Survival, 1930–1941

*We are all ruined for lack of rain.*

WASP NEST FARMER,
*1930*

*Going to school is the children's occupation; picking cotton is the adult's job.*

CARDEN BOTTOM FARMER,
*1930.*

*I don't mind the burglars breaking open our safe, but I hope they are discreet and will not tell anybody it is empty.*

OLA STORE OWNER,
*1935*

*The Japs have bombed Pearl Harbor. I'll never see my Ted again!*

RUTH SEXTON,
*Carden Bottom resident, December 7, 1941*

## Introduction

By 1929 Arkansas ranked forty-sixth out of the forty-eight states in per capita income and first in the nation in per capita indebtedness. The average day wage for a farm laborer in July 1929 was $1.65, which was approximately one-half of the average wage in nonsouthern states. Between 1930 and 1932, 35,000 industrial workers in Arkansas lost their jobs, amounting to approximately 12 percent of the industrial workforce. In total, approximately 38 percent of all the state's laborers were out of work. During the same period, Arkansas bank deposits declined by more than 45 percent and the state's overall income level declined by 25 percent. By 1932 private social agencies and most welfare bureaus had exhausted their relief funds.[1] In Arkansas—like in most states at the time—suffering existed on a grand scale.

## Weather and Economic Calamities

By late 1930, nearly one hundred Arkansas banks had closed. The economy was in shambles. Tenant farmers were working for 75 cents a day, and feeding their families with raccoons, opossums, and fish. When available, farmers would supplement their diets with winter-garden produce of greens, turnips, and onions.[2] In the summer of 1929, the price of cotton stood at 19 cents a pound, but by April 1932 it had plummeted to 6.1 cents a pound.[3] Three months later, the price of cotton was 5.1 cents a pound, the lowest price on record since 1897.[4] Nationally in 1928 cotton farmers had earned $1.5 billion, but in 1932 they only received $0.5 million. During the World War I years, the average national price of cotton was 35.2 cents a pound. The price see-sawed downward during the 1920s, and in June 1932 cotton prices averaged nationally 4.6 cents per pound.[5] Cotton's journey from the time of World War I to the early 1930s was a path to annihilation. Cotton was in crisis.

During the first three weeks of 1930, the temperature in Dardanelle dropped to minus 10°F on three separate occasions with the highest temperature reached during the period being only 26°F. As the snow fell and tons of three-inch-thick blocks of ice floated down the Arkansas River, business and farming activity in and around

Dardanelle came to a near halt, while religious leaders raised charity funds for the "suffering humanity."[6] By late summer, the weather continued to bring misery and hardship, as the rainfall ceased and soaring temperatures reached 110°F. By late August, Dardanelle and the Bottoms were experiencing severe drought conditions, and government officials were urging citizens to conserve their resources.[7]

As the Great Depression caused the loss of jobs and wages, forced home and farm foreclosures, closed banks, and destroyed savings, weather woes worsened the general level of misery and anxiety. A resident of Wasp Nest in the Lower Bottoms summed it up: "How is everybody taking the hot winds and sun now? It has almost burned us up!"[8] The local Red Cross chair, Dr. Charles W. Anderson, urged the townspeople to cease using coal and purchase wood from destitute farmers, thereby affording them some means of earning an income.[9] One-third of the United States was baking in the drought of 1930, exacerbated by less-than-average rainfall during the previous winter. In fact, records show that the rainfall total from December 1929 through August of 1930 was half the usual average rainfall. Kentucky blue grass turned white, rivers and creeks ran dry, crops burned up in the fields, livestock suffered and some died from heat and a lack of water, fruit hanging on the trees burned to a crisp, and the average daytime temperature from Arkansas northward ranged from 106°F to 108°F for weeks on end. The crops most affected included cotton, corn, fruit, and hay.[10]

In the Dardanelle Bottoms, approximately 75 percent of the cotton, corn, and hay crops were destroyed, and farm families were experiencing hunger.[11] Spring gardens dried up and, thus, no canning of fruits and vegetables occurred, a necessity for the farm family larder. By August 21, 1930, Dardanelle and the Bottoms had been rain free for eighty-three consecutive days and late summer/early fall gardens would be impossible unless it rained before mid-September.[12] Estimates are that some 20 percent of Yell County schoolchildren did not enroll in school due to a lack of funds to purchase clothing, much less schoolbooks.[13] By early September state officials were urging farmers to keep their milk cows if possible and try to sow some winter wheat or rye with seeds available from the Red Cross.[14]

By mid-September sufficient rain had fallen statewide to allow farmers to plant winter wheat, and the Red Cross donated $2,000 for seed and engaged in a countywide effort to raise funds for additional seed.[15] State agricultural officials were calling for the immediate planting of radishes, lettuce, spinach, and turnips in order to provide food for farm families.[16] At the same time, Arkansas governor Harvey Parnell and the chair of the Drought Relief Committee, Harvey Couch, each concluded that state food relief aid was not warranted since local charities provided the proper channel for such relief. Further adding to the distress, some plantation owners, especially in Arkansas's Delta, believed that providing food relief to African American sharecroppers and tenants farmers would "destroy the incentive of our negroes to work . . . and ruin our labor force."[17]

As early as July 1930, Senator Joe T. Robinson (D-Arkansas) had called for federal government assistance, and he was soon joined by Senator Thaddeus Caraway (D-Arkansas) and Representative Wright Patman (D-Texas) in a congressional proposal for $60 million in aid. In December, President Herbert Hoover urged that emphasis be placed on Red Cross charity efforts and, although the United States Senate approved the $60 million aid bill, the House sided with the president. The national chair of the American Red Cross, John Barton Payne, informed President Hoover in late December 1930 that he was certain private charity could manage the problem.[18] Fearing that charity in the form of food relief would "drain the strength and weaken the moral fiber," the Red Cross concentrated their focus on self-help efforts, such as pasture and garden seed disbursements to starving families. Turnips were a drought and depression era stopgap measure against starvation. Six decades later, Bill Garner, who was a child in Dardanelle during the Depression, remarked that every time he saw a turnip he immediately thought of the Depression and his family's struggle against hunger. He said he had not eaten a turnip since the 1930s and would never again eat another.[19] By the fall of 1930, the Red Cross had twenty-nine active local chapters in Arkansas directing local relief programs for the estimated 100,000 to 200,000 families in dire need of food.[20] Red Cross officials estimated that 250,000 Arkansans were in need of their assistance and that their $5 million budget was insufficient to manage this crisis.[21] The Red Cross, like all privately funded social service and religious organizations, was overwhelmed by the extent of size of this crisis and the number of people affected.

This inability of private groups to properly address the suffering of hundreds of thousands to millions of people nationwide evidenced the immense scope of the Great Depression.

Following the national reports of the January 3, 1931, "Food Riots" in England, Arkansas, Senators Robinson and Caraway managed to get a $15 million food-loan relief bill through the United States Congress, and—after considerable difficulty—President Hoover signed a version of the bill on February 14.[22] Through its local chapters, the Arkansas Red Cross began food programs that continued providing food to 35 percent of all Arkansans until April. This aid, which represented a $2.00-a-week food allowance per family, primarily consisted of lard, flour, pinto beans, and potatoes and required the recipient to work two days a week as directed by the local Red Cross chapter.[23] Absent from these rations were meat, milk, fruit, and sugar.[24] Many rural families were depending on squirrel and rabbit meat, as well as an occasional stolen chicken or hog to stay alive. From January to April 1931, the Red Cross gave 460,240 families clothes and food, and $3 million was expended.[25] Even with this food assistance—meager and not terribly high in nutritional value—outbreaks of pellagra (caused by a niacin deficiency) occurred from late 1930 into 1931, especially among the poorest rural residents.[26] At the same time, reports of typhoid fever were noted. While not directly related to diet, these reports were indicative of the deteriorating general health condition, especially among Arkansas's poorest citizens.

By February 1931, Arkansas livestock were dying, hunger was widespread, and the Red Cross was running dangerously short of funds. These realities, among others, permanently shattered President Hoover's reputation as a great humanitarian.[27] Under the Franklin D. Roosevelt administration, food relief was handled differently. Beginning in 1933, thousands of Arkansas families started to receive monthly food support in the form of commodities, school lunches, or food stamps.[28]

The drought of 1930–1931 entered the record books at that time as the most severe in Arkansas history, but recurring dry weather continued periodically in the 1930s creating ongoing drought concerns.[29] While twenty-three states located in the Mississippi River Valley, the Ohio River Valley, and the mid-Atlantic region were affected by the drought of 1930–1931, the most severe conditions were in the southern states, and Arkansas experienced drought conditions 16 percent worse than did other southern states.[30] The period of 1930–1931 continues to be deemed Arkansas's worst drought of the twentieth century.[31] It reduced farm income statewide by 62 percent, causing numerous overextended and cash-poor local banks to fail, thus leading to a credit deficit in numerous small towns and rural areas statewide.[32] This crisis also caused some to rethink the role of the federal government vis-à-vis that of private charities in providing for the needs of distressed citizens. The drought created varied types of human misery and planted the seeds of reform and change.

The editor of the *American Guardian,* an Oklahoma socialist publication, reported that in Arkansas in 1930 he "saw cotton rotting in the fields because cotton pickers could not exist on the 35 cents paid for picking 100 pounds."[33] In short, by 1930 Arkansas was unable to meet the needs of its hungry citizens.

Terrible weather and the havoc it caused seemed a fitting backdrop to the despair of the early years of the Great Depression. The 1930 census figures were also a cause for concern, although few people noticed given the urgency of more pressing, apparent problems. In the Bottoms, Wilson Township lost 216 residents and Galla Rock Township lost 41 while Dardanelle Township declined by 152. Census records show that Yell County's population declined by 3,205 residents during the decade of the 1920s.[34] In short, good news was hard to find in 1930, while bad news never seemed to end.

Additional weather-related traumas occurred during the 1930s as a general shortage of rainfall persisted until early January 1937.[35] In 1936, temperatures soared to 110°F, an all-time record high recorded on July 18, but this was mercifully broken within three days by several inches of cooling rain.[36] While crops were damaged, the corn crop appeared ample, and Yell County was in a comparatively better condition than the rest of Arkansas.[37] In 1930 Yell County contained 3,133 farms, a number that remained remarkably steady with 3,128 farms in 1935, then the number dramatically declined in 1940 to 2,454. This represented a 29 percent decline during the decade of the 1930s, with terrible weather and a bad economy being the primary culprits.[38] More dramatic weather events centered upon three separate tornadoes.

On October 18, 1937, at approximately midnight, a tornado tore a one-hundred-yard path through Carden Bottom. Four houses were demolished, and four additional homes were damaged. There was also severe damage to Carden Bottom High School, with complete destruction of the new gymnasium. In addition, damage occurred to the McClure Gin, plus the loss of farm implements, wagons, several barns, and more than two hundred bales of cotton and three hundred bales of hay. The gymnasium alone represented a loss of $25,000.[39] As it had in previous disasters, the community banded together, repaired, and rebuilt; the school and its gymnasium were opened again eleven months after the destruction.[40]

A tornado rolled through parts of Yell and Pope Counties on May 21, 1938, demolishing buildings near Centerville and New Neely while causing injuries and home demolition in western Yell County, as well as in Riverside in the Upper Bottoms.[41] Then, on October 26, 1941, another tornado destroyed a large swath of the south end of Dardanelle, resulting in the complete leveling of numerous old and venerable homes, and bringing about widespread destruction and multiple injuries. Sadly, two deaths were also reported: an African American woman and her young baby, whose bodies were found wedged in the branches of a tree near the riverbank.[42] As a consequence of the October tornado and its accompanying storm, a total of thirty-seven families who suffered significant property damage in Dardanelle received Red Cross aid totaling $1,979.58.[43]

During the 1941 storm, Pauline Bata, approximately twenty-two years old and a four-year employee of the Western Arkansas Telephone Company, courageously stayed at her post answering and connecting switchboard calls and taking distress calls. Even when told her own home had been demolished, she continued to work, directing ambulances to those needing help. When asked later why she did not leave and seek shelter during the tornado, Ms. Bata replied, "I don't know. I just didn't think of leaving my board until I found someone to take my place."[44]

## High Water and Floods

Ironically, as it had in the previous decades, high water and flooding remained the most imposing weather-related dangers for Dardanelle and the Bottoms. During the 1930s, several floods caused massive damage and financial losses as well as the displacement of people and livestock. In June 1935 heavy rains in the upper Arkansas River watershed resulted in a rise of the river level to 24.1 feet. The Carden Bottom Levee on the Petit Jean River broke and land in the Lower Bottoms not protected by levees flooded for the fourth time in one year.[45] Just one week later, the Arkansas River posed a serious overflow threat for the fifth time as it reached 24.3 feet, 1.3 feet above the Dardanelle flood stage. While the levees remained secure, land in the Lower Bottoms was flooded as water topped the river's banks; in the Upper Bottoms, the lowlands were flooded by the rain. At Fields Chapel the riverbanks were caving badly, prompting Marie Shepherd's father to move his family's house approximately one-half mile away from the river, using a moving crew from Little Rock with mules. Grace Hatch McClure's family, the Shepherd's neighbors, also moved their home.[46]

Then, on early June 17, 1935, unusually heavy rainfall on the upper Arkansas River caused river waters to rise to 26.1 feet at Dardanelle. Consequently, the levees at Riverside, New Neely, and Holla Bend failed and 25,000 acres were flooded (see Appendix, fig. 4). Residents from the Lower and Upper Bottoms fled with household goods and livestock to higher ground as the Petit Jean, Arkansas, and Fourche Rivers all overflowed. Some eight hundred families were displaced and required aid. Given the fact that this flood occurred well after the end of the planting season, the flood of 1935 was more financially destructive than was the more infamous flood of 1927. Following the receding of the waters, the levees were repaired and rebuilt, and the county health department and the Red Cross worked to avoid an outbreak of typhoid and malaria.[47] When the levee was breached near Riverside at Stringtown, a ninety-two-pound alligator gar swept past the men trying to reinforce the levee. It took four men to kill it.[48]

On Friday, June 21, the Cotton Town levee gave way, creating a 1¾-mile-long opening. As a consequence, water swept into previously protected fields (see Appendix, fig. 5). In the end, the only levee not damaged in the 1935 flood was the Fields Chapel section of the levee. In response to the flooding, the Red Cross provided food and clothing to some 225 displaced persons and set aside $2,500 for disbursement relief funding. The highest water level recorded at Dardanelle during the flood of 1935 was 29.5 feet on June 21.[49]

One of the long-term effects of the 1935 flood was the impossibility of replanting cotton so late in the year. As such, farmers were urged to quickly replant corn, sorghum, hay, or soy beans.[50] Local leaders met with engineers from the federal government to inspect and begin the process of levee rebuilding, including the damaged Carden Bottom levee and the Dardanelle Drainage District No. 1 Levee. The government assured local officials that $6,000 would be made available immediately.[51] Near the one-year anniversary of the flood of 1935, the Omnibus Budget bill passed by Congress allocated $93,200 for rebuilding six miles of the Dardanelle Drainage District levees in order to render protection from a 36-foot flood stage surge of the Arkansas River at Dardanelle.[52]

In mid-February 1938, high water and intense rains were causing the Arkansas River to rise again. As the river level reached 25.5 feet at Dardanelle, observers noticed wooden bridges and underground gasoline storage tanks bobbing in the swift-moving yellow torrent. Families in Carden Bottom were beginning to pack up and move to higher ground as the Dardanelle and Carden Bottom levees were being patrolled.[53] The anticipation of danger and damage was great as all eyes focused on the river gauges and the levees.

The Arkansas River crested at Dardanelle on February 20 at 29 feet. Large areas of the Upper and Lower Bottoms were flooded in 10 or more feet of water, but no loss of life or property occurred and limited crop damage was reported. All the levees, except a section at New Neely, held, but the water flowed from the creek banks and the Petit Jean and Arkansas Rivers, and water also backed up in these rivers and creeks and topped the levees. At Fields Chapel, the Arkansas River caused intense riverbank caving and reached within ten feet of the Hatch home. Some 250 Bottoms' families who fled the high waters sheltered with relatives and friends while the Red Cross issued food certificates to the displaced, which local merchants honored.[54]

The flood of 1938 was comparable in its impact to the flood of 1935, with the exception that in 1938—as in 1927—the high waters occurred in winter and thus did not damage already planted crops. This was not the case in the summertime flood of 1935 that resulted in extreme economic complications and created severe want for farm families. There have always been good reasons to fear heavy rain and rising waters, and in late March 1938 anxiety increased as intense rains returned, leading to a sense of urgency to complete levee repairs.[55]

Spring 1939 brought worrisome April showers also. During a twenty-six-hour period (April 15–16) 8.4 inches of rain fell in Dardanelle, causing major flooding in the Bottoms and throughout Yell County. The county suffered between $8,000 and $10,000 in losses, as seven large bridges and numerous culverts were swept away. Furthermore, hundreds of families scrambled to remove themselves and their livestock from imminent rising waters. The Carden Bottom levee failed and, in some places, the waters of the Petit Jean River were spread out several miles wide. Thousands of acres of cotton, corn, and alfalfa—nearly ready for cutting—became submerged under feet of water. The Upper Bottoms were also flooded, as Mill Creek and Smiley Bayou ran over their banks, flooding fields of cotton and corn. Even upland farms in Yell County suffered with an estimated $200,000 in damages from soil erosion.[56]

Two years later (1941), high water was once again a problem. At Stubbs Town in Carden Bottom, all residents moved out as the Arkansas River levels rose. Riverside residents anxiously watched as waters began to top the levee there and some fields were flooded. In response to the dangers, fifty Works Progress Administration (WPA) workers placed hundreds of sandbags along weak points of the levees in both the Upper and Lower Bottoms. On April 23, 1941, the river gauge at Dardanelle measured 27.2 feet, with thousands of previously planted acres already inundated.[57] Sadly, the "big" flood of 1941 was still to come.

On November 5, 1941, the Arkansas River crested at 32.1 feet, the highest level recorded at Dardanelle since the terrible flood of 1927, when levels reached 33.5 feet. All the levees were either topped or failed. Fifty thousand acres of Bottom land were flooded. Water 2 feet deep shut down Highway 7 two miles south of Dardanelle at Smiley Bayou; and 14 feet of water also stood west of town, causing the closure of Highway 22. Thousands of farm families moved to Cotton Town (the highest elevation in the Lower Bottoms) or to Dardanelle, where refugee centers had been established at the National Guard Armory and the American Legion Hut. Townspeople worked with the local Red Cross to provide food, clothing, and shelter for the displaced. These people waited some ten days before the waters receded sufficiently enough to allow for their safe return to their wrecked, mud-encrusted homes and farms. It deserves to be mentioned that the rushed effort by the townspeople to organize and to assist their flooded neighbors occurred less than two weeks after Dardanelle had been wrecked by—and suffered greatly because of—the October 1941 tornado, as described above.

Fortunately, most of the livestock in the Bottoms had been saved, having been driven to higher ground. However, thousands of poultry were lost, along with 250 bales of stored cotton and thousands of acres of alfalfa and corn. As a result of the flooding, several feet of river sand were deposited on some of the land in Carden Bottom, including all the area of Stubbs Town, seriously and permanently damaging its productive capacity. Intense riverbank caving at Fields Chapel necessitated the removal of numerous structures sitting on the brink of collapse into the river.[58] Slowly, after a series of successive high-water events, Fields Chapel was caving into the Arkansas River.

The *Dardanelle Post-Dispatch* reported that the Red Cross assisted 341 families, for a total expenditure of $2,713.63. While most of these funds involved emergency food costs, 42 families received funds to help pay for livestock feed and 3 families were given funds for furniture since they had lost all of their household property in the high waters.[59] Assuredly, the flood of 1941 damaged crops, farms, lives, and futures.

## Suffering and Deprivation

Given the grip of the Great Depression—coupled with weather and flooding disasters—the Dardanelle Bottoms and, to a lesser extent, the people of Dardanelle, were frequently in need of assistance during the 1930s. Prior to the implementation of the New Deal in 1933, most relief aid came from private charity organizations and churches. Given their importance, a brief summary of these relief efforts is warranted in order to offer insight into the relationship of the town to the country as well as the nature of class and race relations in onerous times.

In December 1930, the local Red Cross chapter asked for clothing donations (coats, dresses, pants, and shirts) so that destitute children might have warm clothing and be able to attend school. Additionally, the chapter sought two heating stoves that might be donated to destitute families.[60] A *Dardanelle Post-Dispatch* editorial outlined the problem:

> [S]cores of able bodied men are begging for work—at any price, work at 75 cents, even 50 cents a day—in order to procure food to sustain their families . . . scores of men, women and children in Yell County suffering the pangs of hunger . . . eight hundred, or even a thousand destitute families . . . President Hoover and his administration turns a deaf ear to the appeal . . . the problem is up to us![61]

The economic depression was part of the reason for this deprivation, but the drought of 1930 intensified the hunger problem. Life in Yell County in the early 1930s was rough, including overly indebted landowners (many of whom lost their savings in failed banks), families of sharecroppers and tenant farmers starving and nearly naked, looming farm foreclosures, and bad weather. In addition, the Red Cross was faced with demanding needs and dwindling funds. Local merchants and businesses of all kinds were also stressed, but because some had more resources than others, they were not in such a state of deprivation as were the rural people, the poor, and the African Americans.

In early 1931, the Yell County Red Cross provided work for the rural poor shoveling and hauling gravel for county roads. For a man with a team of mules and a wagon, the gravel work paid 40 cents for hauling one yard of gravel one mile, 60 cents for two miles, and 75 cents for two to three miles. For the needy in town, the offer consisted of work on streets and public areas, at a rate of 15 cents an hour. In order to maximize Red Cross funds, each head of a family would be allowed only enough work to provide for basic family survival. This was implemented as follows: for a five-person family, the man would be allowed $6.00 of work in a two-week period; families of six to eight were allowed $8.00 of work within a two-week period; and families having more than eight members were limited to $10.00 of work within a two-week period.[62] Limited as this was, it was at least something. Within its first month of operation, this program was assisting 2,338 families in Yell County and, thereby, providing food for approximately 11,690 persons in a county with a total population of 21,313.[63]

In late January 1931, the Red Cross allocated $300 to start a hot lunch program in county schools for children who had little or no food at home. The program was administered by the various schools' home economics and Smith-Hughes vocational agriculture teachers, with money allocated to each of Yell County's twenty-three school districts based on enrollment.[64] In February 1940, the Dardanelle Parent-Teachers Association and the chamber of commerce, working with the federal Works Projects Administration, established a school hot lunch program operating out of the kitchen in the American Legion Hut. Students brought one item from home to exchange for one hot meal ticket. This program served a complete hot lunch for 185 children daily, and when the school term ended, the lunch workers began canning foods from the school's garden for the upcoming year's needs.[65]

In early 1931, the Red Cross agreed to pay doctors for brewer's yeast given to patients suffering from pellagra.[66] United Drug Company, working with the American Red Cross and the Rexall Drug Store chain, agreed to provide prescription medicines free of charge to drought-stricken individuals, and the Singer Drug Store in Dardanelle filled twenty-five free prescriptions during the first week of this program.[67] In the fall of 1931, the economic situation was still dismal, as indicated by the late start to the school term and poor early term attendance. Children simply stayed out of school in order to work the fields as hiring workers was unfeasible.[68]

The drought of 1930 passed, though the problems of the Great Depression continued. As such, though not a great year, 1931 was less dismal than the previous year, as summarized in the *Dardanelle Post-Dispatch*: "1931 may not go down as a money-making year for the farmers and businessmen of Yell County, but it is a wonderful improvement over 1930."[69] In early 1933, a self-help county group was formed to engage in educational uplift and to help citizens avoid the pitfalls of prolonged reliance on charity. Shortly after that, the Red Cross announced that aid to residents in Yell County would completely cease at the end of March.[70]

In order to have some insight in Arkansas's comparative economic standing during the early years of the Great Depression and in the decades to follow, one has only to compare Arkansas per capita personal income statistics with those for the United States. The following figures are cited in current dollars and are not adjusted for inflation. Arkansas's per capita personal income averages from 1929 through 1941 and those for the United States are displayed below.

## Comparative United States/Arkansas Economic Data

| YEAR | PER CAPITA PERSONAL INCOME UNITED STATES | PER CAPITA PERSONAL INCOME ARKANSAS |
|---|---|---|
| 1929 | — | $302 |
| 1930 | $621 | $224 |
| 1931 | $529 | $207 |
| 1932 | $402 | $152 |
| 1933 | $376 | $153 |
| 1934 | $427 | $182 |
| 1935 | $428 | $204 |
| 1936 | $540 | $243 |
| 1937 | $579 | $253 |
| 1938 | $532 | $228 |
| 1939 | $562 | $246 |
| 1940 | $601 | $257 |
| 1941 | $734 | $344 |

Source: Archival Federal Reserve Economic Data, Federal Reserve Bank, St. Louis, Missouri. https://alfred.stlouisfed.org.

The initial phase of the Great Depression—from late 1929 until early 1933—was a particularly dark time for the people of Dardanelle and the Bottoms. The above income figures certainly underscore this. Additional economic statistics only underscore this truth. For instance, in 1930 an Arkansas farm income was only 40.9 percent of what it had been in 1929 and by 1935 it had increased to only 68 percent of its 1929 level. In 1935 Arkansas's wages and salaries were only 72.7 percent, farm proprietors' income only 66.9 percent, and nonfarm proprietors' income only 66.9 percent of their respective 1929 levels.[71] In comparing personal income in Arkansas and the United States and using 1929 as a base year, Arkansas's 1930 personal income was only 74.3 percent of its 1929 levels while the nation's 1930 personal income level was 89.7 percent of their 1929 level. Likewise in 1935 the Arkansas percentage was 68.9 percent while the national percentage was 71.3 percent.[72]

These poor in Yell County were almost a forgotten people, except for limited local relief efforts and some small amounts of national charitable assistance they received during the early and most difficult days of the Great Depression. As New Deal programs began to materialize and relief efforts intensified, the old agricultural system transformed. The Great Depression ushered in a torrent of new programs and agricultural management systems, all of which rushed over Dardanelle and the Bottoms creating a cascade of change. The first hint of this change was the abolishment of Arkansas's Office of the Commissioner of Mines, Manufacturing and Agriculture on January 31, 1933.[73] Originally created in 1907, this office had served as a conduit of information and advice to farmers. Now, its need was gone as federal agencies and programs filled that role. The New Deal had arrived in Arkansas, and increasingly the federal government working through local committees would direct policies and influence the lives of the citizens of the area.

The United States Department of Agriculture announced its regulations for 1933 loans under the Reconstruction Finance Corporation to include a 30 percent planting reduction of cash crops with individual loans limited to $300. It required planting a home garden and feedstuff production sufficient for one's livestock. Furthermore, these loans were not to be spent on the purchase of machinery, livestock, or the payment of debts, taxes, or interest on debts.[74]

Local relief efforts continued. The chamber of commerce supported and promoted the idea of using vacant lots in Dardanelle for vegetable gardening in support of the needy, as well as securing Reconstruction Finance Corporation aid in offering $8.00 worth of free seed per household for this gardening program.[75] The real focus, beginning in 1933, however, centered on the explosion of New Deal legislation and programs.

By November 1933, some 3,000 needy and unemployed men resided in Yell County. Although all were eligible for temporary work under the Civil Works Administration (CWA), the original maximum county allotment was only 533. On November 27, male heads of household began to complete applications for CWA jobs, and within ten days, 245 men were assigned to the thirteen CWA projects in the county.[76] By mid-December, the county's allotment had been increased to 733 workers, and additional projects were being proposed and approved.[77] Before the Civil Works Administration could get its program firmly established, however, it ended its work in Yell County (in March 1934), having expended $126,127. It was announced that a new rural rehabilitation program would replace it.[78]

## Home Demonstration Clubs

While the record of the Civil Works Administration was chaotic and short lived, the US Department of Agriculture's Home Demonstration program was not. The first Home Demonstration Club in Arkansas had begun in 1912 and Yell County had employed a home demonstration agent in 1920. Therefore, while not specifically a New Deal program, the Home Demonstration program was well funded and supported by the county quorum court during the New Deal era as a means of improving the deficiencies of rural life.

The Home Demonstration program quickly became an established part of the rural setting. On January 1, 1934, the Yell County Quorum Court appropriated $1,000 to hire a home demonstration agent. Within months, the new county home demonstration agent, Lenore Abboud, had organized clubs in the Dardanelle Bottoms at Lakeview, Centerville, Liberty Hall, and Fields Chapel, as well as in numerous other Yell County locations. Abboud worked with great energy and efficiency, and also created a countywide club council that met on a regular basis. The rural women who were active members of these clubs learned about improving health and sanitation; the appearance and safety of their homes, the health of their families, and the care of their children; as well as about home sewing, construction and beautification projects, and landscaping. Contests were held featuring clothing, apron, curtain, and hat designs; and demonstrations were made on weaving rugs, making mattresses, and small home building projects. In addition, the Home Demonstration Clubs emphasized food preservation and canning, both of which provided rural women with a way to improve their homes and learn new skills at minimum cost. But perhaps the greatest benefit of Home Demonstration Clubs was in providing their members with a sense of community. The clubs afforded rural women the opportunity to meet regularly, enjoy the support and instruction of the HD agent and fellow members, and create and enjoy the camaraderie of a community of women who shared similar problems, stresses, needs, and goals.

Members of the Home Demonstration Clubs were also interested in substantive ways to improve the quality of their lives by increased economic success. For instance, with a small flock of fifty hens during one month (April 1936), one HD Club member, Mrs. Roy Madden, raised and sold eggs at a cost of 7 1/3 cents each and sold them to the local hatchery for 26½ cents each, earning a profit of $15.89.[79] HD Club members found poultry a feasible means by which to supplement family income.[80] Another HD Club member, Mrs. Ruby Watkins of Belleville in western Yell County, used her wood-crafting skills to build bookends, magazine racks, and shelves, which she placed on consignment at a local store, earning $12.00 during December 1937. She then used the money to install French doors between her living and dining rooms.[81]

The resourcefulness of the women in the HD Clubs was remarkable. With little or no money, they effectively used what was available to improve their homes and their lives. Using discarded cotton scraps and feathers, some women crafted new mattresses. Using native stone, they underpinned their houses to improve insulation and gain greater protection against insects. Using feed sacks and dye, they designed and installed new window curtains. One illustrative example from 1938 was Fannie Tedford of Lakeview in Carden Bottom, who built nine pieces of furniture at a total cost of $4 from discarded wood.[82] The home demonstration agent and other club members encouraged women to select projects—raising poultry, gardening, or home improvement—and share their work and methods with other club members. Young mothers were invited to the agent's child-care presentation and were urged to "bring their little fellows and come to the meeting."[83] Women enjoyed the fellowship afforded club membership and were pleased with their efforts to improve the quality of their lives and that of their families; and, thus, clubs grew in membership and loyalty. At a late 1937 meeting in Carden Bottom, sixty-four members participated.[84] Rural women were devoted to the Home Demonstration Clubs and took seriously the responsibility and opportunities afforded by membership.

By 1937 the Home Demonstration Clubs were large enough in number and of sufficient strength to sponsor a Better Homes Contest in Dardanelle. Here, club members from throughout the county displayed their home-improvement projects including making, repairing, or painting furniture; building a closet in the home or adding a garage; building a fence; planting shrubbery and shade trees; home insulation; painting; and building new kitchen cabinets. The home-canning exhibit alone featured the work of two hundred women and displayed their canned vegetables, meats, and fruits. The Better Homes contests and displays became annual events in Dardanelle, with local merchants providing prizes. In addition, the Home Demonstration Clubs held annual home tours throughout the county, open to visitors and club members.[85]

By late 1939, the Home Demonstration Clubs in Yell County were being celebrated for their efficiency and successes, and agent Lenore Abboud was being praised for her "splendid work."[86] The record was impressive: Yell County had forty-two Home Demonstration Clubs, with 1,396 members; eighty-three meetings had been conducted in the county during the year, with a total attendance of 3,983; and home demonstration agents participated in forty-five additional meetings that were attended by 15,626 people. During 1939 the meeting agendas included subjects such as home gardening, home engineering, poultry, food selection and preparation, food preservation, child development, clothing, home management, house furnishings and handicrafts, health and sanitation, and community activities. Club members in Yell County canned 230,630 quarts of fruit, 121,372 quarts of vegetables, 18,104 quarts of fruit juice, 20,790 quarts of meat, 46,424 quarts of pickles and relishes, and 267,720 quarts of preserves. In addition, they planted 2,742 shade trees and 5,158 shrubs, sodded eighty-seven lawns, and tore down eighty-six old buildings and fences. Additionally, thirty-eight new homes were built, seventy-six were remodeled, and thirty-nine were underpinned with native stone. Yell County club members produced 5,420 pounds of cheese, 367 poultry operations were developed, 5,523 garments were produced for family use, 980 pieces of furniture were built or refurbished, 221 mattresses were constructed, 278 rugs were constructed, and an unrecorded number of hours were spent learning about improved nutrition and engaging in community activities.[87]

In summary, the Home Demonstration Clubs achieved much that was good. They not only improved the quality of homes, diet, and family life in general, but they also allowed rural women greater self-reliance as they created money-making opportunities, provided an arena to share ideas, and created an enlarged and empowered sense of self and community with other women.

## The New Deal

The First Agricultural Adjustment Act (AAA) was signed into law May 12, 1933, by President Franklin D. Roosevelt. This law allowed farmers to contract with the government—through the local county agent—to reduce particular crop acreage. The First AAA called for the immediate and one-time destruction of existing surpluses of cotton, corn, milk, and pigs. Its purpose was to stabilize and increase prices per crop. Farmers who contracted with this program were told to plant some of their land in conservation crops or to leave some acreage unplanted. In 1935 Yell County agent G. M. Measeles urged farmers to plant rented acreage in hay, oats, or rye, and to consider vegetable crops such as tomatoes, sweet and Irish potatoes, peas, sorghum, and peanuts while avoiding cotton and corn.[88] Declared unconstitutional by the US Supreme Court's decision in *Butler v. United States* (1936), the law was replaced in 1938 by the Second Agricultural Adjustment Act, which included many of the first law's features but also guaranteed farmers parity payments on the crops produced. These laws were both recovery- and relief-oriented legislation.

During 1936 Yell County farmers received some $135,000 in AAA payments with 1,908 farms involved. By May 1937, government payments through the AAA programs had reached $102,164.98 for diverting 1936 cotton acres to soil-conserving crops, and $27,288.46 for engaging in soil-building practices on 24,051 acres.[89] For 1937, AAA payments to Yell County farmers totaled approximately $162,000.[90]

By 1940 AAA payments included 1.55 cents per pound for cotton, based on allotted acreage and average yield; and 1.6 cents per pound of cotton in conservation payments to assist in continuing soil-building practices. Also, the farmer was to receive $1.50 if he raised a home garden that met government specifications, plus a minimum conservation payment of $20 per farm depending on soil-building practices used.[91]

While the two AAA programs tackled the problems of crop surplus and pricing, the Production Credit Association (PCA) created by the Farm Credit Act of 1933 offered a new method for farm financing. The local PCA office would give a farmer a loan at a rate of 5.5 percent for a term of between three to twelve months if the farmer offered acceptable collateral. Thus, the days of the furnishing merchant and high-rate agricultural bank loans were addressed. Also, the farmer, by securing a PCA loan, became a voting member of that organization, a cooperative farm-lending agency enjoying US Government support. By the spring of 1934, the PCA office in Russellville—which served Yell, Pope, and Johnson Counties, and part of Logan County—had received 290 applications representing requests for $27,915 in short-term loans.[92] The Emergency Crop and Feed Loan section of the Farm Credit Act allowed farmers up to $100 for seed and land preparation in order to plant winter grain crops in areas—such as Yell County—stricken by prolonged drought. Farmers applied for these loans through their local PCA office.[93]

The Federal Land Bank, originally created in 1916, was busy during the Great Depression selling farms gained through foreclosure. During the first eight months of 1938, a total of sixty-five Arkansas farms were sold through this process each month. Government directives issued in October 1938 ordered that sales be made to persons living within the county of the foreclosed property and requiring a small down payment with the balance requiring yearly payments. It was announced that all twenty-nine Yell County foreclosed properties would be up for sale within two weeks.[94] This new policy would assist farmers in acquiring these foreclosed properties and thus allow the land to stay in operation. This would also keep the Land Bank from having to maintain unused properties for long periods of time. By June 1940, Yell County farmers were carrying $327,000 of Federal Land Bank loans, most of which had a thirty-year term and usually represented the first mortgage on the property.[95]

The various New Deal farm programs had long-lasting effects on the structure of American agriculture. These programs marked the beginning of contemporary American farm cultivation and signaled the demise of the previous "nineteenth-century" approach. The furnishing merchant was replaced with government financing programs, the market was now constricted by government acreage contracts that reduced production, and commodity prices were floored with a parity payment. Because of the New Deal farm programs, some landowners, who still were farmers, would replace their remaining tenants and sharecroppers with tractors and invest in fertilizers and pesticides. Within approximately two to three decades after the introduction of these New Deal programs, farming had become an agribusiness with massive investments in equipment for the cultivation of huge amounts of land. The New Deal's effect on agriculture was profound. The traditional American farm, characterized by one family's cultivation of a small amount of acreage and geared to self-sufficiency, largely became extinct as it was replaced by gigantic, capital-intensive, agribusiness concerns.[96] This went beyond transition: this was permanent, extensive systemic change.

While New Deal programs were offering assistance to farmers, others were helped by the Works Progress Administration. Created as a relief program on May 6, 1935, the WPA employed twenty-five men under the direction of local contractor J. B. Hofstetter to build a new National Guard Armory adjacent to the Yell County Courthouse in Dardanelle. The project began on November 26, 1935, and was completed in 1936 at a total cost of $23,300.[97] Another WPA project was the Women's Sewing Room, which opened on November 13, 1935. Housed in the Masonic Lodge Building on the southeast corner of South Front and Pine Streets in Dardanelle, the Sewing Room employed thirty women who each worked five days a week and earned $21 a month. By 1937 the Sewing Room employed seventy women, working with materials furnished by the Works Progress Administration, Yell County government, and local merchants. These women produced garments that were then given to the local Red Cross for use by the needy of Yell County. By 1940 the Sewing Room employed some African American workers and had six locations at various communities in the county.[98] The Works Progress Administration ended on June 30, 1939, and was replaced by the Work Projects Administration on July 1, 1939. During its four years of operation (July 1, 1939, until July 1943) the Work Projects Administration spent $785,691 in Yell County. Almost all of these funds were for salaries and wages with the largest category of expenditure being road and street construction/improvement expenditures ($450,360 in Yell County). The Sewing Room Project received $70,044, and public buildings were allocated $215,367.[99] Thus, beginning on July 1, 1939, the Work Projects Administration carried on some of the activities conducted previously by the Works Progress Administration, including the Sewing Room. In addition, new programs were added including school hot lunch programs, nursery schools, art and music studios, library and recreation projects, and three courthouse programs.[100]

The Federal Surplus Commodity Corporation and the Surplus Marketing Administration sought to provide hunger relief through an array of federal and state programs, such as the school lunch program, canning projects, surplus commodity distribution, and food stamp programs. However, Arkansas's assistance was limited to a maximum of $10 or less per month per family and thus food became highly valued.[101] Bobby Crow remembered that his mother's family came to Carden Bottom during the Depression looking for any work in the cotton fields. Poor and destitute as a child, upon reaching adulthood, Mrs. Crow kept an extremely well-stocked pantry. As her husband noted: "if Kroger has that item, we have it at home in multiples."[102] The memory of hunger was not easily erased.

By 1937 the New Deal Recreation Project, locally under the direction of Louise Boyce, was involving children in plays, music, dance and drama training, hosting music festivals throughout the county, and working with the Home Demonstration Clubs to create recreational activities in forty-two separate county communities and with the Negro Recreation Project in Dardanelle.[103]

The record of the Work Projects Administration was most impressive. In March 1940, the Work Projects Administration allocated

$264,818 for Yell County roadwork.[104] By later that year, 563 culverts and bridges had been erected, 500 acres of land drained, and more than 13,000 feet of ditches cleared and pipelines installed in mosquito control efforts. In addition, 4,800 feet of levee embankment improvements were completed, thirteen public buildings were either constructed or repaired, and numerous street and alley repairs were completed.[105] In 1933, under the previous Works Progress Administration and in coordination with Yell County judge Morris Moore, the Yell County Commissary had been established in order to provide surplus commodities from the federal government to needy families. By 1940, under the Work Projects Administration, 500 families—representing 1,900 people—were receiving food assistance through the surplus commodities program.[106] In July 1941, an adult education project began in Dardanelle as a coordinated effort of the Work Projects Administration, the state education department, and the Dardanelle Chamber of Commerce. It offered formal educational opportunities for persons sixteen years of age and older. While this program was open to both whites and African Americans, the sites of instruction and registration were segregated.[107] Highly visible in Yell County, the Work Projects Administration accomplished a wide range of good works as well as provided employment for many (241 as of late 1941).[108]

The National Youth Administration (NYA), which began on January 17, 1936, was also active in Yell County, employing 60 high school students from needy families at $10 a month by February 1937.[109] By early 1939, 149 needy youth were employed by the NYA in a variety of construction projects within the county. For example, in Dardanelle 25 NYA boys repaired and painted the vocational agriculture building on the Dardanelle High School campus.[110] In September 1939 it was announced that the Yell County National Youth Administration program would receive $1,872 during the 1939–1940 fiscal year for youth workers, with $432 slated for Dardanelle and $144 for Carden Bottom. The intent of this program was to provide needed part-time employment to students in order to allow them to complete their high school education while also learning employable skills. This was a forerunner of contemporary vocational education.[111]

Another of the New Deal relief measures was the Resettlement Administration (RA) created on April 30, 1935, which among other elements included the Farm Debt Adjustment project. The Yell County Farm Debt Committee (FDC) worked under the State Agricultural Advisory Council to bring worthy, debt-burdened farmers and their creditors together in an effort to develop new and more manageable debt agreements between the parties involved so as to avoid foreclosure and financial loss for all. This is what bankers call a "work-out" arrangement. In July 1936, the Yell County FDC invited applications, and a year later the committee successfully managed ninety applications while fifty-five others were declined because equitable adjustment was not possible.[112] On July 22, 1937, the Farm Security Administration succeeded the Resettlement Administration as the coordinating group for farm-debt adjustment, and the Farm Debt Committee continued to function on the county level engaged in this effort.[113] This transition occurred when Congress passed the Bankhead-Jones Farm Tenant Act, with the intent of assisting tenant farmers, sharecroppers, and farm laborers in buying farms through a low-interest purchase arrangement. Financed through the Reconstruction Finance Corporation and later through the Farm Security Administration, these loans carried a 3 percent interest rate and a forty-year term for small amounts of approximately $5,000.[114] Under this program, the Yell County Farm Debt Committee authorized approximately five to ten tenant farmers yearly to apply for loans and in 1938 six loans were approved. The county committee also encouraged farmers who wanted to sell their farms to list properties with them.[115] In 1935 there were 2,865,155 tenant farmers in the country, with 151,759 of them living in Arkansas (5.3 percent). By 1941, 20,748 tenant farmers nationwide had been given loans, with 1,399 (6.7 percent) of the total living in Arkansas. The reality is that less than 1 percent of the tenant-sharecropper population in the United States received any direct benefit from the Bankhead-Jones Farm Tenancy Act.[116]

Another part of the Resettlement Program was the creation of thirty-five nationwide farming communities composed of selected tenant families. Each family was provided with a small farm complete with a house wired for electricity and having running water; ten acres of cleared land and ten acres needing to be cleared; a barn; a chicken house; and a government-held mortgage. Thirty-five Yell County families, mostly from the Bottoms, were relocated under this program to the Dyess Colony in Mississippi County in March 1936.[117]

In Yell County, 55 percent (1,742) of all farmers were tenant farmers in 1937. That same year, 60 percent of all Arkansas farmers were tenants.[118] Various New Deal programs—such as the Farm Security Administration and the Resettlement Administration—represented efforts to reduce tenancy and increase small farm ownership and self-sustainability. In reality, these efforts were not highly successful. It is true that ample evidence exists, while lacking in uniformity from location to location, showing that many tenant farmers and families were simply evicted, others did not share in the AAA payments due to them, and that generally New Deal agricultural policies favored landowners who had significant capital, not agricultural laborers.[119] It is also true, but the degree of this truth varies from one location to another, that local committees responsible for directing New Deal agricultural programs frequently attempted to aid large landowners over small farmers, especially tenant farmers and laborers.

Near the end of the First New Deal (1933–1937), the *Dardanelle Post-Dispatch* discussed an Arkansas Department of Public Welfare report that addressed the various types of relief that had been granted Yell County and its residents during 1936. The county had received $80,734 in various relief payments—including $12,646.04 in distributed commodities—for 164 persons employed by the Works Progress Administration, 168 Civilian Conservation Corps recruits, and 754 certified drought cases.[120] Consequently, even as the darkest days of the Great Depression were ending, the severity of economic conditions in Yell County remained, and as the above numbers indicate, the need for continued governmental assistance existed.

One of the New Deal's approaches to assisting rural citizens was a subtle but significant agenda to redirect and remake typical rural life. This approach is reflected in the remarks given by Connie J. Bonslagel, assistant national director of Rural Rehabilitation, an agency within the Resettlement Administration, at a Biloxi, Mississippi, conference in 1936:

> [I]f the income of a farm family is suddenly increased, it does not mean that their standard of living rises to meet the income. I have known of low-income families who have suddenly become wealthy. . . . They bought automobiles and electric pianos, but they continued to throw their dish water out the back door and to live in the squalor they were accustomed to. Their standard

of living definitely was not raised simply because their income was increased.[121]

Bonslagel continued by stating that the task of the Resettlement Administration was twofold: to create a desire for a better standard of living and the good things it could provide, and then to teach farmers how to achieve this standard. The same sentiment was enunciated, although less sharply, by J. H. Snapp at a WPA conference held in Little Rock as he called for WPA employment of rural citizens on rural projects:

> In this way, the proposed WPA program would not only work toward supplementing farm income during periods of financial depression and low prices, but would bring to rural communities additional public enterprises which are designed primarily for rural betterment . . . better secondary roads, better health, drainage, and similar beneficial developments.[122]

Certainly, rural residents in the Dardanelle Bottoms had for decades called for improved roads and levees to protect their homes and crops, and surely they must have longed for better health care for themselves and their children; but there remains something almost sinister about government program officials discussing the need to create new visions of rural life in the minds of rural residents. Historically, New Dealers were more of the Progressive Era mindset and, thus, believed that in refashioning people with a proper middle-class set of values, their lives would be improved. It can be argued that the people of the Bottoms did want a better life, and their words and efforts had for decades revealed this; however, given their independent character, some, perhaps many, may have resented attempts by the government to recast their values and daily habits.

Regardless, the New Deal programs and approach seem to have been generally quite successful. As Lucille Watson, home management supervisor for Yell County, noted in the spring of 1939:

> For many years farm families who have weathered financial storms best and made the most consistent progress have been those who followed a live-at-home program. . . . If we have a garden that produces our vegetables, potatoes, and other foods; cows for milk and butter; chickens for eggs and meat; beef and hogs

for meat, we have saved money we would have spent for food.
... With fewer acres in cotton, we ought to be certain to plant
enough corn and grains and hay to supply feed for livestock.
... When we raise our own food and feed, we are protecting our
cash income and assuring our families that they will have a sufficient supply of food during the year.[123]

This approach was not new. What was new in the New Deal were
the governmental programs that helped farmers curtail their surplus production while creating a floor for commodity pricing. These
actions—coupled with better loan and debt-management programs—
were undertaken as other agencies simultaneously and aggressively
educated farmers and farm families in the methods for improving
the quality of their homes, diet, health, and lives. Taken as a whole,
the New Deal worked a miraculous change in American agriculture,
at least for most farmers.

In short, the New Deal worked for many area farmers. One case
in point was the 1939 record of Joe Storment's family near Ola. On
their 112-acre farm, they had four cows that produced $91.26's worth
of cream, calves sales that generated $41.00, and twenty-five chickens
that produced eggs for family use plus $2.34 in sales. At the same time,
Storment's timber sales produced $25.00, cotton revenue generated
$204.99, and his Agricultural Adjustment Act benefits generated an
additional $85.70.[124] This diversified approach, coupled with the "live-
at-home" approach described above, allowed the Storment family to
avoid additional debt and generated a small positive cash flow. The
transitions created by the New Deal permanently changed farming
and rural life in America.

In the fall of 1930, Arkansas's agricultural commissioner stated:

I have been around all over the state and it looked bad to me.
... Arkansas farming will have to undergo a number of changes,
if the farm population of today remains on the farm and makes
a living. ... either the one-crop system or the farmers will have
to go. The partnership has failed.[125]

While the New Deal would eventually facilitate these changes, the
miseries of deprivation—hunger, extreme poverty, and need—had to
first be endured. Indicative of these extreme needs was the fact that

farmers in 1931 were allowed to apply for loans from the United States Extension Service not only for seed and usual farming supplies, but also for food. The Red Cross locally asked for stoves, shoes, and clothing in all sizes for the rural needy, and, week after week during the 1930s, farm foreclosure notices appeared.[126] The fortitude exhibited by the farm families of the Bottoms offered a true profile of courage and optimism in face of great difficulties.

Meanwhile, Fred Smith, the Smith-Hughes vocational agriculture teacher at Dardanelle, continued to hold night classes for farmers throughout the county, four in Carden Bottom alone in 1930, in order to help develop new crops and a broader level of agricultural expertise.[127] Transitioning from a cotton-based economy was not a quick or painless task. In 1931 two cotton gins operated in Dardanelle and seven others were operating in the Dardanelle Bottoms.[128] Reminiscent of Henry W. Grady's 1889 remarks imploring the South to develop a "New South" economy, Loy E. Rast, an Arkansas cotton farmer, commented in 1931 on the subservient condition of the southern farmer.

> They get up at the alarm of a Connecticut clock, put their Chicago suspenders on a pair of Detroit overalls, wash their faces with a cake of Cincinnati soap in a Philadelphia wash pan, sit down to a Grand Rapids table and eat Indiana hominy fried in St. Joseph lard, bacon from Kansas City, potatoes from Maine, biscuits made of flour from Illinois, cooked in a St. Louis stove and finish their meal with a cup of coffee from South America or tea from China. They go out to a lot fenced with Pittsburgh welded wire and put a St. Louis bridle on a Missouri mule, ride to the field in a Springfield wagon, hitch up to a Syracuse plow and work all day on a farm covered by an Ohio mortgage. At night a few of them read from a Bible printed in Chicago and a prayer written in Jerusalem, get into a bed made in Michigan with a blanket from New Jersey just to be kept awake half the night by the howling of a hound dog—the only home raised product on the farm![129]

This represents, of course, a great deal of exaggeration since most Arkansas farmers did not possess the extensive household goods described and since many were already fairly self-reliant. Nonetheless, this satire does underscore the frustration that farmers, especially the

cotton-dependent farmer, felt toward the pre–New Deal economic system. Once the New Deal began on March 4, 1933, changes took place.

Under the First Agricultural Adjustment Act, the US Government
began (in 1933) signing contracts with landowners and landowning
farmers for the voluntary reduction of cotton production by 21 to 31
percent, with implementation beginning with the 1934 crop. Farmers
were paid 3.5 cents per pound on the adjusted production, based on
a five-year average. The 1935 cotton reduction plan functioned with
the same guidelines.[130] This program hoped to reduce cotton acreage
nationally by 10 million acres with just over a 1-million-acre reduction
in Arkansas. This goal was exceeded as a 1.3-million-acre reduction
was achieved in total Arkansas cotton plantings. State officials warned
farmers that failure to sign up for this voluntary program would lead
to cotton prices in the 3-to-4-cent-per-pound range, "black ruin!"[131]

Tenant farmers and sharecroppers were not directly involved in
these contracts, and thus many were "removed" by the landowners.[132]
This was not a frequent occurrence in Yell County, although in the
Arkansas Delta, eviction was quite common. In order for the tenant
or sharecropper to be a party to the cotton contract, his name had to
appear with the landowner's on the government contract and this was
rarely done. While the Agricultural Adjustment Act programs directly
benefited a majority of Arkansas's almost 100,000 cotton growers and
indirectly aided many others linked to the cotton trade, an indeter-
minate number of Arkansas tenant farmers and sharecroppers were
excluded from the program and its benefits.[133]

There were several attempts in September 1933 to organize cotton pickers in the Dardanelle Bottoms in what the *Dardanelle Post-
Dispatch* referred to as "night-riding" incidents by a group calling itself
the "Workers' Legion for Justice of America" and three of its members
—Ed Davis, J. R. Fulford, and C. B. Lewis, all from Russellville—
referring to themselves as the national organization's leadership. The
group was soliciting cotton pickers as they worked in the fields, urging them to stop working unless paid 75 cents per hundred pounds
of cotton picked, as well as to demand that cotton laborers be paid
20 cents an hour based on an eight-hour workday. The organization
visited numerous fields in Yell and Pope Counties, usually in groups
of fifty to one hundred members, resulting in a large (but unspecified)

number of cotton pickers stopping work. Yell County sheriff Buford Compton arrested nineteen people including Ed Davis, the president of the organization, and charged them with night riding. According to Davis, the organization had a contact with the American Federation of Labor and Hugh Johnson, director of the National Recovery Act. Davis contended that both supported their efforts to engage in peaceful activities designed to raise cotton pickers' wages. Also, according to Davis, the organization had some seven hundred members in Pope and Yell Counties and had local organizations in Fields Chapel, Dardanelle, Prosperity, and Slaty Crossing.[134]

A week after these arrests were announced, an awkward paragraph appeared in the "Carden Bottom Items" section of the *Dardanelle Post-Dispatch* in which the correspondent referred to hundreds of cotton pickers working from sun-up to nightfall picking from between one to one and a half bales of cotton per acre and all the while "singin' and whistlin' and waving a 'cheery' hello as one passes."[135] It is unclear how realistic this portrayal was or whether it was a snub, or rebuffing, of the union organizing efforts. If so, was it the correspondent or the newspaper editor who wrote about happy, singing cotton pickers? These remain unanswered questions. What can be ascertained is the strong anti-organizing predisposition of landowners and many Dardanelle businessmen, all of whom depended on cotton pickers and farm day laborers to bring in the crops upon which their successes depended. Opposition to unionization of farm laborers was again bolstered in 1938, when the United States Congress, given strong lobbying from the American Farm Bureau, added an amendment to a farm wage bill that exempted rural laborers engaged in "the area of production, handling, packing, storing, ginning, compressing, pasteurizing, drying or canning of farm products, and in making cheese and butter" from coverage. The plight of farm laborers resulting from low wages and abusive working conditions continued for decades.

While cotton production was intentionally reduced, it was not eliminated, although serious outbreaks of armyworms, along with grasshopper and boll weevil infestations—especially during the 1930s—made some wonder whether cotton would survive.[136] Other crops were beginning to crowd cotton's old monopoly. As dairy cattle operations continued to grow and flourish, the Blue Valley Creamery was established in Dardanelle in 1932. The business prospered and 7,500 people participated in the plant's celebration of its third anniversary.[137] In 1938 this operation was purchased by Sugar Creek Creamery and was later moved to Russellville in 1945. The expanding poultry industry also was establishing its presence in Yell County. By 1935 the county reported a $200,000 annual poultry income, including $50,000 in the Dardanelle egg market. The county had three hatcheries (Ola, Dardanelle, and Danville) that together sold more than 75,000 baby chicks annually by the mid-1930s.[138]

A comparison of agricultural prices before and after the New Deal began reveals noticeable changes in the market price paid to farmers for certain commodities.[139]

| COMMODITY | FEBRUARY 1932 | FEBRUARY 1936 |
| --- | --- | --- |
| Cotton (per pound) | 5¢–6¢ | 12¢ |
| Corn (per bushel) | 15¢ | 60¢–75¢ |
| Hay (per bale) | 15¢ | 25¢–60¢ |
| Hogs (per pound) | 2¢–3¢ | 10¢ |
| Cattle (per pound) | No Market Data | 9¢ |
| Eggs (per dozen) | 6¢ | 25¢ |
| Poultry (per pound) | 7¢ | 21¢ |

In addition to these impressive farm price gains, measurable agricultural structural differences had occurred by 1936. Cotton farmers had used New Deal programs and instruction to improve soils, resulting in enlarged yields. The average yield per acre for cotton was 325 pounds in 1939, whereas it had been 304 pounds in 1938 and 193 pounds in 1928. Soil improvement efforts helped to enhance productivity. Acreage removed from cotton production during the 1930s had led to big increases in acreage devoted to other crops. This resulted in better-fed livestock as well as greater diversification and improved soil nutrition: 243,000 acres in corn, 42,500 acres in grain sorghum, 202,800 acres in soybeans, 312,000 acres in hay, and 257,000 acres in cowpeas. By comparing 1939 totals for head of stock to those of the five-year average of 1928 through 1932, impressive increases are seen: 258,600 more cattle,

380,400 more hogs, and 14,400 more sheep. Thus, the New Deal, particularly the Agricultural Adjustment Act, had transformed agriculture in Arkansas as elsewhere. From 1933 through 1939, Arkansas farmers received $100 million in benefit payments, which resulted in notable advances in productivity, improved care of the land, a more balanced set of crops, and improvement in the rural quality of life.[140] The New Deal worked, at least on a macroeconomic level.

Proof that cotton was not dead, at least not yet, was evident as two new cotton gins opened in Dardanelle between 1936 and 1941. The Farmers Gin—owned and managed by W. H. McClure and located on the south side of Front and Mill Streets—operated on the site of the old Arkansas Valley Cotton Oil Company and opened on August 1, 1936, with $20,000 worth of updated equipment.[141] The Tilmon Gin—operated by Dan Keenan—opened in the space that once housed the Thomas Cox Machinery Company on the north side of Front and Oak Streets on August 1, 1941, following $20,000 worth of investment in updated equipment. For the next fifty years the McClure and Keenan families played a major role in agriculture in the Dardanelle Bottoms.

## Transportation

Even the trauma and demands posed by poor weather and the Great Depression, dominating forces that they were, did not erase other pre-existing, longstanding problems. One of these fundamental problems was transportation, especially in the Bottoms. In 1935, M. L. McBride of Carden Bottom wrote an eloquent and enlightening essay in the *Dardanelle Post-Dispatch* regarding the impact of the deplorable condition of the roads in this area, referring to Carden Bottom as "a land of suction and production," heavily populated and having roads so bad as to generate excessive hardship and constant profanity. McBride points out the irony of farmers having automobiles that sit idle during the winter months because roads are impassable. He noted that mud-holes swallowed up cars, trucks, and even wagons; forced people to use horses and mules; and required the population to trudge in mud up to their ankles in order to move from place to place. Consequently, people kept their children home from school and kept their mules in the barn in order to protect them. Mail carriers were forced to park their cars and walk miles trudging through the slick mud in order to deliver mail to the five separate Bottom's stores that served as mail stations. McBride demanded road improvement.[142]

On March 11, 1930, a special election revealed overwhelming approval (2,838 to 67) for the establishment of a new county highway plan to be developed and managed by a county road commission composed of three members, one of whom must be the county judge.[143] By late 1930, Yell County judge F. D. Majors had purchased new road equipment, and thus the county then owned three caterpillars and three graders and reported the county roads in good shape, although there was a need for many new culverts.[144] The truth is that, although the need was great, very little improvement was made on rural roads during the 1930s. Not until dirt roads were upgraded to asphalt or concrete—which only began in the 1950s—would the problems of mud and "suction" and the resulting impassability be solved. Even in the 1950s and 1960s, children living on county or farm roads would remove their shoes and walk in deep, sometimes nearly frozen, muddy slush—sometimes up to their ankles—in order to reach the school bus pick-up point frequently up to two miles from their homes. Such had been the case since school buses came into use.[145] These facts were obvious in 1932 when heavy rain made the dirt roads impassable to school buses. School was dismissed in Dardanelle for two days and a collection of faculty, students, and patrons spent the days trying to improve the roads so that the district's nine school buses could safely traverse their routes.[146] In 1936 one vacationer on Mount Petit Jean observed that the road from Centerville through the Bottoms (Highway 154, a graveled dirt road) was "nothing to brag about but it is passable—by being careful."[147] An Arkansas road map printed in the *Dardanelle Post-Dispatch* in late July 1930 documented no paved roads into the Dardanelle Bottoms.[148]

The greatest interest in road improvements on the part of the townspeople dealt with the major state highways (Numbers 22, 27, and 7), three of the four state highways that directly connected with Dardanelle. In 1930, the Highway Number Seven Association was formed to advocate for the completion of Highway 7 from Russellville to Hot Springs, although it would be 1952 before Highway 7 was paved between the two cities.[149] The concrete resurfacing of Highway 22 from Dardanelle to Fort Smith was completed by the spring of 1930 and most of Highway 27 from Dardanelle into Sebastian County was completed by the same time.[150] Rural roads, however, remained unimproved (see Appendix, fig. 1).

Two additional transportation transitions took place during the 1930s. First, in February 1938, the Interstate Commerce Commission authorized the abandonment of the twenty-six-mile railroad line from Scranton (Logan County) to Dardanelle. They had previously authorized the abandonment of a branch line of the Chicago, Rock Island and Pacific (originally known as the Dardanelle, Ola, and Southern Railroad) from Dardanelle to Ola. The only rail service into Dardanelle was, thus, the Dardanelle and Russellville (D&R), a short line carrying passengers and freight to and from North Dardanelle and Russellville over a five-mile route. Although the D&R remains a working short line rail today, all other railroad services to Dardanelle ended in 1938 (see Appendix, fig. 7).[151] Second, in June 1938, the Arkansas Legislature relieved the taxpayers of the Free Bridge District in Dardanelle of their existing $16,818.75 debt ($11,000 in bonds and $5,818.75 interest due before September 1, 1938) on the Dardanelle "Free" Bridge, which opened in 1929.[152] These changes during the 1930s were indicative of the decade's transportation's transitions as emphasis on rail reliance declined while growing concern over highway developments increased.

## Education

Education also experienced important transitions during the 1930s. In 1929 Arkansas had 3,193 school districts that employed 12,953 teachers. The funding for many schools, especially rural one-room schools, was limited. As the Depression worsened, teacher salaries—which averaged $643 annually in 1931—fell to $540 in 1932, with some teachers paid only partial salaries or none at all. By 1933, Arkansas had 725 school closures and another 1,200 announced shortened terms due to a lack of local and state funding.[153] Public education was in crisis.

The Dardanelle Chamber of Commerce launched a school consolidation effort urging the county board of education to approve bringing fourteen of the separate school districts in Yell County together.[154] Of these fourteen schools, two were in the Upper Bottoms: Fields Chapel and Riverside. The county board approved their consolidation with the Dardanelle District on May 16, 1930.[155] Following this consolidation, the Dardanelle School District became the largest in Yell County, reporting a total enrollment of 1,565 with an operating budget of $1,419,080, double both figures for the nearest-sized district, Danville.

Most rural residents were much in favor of consolidation, arguing that a consolidated district could provide a higher quality of education than could the numerous smaller rural districts.[156] In late June 1930, the Dardanelle District began advertising bonds in order to secure funds for a new high school building, estimated to cost $60,000. The foundation of this structure, located on the northeast portion of the city block between North Second and West Streets, was completed in June 1931, with the building opening in September 1931.[157] Meanwhile, the Carden Bottom Consolidated High School, School District No. 67, continued its operations with a 1931 enrollment of six hundred students, a faculty consisting of thirteen teachers, and its first graduating class of eleven students.[158] By 1932, Yell County had eight consolidated high schools and twenty-two total school districts within its 955 square miles.[159]

Obviously education was a priority for most Yell County citizens. Trouble was brewing, however, given the excessive numbers of delinquent property tax receipts first noticed in 1930. By 1932 these delinquencies posed a major financial problem for the schools. Between 1930 and 1931, schools lost 20 percent of their funding, as delinquencies in property tax payments increased statewide. The $2,189,658.67 decrease in tax revenue was the primary cause of a total decrease in school funding of $3,715,157.63 in 1931.[160]

In early November 1933, the Dardanelle District was forced to close briefly because of insufficient funding. School officials requested federal funds but only received short-term assistance from the Arkansas Emergency Relief Fund that allowed the schools to reopen on November 29.[161] In 1934 the schools did not open until October 15 as officials were waiting and hoping for federal aid disbursement to arrive. Staff was severely reduced, requiring the placement of fifty-five to sixty students in each class.[162] On February 28, 1935, all federal aid to Arkansas schools was withdrawn, but the Dardanelle schools continued to operate as teachers worked without pay. In lieu of salaries, the Dardanelle School District issued warrants to teachers that were honored by J. J. Boyce at the Dardanelle Mercantile allowing teachers to purchase groceries, dry goods, shoes, and livestock feed.[163]

In February 1935, a federal lawsuit was filed against the Dardanelle schools for nonpayment of interest and bonds. As this case was awaiting trial, the Dardanelle District, without any disbursement of operating funds, could not open school until a settlement or judgment was reached. A temporary disbursement was ordered by the district court and schools opened on September 30, 1935.[164] The case was settled and the school began to require a small tuition payment as it continued to operate with reduced and unpaid staff. By 1937 state funding for public schools had slightly increased, primarily because of improved general revenue collection efforts, and, although property tax delinquencies remained high, they had decreased since earlier in the 1930s.[165] This lingering basis for the school's financial problems became obvious as the Dardanelle schools closed on April 11, 1941, because of a lack of funds based on falling attendance numbers, a reduction of 50 percent in property tax assessments, and hundreds of delinquencies in property tax payments. The only way to avoid the loss of the school term and to reopen the schools was to charge tuition. The Parent-Teacher Association president, Lucy May Williams, and Dardanelle mayor, Reese Batson, held a well-attended public meeting on April 15, 1941, calling for support of the tuition plan and asking local businessmen and school patrons to donate funds so that families who could not afford to pay tuition might still be able to have their children in school. The tuition plan required a $3.50 tuition payment for students in grades nine through twelve, a tuition payment of $3.00 for those in grades seven and eight and $2.00 per student in grades one through six.[166] The 1941 school term was completed in May and again, as in previous decades, the citizens of Dardanelle demonstrated their support for education.

The back story of education funding in Arkansas from 1930 to 1937 involved the question of who—federal, state, or local governments —was responsible for funding. Added to this debate, which transpired during a time of dwindling funds, was the tension caused by the different viewpoints of the fiscally conservative governor Marion Futrell, the Arkansas General Assembly, and William Reynolds Dyess,

Arkansas's Federal Emergency Relief Administration (FERA) administrator. Dyess pushed for federal funds to aid financially distressed school districts. Harry Hopkins, FERA's national administrator, did not want federal funds disbursed to local school districts. Caught in the middle of this confusion and turmoil were 3,193 Arkansas school districts and their 12,953 teachers. Sadly, Dyess was killed in a plane crash; Hopkins refused to issue additional FERA funds to operate Arkansas public schools after 1936; and the General Assembly began to enact new school funding tax legislation. Had it not been for FERA funds from 1933 to 1936, a time when the governor and legislature were doing nothing to solve the funding crisis, Arkansas public schools would have ceased operations.[167]

## Health and Disease

Another area in which transition was the primary theme during the 1930s was health care, which can be characterized as taking two steps forward followed by one step back. The work of previous decades clearly had created more institutional systems and procedures for addressing health needs. Thus, during the 1930s, the residents of Dardanelle and the Bottoms received improved health care, but many of the old diseases and maladies remained. The Yell County Health Department rendered excellent service, continually informing citizens of the causes and preventive measures needed for diseases like typhoid fever, as well as holding clinics for smallpox and diphtheria immunization.[168] In the fiscal year ending on June 30, 1930, alone, they administered 7,283 typhoid doses, 3,465 toxin-antitoxins, 1,738 additional vaccinations, performed 3,068 preschool and school health examinations, issued 5,196 health informational bulletins/presentations, and performed 1,511 sanitary inspections.[169]

As the Great Depression grew worse and the health of many citizens declined accordingly, in May 1931, a local health unit was formed by medical personnel from the county health department and twenty-nine women from prominent Dardanelle families. Its purpose was to provide free health care for indigent citizens.[170] In addition to "normal" outbreaks, such as the influenza cases in late 1932 and early 1933 in both Dardanelle and the Bottoms, the 1936 smallpox outbreaks in the Bottoms, the sixty-four cases of trachoma diagnosed and treated in 1941, and the seventeen cases of rabies treated in 1935, the Yell County Health Department treated a variety of other health problems.[171] In 1935 alone, they dealt with 173 cases of pellagra, 258 cases of scabies, 7 cases of gonorrhea, 37 cases of tuberculosis, 183 cases of malaria, 26 cases of measles, 18 cases of typhoid fever, 16 cases of whooping cough (pertussis), and small numbers of other diseases. In addition, the department aggressively performed immunizations, pre-natal care, sanitation inspections and improvements, and performed several thousand infant, preschool, and school examinations.[172]

The predominant nutrition-related disease in the state, as it had been during previous decades, was pellagra. As noted earlier, pellagra is caused by a niacin (Vitamin B3) deficiency and causes its victims to present with extreme lethargy coupled with progressive skin disor-ders, weight loss, and ultimate organ failure. The food shortages and the large degree of malnutrition people endured during the drought of 1930–1931 and in the Great Depression, similar to but in much longer duration than those suffered following the flood of 1927, heightened the number and the intensity of pellagra cases in Arkansas. Even prior to the most severe years of the Great Depression, in 1929 alone 657 persons in Arkansas died from pellagra.[173]

As noted above and irrespective of the severity of numerous seri-ous health challenges during the 1930s, public health efforts in Yell County were far-reaching and effective. This was possible given the efforts of earlier decades that set a foundation for public health out-reach programs. These efforts appeared to unite both town and rural citizens. While the more affluent townspeople actively promoted pub-lic health activities, the poorer rural residents also participated in large numbers and, thus, social class did not inhibit one's engagement in improved public health, although it did determine the form of one's involvement. The affluent lectured and organized, while the poor lis-tened and participated.

While one can conclude that public health as a separate field was maturing and developing during the 1930s, its emphasis was still pri-marily on the diagnoses and treatments of major diseases, whereas the contemporary focus of public health has advanced to the point of emphasis on prevention via the adoption of healthier lifestyles including improved diets, nutrition, and lifestyle choices. Certainly this was not yet the case in the 1930s, as seen in a 1937 exchange between two women from Liberty Hall:

> One of my neighbors came to call this morning. I saw her face was smeared with grease. I said, "My goodness, Mrs.——, you have grease from ear to ear!" She replied, "That proves that I've had breakfast." I really know sausage or maybe it was spareribs were served at her home this morning.[174]

## Women

If education and health were transitioning elements during the 1930s, women's roles were not. They remained fairly static based on social class and race, although minor changes occurred. During the first years of this decade, women's clubs pursued their longstanding agendas, such as community clean-up campaigns and keeping town chickens properly penned.[175] Many long-established women's clubs, such as the United Daughters of the Confederacy, continued to function, as did more recently formed organizations such as the Mozart Club and the Philharmonic Club.[176] Women's church organizations continued to meet and hold their usual functions, but the turnouts were usually smaller and somehow they seemed less festive than in earlier years.[177]

Regardless of the continuity of women's organizations' agendas and functional style, there was a difference. So many of the women of the past two decades and earlier, who had spearheaded civic efforts and organized Dardanelle's women into effective workers, were now gone. For example, Ella Crownover, who had managed Dardanelle's World War I Red Cross workroom, and Mrs. L. C. Hall, previous UDC local president and regional and national vice president and founder of the Ladies Auxiliary of the Presbyterian Church, both died in late 1931. The new generation of women who were assuming leadership roles were younger and not always as privileged in wealth and time as had been their predecessors. The *pro forma* of women's clubs, their activities and stated purposes, remained largely unchanged, but there were subtle differences beginning to emerge in their leadership. In March 1932, a new women's club, the Philharmonic Club, organized as the established groups, such as the Civic Club, the United Daughters of the Confederacy, and the Cemetery Association continued their work.[178] Of course, some people maintained the belief that women should remain primarily domestic and uphold strict standards of modesty and virtue. As one Ola citizen noted in 1935, "on our way back to normalcy, isn't there something we can do to get the girls' nails out of the red?"[179] The answer, of course, for many women was "No" as skirts remained shorter and nails were painted red. These were small, but emblematic, symbols of more far-reaching gender-role prescriptions.

In the Bottoms, women's clubs were primarily the Home Demonstration Clubs. Entertainment in the Bottoms was not the sole prerogative of women. A 1932 party in Centerville hosted both young and older men as well as women and featured games; songs with violin, guitar, and harmonic music; candy making; and roasted peanuts and popped corn and reportedly provided a delightful Saturday night.[180] When there was a "women's party" in the Bottoms, it was usually a demonstration of community spirit and self-help. For example, on February 14, 1933, Miss Modean Cain of Centerville hosted a gift shower for Mrs. Percy George, whose Ola home and its entire contents had been destroyed by fire six days earlier. Approximately eighteen people attended, enjoyed a lovely Valentine's theme luncheon, and presented Mrs. George with useful and beautiful gifts as did others who were unable to attend in person.[181]

Doris Hundley Hickey was born in 1929 at Bryant's Cove, a little hamlet just south of Carden Bottom. She recalled that "everybody took care of everybody else. . . . there wasn't a lot of greed and envy among the people down there. If you could help somebody, you just did it. Nobody had to nudge you, you just did it. Roots run deep. It was a wonderful place to live."[182]

The differences between the "old-fashioned woman" and the woman emerging during the 1930s were described in two different writings appearing in the *Dardanelle Post-Dispatch*. First, a 1930 letter to the editor deplored modern changes in women's lives:

> When I was a boy the hired girl cooked, cleaned house and did the family wash and every Saturday night drew the fabulous sum of $2 and felt her importance. A bobbed-haired woman was considered a "high stepper," and a skirt that did not completely cover

the ankle was an unknown article in feminine wearing apparel. . . . Today . . . everybody rides in automobiles . . . they play golf, shoot craps, dance the Charleston, . . . go to the movies nightly. . . . These are the days of suffragetting, profiteering, short skirts, bobbed hair, excess taxes and prohibition.[183]

Second, a 1937 editorial presented a somewhat more appreciative, although skeptical, view of the modern woman:

For the past several years I have been viewing with alarm the encroachment of women upon the rights and prerogatives of men. My attention was first focused upon this matter in the schools of the state. It is a matter of common knowledge that more girls are graduating than boys. This means that more girls are going to be qualified for the white-collared jobs than boys, which finally means that more women are going to be prepared than men. Now, this thing seems to have no ending. Women's clubs, political if you please: women sheriffs, women senators and representatives—women taking over most everything. . . . I'm not complaining. . . . But I am saying that men had better look out or they are going to lose out. . . . All that a man has left absolutely for him and for no one else is singing bass.[184]

Thus, it is quite apparent that women were experiencing subtle but meaningful changes during the 1930s, but still they remained more like those of previous decades when compared to the whirlwind of changes that would occur and alter women's lives in later decades. The nature of women's lives including educational attainment, employment opportunities, leisure activities, health care, and their status within society were still primarily determined by their social class and race.

## Crime

During the 1930s, crime was prevalent in and around Dardanelle. It could be classified frequently as associated with one of four categories: liquor, economic survival needs, passion, or greed. The following are representative case studies illustrating these categories of criminal motivations.

First, liquor reappeared legally as prohibition was repealed by the Twenty-First Amendment to the US Constitution on December 5,

1933. Then, in a special election held on July 18, 1935, Yell County voted to repeal the countywide ban on alcohol by a vote of 792 for and 675 against.[185] A few months earlier on March 30, 1935, the Sullivan Liquor Store was opened on the northwest corner of Front and South Main Streets directly across from the Singer Drug Store. For the first time since 1899, liquor could be legally sold in Dardanelle, although illegal liquor activity had been a constant, longstanding fact.[186] Strong opposition in Dardanelle to liquor sales was warranted by factual evidence. Earlier, in July 1934, Elmer Coffman died following an afternoon and evening of gambling and drinking on the riverbank. This resulted in a broken leg following a "friendly scuffle" with a fellow participant. Although he was seen by a doctor, his companions found Coffman deceased the next morning.[187] Then, in November 1938, Dardanelle's city marshal received significant knife wounds to his arm and neck while successfully arresting a man on Sunday afternoon for public drunkenness.[188] In early 1939, prosecuting attorney A. B. Priddy urged citizens to take more interest in law enforcement and support a crackdown on rowdy beer joints because "they are nuisances, crime breeders, the scenes of frequent fights or disturbances . . . with beer or whiskey being sold to minors or to habitual drunkards."[189] Nonetheless, another liquor permit was issued for a Front Street store the following month and legal liquor continued to flow in Dardanelle until the mid-1950s, a fact that regularly resulted in violence.[190]

A second category of crime during the 1930s was based on simple survival needs. In January 1937, a Dardanelle grocery store was robbed of three sacks of flour, two buckets of lard, some tobacco, several pairs of overalls, and one dollar's worth of pennies.[191] The White Castle Restaurant in Dardanelle was robbed in April 1935 with the offenders taking cash and food.[192] Other small store burglaries occurred as well as several area bank robberies during the 1930s. While not a crime (other than trespassing), but certainly a tale that underscores people's economic plight, in 1935 two families moved themselves into a chicken house for shelter and evicted the chickens to the trees and the yard.[193] Crimes of apparent need—and perhaps also greed—include a series of gasoline robberies in 1932 involving the cars of Mayor Reese Batson, a Dardanelle police officer, and a visitor to Dardanelle from Little Rock. The culprits escaped even though the police officer, Jeff Ellis, emptied his revolver at the vehicle.[194]

As with any era, there were also some grisly violent crimes involving passion during the 1930s. One in particular was that of J. A. Coleman's stabbing of his stepdaughter and wife prior to setting his house on fire and burning their bodies. Then, he took poison as police tried to arrest him in North Dardanelle. All of this was witnessed by the stepdaughter's two young children and Coleman's nine-year-old son.[195] Another attempted murder-suicide (husband-upon-wife-crime) occurred in Danville in 1933. In addition, the murders of four African Americans from 1933 to 1939 and several rape cases highlight the crime during this period.[196]

There were also crimes motivated by greed such as the 1934 stabbing death, in the middle of *El Dorado* ("Tuff" Street) in Dardanelle, of Lucius Shilling by his former restaurant business partner, Claude Cook, over the ownership of a cooking stove.[197] Other crimes of greed involved arson of a competitor's business as well as robbery and fights over the control of illegal liquor.[198] Of course, gambling violations continued to be quite common, as in previous decades, with ninety-five arrests and seventy-five convictions for gaming in April 1932 alone.[199] Moonshining and bootlegging were also still fairly common and occasionally were prosecuted.[200] Election fraud, however, while discussed and debated with great interest, was not prosecuted.[201]

## Race

In this Jim Crow era, the state of race relations also reveals a side of the area's social history. By 1930 the African American population of Dardanelle and the Bottoms and their white counterparts had settled into an accepted, static state of segregation with both groups needing continued reassurance. Whites relied on Jim Crow practices as proof of their racial superiority, and African Americans used this racist system to allow for their cocooned safety within the segregated status quo system. This was a carefully executed dance, a balance catering to the demands of the status quo while tipping one's hat to the accepted boundaries of inequality that the system imposed, while simultaneously nurturing some practice of racial acknowledgment but not inclusion. This all worked well, as long as both African Americans and whites stayed in their appropriately assigned societal "place." The 1930s, therefore, was an incredibly racist period in the history of

Dardanelle and the Bottoms, since most people seemingly accepted these racist concepts and practices. As people are fond of saying, it was a different time, a time of unprotested racism.

The effects of these racist practices were extensive. This reality can clearly be seen in the notice of death of Gus Scott, who died on July 11, 1931, following several years of declining health after suffering a knee injury that was never medically treated. The notice of his death below—not a true obituary—says much about this almost innate level of racism:

> Gus was a negro of the type the true Southerner loves. A giant in stature, he had the native gentleness of a woman and a heart as big as all outdoors. Respectful, kindly, courteous, there was yet nothing servile about him, and he possessed in a marked degree the true dignity that marks the real man. . . . Though proud of his boundless strength, he was never boastful. . . . The writer has known Gus for more than 30 years, and has always admired his sunny, cheerful disposition, his kindly, considerate nature and his magnificent, beautifully muscled body . . .he faced the Grim Reaper as he faced every other contingency of life, smiling and unafraid.[202]

Ironically, directly preceding this notice was the announcement of the death of another Dardanelle African American, ninety-eight-year-old "Uncle Cairo" Toney, a former slave. Again, one can detect the racist undertone thinly cloaked in superficial praise: "though not an ordained minister, 'Uncle Cairo' was a religious lecturer of more than local repute, and also a great debater on subjects both religious and secular."[203]

In either notice no mention was made of the deceased men's families, personal histories, or place of interment. These notices were not to honor the two deceased African American men but rather were written to address the sense of loss their deaths caused the white community, the loss of a "colored man" that a real southerner could appreciate given his "gentleness of a woman and sunny disposition" and a dedicated but, of course, untrained "religious lecturer." Furthermore, these men's lives were celebrated only to the degree and in the manner they "fit" into the white concept of race and societal place in the 1930s.

The white citizens of Dardanelle were careful to include the "colored people" in public efforts, such as the solicitation of Red Cross donations and the public presentations by the African American school (the Douglas School) in the Tuberculosis Easter Seal Drive.[204] Even when being publicly acclaimed for their voluntary public-spirited efforts, African Americans were reminded of their subservient place with "complimentary" language like "Dardanelle has the most patriotic industrious and law-abiding citizenship in Dixie ... [who] ... in every worthy undertaking lend whole-hearted support and fullest co-operation."[205] Indeed, nothing delights the heart of a racist as much as the presence of good colored folks who know their role, their place, and do their public duty while not causing trouble or disturbing the status quo of the accepted societal racial model.

Racist jokes that suggested most African Americans were liars appeared on the front page of the *Dardanelle Post-Dispatch* fairly regularly; and the editor related the fact that he was asked by an illiterate African American to write a letter to the man's wife, who was confined in a Little Rock hospital, to inform her that their two sons had died. Few if any residents of Dardanelle understood the racism these stories manifested. At least, no one objected.[206]

Meanwhile, African Americans did what African Americans had grown accustomed to doing: they persevered. African Methodist Episcopal ministers spoke out against stores opening on Sundays and breaking the Sabbath. African Americans in Riverside held picnics. Newspaper reports insinuated that Aunt Easter Rosebud, whose home burned to the ground, was happy knowing she had a "Home on High Left," even though on earth she only had two quilts and the clothes she was wearing. An attempt to raise money for an elderly African American couple, former slaves from Mississippi, whose home and belongings were destroyed by fire, failed, while newspaper reports called them respected, good citizens.[207] Racism was manifested in every facet of life.

It was almost appropriate that, as the last of the surviving former slaves living in Dardanelle—"Uncle" Paul Fowkles—was dying in the late 1930s, so too was the last Confederate soldier from Yell County—Joseph J. Jackson—who died on March 1, 1941.[208] And, just as in life, the reports of these deaths were also inequitable. Mr. Fowkles was given a seven-line public notice with minimal information on page five, whereas Mr. Jackson's obituary was 112 lines and seven paragraphs in length, filled with extensive personal information and history and appeared on page one. During the 1930s, racism was present in death as in life as it had been for many decades. Racism was so apparent that no one seemed to notice it.

## Leisure and Recreation

In other areas, such as leisure and recreation, activities appeared fairly simple during the 1930s. Of course, the Great Depression was a fundamental reason for this, but the reality was that a new generation of Dardanelle women did not seem as inclined toward lavish or refined entertainment as were those of previous times. Entertainment in Dardanelle was sparse and lacking ostentatiousness. Afternoon bridge games, a few women's club sponsored events, and church forums characterized most of the 1930s entertainment venues. In 1931 the Civic Club sponsored a "proper" benefit party to raise funds for town beautification projects. The afternoon party included bridge games, refreshments, and a performance by an African American all-male choir.[209] Certainly, this was a "nice" affair, but it was not the high tone, glittering entertainment that Dardanelle's leading families engaged in during previous decades.

In the Bottoms, entertainment usually consisted of community singings of which there were many throughout the 1930s in various locations, as well as school or church-related events. One noteworthy example of the spirit of community so characteristic of the Bottoms was the all-day picnic and swimming excursion sponsored by Mrs. G. L. Potts for forty-four senior members of the Lakeview Sunday school that included three far-flung swimming sites and a huge picnic at each location.

> Anyone looking upon that lunch provided by those farm boys and girls would never associate the word "depression" with the Carden's Bottom country and the Lakeview community. Nothing was omitted from the fried chicken to the ice cream and cake— cakes rather, which made up the dessert ... Late in the afternoon (after the third swimming venue) there was a watermelon feast. ... This was really the "end of a perfect day."[210]

While Mrs. G. L. Potts was a celebrated hostess who managed gracious and sometimes quite elaborate social events, most of the entertainment in the Bottoms was much simpler, consisting of dances at home and popcorn parties, but always well attended and full of fun. Gordon Crain, born in 1926 at Stubbs Town, recalled the home dances held outside in people's yards, which generally attracted fifteen to twenty young people. Many people played music and he particularly recalled Harrison Manes, a fiddle player, and his son, Red, who played the guitar. Not trained musicians, Mr. Manes would use his foot to press down on Red's foot when the music called for a change in key, which sometimes caused Red to cry out in pain.[211]

Church socials, revivals, and prayer meetings were also a big part of rural social life as the church was a center for social gatherings, a community cornerstone in a hard but simple life.[212] Gordon Crain recalled that he and his twin brother, Jack, would even go to church because that was a good place to meet girls.[213] There were baptisms in the Petit Jean River near Pontoon with church members, families, and observers sitting on the slate riverbanks.[214] Church was as much a social gathering place as it was a place for religious observance: "Lots of people went to church, nowhere else to go!"[215]

In the dry summers of the early- to mid-1930s Gordon Crain remembered that frequently ten to fifteen boys would walk across the low-level Arkansas River at Stubbs Town and go to Atkins, some six miles away, to take in the movies. "The shows started at ten in the morning and ran all day and the river, when the river was low it was only ankle deep then. As a young kid we were always looking for something to do."[216]

In Carden Bottom, especially, entertainment centered around Carden Bottom High School as both school and community events were held there and almost always guaranteed a large community turnout. Carden Bottom was a highly cohesive area, some would say clannish, and its communities and residents supported one another and exhibited great pride in and loyalty to all things in Carden Bottom. Doris Hundley Hickey recalled:

> An organization in Carden Bottom would have 90 percent participation for the simple reason those people didn't have anything else to do. They couldn't go to Oklahoma and gamble or drive to Wal-Mart to buy something. Everybody used Carden Bottom High School. The HD Club used study hall for cooking classes and we had pie suppers for fund-raisers. Any worthy

cause and everybody would jump in and support it. There was a closeness, a friendliness in Carden Bottom. Yes, Carden Bottom people were clannish![217]

Gordon Crain also remembered the closeness of the Carden Bottom people, stating that they were "like a family and it's still that way, but we're all dying out now."[218]

In the other areas of the Bottoms, life was slightly less community centered and the most typical forms of entertainment involved singings held at the school, at the church, and at the annual Decoration Day activities. The Hartford Music School (Hartford, Arkansas), which published shape note singing books and employed numerous singing instructors, frequently held well-attended singing conventions in the Bottoms. Locals enjoyed the social side of these singing schools as well as the music. These gatherings were well advertised and extremely popular. While singing schools were more of a rural affair and were not held in Dardanelle, the Dardanelle Decoration Day at Brearley Cemetery was also a major formal event just as the more informal cemetery clean-up and decorating ceremonies were in the Bottoms.

Although rare, there were some entertainments in the Bottoms similar to those in town. An example was a Centerville card party, hosted by Olita Chandler, with prizes awarded for the high scores, refreshments served, and the home "artistically decorated with dogwood blossoms and narcissus."[219]

One form of entertainment popular in Dardanelle and the Bottoms was baseball. As previously noted almost everyone was a baseball fan or player. Dardanelle had produced some skilled major and minor league players, notably Carey Selph, third baseman with the Chicago White Sox, and Dizzy and Paul Dean from Chickalah (twelve miles west of Dardanelle), each of whom became major league baseball players. Dizzy soon become a star pitcher for the St. Louis Cardinals. Dizzy and brother Paul had chopped and picked cotton for Charley Shepard in Fields Chapel in the late 1920s and spent part of the winter of 1931 with their family hunting around Dardanelle.[220] In November 1931, Dizzy and Paul played a Sunday afternoon game in Dardanelle with Dizzy playing for the Dardanelle team and Paul playing for the Plainview team.[221] Baseball was played throughout the Bottoms with numerous hamlets having their own teams and playing an organized season of games with other town teams. In Lakeview, G. L. Potts allowed teams to play Sunday afternoon games in the pasture directly across from his store. He did a steady business of selling cold drinks and snacks to those attending. Occasionally, he arranged for African American teams to play there. This brought out a big crowd of observers.[222] In Liberty Hall, Isodore Thompson, the son of an African American tenant farmer, also loved to play baseball and recalled that a game could be played on a schoolyard, a pasture, or a vacant field.[223]

Young Isodore also loved to play music. His parents, Mr. and Mrs. Elton Thompson, were singers in the Sweet Home Baptist Church Choir, an African American congregation whose members took part in singing conventions as far away as Fayetteville and Fort Smith. Isodore played string instruments—the guitar, fiddle, and banjo—by ear. He and friends would play every night at someone's home. When he became an adult, he formed a band called the "Sunrisers." The band played at juke joints like the Blue Moon Café in Dardanelle during the 1950s and 1960s.[224] Entertainment venues during the 1930s, like other aspects of life, were strictly segregated, although Isodore said that, by the 1950s and 1960s, the Sunrisers had attracted some white fans.

By 1940 a hint of the old entertainment elegance had returned to Dardanelle. The Dardanelle Garden Club Tea, hosted by its one hundred members, displayed more than fifty floral designs and was held in the Reese Batson home, which was fully decorated with fresh flowers. The hostesses served punch and refreshments from a lace cloth, presented several readings, and the entire affair was managed by nine senior club ladies in full-length afternoon gowns.[225] Yes, this was a gracious social function that would have made the Dardanelle ladies of twenty-five years earlier feel at home. Although, for most people, entertainment was less elaborate: taking in a movie, watching a baseball game, attending a church social, or just enjoying a piece of homemade pineapple pie at the White Castle Café on Union Street in Dardanelle.

## Depression Era Transitions

The decade of the 1930s was a hardscrabble time for Dardanelle. The town's dichotomous relationship with the Bottoms was one reason for this disastrous decade of economic difficulty. Dardanelle remained tied to its role as a regional farm-to-market town and, as farming changed due to the new Depression era governmental policies, the town needed to adjust its role and rethink its basis for existence. Unfortunately, this did not happen or it only marginally occurred. There were attempts to bring new businesses to Dardanelle, but they were agriculturally based, and so the town did not break out of its original mindset as a hub existing primarily to serve and benefit from its rural agricultural surroundings. One could still make money in Dardanelle, but now it required more skill, greater risks, and a willingness to change with the changing times. Coincidentally, during the 1930s (more precisely, from 1903 to 1938) Russellville, the little town to the north in Pope County, began to grow and develop as it transformed itself from "a straggling country town to one of Arkansas's most progressive small cities."[226] Why? Leadership that resulted in a more balanced economy and new businesses that were not solely/directly dependent on agriculture seemed to be the answer. Meanwhile, Dardanelle remained steadfast in its adherence to a nineteenth-century agricultural-based economy. And still, for another four decades or so, this more or less worked, although the frayed places in Dardanelle's economic fabric were beginning to show during the 1930s.

Despite the Great Depression and recurring drought, there were some brighter moments in 1931, such as a brief stop by humorist Will Rogers in Dardanelle while en route to a fund-raiser at the Arkansas Polytechnic College Armory for the Red Cross. Rogers's performance was an effort to emphasize courage and optimism, although, by 1931, most people were experiencing dark and difficult days.[227] More and more families were seeking aid from the Red Cross, increasing numbers of property owners were unable to pay their property taxes (the largest list of delinquencies ever compiled as of May 1931), and the Dardanelle School District announced it might have to close after a seven-month term due to lack of operating funds. Then, on January 22, 1931, the First National Bank suffered a run, closed its doors, and left the town without a bank for the first time in forty-three years.[228] Fifty-five farmers had already applied for government loans by mid-February 1931, but the processing was delayed for six weeks due to the use of improper application forms.[229] Meanwhile, by late February, Singer Drug Store—the local Rexall franchisee—announced it would fill customers' prescriptions free of charge, and parents throughout Yell County were enrolling children in school in order to have them access the free lunch.[230] The same newspaper edition in late March carried the report of the death of Colonel Marcellus L. Davis, Dardanelle lawyer, respected resident, former United States consul to Trinidad and the Yucatan, Arkansas adjutant general (1902–1904), and the person who had eloquently nominated the racist demagogue Jeff Davis for governor in 1900. Also included was the report stating that only ten living Confederate veterans remained in Yell County.[231] These were bleak times for sure that seemed to almost signal a changing of the guard, the end of something and the beginning of some new but yet undefined life.

Nonetheless, amid the uncertainty and anguish—and there was much of both from 1930 through 1932—the tenacity and determination that had long characterized Dardanelle and the Bottoms had not vanished. A group of local businessmen organized an intermediate credit bank that was set to open on April 1, 1931; and in late March, a new general merchandise retail operation, the Dardanelle Mercantile Company, held its formal opening with great ceremony and celebration.[232] Farmers and townspeople decided to forego the expense of automobile license fees, gasoline, and oil and once again Dardanelle's alleys were filled with mules, wagons, and horses. A young University of Arkansas student, determined to earn the money to continue his schooling, reopened for a second summer his River Oak Miniature Golf Course on North Front Street.[233] Depression, drought, and difficulty did not break the people of Dardanelle or the Bottoms. For a few, the stress was too much and, sadly, reports of suicide were too frequent, but most people coped and, as change came, they adapted and moved forward.

The Blue Valley Creamery Company established a butter plant in Dardanelle opening on May 18, 1932, a result of the dairy program that had been created among area farmers during the previous ten years.[234] The poultry farmers of the area began to organize in order to develop a marketing plan for their chickens and eggs.[235] Fred Smith, respected agriculture educator and promoter, began to advocate a move away from cotton and toward cattle, citing the presence of abundant twelve-month-a-year grazing lands coupled with less overhead costs and a better livestock market.[236] Even among some good news, the local newspaper in 1932 contained two to three full pages of delinquent property taxpayers' names, multiple foreclosure notices every week, business liquidation notices with property for sale, and numerous church suppers and prayer meeting announcements. No doubt about it, these were tough times. Thus, it was sad but fitting that, on December 29, 1932, it was announced that the old Jacoway home was now vacant. The intersection of South Main (now Market Street) and Third Streets had once been the site of four gracious homes belonging to four powerful, moneyed Dardanelle families: the Jacoways, the Crownovers, the Bullocks, and the Kaufmans.[237] Now these lovely structures were either gone or vacant and their previous occupants had moved from Dardanelle or were now deceased. Likewise, the younger members of the Catlett family had mainly moved to Little Rock a few years earlier. Transition and change were definitely taking place as Dardanelle was losing its best "old families," the ones who had long been the backbone of the town, both socially and economically. Structures and businesses could be replaced perhaps, but the tenacious leadership and successes earned by leading businessmen could not. Their loss would affect the town and the Bottoms. However, few people took notice of this in the early 1930s as most folks were simply trying to stay alive and keep their livelihoods afloat. Besides, change was soon to be the watchword as New Deal Depression-fighting methods and programs rolled out of Washington and into the lives of the citizens of Dardanelle and the Bottoms.

The Agricultural Adjustment Act sought to reduce cotton acreage by 40 percent and thus hold prices higher while also providing an incentive parity payment to farmers based on the buying power of the 1909 to 1914 average cotton price. The local logistics were administered by a county allotment committee, which executed contracts with the government and presented farmers with their payments for reducing cotton acreage. When first announced in 1933, it was hoped that the AAA would create 10-cent-a-pound cotton.[238] A small testimonial as to the great need for this program was the fact that some tenant farmers from Slaty Crossing went to Missouri in the fall of 1933 to find work as seasonal cotton pickers.[239] By early 1933, estimates showed that a potential 1933 production of 17.5 million bales of cotton (without the

AAA implementation) would have yielded 5-cents-a-pound cotton and a total crop income of $437.5 million, whereas, given the AAA plan for plowing up cotton fields and reducing acreage, the actual 1933 production was 13.1 million bales with an average price of 9-cents-a-pound and a total income of $749.5 million.[240]

As New Deal programs stabilized the cotton market, other related businesses also improved. By 1935 the local Planters Compress Company was installing $25,000 worth of new equipment, including a modern steel water storage tank and sprinkler system, and was able to produce tens of thousands of bales of cotton annually.[241] The New Deal's AAA saved the cotton farmer, although many tenant farmers and day laborers were displaced. In Arkansas, this appeared to be more of a problem in the Delta than in the Dardanelle Bottoms. As Pete Daniel and other historians point out, however, the New Deal, through programs like the AAA, primarily benefited the larger land-owners and began the permanent alteration both in how agriculture was conducted and in the farmer's relationship to the government.[242] New Deal policies created sweeping change. At least, the boll weevils and armyworms remained unaffected.

The Civilian Conservation Corps (CCC) also posed a mighty presence in Dardanelle. The Veteran Civilian Conservation Corps (VCCC) Camp No. 1780 was located on Mount Nebo. Some two hundred veterans of World War I served in this organization, and they reinvigorated the mountain with their works and their presence. None of these men was from the immediate Dardanelle area and, thus, within several months of their arrival on the mountain in late 1933, they rented the summer cottages of locals and moved their families to the Mount. They soon demanded a school for their young children, leading to the remodeling of the old normal school building that had been used in the 1890s; a teacher from Dardanelle was hired and soon some thirty children were attending school daily.[243] They wanted a Sunday school and some religious observances and thus the nonde-nominational Mount Nebo Sunday School was formed. The VCCC men and their families also enjoyed entertainment, such as Saturday night dances with music provided by various members of the camp and refreshments provided by the wives. They had Christmas and Easter services and enjoyed leisure activities such as baseball games.

They developed a community on the mountain and interacted with pleasure with the people of Dardanelle, who frequently participated in the VCCC's entertainment activities. A weekly column appeared in the *Dardanelle Post-Dispatch* on the work of the VCCC Camp, along with items dealing with personal reports of their families' events.[244] Thus Mount Nebo Veteran Civilian Conservation Corps Camp became a vibrant and respected part of Dardanelle life.

The work of VCCC No. 1780 was impressive. They dismantled the old deserted buildings on the Bench (the mountain's rim, approximately one mile below the summit of the mountain), salvaged the usable lumber, and built for their use a barracks, mess hall, hospital, officers' quarters, car shed, carpentry shop, pump house, and recreation hall. They widened the road from the base to the top of the mountain, created a firm roadbed, and straightened some of the more dangerous curves. It remained a dirt and gravel road, but it was definitely a marked improvement compared to the old road. They placed the telephone line from the top of the mountain to Dardanelle; constructed twelve cedar-and-rock cabins and a 3,000-square-foot rock-and-cedar beam pavilion overlooking the valley below; laid the foundation for a lodge that was never completed; cleared acres of deadwood and brush; built six extensive walking trails around the Bench and on the mountaintop; built culverts, small bridges, campsites, and rock retaining walls; planted trees, flowers, and shrubbery; and created new and refurbished existing recreational facilities. As with all CCC units, the Mount Nebo men took educational classes—some required and some selected—including elementary reading and writing, English, stone masonry, general agriculture, poultry farming, carpentry, forestry, auto mechanics, first aid, shorthand, and business courses. By late 1934, it was reported that all the men were now able to read and write and were making progress in their other areas of study.[245] It is noteworthy that the CCC program allowed thousands of young men an educational opportunity that aided in their improvement long after the Great Depression ended.

On October 25, 1935, VCCC No. 1780 was disbanded and the men were sent to various other Civilian Conservation Corps camps, including those at Petit Jean Mountain, Magnolia, and Devil's Den. In its two years of existence, VCCC Camp No. 1780 had achieved lasting improvements on Mount Nebo, many of which are still in use today, and had made close friendships with many people in Dardanelle. Most men, upon departing, expressed their genuine sadness at leaving. As one man said, "I have fallen in love with Nebo and after living there two years would like to spend the rest of my life there!"[246]

Mount Nebo had been designated a state park in 1927, the second oldest in Arkansas (Petit Jean being the first designated Arkansas State Park). Many property owners were unable to pay their property taxes during the early years of the Great Depression and thus the land reverted to the state park system. Others, especially during the 1930s, donated their property to the park.[247] Thanks to these additions— coupled with the excellent craftsmanship and work performed by the men of VCCC Camp No. 1780—Mount Nebo had gained a second lease on life. This would propel it successfully into the middle and latter twentieth century, including its current resurgence.

Although still present, by 1936 the Great Depression had decreased in severity, and many in Dardanelle felt the economic improvement. Several new businesses had opened, the national economic outlook was the best since 1929, and the delinquent property tax list for Dardanelle was "substantially smaller than that of last year, a certain indication that 'times are better.'"[248] Perhaps it would now be possible, notwithstanding all the new programs, to return to the old economic relationships that worked well (for some) for decades. Many merchants exhibited this mindset as seen in a two-page 1937 advertisement that promoted Dardanelle as the "best cotton market in this section of the state," while urging farmers to "buy merchandise here for less than you would have to pay in the larger cities."[249]

Given this mindset, a farmers and businessmen picnic was held on May 7, 1937, under the auspices of county agent Walter Cooper and several Smith-Hughes vocational agriculture teachers from various Yell County schools. This meeting was billed as a "get together" to create a countywide organization of farmers and businessmen with the goal of learning more about existing federal agricultural programs in order to secure all the good things to which farmers are entitled. Women were also encouraged to attend and especially encouraged to bring lunch baskets![250] Perhaps life was returning to "normal" after all.

New Deal programs, which had provided local employment as well as needed projects, were being completed. The National Guard Armory in Dardanelle, Works Progress Administration Project No. 1253, which was begun in November 1935, was nearing completion as officers of Company F, 153rd Infantry of the Arkansas National Guard, were beginning to plan the dedication ceremony and town leaders were planning a community dance to follow.[251] On April 30, 1935, a new American Legion Hut was dedicated and opened with $4,300 worth of WPA funds and $2,000 in private donations.[252] This facility is still in use and has over the years served not only as an American Legion Hall, but as the home of Dardanelle's first public lending library, numerous civic meetings and social gatherings, as well as an election polling station. On July 9, 1937, the Rural Electrification Administration (REA) completed the Spring Creek Dam, fifteen miles west of Dardanelle, and thus Spring Lake was formed. The lake would soon be filled with fish, and plans called for the construction of a recreation area complete with cabins, a sandy beach, and a boathouse.[253]

Although merchants reported in June 1934 that business had improved and that they hoped to extend their trade territories, efforts to attract large commercial businesses were not particularly successful.[254] In August 1937, attempts by local businessmen to bring a cannery to Dardanelle and entice local farmers to plant spinach and green beans for commercial use failed. Discussions, it was announced, would continue, but nothing ever came of this effort.[255] On February 23, 1939, Blue Valley Creamery Company announced its sale to Beatrice Creamery Company effective March 1, 1939. Several months later, on December 1, 1939, Beatrice Creamery Company sold the Dardanelle plant to Sugar Creek Creamery Company of Danville, Illinois. There were several changes in plant management, but the general operations, purchases from local dairy producers, and employment levels remained the same, until the business was relocated to Russellville in 1945.[256] Dardanelle was beginning to experience the swift chill of change associated with absentee corporate ownership of local assets.

## Passage toward Modernity

As the 1940s began, Dardanelle's population was one less than was Centerville's and only 388 more than the combined townships of Wilson and Galla Rock, which composed most of the Lower Bottoms. However, most people were unconcerned about the census results, noting that Dardanelle had only a decline of 27 people as compared to the 1930 census.[257] Few people were overly concerned when Dr. Roy Millard, who had practiced medicine in Dardanelle since 1936, moved into a new office in Russellville and began employing his own medical assistants.[258] Of course, Dr. Millard continued to see Dardanelle patients, but his practice would increasingly become more Russellville centered. As long as Dardanelle businesses were profitable, farmers had some money to spend, banks made loans, and young men were employed and not leaving town as soldiers, most people felt secure. Life was good in Dardanelle when these reliable and predictable fundamentals were working.

Merchants revived the Trade Day promotion in order to attract buying customers into their businesses. In October 1938, "with every business house in the city co-operating to the fullest extent and all offering special bargains," Dardanelle had 2,500 people in town and a burgeoning community of supportive local merchants and business houses.[259] This was the sort of economic activity that Dardanelle understood. It was not commercial plants or industry or corporate planning. No, Dardanelle was tied to its roots and its quintessential economic relationship between the rural customer and the town businessman. This is clearly seen in the fall of 1941 in a *Dardanelle Post-Dispatch* report on recent business activities.

> Reminiscent of the days before the building of the Rock Island Railroad, when Dardanelle was the trading center of three Counties, one of the largest crowds of shoppers ever gathered in Dardanelle packed the streets and business houses here last Saturday . . . merchants had stacks of every line . . . ample to meet the heavy demand . . . another immense crowd is expected next Saturday. . . . Dardanelle is a popular trading center . . . one of the best cotton markets in the State . . . parking space in or near the business section is hard to find on Saturdays.[260]

This outdated economic model to which Dardanelle clung so tenaciously would continue to produce fairly good results until the late 1960s. Ultimately, of course, as the model became defunct, Dardanelle suffered. But before this all happened, some thirty more years would pass.

## Conclusion

By August 1940, world events were beginning to crowd in on Dardanelle and the Bottoms. Company F of the 153rd Infantry Division of the Arkansas National Guard—which included many "local boys"—was involved in summer camp in Minnesota. Rumors were, which proved true, that they would be nationalized and sent to Dutch Harbor on Amaknak Island, Alaska.[261] On September 26, 1940, a peacetime military draft was implemented in the United States.[262] Anxiety and concern were high, leading the local newspaper to not print "Letters to Santa" in 1940. On December 23, 1940, Company F was federalized into the United States Army, and the 107 Dardanelle area troops were sent home for Christmas. The men were honored at a community ceremony on January 2, 1941, and departed for Camp Robinson on January 3, 1941.[263]

As the country prepared for possible war and anxiety soared along with patriotism, there were increasing instructions to citizens to save all waste paper for national defense purposes and more draft notices were received.[264] Again, the newspaper did not print its traditional "Letters to Santa" in 1941. It seemed everyone was waiting for something: the future.

In Carden Bottom, eleven-year-old Doris Hundley Hickey accompanied her mother to visit a neighbor, Mrs. Sexton, who had been ill. They knocked on the front door and sat down on the porch swing to wait. Mrs. Sexton was listening to her battery-powered radio. In a few minutes, she walked out onto the porch. Doris remembered her hair was parted in the middle with tiny, neat braids covering her entire head, and she was crying, her eyes red and swollen. She shouted to Mrs. Hundley, "the Japs have bombed Pearl Harbor! I'll never see my Ted again!"[265] It was Sunday, December 7, 1941. The future had arrived and modernity was about to sweep over Dardanelle and the Bottoms in a most unceremonious way.

## CHAPTER 6

# Modernity and Transformation, 1942–1970

*It seems sad and lonesome in our community this week, as there have been so many of our young men called to the United States Army within the past few days.*

RIVERSIDE RESIDENT,
*December 1942*

*We have learned—the hard way—that our prosperity lies within the top foot or two of our soil.*

DARDANELLE CHAMBER
OF COMMERCE,
*July 1948*

*Cotton died in the Bottoms in the mid-1970s. Pesticides and machinery were expensive, farm laborers were scarce after 1955, the Bottoms were too small geographically to compete with the Delta, and the gins all closed down by the mid-1970s. Cotton was dead.*

DELMA MERRITT,
*July 2014*

# Introduction

The period from 1942 through 1970 witnessed profound changes for the Bottoms and for Dardanelle. Population shifts, permanent changes in the relationship of the rural area to the town, and a decline in Dardanelle's importance as an Arkansas community occurred. By 1970 the rural population had significantly dwindled in size and importance, the town's economic base and its leadership component had been altered, and the area's role as an important segment of the Arkansas economy had declined. In order to analyze these changes, this chapter will be subdivided into three sections: from 1942 through 1945, 1946 through 1960, and 1961 through 1970.

# 1942–1945—World War II

In early 1942, several hundred young men—many of them area students attending Arkansas Polytechnic College in Russellville—walked together from the college campus to the train depot in order to depart for military basic training. A large number of Tech students, faculty, and staff as well as family members and townspeople had gathered along the several blocks to see the boys off. Marie Shepherd, then a college freshman, remembered how sad she and other students felt: "You just didn't know if you would ever see those boys again. They were just boys and now they were going off to war. It was so sad."[1]

As throughout the world, World War II held tremendously important implications for Dardanelle and the Bottoms. Government controls created new problems and some opportunities for agriculture. While war efforts generated changes in the area's population, local Red Cross activities were reenergized and race relations were affected. For the Dardanelle area, hundreds of local young men and women participated directly in the war effort.

Agriculture would be permanently changed as a result of War World II government programs. In early 1942, E. A. Hansen, Yell County extension agent, warned farmers about a possible availability shortage of chemicals used by cotton farmers, particularly ceresin, which increased yields when applied to seed a month prior to planting. The new reality was that ceresin was needed for the war effort, given the wax's high mercury content.[2] At the same time, Hansen urged the planting of peanuts, with their high oil content, an item also needed for the war effort. In response to this need, Yell County farmers pledged to plant 10,000 acres in peanuts.[3] Meanwhile, Raymond Pledger, Yell County Farm Security Administration supervisor, urged farm families to make every effort to produce large quantities of food and fiber in order to reach the goals of the "Food for Freedom" program. These wide-ranging goals included farm self-sufficiency in foodstuff production of items such as pork, beef, dairy, poultry, eggs, vegetables, and sorghum; a 25 percent increase in home canning; and an increase in commercial truck farming.[4] Home demonstration agent Josie Benton worked to educate farmers' wives on how to cook using less sugar and how to maximize the greater use of and the cleanliness of home dairy production.[5]

Rationing for the civilian population began in early 1942 as families made their application for a War Ration Book. Sugar was one of the first rationed commodities.[6] By September 1942 the War Production Board Foods Requirement Committee announced plans to begin meat rationing to 2.5 pounds a week for the civilian population as soon as possible and, certainly, within four months.[7] Likewise, paper bags disappeared as the material was needed for packing weapons, and civilians were urged to return used toothpaste and shaving cream tubes—given their metal content—to their local drugstore for government use.[8]

As scrap metal collection became an important wartime activity, in late September 1942 citizens were urged to donate all available scrap metal to the government drive. October 8 was designed as the scrap metal collection day in and around Dardanelle, with Harold Snyder, Dardanelle's vocational agriculture teacher, serving as the drive's chairman. Some 29,000 pounds of metal (14.5 tons) was donated at various collection points in the Bottoms and Dardanelle, to be hauled to the Dardanelle and Russellville Railroad yard for rail transport on October 14, 1942.[9] On that day, two thousand people attended a patriotic celebration to see the area's first (rail) load depart for the steel mill.[10] Mattie Harrison, a resident of Mount Nebo, was inspired to conduct an on-foot, house-to-house canvass of Dardanelle, through which she personally collected over five hundred keys that she then mailed to the government.[11] With aluminum, stainless steel, copper, brass, and tin deemed essential war production materials, cooking utensils underwent a change during World War II, and Agent Benton advised the use of glass, enamelware, and cast iron as alternatives through her Home Demonstration activities.[12]

W. H. Nichols, a member of the Yell County Ration Board, urged people to conserve their tires as a rubber shortage would soon occur.[13] Gasoline rationing began in Arkansas on November 22, 1942.[14] Even the four World War I brass cannons that sat in front of the Yell County Courthouses, two at Danville and two at Dardanelle, were sacrificed to the war effort. Sold for $361.70 to Henry Esch, owner of Dardanelle Tire and Auto Supply, the cannons then were surrendered to the government's metal collection efforts.[15] To this day there are citizens of Dardanelle who begrudge their loss, and the concrete bases upon which the cannons once sat remain empty in front of the Dardanelle courthouse. Emblematic of the depth of civilian participation in the war effort was the cancellation of the Yell County Fair from 1942 to 1945.[16] Not simply a recreational gathering, the fair had long been a serious means to promote agricultural pursuits as well as the pride of rural families in demonstrating their achievements. In addition, the county fair provided an opportunity for the diverse people of Yell County to mingle and enjoy one another's company. In the end, however, it too took a back seat to the war effort.

As young men were drafted into the military and civilians began to leave the area for jobs in war-industry plants, a local labor shortage ensued, especially on the farms. Lonnie Dickens, a young African American tenant farmer, recalled that many of his relatives moved to Detroit and found jobs in the Ford Motor Company plants building military equipment.[17] In June 1942, a Riverside landowner posted a call for cotton choppers, noting that "most all the young men are now in Uncle Sam's services" and we "have lots of work to do."[18] By late August 1942, there was a serious shortage of cotton pickers throughout Arkansas.[19] The opening of the Dardanelle Public Schools was delayed until either the first or second Monday in October (depending on need), as rural students were needed to work in the fields with the cotton harvest and several faculty vacancies had yet to be filled.[20] The Dardanelle schools opened on October 12, 1942, with eight high school teachers and six elementary teachers plus one superintendent and one principal; Douglas School opened its 1942 school year with one principal and six teachers.[21] By late October 1942, the assistant director of the Agricultural Extension Service in Arkansas, Aubrey Gates, predicted a continued severe farm labor shortage. While farmers were compensating for this shortage by pooling their laborers and machines, a realistic remedy for the labor shortage still had to be found.[22]

The Farm Security Administration stressed the essential need to produce foodstuffs as farmers enjoyed higher prices and greater product demand. At the same time, however, they also had to contend with a labor shortage.[23] In 1940, Yell County reported having 3,080 family farmworkers and 617 "hired" farm laborers; by August 1942, the total number of farm laborers had decreased by 59 percent as the military draft and enlistments, higher farm wages, and available war-industry jobs accounted for a massive decrease in farmworkers. Despite this problem and a lack of farm machinery and supplies, farmers managed to increase their overall production yields and reduce their crop spoilage losses.[24] In order to increase food production, the Farm Security Administration announced in December 1942 that it would lend money to low-income farmers to assist them in their efforts at increasing food production and attaining greater self-sufficiency. These loans, forty years in length with a 3 percent interest rate, would be made to landowners, tenant farmers, and sharecroppers who could prove ownership or leases of farms.[25]

The effects of farm labor shortages were exacerbated by the attraction of good-paying defense plant jobs. For instance, in April 1942, two sisters from Carden Bottom, Gladys and Saramae Merritt, approximately ages seventeen and nineteen, left for employment at the Ordnance Plant in Jacksonville, Arkansas.[26] By midsummer, three Centerville citizens, Clarence Keeling, O. C. Pockrus Jr., and Mrs. Bert Yeager, were also employed at the Jacksonville plant.[27] About the same time, the Matt Miller family of Dardanelle moved to Tulsa, Oklahoma, where Mr. Miller, an army pilot during World War I, had been employed as a test pilot and inspector at a plant building Army Air Corps bombers.[28] Many Bottoms and Dardanelle residents found the pull of higher-paying defense industry jobs too alluring to ignore. While some area residents moved away to find better economic opportunities, most never forgot where they came from, as demonstrated by the number of people from Dumas and other Delta towns, as well as Detroit and Brooklyn, who periodically returned, especially to the Bottoms, to visit relatives at "home."[29]

What began as a trickle in a patriotic gesture—as well as a chance for a good-paying job—became a major exodus from the Dardanelle Bottoms during the war and postwar years. In 1943, a national shortage of farm laborers prompted 160 Yell County men to travel to Maine to work in the potato harvest, while more than 100 farm families went to the Delta towns in eastern Arkansas to work as cotton pickers.[30] Some of these workers returned to the area; some permanently moved. California, the Imperial Valley in particular, offered better wages for farm laborers and drew hundreds of Bottoms families during the late 1940s and early 1950s.[31] Farmers during the war years had to deal with a host of problems: drought, floods, boll weevils, armyworms, labor shortages, and gasoline shortages. Thus, one can understand the allure of moving away to earn better pay with less uncertainty and deprivation. In rural America, life on the farm was poised for change.

As the nation geared up for war, the local Red Cross chapter pitched in to assist. Mrs. Howard Hunt served as Yell County chair for the American Red Cross, Mrs. Paul Parks served as the Home Service chair working as a communication link between local families and their military relatives, and Mrs. Stickney Meek served as the county chairperson for war production.[32] Whether it was making surgical dressings, manning sewing rooms for making garments and knitting helmet covers, learning first aid techniques, gathering reading materials for military hospitals, sewing draperies for military facilities, preparing and delivering telegrams, or ferrying emergency messages to and from family members and their servicemen and relatives, the women of Dardanelle and the Bottoms volunteered time and talent at various locations in their ongoing support of the war effort.[33]

As they had during the First World War, local civilians became involved in the purchase of war bonds. The people of the Bottoms offered their financial support as evidenced by the partial reports from the first bond drive in June 1942, which noted $4,131.25 worth of bonds purchased in New Neely and $1,556 in Carden Bottom.[34] For their part, the school districts in Yell County conducted their own war bond drives.[35] Throughout the war, Dardanelle and the Bottoms continued to reach and exceed their war bond quotas. It was clear that there was broad civilian support—in multiple ways—for the war effort.

While the civilian population, both town and rural, began to play its domestic wartime role, local reports of military inductions and news from the warfronts were omnipresent. Three Yell County soldiers were reported missing following the fall of the Philippines.[36] One of these was Grady "Ted" Merritt, the twin brother of Mrs. Ruth Sexton of Carden Bottom, the woman who tearfully reported the Pearl Harbor attack to Doris Hundley Hickey's mother. Ted had been reported a Japanese prisoner of war, taken at Corregidor during the first week of May 1942.[37] Casualty reports were common in October 1942, and the Naval Department reported that Guye R. Winfield, formerly of Carden Bottom and a survivor of the USS *Oklahoma* at Pearl Harbor, was killed in the sinking of the USS *Jarvis* in the Southwest Pacific.[38]

As early as March 1942, the County Selective Service Board announced it had exhausted its quota of 1-A deferments and would begin draft number drawings for all men ages eighteen to forty-five. In addition, the board noted large future monthly induction calls.[39] A young man could escape the army draft by enlisting in the navy, and three African American Dardanelle men, Levester Shurn, J. C. Nichols, and Theoplis Jack Enoch, enlisted in the navy as mess attendants, third class, during or before March 1942.[40] In July 1942, the navy lowered its physical restrictions and urged new enlistments of men seventeen to fifty including African Americans and especially those with carpentry, mechanical, and electrical trade experience.[41] Beginning in April 1942, the Selective Service required all men between the ages of forty-five and sixty-five to also register, and in September, Major General Lewis B. Hershey, national director of Selective Service, said that married men with children and eighteen- and nineteen-year-old youths could be drafted during 1943 as the pool of unmarried draft-eligible men was depleted.[42] In late October 1942, 115 Yell County men were inducted in the US Army and departed for basic training, as a larger county induction quota—125—was set for November, and included married men. The draft registration of eighteen-year-olds was to begin on December 11, 1942.[43] The county's registration quota for December was 328 men, which included 303 whites and 25 African Americans; while the January 1943 quota was preliminarily set at 115, which included 78 whites and 37 African Americans.[44] As of early October 1942, volunteer enlistments for Arkansas revealed that 3 percent of military enlistments statewide involved African Americans, whereas Yell County enlistments and inductions of African Americans were higher.[45]

The various local elements of the war effort continued to consume much attention and energy in 1943. The first war bond sales in December 1942 netted $24,175 and were sold to over four hundred people, while the March 1943 Red Cross War Fund Drive—which had yet to be completed—had already exceeded its quota with generous support from both African American and white area citizens.[46] The final tally revealed that Yell County citizens had contributed $3,699.15, which was $1,099.15 over its quota. Included in this total were donations from the Bottoms: Centerville ($30.44 given by thirty-one people), Liberty Hall ($16.25 given by twenty-seven people), and Carden Bottom ($90.00 given by eighty-one people).[47] In April 1943, Dardanelle citizens purchased $28,562.50 in war bonds, which greatly exceeded its quota of $20,000 for the second war bond drive.[48] The staggering sum of $126,000 was announced as the county's quota for the third war bond drive, and then it was increased to $241,000. By early October, the quota had been met and exceeded by $46,874.75.[49]

Dardanelle women continued to volunteer throughout 1943 as Red Cross workers. During the first two months of the year, volunteers in Dardanelle and the Bottoms donated 954 hours and prepared 7,000 sponge bandages to be used in the war effort. Red Cross volunteer centers were open weekly six hours a day from Tuesday through Friday, with three additional hours on Tuesday and Thursday evenings.[50] A small but loyal contingency of Dardanelle women, many well into their sixties and seventies, worked tirelessly as volunteers in these centers. For example, on a single day, April 8, 1943, forty-two women volunteered a total of 169¾ work hours and completed the preparation of 1,250 surgical bandages.[51] The *Dardanelle Post-Dispatch* noted that Dardanelle women worked 691 hours in April; 319¼ hours in July; and 237½ hours in October, with several women working 30 hours a week.[52] The core of the volunteers remained a loyal, hard-working group of women who consistently made their Red Cross volunteer work a major part of their daily lives. These selfless volunteers, many of whom were from prominent Dardanelle families, worked a total of 259 hours in November 1943.[53]

Women were also serving as clerical workers in government offices, in the armed forces, and in various defense industry plants. Tomelia Wright Kennan of Centerville spent World War II in the United States Navy (WAVE) within the intelligence division, and Pauline Bata—the heroic telephone operator during Dardanelle's 1927 tornado—spent the war years working at the Jacksonville Ordinance Plant and at Camp Robinson. A Centerville native, Geraldean Kinser (age twenty), worked at the Pine Bluff (Arkansas) Arsenal, where she was killed in an accident on June 29, 1943.[54]

For rural women, World War II frequently meant the undertaking of additional field work, given the agricultural labor shortage. The Women's Land Army, a division of the United States Crop Corps, administered by local home demonstration agents and the Agricultural Extension Office, was designed to develop a female agricultural workforce with women working for and paid by local farmers.[55] Most women in the Bottoms simply assumed additional farmwork as husbands, sons, and male relatives were away at war. Certainly, the agricultural labor shortage during World War II was a factor in the shift toward greater agricultural mechanization, which became increasingly apparent following the war.

The civilian population was experiencing severe rationing restrictions by 1943, encompassing a diverse array of goods that included canned and processed foods, meat, cheese, butter, fat products, sugar, canning sugar, coffee, gasoline, tires, and shoes.[56] In September of that year, the shoe ration limited civilians—except for infants—to two pairs of shoes a year.[57] In October, the Office of War Information announced that civilian gasoline supplies would soon "become progressively poorer," forcing some to undertake creative thinking in order to deal with the rationing.[58] One young airman, Jack Guice, whose mother hailed from Dardanelle, possessed such daring and engineering mentality. In order to get himself and his new bride to his new posting in California, he mixed kerosene with the scant amount of gasoline he had available, thus enabling his 1938 Oldsmobile to just barely ascend the Rockies.[59]

While the war certainly affected civilian lives, the primary concern during those years was military service. The *Dardanelle Post-Dispatch* regularly updated its readers in 1943 with induction numbers, including 33 men from Yell County being inducted into the army in February; 126 men in June; 65 men in July; and 21 men in October, as the army announced it would soon induct married men with children. In April, the paper also carried a notice that the navy had announced its need for seventeen-year-olds to enlist.[60] By October 1943, more than 2,000 Yell County boys were serving in the United States military and another 90 men were inducted in December.[61]

African Americans continued to be inducted into the army and others enlisted in the navy. According to newspaper records, fifty-four African Americans from Yell County served in the military during World War II.[62] In November a short item in the local paper, while attempting praise, strongly hinted at the always present racist undertone of the times:

> We have noticed several fine looking colored soldiers on the streets this week—local boys home on furlough or leave—but we failed to learn their names. Dardanelle has the finest colored folks on earth, loyal, patriotic, industrious citizens all, and they always do their full duty in every undertaking.[63]

As the war slowly marched on, periodic reports appeared when local boys were captured as prisoners of war, wounded, or killed in action. The lack of definitive information regarding military personnel and military actions in comparison with contemporary immediacy provides a stark reminder of how far "instant communication" has evolved since the 1940s. Throughout the war, Mrs. Paul (Louise Dunbar) Parks worked as the local Red Cross communications director supplying available and much-appreciated information to families about their servicemen and women.

During 1944, activities that had marked the previous two years continued as wartime circumstances had become the new daily reality. Women worked as Red Cross volunteers and some volunteered for military service, young men were inducted, successful war bond drives were held, local citizens departed for work in war defense plants, agricultural labor shortages continued, rationing persisted, and occasional reports regarding soldiers and sailors were attained. This was Dardanelle and the Bottoms on a wartime footing.

In the fourth war bond drive, Yell County exceeded its county quota of $191,000 by $90,560.75.[64] This patriotic financial support continued as the county, now on its fifth war bond drive, exceeded its $225,000 quota by $70,800, and in its sixth war bond drive, the $175,000 quota was exceeded by $36,600.[65] The final war bond drive ended in mid-June 1945 with Dardanelle and the Bottoms exceeding their $61,000 quota by $22,000.[66] It was clear through all seven war bond drives that residents of Dardanelle and the Bottoms supported the war effort and performed their patriotic duty during World War II.

The people of Dardanelle and the Bottoms also generously contributed to the Red Cross War Fund Drive. In 1944 Dardanelle exceeded its quota of $1,500 by $871.29 including $38.00 contributed by "colored citizens," while the Dardanelle Bottom communities of Centerville, Lakeview, and Fowler in Carden Bottom, and New Neely donated $531.73 with $344.48 of the total contributed by Carden Bottom citizens.[67]

Continued weekly appeals were issued throughout the war years for women volunteers in the preparation of the always needed surgical dressings. Some twenty-six to thirty women, usually the same individuals, dutifully gave on average a total of from 146 to 220 hours a week in this effort.[68] From 1943 through 1945, some citizens moved to Bauxite, Arkansas, to work in the aluminum war plant as others enlisted in the navy, such as former Dardanelle vocational agricultural teacher Harold Snyder, or were inducted into the army.[69] Private first class Kitty Jo Clark of Dardanelle, a marine, served as a general clerk at the Marine Corps Air Station, Cherry Point, North Carolina.[70] Mimzie Dobson, a marine private from Dardanelle, was photographed with a group of United States Marines raising the American flag over Okinawa at the conclusion of that battle.[71]

Increased numbers of casualties as well as military inductees were reported as 1944 dragged on and into 1945. Between February 17, 1944, and August 9, 1945, 376 Yell County men were inducted into the army.[72] Another 42 men joined the navy in 1944.[73] Two of the navy recruits were Jack and Gordon Crain, twins from Carden Bottom who joined the navy as seventeen-year-olds and were described as "alike as two peas in a pod."[74] On May 27, 1944, Staff Sergeant Lemoyne Coffey of Dardanelle, an Army Air Corps engineer and gunner, was reported as missing in action over Germany. Coffey was taken as a German prisoner of war (POW) for the remainder of the conflict.[75] Lieutenant John Phillip "Flip" Cowger met a similar fate as his B-24 bomber was shot down over Germany in July 1944.[76] Stanley W. Wesley of Dardanelle, an infantry soldier, was also a German POW.[77] Coffey, Cowger, and Wesley survived the war and returned to Dardanelle for the rest of their long lives. Lieutenant Colonel Thomas Willson of Dardanelle was one of 513 American POWs freed after thirty-six months of captivity, as American forces captured Cabantaun Camp from the Japanese in Luzon, the Philippines, on January 31, 1945.[78]

In May 1944, Private First Class Charles McClure, US Marine Corps, was killed in action on Saipan.[79] Other war deaths reported between August 1944 and August 1945 included Morris Cain, Foy Clark, and Lloyd Sheets of Centerville; Leo Hamburg Jr. of Mount Nebo; Hollis McGlothin, William Oscar Barnes, and John F. Keeter Jr. of Carden Bottom; and James George Jr., Delbert Garrett, James Cunningham, James E. "Pinky" Harmon, George R. Pfeifer, Wilson Word, Bill Dawson, and Harold W. Howsley of Dardanelle.[80] Just a few weeks after the Japanese surrender, Private First Class Grady "Ted" Merritt's family—including his twin sister Mrs. Lee (Ruth) Sexton—was notified that he had been killed when a Japanese ship loaded with American POWs was torpedoed and sunk in Subic Bay, Luzon, the Philippines.[81]

By July 1946, the United States Army listed thirty-one Yell County servicemen killed in action, four deaths due to combat injuries, twenty deaths due to noncombat causes, and three soldiers previously listed as missing in action were declared dead.[82] This figure does not include US Navy, Marine Corps, and Coast Guard losses. Funeral and memorial services for deceased military personnel continued to be held in and around Dardanelle into the late 1940s.

Numerous local military personnel were wounded and experienced some harrowing escapes. Included here, along with others, was army sergeant Buck McConnell, who grew up in the Ard community five miles south of Dardanelle and who lost both legs in a Pacific island invasion.[83] Once released from the hospital and returned home, McConnell was embraced by the community, and the Garner-Hudson Post No. 69 of the American Legion in Dardanelle spearheaded a fund-raising campaign to purchase a modified automobile for McConnell's use. The car, a Ford, was obtained and presented to McConnell in late August 1946.[84]

News of the German surrender was announced in Dardanelle in the morning hours of Tuesday, May 8, 1945, to the sounds of ringing church bells, fire sirens, and mill whistles. Businesses closed, an impromptu Front Street parade was staged, and a public prayer service was held on Front Street.[85] The only thing tempering this celebration was the knowledge that Japan still had to be defeated. When that news was heard in Dardanelle at 6:00 p.m. on Tuesday, August 14, 1945, a similar pattern of events occurred but the relief and thanksgiving evidenced by the end of the war was even greater: "rejoicing continued until the early morning hours, but there was no rowdyism and but little drinking."[86]

On Wednesday, August 15, 1945, all business in Dardanelle was suspended for one day as people continued celebrations, prayer services, and private reflections regarding the ending of a monumental conflict that profoundly rearranged and permanently altered their lives and world.

While the public's attention was primarily focused on war concerns from late 1941 through 1945, there were other important events. The war had not completely destroyed poverty as evidenced by the Yell County Welfare Department's continued distribution of food, potatoes, and eggs, primarily to needy families.[87] In one month in 1942, the welfare commodities program in Dardanelle distributed $3,996.45 worth of food, while a total of 3,817 Yell County citizens—of which 3,267 were children—were recipients of food welfare.[88]

From 1943 to 1945, the agricultural labor shortage grew. The Yell County Farm Labor Committee met in February 1944 in an effort to find solutions to the "desperate labor situation in Yell County."[89] Noting that fertile land would lie idle unless solutions were found, the committee urged greater use of farm machinery, assistance in obtaining financing for machinery, community help in getting laborers into the fields, and the encouragement of young women from the hill country to aid in hay and spinach harvests and in cotton picking.[90] As one Carden

Bottom farmer, Erby Moore, noted in mid-1944: "due to an acute shortage of farm labor, fully 20 percent of the cotton land in the Bottom
will lie out this year."[91] These farm labor shortages affected the start of
the Dardanelle school year, which was much later than usual "due to a
heavy yield of cotton and an acute shortage of pickers. By October 16,
the majority of farmers will have their cotton picked or will at least be
far enough along with the picking that the boys and girls of school age
can leave the fields and attend school regularly."[92] In July 1944, the Farm
Credit Bureau, a division of the Farm Credit Administration, opened
an office in Dardanelle.[93] The farm labor shortage caused by World War
II spelled the beginning of the end of the traditional way of life in the
Dardanelle Bottoms and signaled a fundamental forthcoming change
in the fortunes and significance of Dardanelle.

The last several months of 1945 and into 1946 offered a strange
blend of war news and facts and a movement back toward civilian
life. Servicemen and women began returning home, small numbers of
new military inductees departed, memorial services were conducted
for some of the fallen, and in yet another war bond drive, the eighth
since 1942, Yell County led all other Arkansas counties and more than
doubled its quota by purchasing $330,678 worth of government secu-
rities.[94] A sure sign of a return to civilian life was the announcement
of the return of Dardanelle High School football during the 1945–1946
term, its first season since 1941. The Yell County Fair also returned
in 1946.[95]

Perhaps the best area summation of World War II was offered by
a Centerville citizen who with matter-of-fact rural precision offered
the following in the *Dardanelle Post-Dispatch*:

> Well, it looks like the "Rising Sun" is about to set, and we all
> hope it stays set! "Peace Days" were just about like any other days
> at our town—not much of a celebration, but a lot of thankful
> hearts! So far as I know, this community has lost three boys killed
> in action: Morris Cain, Foy Clark and a son of Elisha Sheets.
> Quite a few have been injured, and a few have been prisoners of
> war. The atomic bomb was a fearful thing, and its use staggers us
> all to even think of it; but if it stopped the Japs, that is fine! Let's
> hope it need never be used again.[96]

## Rising Water and Floods

While World War II consumed much of people's energy and attention, it was not the only major event in Dardanelle and the Bottoms from 1942 to 1945. The age-old nemesis of rising river waters and floods captured much attention during 1943 and 1944. On May 14, 1943, the highest Arkansas River level ever registered at Dardanelle was noted at 33.8 feet, surpassing the 1927 flood record of 33.3 feet. The waters destroyed most of the levees in the Bottoms, flooded 25,000 acres of planted cropland, and forced three hundred families to evacuate, resulting in the loss of all or part of their worldly possessions. Many tenant houses were washed away and all the wells were deemed unsafe for use.[97] The misery caused by the flood of 1943 was caught in a poem written by a tenant farmer working for A. S. "Sid" McCray, a Dardanelle planter and banker. The following writing was sent to McCray on a postcard on May 17, 1943:

> Pigs outside, hens won't lay;
> Mules in the pasture, plum out of hay.
> Boys in the Army, wife in bed,
> Got such a headache, darn near dead!
> Corn washed away, cotton all rotten—
> Say, Uncle Sid, you'd better come strottin'.
> 'Bout out of groceries, credit shut down—
> And the water's backed up near the old school ground![98]

As the floodwaters gathered strength, hundreds of families in the Bottoms went to Cotton Town, the highest elevation in the Dardanelle Bottoms, to wait out the flood. J. J. Boyce operated a satellite store of the Dardanelle Mercantile Company there and supplied rations to these families. Others huddled in the Carden Bottom High School, which was soon filled with floodwaters. Every road leading out of Dardanelle, except a portion of Highway 27, was covered with three to five feet of water and remained so from one to two weeks. The Dardanelle and Russellville Railroad suspended operations due to at least a foot of scattered debris and fast-moving water overflowing its tracks. A massive amount of timber was washed into the Arkansas River for a quarter mile south of Dardanelle and was deposited in the Holla Bend area of the Bottoms. Large tracts of fertile cropland were overtopped in three to twenty feet of sand, rendering it virtually unusable. The Hunt land in the Upper Bottoms, the land farmed by Elizabeth Hart—"Auntie Hart" during the Civil War—was rendered worthless as cropland by an estimated five feet of sand deposits. Howard Hunt and his son Charles used two Caterpillar dirt movers to mix soil with the deposits of sand and ended with a sandy soil rather than the original and much richer black loam clay soil. They also "dug out" the barn from the sand and built two new barns, four box tenant houses, a tractor shed, and a smokehouse. After years of turning and working this sandy loam, which Tommy Hunt, Charles Hunt's son, refers to as "The Desert," the land today will primarily produce hay and serve as grazing land. "The 1943 flood jumped the levee and sanded all the flat land south of the river."[99]

The Arkansas River ultimately reached 34.05 feet on May 25, 1943, its highest flood stage ever recorded.[100] The Yell County chapter of the American Red Cross, led by Mrs. Howard Hunt, worked with county home demonstration agent Josie Benton and county extension agent D. S. Lantrip to gather donated garden seeds for distribution among displaced farm families in order to ensure their food source.[101] The flood of 1943 was massive, creating permanent devastation on both a personal and collective level across the county.

For one tenant farm family living in Stubbs Town, the 1943 flood marked a turning point in their lives. Young Joe Grimes, approximately seven years old, lived with his grandparents, Mr. and Mrs. Jess Manes. His father, Carl Grimes, was away serving in the military and his mother was not present. Late on the night of May 13, a neighbor, Hence Crain, warned Manes to move out immediately given the fast-rising waters of the nearby Arkansas River. Joe recalled that he and his grandfather hitched up their mule to the wagon and hastily packed it with a few possessions and then he and his grandparents began the terrifying trek down the dark dirt road to Cotton Town, stopping periodically to walk over near the river in order to gage the height of the water. The night was black and it was difficult to know if they were on the road as they continued to hear the sound of the river's rushing torrent. They reached Cotton Town by late morning on May 14, 1943. The tenant house they left and most of Stubbs Town was washed away in the floodwaters. Joe and his grandparents continued their lives living in one of two tenant houses near Cotton Town, both of which were without electricity and running water. Soon after the flood of 1943, his grandmother suffered a paralyzing stroke, and though she lived another two years, she never regained her health. He and his grandfather struggled on but with difficulty. Hunger was a constant problem as they lived mostly on pinto beans and fried potatoes and whatever kind of fish they could take from the Arkansas River. Planting, chopping, and picking cotton consumed their days. "I think we might really have starved to death had it not been for the little bit of credit given us by J. J. Boyce. That allowed us to buy a little food and some needed supplies. Boyce was a good man. He saved a lot of farmers from starvation, but he was the meanest Son of a Bitch I ever knew."[102]

J. J. Boyce was indeed a tough, hard-driving businessman. Orphaned at the age of two, he was raised by his two uncles, Millard and Thomas Boyce, who operated Boyce Brothers General Mercantile in Dardanelle from 1882 to 1909. At the age of ten, his uncles told Jack, as he was called, that he was now a man and had to quit school and go earn a living. He did and ultimately he opened his own store. Three times in his sixty-year business career his store was destroyed by fire, twice by arson from competitors. Every time, he rebuilt and ultimately opened the Dardanelle Mercantile Company on Front Street in Dardanelle, which he owned until his death in 1954. His granddaughter remembers Boyce's fierce temper as she witnessed his profane dressing down of a workman whose work was defective and whose bill was excessive. "By the time Big Daddy was through talking, that poor man was shaking, crying, and apologizing. He could just make people melt away when he criticized them."[103] Boyce extended credit to many a struggling farmer and did not foreclose on a man's property for nonpayment as long as he judged the man honest and his credit worthy, although he would hunt down a dishonest man and he would not rest until he obtained financial restitution. As such, Boyce was representative of the honest, hard-working businessmen of Dardanelle who were both compassionate to the struggling, hard-working poor and totally unforgiving of dishonesty in any form. Certainly, Joe Grimes's family benefited from their association with Jesse Jackson "Jack" Boyce.

By early June 1943, Yell County officials had compiled their initial flood damage report, which listed crop damages of $1,149,000, stock losses of $95,500, and soil damages of $500,000. Damages to roads and bridges in the county were estimated at $114,000. Thus, the flood of 1943 cost $1,858,000—not including the housing losses and personal private damages—as well as the toll caused in displacement and hardship.[104] County judge Jack White traveled to Washington, DC, to gain assistance from the United States Army with the debris-removal process, and with repairs to roads and bridges or, when completely destroyed, with their rebuilding. By late July, this work was complete and the army engineers had let contracts for the rebuilding of the levees in the Upper and Lower Bottoms.[105] As in previous disasters, notably floods and droughts such as the flood of 1927 and the drought of 1930–1931, the American Red Cross engaged in relief efforts and provided assistance. Red Cross relief was extended to 382 families for emergency food aid; 73 families received some amount of replacement household goods, including 60 mattresses; and 1,055 shots were administered to combat typhoid. The Red Cross expended $10,225.13 in various forms of relief assistance in Yell County.[106] To put it mildly, the flood of 1943 was a major catastrophe.

Jack and Gordon Crain, the twin brothers from Stubbs Town who entered the United States Navy in late 1943, had vivid memories of the 1943 flood: "people left Stubbs Town after the 1943 flood, lots of destruction. Usually during high water people would be gone about a week and then return and clean up, but the 1943 flood just destroyed everything. So folks scattered throughout the Bottoms or left for good."[107] Gordon Crain joked that people in the Bottoms were so accustomed to high water departures that, when it rained, the chickens would cross their legs waiting to be tied up for removal and the cattle move on their own to higher ground. He also remembered the saying that warned in high water "you must take your livestock, but you could leave the kid."[108]

During the Second World War, given the government's emphasis on increased food production, events such as the 1943 flood or any event that disturbed agricultural production was seriously reviewed. Therefore, for the first time, serious consideration began to be given to the construction of flood control dams on the Arkansas River. By 1944 Dan Keenan of Dardanelle and attorney Reece Caudle of

Russellville testified before the Facilities Review Committee of the War Production Board in Washington, DC, in support of the building of dams upstream from the Arkansas River Valley.[109] In early 1945, a public meeting between United States Army Corps of Engineers personnel and members of the Arkansas River Flood Control Association was held in Russellville to discuss the possibility of a Dardanelle dam to provide flood control.[110] It would be another twenty-plus years, many meetings, and much lobbying before this initial discussion transformed into a dam, but the effort began in 1944.

The Arkansas River continued to cause misery in the region. In April 1945, the Arkansas River crested in Dardanelle at 33.5 feet and 19,000 acres in the Upper and Lower Bottoms flooded, forcing families to evacuate their homes and seek higher ground. German POWs from Camp Robinson in North Little Rock worked under the supervision of army engineers in an unsuccessful attempt to save the levees in the Upper Bottoms. The Red Cross administered aid to 119 displaced families for the loss of household furnishings and some loss of livestock.[111] Just as crops were replanted, on June 11, 1945, the river crested at 29.68 feet and 20,000 acres were flooded and all the levees failed, weakened by several earlier floods.[112] In early October, a river crest of 27.76 feet resulted in the flooding and destruction in Carden Bottom just prior to harvesttime. While the levees in the Upper Bottoms held due to their recent repair, all of the levees in the Lower Bottoms failed (see Appendix, figs. 4 and 5).[113] These floods served to emphasize the need for improved levees and a dam on the Arkansas River.

With the war over and the return of military personnel to civilian life occurring as a trickle during 1945 and 1946, one could detect an undercurrent of change. As Joe Grimes put it, "those men had seen things, new things, and they were not willing to come back home to settle down into the hard life of a tenant farmer."[114] Also, some former residents who had taken defense industry jobs during the war did not return when the conflict ended.

Another change the returning GIs advocated was the ending of Yell County political corruption. On August 5, 1946, two hundred automobiles packed with returned GIs converged on the American Legion Hut in Dardanelle for a meeting to discuss plans to fight political corruption.[115] A follow-up meeting of 1,200, mostly former GIs, convened on August 9, 1946, in Danville and defiantly protested that July's Democratic Party Primary—which had allegedly been rife with voter fraud and corruption. This protest marked a departure from the long-held political power of the status quo in Yell County. Dr. Kent Grace, of Belleville and former lieutenant-colonel, US Army Medical Corps, spoke for the group: "this meeting was not inspired by Jack White or John Chambers or Buford Compton, or "Buster" McClure. It's a spontaneous outburst of indignation on the part of the GIs, who are determined to stop the thievery that has made a mockery of Yell County elections for years."[116] On August 23, 1946, the GIs announced a full slate of Yell County candidates. Only two candidates, Ed Isom of Ola and W. W. "Wibb" Warren of Dardanelle, were not residents of far-western and southern Yell County.[117] The Yell County GIs had been in conference with the young, dynamic Sid McMath of Garland County, who had led a "GI Revolt" there and successfully removed the Leo McLaughlin political machine from power. McMath had advised the Yell County group that they would have an easier time "overthrowing the political dictators of Yell County" than he did in "smashing the Garland County political machine."[118]

In the GI Revolt, which incidentally was a play on words to gain the attention and interest of returning World War II soldiers, the initials actually stood for "general improvement." It was an effort to remove fraud from elections and governmental practices. Particularly, participants in the GI Revolt were opposed to entrenched incumbents and the "political machines" surrounding them, the misuse of the issuance of poll tax receipts, and practices of election fraud such as lost ballot boxes, double voting, and the voting by election officials and party hacks of deceased individuals. During the late 1940s this movement had identifiable organizations in six Arkansas counties: Cleveland, Crittenden, Garland, Montgomery, Pope, and Yell as well as in the city of Pine Bluff in Jefferson County. This particular government improvement effort was most focused around the 1946 elections and faded away during 1950. The GI Revolt did elect some of the candidates it supported, but generally failed to develop a broad-based agenda and a cohesive internal organizational structure—both of which were needed to attract large numbers of voters, create successful political outcomes, and establish a cohesive political presence for itself and its participants. Nonetheless, the GI Revolt did bring greater attention to the problem of election fraud and machine politics in Arkansas and certainly to the particular locations in which it was most active. As a result, the GI Revolt created a greater incentive for others who followed, mostly during the 1960s, such as the League of Women Voters, the Election Research Council, and investigative journalists who called out corrupt politicians and sought to curtail election fraud.[119]

As the Yell County GI Revolt centered on ending election fraud, its specific goals included prohibiting the county judge from direct engagement in other political campaigns, ending the selling and giving away of liquor on election day, and ending more obvious fraudulent activities such as miscounting or the intentional destruction or hiding of ballots, as well as bribery of election officials and voters with money and/or gifts.[120] While one could note numerous examples of election fraud in Yell County, one example will suffice to highlight its overt nature. In September of 1933 Governor Futrell urged the General Assembly to allow his appointment of a person to fill the recently vacant Fifth Congressional District seat without holding a special election. A special election was ordered and Brooks Hays in a runoff election was defeated by a slim margin. Hays, an opponent of Governor Futrell and Homer Adkins (the former Pulaski County sheriff, Arkansas Klansman, and then Arkansas commissioner for the federal Internal Revenue Service), campaigned aggressively in Yell County. In Yell County the anti-Hays faction, all entrenched and powerful Yell County politicians, rallied behind the Futrell/Adkins faction and 2,454 votes were cast in the runoff giving Hays's opponent a three-to-one victory. At the time only 1,651 registered voters lived in Yell County.[121] This was the sort of long-established machine politics and voter-fraud practices the GI Revolt of the late 1940s was attempting to end.

The "independent" GI candidates in Yell County lost every office "by substantial majorities" in the November 5, 1946, general election.[122] Despite their electoral defeat, their call for an end to political corruption struck a chord with many citizens as evidenced by future hard-fought races during the late 1940s and 1950s pitting younger candidates against traditional, entrenched officeholders. The spirit of political reform in Yell County was ignited by the county's "GI Revolt" of 1946 as it was in certain other areas of Arkansas as well.

During World War II, Yell County agriculture sustained notable alterations. From 1940 to 1945, the number of farms decreased by 719 and agricultural acreage declined from 243,737 to 207,206 acres. Conversely, the size of the average Yell County farm increased from 99.9 acres to 120.4 acres. Every agricultural index, including number of cows, mules, hogs, pigs, chickens, and eggs produced, also dramatically decreased from 1940 to 1945. Crop production, including corn, wheat, sweet potatoes, sorghum, hay, and oats, as well as the number of acres devoted to their production, noticeably declined. Perhaps most telling was the decline in the acres of cotton production—down 50 percent, representing 14,956 fewer acres, resulting in a decline in the number of cotton bales produced from 13,788 bales in 1940 to 8,958 bales in 1945.[123]

Changes in agriculture were reflected by changes in demographics. The pattern of depopulation in the Dardanelle Bottoms, which had begun during World War II, was accelerated during the period from 1946 through the 1970s. Young Joe Grimes serves as an example of this. Following his return from the war, Joe Grimes's father, Carl, farmed with his brother for a year and then took his family to California for a year and then on to Dumas, Arkansas. Joe returned to live with his grandfather in Cotton Town for approximately two years and then, in 1955, left for a career in the United States Air Force.[124] Bottoms families left for better pay and more opportunities primarily in California and the eastern Arkansas Delta. By 1948, the weekly Carden Bottom reports published in the *Dardanelle Post-Dispatch* began to contain numerous items on the visits of former residents now living in Moscow, Wabbaseka, Dumas, Little Rock, and various Oklahoma and West Coast locations. With regret, a report noted the departure of the Fred Hickey family from Carden Bottom in early 1950 as it praised Hickey for his twenty years of leadership in his church and the Carden Bottom School: "one of the best and progressive farmers in the State—the type of citizen a community can ill afford to lose."[125] During the decade of the 1940s, Yell County's population declined from 20,907 to 14,037, a 33 percent decline. Most of this decrease came from the depopulation of the rural areas with some residents moving to town and others leaving the county altogether.[126] By 1946 several Bottoms communities, Riverside, Liberty Hall, Lakeview, Stubbs Town, and Wasp Nest (the latter three in Carden Bottom) and Fields Chapel were either completely gone or contained only a few scattered homes and residents. The river's constant gnawing and chewing away at its banks caused Fields Chapel to completely fall into the abyss and disappear. Stubbs Town was so destroyed by the 1943 flood, that it too all but disappeared (see Appendix, fig. 6). Depopulation due in part to wartime relocations and in part due to the devastation caused by the floods of 1943 and 1945 had transformed these once-thriving and proud rural hamlets into places that existed primarily in collective memory rather than as truly functioning communities of residents. Wherever their destination and whatever their reasons for departing, following World War II rural residents were leaving the countryside. Later reunions would attest to the fact that while many moved away, their hearts and sense of place were still deeply rooted in Bottom soil. For these people the reunions were truly a coming home.

In the 1960s, former residents of Carden Bottom began holding "Old Timers Reunions." On July 9, 1965, a picnic supper was held at Council Oaks in Dardanelle with fifty-two former Carden Bottom residents in attendance.[127] Two years later, five hundred people attended the reunion, which was held at the old Carden Bottom High School. Mrs. G. L. Potts, president of the Carden Bottom Association and a prominent member of the Lakeview Extension Homemakers Club, which hosted the event, was so overcome with emotion that she was unable to deliver the welcome.[128] Mrs. Potts left her home in Carden Bottom in 1966 and moved to Russellville to live in her sister's home.[129] For two generations, it would have been difficult to imagine life in Carden Bottom without Mrs. G. L. (Orra) Potts. When she died on February 13, 1979, at the age of ninety-two, she was laid to rest in the Oakland Cemetery (Russellville) near the graves of her two infant daughters, Dorothy and Grace, and her husband.

The most recent Carden Bottom Reunion—the first one in many years—was held in Dardanelle on October 19, 2008, with approximately one hundred people in attendance. As one person noted, "the train has left the station and we are the last to see it go. It is good, but so sad to remember."[130] Many former residents remained psychologically connected to the Bottoms and Dardanelle and kept informed of events by subscribing to the local newspaper. One such person was Alice Floy Hawkins, who, while residing in Garden Grove, California, continued to hope to return to Dardanelle prior to her death. Meanwhile, one of her granddaughters was given the name "Dardanelle Lynn."[131] The sense of place was a powerful magnet for former residents.

## 1946–1960—Postwar Transitions

For rural residents who remained after World War II, life would offer some improvements. In March 1949, representatives of the Western Arkansas Telephone Service met with Dardanelle Chamber of Commerce members to outline the necessary steps to bring telephone service to Carden Bottom.[132] Roy Tillman Jr. recalled that most residents received telephone service between 1954 and 1957 and party lines, as opposed to private lines, were the only option available to rural residents.[133] Transportation improvements also offered greater benefits to Bottoms residents. In early 1944, the construction contracts for two new graveled roads, the Elberta to Neely Road and the Lakeview to Carden Bottom Road, were announced by county judge Jack White.[134] Then in June 1945, the Arkansas State Highway Commission offered assurances that repairs would be made to the Elberta-Neely Road, State Highway 155, given its then all but impassable condition due to recent overflow damages.[135] In June 1945 the county built a new wooden bridge over Smiley Bayou off Highway 7 and also improved the Bottoms road running from Liberty Hall to Slaty Crossing to Neely (see Appendix, fig. 6).[136] In June 1954 a proposed new road linking Carden Bottom to the top of Petit Jean Mountain was discussed. Winthrop Rockefeller, who had recently created his farm and residence atop the mountain, was supportive of this effort. Among its various attributes, the new road would replace the old swinging bridge over the Petit Jean River between Carden Bottom and Bryant's Cove, which had long been inadequate and could not support heavy truck or school bus traffic. For years, school buses stopped on the Carden Bottom side of the bridge and children walked across the swinging bridge to board or exit the school bus.[137] The graveled dirt road from Carden Bottom to Centerville was heavily traveled and quickly became a "dust path," as one resident described it, making it dangerous to gage oncoming traffic and requiring slower speeds. The county attempted to ameliorate this problem by periodically coating the gravel with oil, a temporary fix at best.[138] One Dardanelle resident observed that driving the road from Centerville to Carden Bottom could only be compared to driving on an Oklahoma road during the Dust Bowl years "when visibility during the daytime was about 10 feet . . . during the busy seasons when hundreds of workers are transported to the fields . . . and when farmers are bringing their products to market, travel is extremely hazardous."[139] After many delays, the state included the 14.5-mile Highway 154 expansion and blacktop work in its July 9, 1958, contract bids. The new Highway 154 was completed and dedicated on June 28, 1959 (see Appendix, fig. 1).[140] Finally, after some eight decades of struggle and effort, a paved road into the Bottoms was a reality: "it was a blessing for farmers—faster, safer and easier. Now you could run to Dardanelle from the Bottoms and not be covered up in inches of red dust."[141] Transportation improvements also included the straightening and relocation of Highway 7 between Dardanelle and Russellville, which both shortened the distance and improved the road's safety.[142]

During the 1940s, other changes in rural life were obvious. One resident from the Bottoms wrote in mid-1944 that the days of cotton were fading: "some few years ago the majority of people in our section raised cotton to pay most of their obligations, but today it is quite different. People no longer look to cotton, but depend largely upon cattle, chickens and hogs."[143] As farming changed and the rural areas experienced continued declining populations, other small events were indicative of transition. In 1945, the gristmill at New Neely, which had operated since before the Civil War, was advertised for sale.[144] By early 1945, the Sugar Creek Creamery had moved from Dardanelle to Russellville, and, in late 1953, the Clement-Byrd Feed Store also relocated to Russellville.[145] These transitions did not appear as a tidal wave, but their effects over time would prove highly significant.

Savvy Dardanelle businessmen were aware of the undercurrents of economic change taking place, and positioned themselves accordingly. Dan and Bobby Keenan, the father and son owners of extensive Bottom land and of the Keenan Cotton Gin, purchased a Russellville John Deere dealership in mid-1949, moved it adjacent to their Front

Street gin, and began operating it as Keenan Implement Company.[146] The Keenans aggressively promoted their farm machinery lines in a series of rural community trade shows, including one staged at Carden Bottom High School in January 1950. Additionally, in February of the same year, the company held John Deere Day in Dardanelle to which farmers and their families were invited for a movie show celebrating the farming life, followed by a free luncheon and a display of the newest farm machines.[147]

# Agriculture

Cotton continued to be grown in the Dardanelle Bottoms until the mid-1970s. Its traditional hold on area agriculture did not simply vanish, but slowly faded. Nonetheless, on September 1, 1949, a third cotton gin went into operation in Dardanelle, the Yell County Gin on South Second Street. The McClure Gin and the Keenan Gin were already established in Dardanelle, and two gins were operating in the Bottoms, one owned by the Keenans and the other owned by the McClures.[148] In 1953 the three Dardanelle facilities turned out 7,421 bales while the two Bottom facilities produced 2,835 bales. At a selling price of $195 per bale, Yell County cotton generated a $2 million crop in 1953.[149]

Meanwhile, both the McClure and Keenan operations opened grain elevators in 1955 for storage of soybean and corn.[150] The operations of the new Dardanelle Arkansas Valley Feed Mill, which produced corn-based poultry feed primarily and used approximately 500,000 bushels of corn annually, became an attractive alternative to cotton farming. Representatives from General Mills also encouraged Arkansas River Valley farmers to grow corn rather than cotton, noting that the demand for corn was great given the emerging poultry industry in Arkansas and local farmers could easily sell their crop and avoid high freight cost associated with shipping it north and east.[151]

As cotton's supremacy began to decline, the poultry industry and soybeans began to emerge. Farmers turned to soybeans as a cotton replacement. The decline of cotton did not cause the development of the poultry industry; rather, the rise of poultry was simply coincidental with the timing of cotton's decline. Chronic labor shortages continued to be a constant problem for cotton growers. In 1955 the Arkansas

Employment Security Division launched a campaign to recruit "native farm labor" for the fall harvest, noting that "all available labor will be needed" even given a 7 percent forecasted decline from the 1954 cotton crop levels and a 14 percent decline in the planted cotton acreage.[152] The only way to skirt the constant need for increased numbers of farm laborers to hoe and pick cotton was to invest in farm machinery, a costly option that was not feasible for small-farm operations. An additional costly element in growing cotton was the increasing need during the postwar period to invest in the fertilizers and pesticides required to develop good crop yields, an element that many small farmers could not do or could only do to a limited degree.[153] As had been the case in so many previous decades, cotton had a growing list of difficult production obstacles.

Beginning in 1950, and upon the requests of residents, the Yell County Malaria Control Unit began using DDT and Chlordane to spray outbuildings for mosquito control. The same chemicals were being used in Dardanelle for control of the fly population.[154] By July 1950, the Dardanelle Bottoms had ten crop-duster airplanes spraying cotton fields with both liquid and powder DDT and "emitting a dense cloud of poison," in an effort to kill the boll weevils.[155] While crop dusting was costly and effective, it also had unintended consequences. By August 1955 reports of human and livestock illnesses were being tallied. The use of chemical crop dusting was blamed, especially during periods of high winds as the chemicals descended upon untargeted pastures, livestock, homes, people, and fields.[156]

One of the more bizarre events involving the use of crop-dusting planes occurred in the fall of 1949. District game wardens arrested Charles Stewart for using a crop-dusting plane, which belonged to two Little Rock men operating their dusting service from Morrilton, to kill migratory waterfowl. Approximately one dozen geese were found on the sandbar of the Arkansas River in the Upper Bottoms, which prompted the wildlife officers to investigate further. They found that Stewart was using the airplane to flush birds into the air, drive them over the sandbar, and then used a shotgun at close range to kill them. Stewart was arrested for shooting waterfowl from an airplane, a violation of both federal and state game laws. He was fined $100.[157]

By the mid-1950s, agricultural diversification was again being praised as a means by which to maintain agricultural leadership in Yell County. Spinach growing in Carden Bottom was promoted, as were soybeans, and the broiler and turkey growing industries were seen as suitable hill country pursuits. In addition, beef and dairy cattle were noted as profitable farming activities.[158]

# Poultry

The broiler industry in the Arkansas River Valley was first discussed at a Dardanelle Chamber of Commerce meeting on October 25, 1944. Conversations and presentations continued into early 1946, and by 1949, the group was promoting the idea as a million-dollar-a-year industry that could double or triple a farmer's annual income.[159] In February 1949, the first broiler house in the area was completed near Centerville and placed in operation with 6,000 chicks, while eighteen additional broiler houses were under construction. The new poultry-based industry had begun due in no small part to the partnership between the broiler producers with Arkansas Valley Feed Mill and the promotion of the Dardanelle Chamber of Commerce.[160] By July 1949, Dardanelle area poultry farmers had raised and marketed 50,000 broilers, and the chamber of commerce continued to promote the industry with potential new growers.[161]

Arkansas Valley Feed Mill, located in North Dardanelle near the Dardanelle and Russellville Railroad yard, opened in early 1947. The operation consisted of a feed mill capable of producing feed for a variety of livestock, a grain elevator, a dehydration plant, and a retail seed store, all designed to serve farmers in Yell, Logan, Pope, Johnson, Conway, Perry, and Franklin Counties. Its original officers included W. H. McClure, Stickney Meek, and Harold Snyder.[162] Within one year, manager Harold Snyder announced a massive expansion of the mill and noted a desire to support and grow the poultry industry in west-central Arkansas.[163] As the Dardanelle Chamber of Commerce worked toward developing a broiler industry, the presence of Arkansas Valley Feed Mill proved essential in providing the required balanced feed to the growers.[164] On August 29, 1959, Arkansas Valley Feed Mill became part of Arkansas Valley Industries, Inc. (AVI) as did Ark-Val Hatcheries and Valley Poultry Company. Its original incorporation stock-offering of 30,000 shares was capitalized at one million dollars. Harold Snyder was its chief executive officer.[165] As AVI—an integrated agricultural corporation engaged in the milling of feed and the growing and processing of broiler chickens—the company became a major producer of poultry and livestock feed during the 1960s. As the new company continued to grow and expand, numerous new management positions developed with scores of new managerial positions being filled by educated men with corporate experience. They and their families moved to Dardanelle during the 1960s.[166]

Prior to this, in May 1951, the chamber of commerce had almost completed an aggressive fund-raising campaign to acquire $80,000 to build a poultry processing plant in Dardanelle to be operated by Fox DeLuxe Foods, Inc., of Chicago, Illinois. The contract between the chamber's newly created corporation, Dardanelle Industries, Inc., and Fox DeLuxe was signed on June 14, 1951, and called for the employment of between 150 and 200 people, mostly women at the rate of 75 cents an hour, with an expected weekly payroll of $5,000.[167] The plant opened for operation on April 1, 1952, and anticipated processing 20,000 broilers weekly.[168] Beginning in July 1951, the *Dardanelle Post-Dispatch* began the practice of posting broiler and fryer area wholesale prices weekly.

The evolution of the poultry industry in and around Dardanelle and how it initially developed and what it ultimately became can be seen as part of a southern regional phenomena with its beginnings in the northern piedmont region of Georgia. There, in the 1920s, feed dealers encouraged cotton farmers who were experiencing terrible boll weevil infestations to raise chickens for shipment to Atlanta and other urban markets. By 1923 chicken production had become a major agricultural pursuit in the Delmarva Peninsula of Georgia. Feed mill operators financed the chicken farm operations while simultaneously selling them feed, and by 1926 one million birds were annually being shipped to major East Coast markets. The Delmarva experience, which was abruptly ended by World War II as the United States military became the chief purchaser of poultry, nonetheless led to the development of the new supermarket concept in retail food stores featuring ready-to-use foods such as fully dressed, ready-to-purchase-and-cook poultry, as well as the mass production of broilers, which then decreased production costs based on economy of scale principles. Bankers had also learned from the Delmarva experience that there was profit to be made in the financing of vertically produced poultry involving hatcheries, feed mills, farmers raising chickens commercially, production plants, and trucking, all of which began with an egg and ended at the family dinner table—a journey capable of netting multiple dollars along the way.[169]

As perhaps a final signal that the poultry industry had taken center stage in Dardanelle, it is worth noting that by the late 1960s, the *Dardanelle Post-Dispatch* would cease its decades-long practice of publishing the announcements of the first cotton bloom and first ginned bale of cotton produced in the Bottoms. The paper had ceased quoting cotton prices at Dardanelle in the 1940s, and by 1965, the long-standing tradition of Dardanelle businesses of offering prizes (cash, goods, or services) to the farmer ginning the first bale of cotton had ceased.[170] An agricultural transition was surely underway.

During 1952 and 1953, the Dardanelle processing plant annually handled over 4.5 million broilers and generated a payroll of $454,818.87 for 225 employers, while poultry farmers were paid $3,357,129.31 in 1952 and over $4.5 million in 1953. Conversely, during 1953, $2 million worth of cotton was produced in the Dardanelle Bottoms.[171]

In 1958 Fox DeLuxe announced an expansion of the Dardanelle plant in order to allow for the processing of 14,000 chickens per hour and the construction of a new processing facility in Springdale, Arkansas. The expectation was that the plant expansion would generate an increased annual demand for three million more chickens and one million more turkeys.[172] In January 1959, plant officials announced that the Dardanelle plant had experienced a new record level of production, had 328 employees—the largest number ever—and that high levels of production were anticipated to continue throughout the year, resulting in increased demand for locally produced poultry.[173] The availability of fairly good wages at the poultry processing plant made it even more difficult for the remaining cotton farmers to secure farm laborers.

On December 28, 1960, the voters of Dardanelle overwhelmingly approved the issuing of $450,000 bonded indebtedness in order to allow the city to buy all processing plant equipment and facilities from Fox DeLuxe and lease them to Arkansas Valley Industries for twenty years with the leasing proceeds to fund the city's retirement of the bonded indebtedness.[174] On February 27, 1961, AVI assumed total operational control of the Dardanelle Processing Plant, announcing its target of 400 employees, approximately 100 more jobs than the plant had under Fox DeLuxe ownership.[175] Dardanelle hosted an "AVI Appreciation Day" on March 25, 1961, featuring floats; AVI vehicles and personnel; the high school band; Brownie, Girl Scout, and Boy Scout troops; local civic leaders; and AVI executives. The windows of local businesses splashed welcoming and congratulatory messages for AVI, as some 6,000 people attended the festive events with Front Street in Dardanelle assuming a carnival-like atmosphere.[176]

In April 1961, AVI's Harold Snyder made application to open a new bank in Dardanelle, Arkansas Valley Bank, with initial capitalization of $150,000. This occurred at the same time that AVI set up its corporate headquarters on Front Street, on the second floor of the old Crownover Building located on the southeast corner of Front and Locust Streets. Arkansas Valley Bank would operate on the first floor of this location.[177] In late 1961, AVI expanded with its opening of a poultry processing plant in Waldron in Scott County.[178] Through the decade of the 1960s, AVI continued to expand as Snyder pushed for more farm contracts to enlist farmers in the production of poultry.[179] As a result of this continued effort, thousands of new "chicken houses" were constructed and farmers signed contracts to produce poultry for the company engaged in integrated poultry production: feed grains, hatchery chicks, farm contracts for raising chickens to maturity, processing plants, and marketing contracts for poultry sales.

By the end of its fiscal year on March 31, 1969, AVI had become one of the top-ten largest poultry producers in the United States. It was ranked nationally as number 768 in total corporate sales by *Fortune* magazine and, based on its net income as a percentage of invested capital, AVI was ranked eighty-fifth among all American corporations. On December 1, 1969, AVI merged with George H. McFadden & Bracy, Inc., of Memphis, Tennessee. Along with the name change to VALMAC Industries, Inc., the corporate headquarters was moved to Little Rock, Arkansas. The new AVI managerial employees and their families, who had flocked to Dardanelle during the 1960s and had added a new level of educated, managerial, and generally sophisticated citizens, now departed.

At the time of its merger, Arkansas Valley Industries included egg production operations, hatcheries, broiler growing, feed manufacturing, and the processing of chickens and turkeys with Arkansas plants located in Dardanelle, Russellville, Morrilton, and Pine Bluff, as well as branches in Dayton, Ohio; Oklahoma City, Oklahoma; Denver, Colorado; and in Los Angeles and San Francisco, California. Ironically, the new corporate owner of VALMAC was one of the world's largest and oldest merchants of raw cotton, and in 1969 McFadden & Bracy, Inc., was pursuing international marketing efforts for fiber, food, and shelter products.[180] Locally the processing plant continued to operate, farmers raised chickens, and all of the other industry-related activities initiated by AVI proceeded as they do today under the corporate ownership of Tyson Foods, Inc.

Unlike the Delmarva poultry production, AVI and Tyson represent integrated poultry corporations. In the 1940s the concept of reducing production cost at each stage of poultry production began to materialize. The individuals who first applied this concept to the poultry industry were referred to as "integrators" and quickly poultry production firms, owned by one individual or corporate entity, emerged. The benefit of the integrated model included reduced production cost at each level of production, improved and carefully developed feed to maximize poultry growth and profits, and increased biosecurity and sanitation standards to protect against bacteria, pests, and diseased birds.[181] Harold Snyder and John Tyson understood the potential of an integrated poultry production business. By 1969 more than 98 percent of American poultry was raised by small farmers under contract with integrated poultry corporations that owned and managed breeder flocks, pullet farms, breeder houses, hatcheries, broiler farms, processing plants, and distribution networks, and Arkansas led the nation in broiler production.[182] Snyder's AVI, like Tyson's, was part of that visionary vanguard that used the earlier Delmarva model, altered it to improve quality of and profits from production, and moved the poultry industry in the United States from a small farm, self-sufficiency effort to a multibillion-dollar worldwide industry.

# The Dardanelle Dam

Another significant effort, which began in 1938, extended through 1947, and completed in 1966, centered on the construction of a dam on the Arkansas River. Originally conceived as a means for flood control, the Dardanelle Dam ultimately was built as a hydroelectric generating facility and navigation project, and as part of a larger series of dams on the Arkansas River in Oklahoma and Arkansas: the McClellan-Kerr Arkansas River Navigation Project. Congressional action financed various early portions of the project that focused on flood-control efforts beginning in the 1940s. The basic plan for the Dardanelle Dam received congressional approval in 1946, although funding was not included at that time. Area organizations, primarily the Arkansas River Basin Association, which included several Dardanelle citizens in key leadership positions, maintained continued public awareness regarding the need for a dam as they promoted and supported its construction.[183]

In late 1950, United States congressman Brooks Hays (D-Arkansas) announced that the upcoming federal budget included $1,000,000 to ensure the construction of the Dardanelle Dam. It would finally be built, although the time schedule was still uncertain.[184] The dam's construction was a part of the era's overall river/flood-control legislative effort, and some parts of this effort pushed forward as others inched behind. It was an uneven movement forward at best.

In late 1951, congressional allocations for $4.1 million were approved for riverbank stabilization and levee repair work in the Dardanelle Bottoms.[185] From this allocation, $800,000 was designated for bank-stabilization work from Dardanelle through the Dardanelle Bottoms to Morrilton. This work was a necessary prelude to the Army Corps of Engineers constructing the Holla Bend Cut-Off, which straightened the Arkansas River's channel by removing some eighteen miles of river curves, as it created a new three-mile river channel ending at the old Reed's Ferry location in Carden Bottom, just north of Fowler. This cut-off would stabilize the banks, offer protection for the levees, and greatly reduce the threat of flooding in the Bottoms (see Appendix, fig. 2).[186] Two Dardanelle men, both gin operators and owners of extensive Bottom lands, Bobby Keenan and W. H. McClure Jr., who along with their attorney Reece Caudle of Russellville, advocated for the creation of this cut-off in order to protect 30,000 acres of rich Bottom land from future flooding and subsequent sanding by river sediment. These men went to Washington, DC, and along with Arkansas congressmen Brooks Hays and James Trimble successfully pushed for funding the construction of the Holla Bend Cut-Off through the House Public Works Committee.[187]

During 1952, riverbank stabilization work from Dardanelle Rock to Reed's Ferry was completed, and later that same year, a $700,000 congressional authorization was approved for the Holla Bend Cut-Off, with work to begin in early 1953.[188] By removing the river's curves and turns, the completion of the Holla Bend Cut-Off in 1955 isolated 4,068 acres between the new Arkansas River channel and the original river channel. Originally rich farmland that had bordered the river, this 4,000 plus acres had now become an area filled with a series of isolated pools of water, hardwood timber, and Johnson grass.[189] Local sportsmen believed that the potential was great for creating a wildlife habitat and furthering sporting recreational activities.

By mid-1957, the US Army Corps of Engineers leased the land to the General Services Administration and a wildlife refuge was established. This land was administered by the Bureau of Sport Fisheries and Wildlife, a division of the US Fish and Wildlife Services of the US Department of the Interior.[190] Known as the Holla Bend Wildlife Refuge, and commonly referred to by locals as the Goose Refuge, the refuge is eight miles southeast of Dardanelle and currently offers sanctuary for hundreds of thousands of migratory birds as well as numerous other game animals and fishing areas.[191] At present, parts of Holla Bend Wildlife Refuge are leased to farmers.

In 1968 the refuge, in order to clarify its eastern, southern, and western boundaries, filed a condemnation lawsuit in the Federal District Court of Eastern Arkansas to claim an additional 2,284 acres, including the area of the original river channel and a narrow strip of land adjacent to the old channel. This action involved the taking of land from approximately one hundred persons at a total cost of $51,500.[192] Creation of the new river channel did, indeed, control flooding of some

Bottom farmland, while the creation of the Holla Bend Refuge resulted in the farming loss of several thousand acres of rich land.

One former landowner, Betty Tilmon Keenan, wife of Dan Keenan, continued to fish on this property even after it officially became part of the federal refuge. While fishing one day, a wildlife officer gently reminded her that the land was now federal property and fishing was not permitted. "Miss Betty" defiantly defended her right to fish wherever she pleased, "This was and still is my land, and by God I will fish here whenever I want to. So, you just go along now and leave me alone." The officer thanked "Miss Betty" for her time and quietly left.[193]

In mid-1955, the Dardanelle Dam project received an additional $450,000 appropriation approval as its funding inched forward.[194] After numerous additional piecemeal appropriations, the ground-breaking for the Dardanelle Dam occurred on June 12, 1957, with Arkansas US senators John McClellan and J. William Fulbright, Oklahoma US senator Robert Kerr, Arkansas representative Brooks Hays, Arkansas governor Orval Faubus, numerous county and local leaders, and a total of 5,000 citizens in attendance. The Dardanelle Dam was designed as 2,683 feet in length and 71 feet in height. It includes a controlled spillway of 1,000 feet; a navigation lock 110 feet wide and 600 feet long; and a powerhouse.[195] The reservoir the dam created, Lake Dardanelle, includes 20,000 acres having a water elevation ranging from 336 to 338 feet, with its government acquisition via eminent domain occurring on September 30, 1964. Land having a slightly higher elevation that ultimately bordered the reservoir was allowed to be leased to private landowners in five-year periods.[196] The federal government took over the first 463.4 acres of privately owned land as part of the dam/reservoir project in 1957.[197]

Construction of the dam slowly moved forward. It would be completed and dedicated on May 13, 1966, at a total cost of $79 million. In attendance at the dam's opening dedication were Senators John L. McClellan and J. William Fulbright, Governor Orval Faubus, and 8,000 others. The reservoir the dam created, Lake Dardanelle, is 2 miles across at its widest point and 50 miles in length, comprising 315 miles of shoreline.[198] In addition to the Dardanelle Dam's purposes of river navigation and the generation of hydroelectric power, Lake

Dardanelle was promoted as a recreation and sporting venue that local leaders hoped would spur area economic development. Flood control is not a primary objective of the McClellan-Kerr Navigation System and its seventeen dams. However, the Dardanelle Dam, by controlling the flow of water, in essence does allow for the control of high water.

## A New Bridge

One consequence of the Dardanelle Dam was the construction of a new bridge across the Arkansas River at Dardanelle. The existing bridge completed in 1929 featured a swing span that would allow for the passage of taller river vessels. However, the new dam's design called for the river channel to flow on the north side of the river, whereas the swing span of the 1929 bridge was on the south side. This dilemma, coupled with the fact that the old and extremely narrow 1929 two-lane bridge was carrying an average of 7,000 cars a day in 1966, caused the state highway department to approve the construction of a new four-lane bridge at a cost of $4.4 million.[199] The bridge project began in 1968 and was fully opened to the public on March 1, 1971, although two lanes had been opened in December 1970.[200]

## The Flood of 1957

Ironically, just a few weeks prior to the dam's initial dedication ceremony, the last big flood of the Dardanelle Bottoms occurred. On May 28, 1957, the Arkansas River reached 33 feet and flooded between 4,000 and 5,000 acres in the Dardanelle Bottoms. Approximately one hundred men had worked for five days and nights to shore up the levee five miles south of Dardanelle in the Upper Bottoms on the Keenan lands, but, shortly before midnight on May 28, due to incessant heavy rain, the water topped the levee and it gave way. The levees in the Lower Bottoms held in part due to the efforts of volunteers and the United States Army Corps of Engineers to strengthen them following the levee overtopping on the Keenan land.

The overflow from creeks, however, spread to most of the Carden Bottom farmland. Consequently, most Carden Bottom families moved to higher ground, and moved their livestock and machinery to safety.

Although a few Carden Bottom homes were severely damaged, none was washed away. Junior and Grace McClure's house near Riverside, which they had sandbagged, received water up to its front door. Bottoms families poured into Dardanelle with their trucks loaded with mattresses and other household goods, although within a week most were able to return home to clean their houses and replant their fields.

The levees on the north side of the river in Pope County did fail, however, flooding several thousand acres. The flooded Dardanelle Bottoms lands were the same lands that had flooded in 1927, 1943, and 1945, and some of these lands caved into the river during the 1957 flood. Crop losses included the grain and cotton crops that had been planted and were already sprouting when they were completely washed away. Given quick drainage and replanting of soybeans and sorghum, farmers believed they might still be able to salvage a harvest.[201] Surplus commodities were made available to unemployed and flooded people, Red Cross and county health officials worked to spray flooded structures for mosquitoes and inspect water wells, and county judge Morris Moore began to organize road and bridge repairs in the flooded areas. In addition, Bobby Keenan and W. H. McClure Jr. met with Governor Faubus in an effort to obtain assistance from the state's emergency fund.[202] In late July 1957, the Dardanelle Drainage District issued a thirty-day contract in the amount of $21,617.50 to repair the broken levee seven miles south of town.[203]

The flood of 1957 was a serious event, but it was not catastrophic. As the Arkansas River roared and ran red with the churning sediments from Oklahoma and other upstream locations, the flood of 1957 would be the last major inundation of thousands of acres of Dardanelle Bottom land. The Dardanelle Dam was soon to be completed and a persistent threat to life, property, and profit—the flood—would soon be only a historical event. That "vile and vicious river," as Doris Hundley Hickey called the Arkansas, would soon be tamed and contained, at least to a degree.

## Rural Transitions

During the late 1950s, quiet and subtle agricultural changes were underway. Dairy herds were being dispersed, beef cattle herds were becoming more common, cotton planters were beginning to diversify as more farmers and landowners planted soybeans, cotton gin owners had begun to carry farm implement lines as they too developed a more diversified business plan, and the slow but steady depopulation of the Bottoms quietly continued. In 1947, Mr. Reuben Harnell, who had left Carden Bottom in 1938 for North Little Rock, but returned periodically to visit with old friends, said that he "still thinks of Yell County as home and feels a deep interest in its welfare and progress."[204] As people moved away, many rural hamlets disappeared in all but memory and name—Fields Chapel, Riverside, Stubbs Town, Wasp Nest, Fowler—and those that remained became smaller with each passing year—Lakeview, Bryant's Cove, New Neely, Slaty Crossing, Cotton Town, and Carden Bottom. By the 1950s, Roy Tillman Jr. was using the old Wasp Nest School as a hay barn, while rural churches disappeared as their congregations moved away.[205] County singings and traditional gatherings were fewer or had completely vanished. In July 1957, as noted earlier, some forty Carden Bottom residents received telephone service, delayed by several months due to the flood damage earlier that same year.[206]

In the summer of 1957, as work began on the new steel bridge across the Petit Jean River, a replacement of the old swinging bridge near Bryant's Cove, Carden Bottom High School graduated its last senior class, seven members strong. On July 14, 1957, the Carden Bottom School Board voted to consolidate its high school with Dardanelle. While it retained grades one through six for several more years, with the closing of the high school, the heart of Carden Bottom disappeared. Dwindling enrollment, lack of funds, and the realization that they could no longer provide the best available education for their students were at the heart of the difficult and controversial decision by the school board members to let Carden Bottom High School die.

One man who advocated the closing of Carden Bottom High School was Les Thone, then president of the Carden Bottom School Board. A few days after the vote was taken to consolidate, Mr. Thone was stopped on the road by a truck blocking his passage. Two men walked to Thone's truck and as one reached through the window to grab him, Thone violently threw open the truck door, knocking his would-be attacker on his back. He then grabbed the second man and sent him hurling to the ground. Thone shouted at the third man, still sitting in the pick-up truck, asking if he wanted to "discuss" anything. The man shook his head no, moved the truck, and Thone drove away.[207] School politics stirred strong emotions. In 1963, Les Thone moved his family to Dardanelle. One of his sons, Mark, retains farming interests in Carden Bottom to this day, and was elected Yell County judge in 2010.[208]

In 1962, Carden Bottom residents voted 92 to 22 against annexation of the Carden Bottom School District by Dardanelle.[209] During the 1962–63 term, Carden Bottom had three teachers for students in grades one through six. Then during the 1963–1964 term, for the first time Carden Bottom elementary-age school students began attending the Dardanelle schools. During this first year, there were twenty-eight Carden Bottom students attending Dardanelle High School and approximately forty-two elementary students. Carden Bottom paid tuition in the amount of $250 per student or a minimum of $15,000 annually for attendance in the Dardanelle schools. The Carden Bottom School District continued to operate its own school buses and continued to operate its school building, although as a community center. Even as Carden Bottom's population declined, the remaining residents were defiantly independent, and Carden Bottom residents continued to pay a 30-mill property tax in order to maintain their school district.[210] The Carden Bottom High School Building continued to serve as a community center for several years in the late 1950s and early 1960s. Beginning in 1966, the site hosted adult education classes, which offered free General Education Development (GED) preparation classes taught by faculty from Dardanelle High School and leading to a high school equivalency diploma.[211] Today, the building sits vacate, as does Carden Bottom. Vines grow through its windows as trees cover the once open playground. Carden Bottom High School, a monolithic expression of human will, independence, and love, is receding into the land.

Throughout the 1950s and 1960s, the poultry processing plant and the introduction of chicken farming drew rural residents away from their established way of life. Many moved to town while others drove in each day to earn wages. For small farmers who wanted to continue their rural way of life, their wives often worked at the processing plant

in order to pay for a small farming operation.[212] Many farming operations became contracted chicken (broiler) producers. Traditional
farming was declining and with it a complete way of life was vanishing
or, at least, being radically altered.

On April 4, 1964, Rollow H. Carden, the great-grandson of the
founder of Carden Bottom, died in Russellville; his wife, Gladys
McNew Carden, lived on until 2011.[213]

In 1968, a former resident took a nostalgia-filled sojourn to once
again visit his childhood home. He found that "the cotton fields and
corn fields once enclosed by rail fences have been converted into
tightly wired pastures where sleek cattle graze, while much of the timber is gone." He concluded that it was a journey "to seek something we
may never find again."[214] The rural community and all that it once so
proudly entailed had disappeared.

Historian Donald Holley argues that "from the late 1930s to the
1970s cotton moved from a labor-intensive crop to a capital-intensive
one . . . [and that] . . . the invention of the mechanical cotton picker was
the center piece of the brave new world of agricultural technology . . .
[and that this] . . . transformation uprooted thousands of people who
moved to towns and cities as well as out of state."[215] Reduced cotton
acreage due to government programs—such as the First and Second
Agricultural Adjustment Acts—allowed farmers to experiment with
new crops. Less cotton meant a reduced need for tenant farmers,
and between 1935 and 1940 their numbers declined by 23.9 percent.
Landowners began to rely increasingly on seasonal, nonresident
wage hands for cotton chopping and picking. Subsequently, World
War II increased the "pull" away from tenancy, and from 1940 to 1945
Arkansas lost 28 percent of its farm population. This loss would be
followed by a 22.7 percent decline in the state's population during the
1950s. During the period from 1954 to 1959, 54 percent of Arkansas's
farm tenants disappeared, and the resulting agricultural labor shortage pushed landowners to increase their use of mechanization. Small
landowners could not afford the expensive new equipment, and the
result was the disruption of the traditional agricultural system that
had for decades resulted in widespread rural poverty. By the late 1960s,
90 percent of Arkansas's cotton crop was machine picked, and by 1972
the state's cotton crop was practically 100 percent machine harvested.

Between 1945 and 1969, the number of Arkansas farms declined from 98,727 to 25,353 while the average farm size increased from 77.7 acres to 335.2 acres. While 79.3 percent of Arkansas farms in 1930 were cotton farms, by 1969 the number of cotton farms in the state was down to 25 percent and a continued rapid decline ensued into the 1980s. Mechanization had permanently altered agriculture and the face of rural Arkansas. By the 1950s, Arkansas's major cash crop was the soybean.[216] The transformations to agricultural life in Arkansas were intense, deep, and permanent.

## Town Transitions

In Dardanelle, too, things were quietly changing. Longtime business-men were retiring. Jack Boyce closed out his sixty-plus-year business career, and sold the Dardanelle Mercantile to his son-in-law and daughter in 1952. A big man of almost indestructible character and determination—memorable to anyone who ever met him—Boyce died in November 1954. Singer Drug Store, which had operated for some forty years at the corner of South Main (Market) and Front Streets in Dardanelle, closed in 1950. Cunningham Supply closed its business and liquated its stock in 1957. The Ploss Hotel, a thirty-room rambling structure located at Pine and Second Streets, which for more than seven decades had served drummers and travelers, closed in March 1968 although it reopened briefly in 1970 as an antique shop. The Mount Nebo Chicken Fry, which began in 1949 to promote the area's poultry industry initially attracting 1,500 attendees, had by the mid-1950s become a major political stop for Arkansas office seek-ers. In July 1955, the Mount Nebo Chicken Fry hosted 8,000 people and featured a chicken dinner, political speeches, and a dance and party scene as the day turned to night. The fine once-proud homes of well-to-do citizens, such as the Jacoways, the Kaufmans, and the Crownovers, were razed while other fine old homes lapsed into disre-pair and neglect.[217] Old structures in the business district, including the Joy Theatre, were also almost gleefully replaced, with little regard for their history. Old families died out or left town, and although new citizens arrived, the character of the old town began to change. More women were working outside the home and, thus, the bridge clubs, the Garden Club, Music Club, and Parent-Teachers Association (PTA), while still active, were now managed by women who had employment as well as family responsibilities. With the completion of the Dardanelle Dam, the threat of major floods and all of their terror had disappeared. In 1961 the state highway department let bids for the construction of a Highway 7 Bypass that would skirt the downtown area and make Union Street the primary Dardanelle through street.[218]

## Economic Impact of Rural and Town Transitions

Given the extreme degree and number of transitions that influenced rural and town life during the post–World War II period, a comparison of Arkansas average per capital income versus that of the nation in selected years is insightful. These statistics appear below and are given in current dollars and are not adjusted for inflation. When available, statistics for Yell County are also noted.

| YEAR | AVERAGE PER CAPITA INCOME— UNITED STATES | AVERAGE PER CAPITA INCOME— ARKANSAS | AVERAGE PER CAPITA INCOME— YELL COUNTY |
|---|---|---|---|
| 1945 | $1,256 | $753 | — |
| 1950 | $1,542 | $852 | — |
| 1955 | $1,964 | $1,206 | — |
| 1960 | $2,338 | $1,430 | — |
| 1965 | $2,937 | $1,904 | — |
| 1969 | $3,947 | $2,681 | $2,437 |
| 1970 | $4,216 | $2,920 | $2,493 |
| 1971 | $4,488 | $3,181 | $2,742 |
| 1972 | $4,876 | $3,509 | $3,102 |
| 1975 | $6,329 | $4,780 | — |

Source: Archival Federal Reserve Economic Data, Economic Research Division, Federal Reserve Bank, St. Louis, Missouri. https://alfred.stlouisfed.org.

This data shows that in the three decades following the end of World War II, Yell County was improving economically and moving closer to Arkansas per capita income averages. It, of course, also reveals the disparity between Arkansas and national per capita income averages, a gap that remained persistent throughout these three decades and actually increased beginning in 1965. In fact, although beyond the scope of this study, it is significant to note that this state/national per capita income disparity has yet to be bridged. The 2014 national per capita income average was $46,030 while the Arkansas equivalent was $37,751.[219]

In Arkansas in 1945 wages and salaries were 296.7 percent of their 1929 levels. By 1960 this percentage had increased to 571.5 to 1,264.6 in 1970. Meanwhile, farm proprietors' income in 1945 was only 144.7 percent of its 1929 base level. By 1960 it had increased but only to 149 percent of its 1929 level and by 1970 again it increased to 210.7 percent of its 1929 base level. In comparison nonfarm proprietors' income for the same three years and as compared to 1929 drastically increased by 268.1, 456.2, and 761.1 percent respectively. Thus, the statistics indicate that economic and income growth following World War II in Arkansas was not concentrated or even particularly strong within agricultural. The growth was in nonfarm forms of business and ownership, and it was even stronger among individuals working for wages and salaries.[220]

Thus, even given economic improvements and the numerous transitions that occurred in the Bottoms and Dardanelle from 1942 to 1970, low income, poverty, and limited opportunities for economic improvements remained. Although improvements in these economic areas had occurred and generally economic life was better than in past years, still on average the people of the Bottoms and Dardanelle, as well as Arkansas, continued to face economic challenges. For some, these challenges were severe and had a highly negative influence on their opportunities and their quality of life.

## African Americans

Life for African Americans was also changing. On April 14, several Dardanelle African American community leaders met privately with A. E. Caldwell, superintendent of the Dardanelle schools, to request that the board of education honor their request to integrate Dardanelle

High School. The delegation noted that sixteen high-school-age students (grades seven through twelve) were currently attending Sullivan School, the African American area high school in Morrilton. Given their long daily bus ride, these students were unable to participate in any after-school activities such as sports and, therefore, this constituted an unequal educational opportunity. Also, the long daily bus trip meant that these children were away from home for an undue amount of time during the week.

Lonnie Dickens recalled his daily trip to Sullivan School, resulting in an eleven-hour school day as African American students were collected by the one school bus beginning in Belleville (far-western Yell County), then Danville, Dardanelle, Russellville, Atkins, and finally Morrilton. The bus had seats for only thirty-five students, and from Dardanelle on, students packed into the aisle and stood for the remainder of the trip. Added to this was the fact that the bus driver was a sixteen-year-old white boy who had limited driving experience. The long trip meant that most African American Sullivan School students left for school in the dark of the morning and returned home in the dark of the early evening. When Dickens was seventeen, his stepfather became ill, and Dickens left school for a year in order to manage the family's livestock and work as a fulltime tenant farmer in order to help his family. Upon returning to school the next year, all of his classmates had either dropped out or had graduated, so he, too, left, with a tenth-grade education.[221]

The 1950s, of course, prompted profound changes in the education of African Americans given the 1954 United States Supreme Court decision in *Brown v. Board of Education*. Based on its application of the Equal Protection Clause of the Fourteenth Amendment, the *Brown* decision ended the legal segregation of the nation's public schools. This decision, while welcomed by many as just and constitutionally valid, was also taken by others to be a despicable intervention of federal judicial power rendering the abolishment of centuries of race- and social-based separation. Those who believed in race and social segregation predicted doom for the white race as they railed against the *Brown* decision, the Court and its justices, and what they deemed the unwarranted federal intervention over states' rights and traditions.

In Arkansas, reactions to the *Brown* decision were present both verbally and in subsequent actions. While peaceful school integration occurred in some Arkansas communities such as first in Charleston and in Fayetteville in 1954, this was not always the case. In 1955 in the small northeast Arkansas community of Hoxie, school integration proceeded peacefully until local Klansmen reached out to those with similar beliefs. Soon Hoxie was embroiled in an ugly, loud, public protest as future gubernatorial candidate "Justice Jim" Johnson and thousands of Klansmen and white segregationists descended upon the community in an attempt to intimidate and frighten school officials and townspeople to end their school's integration. White Citizens' Councils and other segregationist groups were formed in Hoxie and in other Arkansas communities to protest against racial integration. The rhetoric was mean, hateful, and appealed to white fears of racial equality. Previously moderate governor Orval Faubus joined the ranks of the southern segregationists in November 1955 in an effort to continue his political career.[222] Hoxie stood firm. On October 25, 1956, the Eighth Circuit Court of Appeals of the United States upheld the Hoxie School Board's right to peacefully integrate their schools without outside interference.[223]

By 1956 the question and "debate" over school integration moved to the gubernatorial race in which Jim Johnson, the staunch segregationist, lost in the Democratic Party primary to incumbent Orval Faubus, who had embraced the segregationist position and then went on to win reelection. The events in Hoxie in 1955 "predisposed the hate groups in Arkansas for action . . . [and] . . . in 1957 when Central High integrated, the segregationists were organized and had learned how to effectively fight integration."[224]

When the Little Rock Central High Crisis exploded as national and international news in September 1957, the people of Arkansas and the nation were divided on their views of school integration as well as their concepts of racial equality. The question of federal authority over states' rights, an old and thorny issue that had for generations interjected passion and fury into many debates, only added to the ferocity of the Central High Crisis. In addition, the contention by segregationists that racial equality was a communist-inspired movement and African American leaders were either communists or communist-inspired intensified the irrational fury surrounding school desegregation.[225]

School integration showdowns would continue through the 1950s and into the 1960s and even beyond. Some, like Charleston and Fayetteville, were fairly peaceful and unnoticed, while others were violent and grabbed news headlines. As the modern civil rights movement pressed forward and increasing amounts of federal legislation and court decisions mandating racial integration of interstate commerce facilities and public universities became law and the Civil Rights Act of 1964 and the Voting Rights Act of 1965 were passed, the debate over racial equality seemed a constant element in American life.

In 1964 in Dardanelle an African American delegation presented a formal petition requesting that the Dardanelle Board of Education take action to integrate Dardanelle High School.[226] On May 25, 1964, the Dardanelle Board of Education ordered the admittance of all African American high school students living within its school district boundaries to attend Dardanelle High School with integration to begin during the 1964–1965 school term.[227] The following year Douglas School, Dardanelle's African American Elementary School serving approximately fifty children grades one through six, was closed and the Dardanelle schools became fully integrated during the 1965–1966 school term.[228] Racial integration at all levels of the Dardanelle schools went smoothly without difficulty or incidents.

Just a decade earlier, an editorial in the *Dardanelle Post-Dispatch* had railed regarding the Supreme Court's decision in *Brown v. Board of Education,* calling the Court's decision "an encroachment on state rights" and believed that "segregation is going to continue in some if not all southern states." Furthermore, the editorial concluded that desegregation "will work a hardship on the Negro race."[229] During the intervening decade, while many segregationists still agreed with this reaction, most area residents were becoming more aware of the need for greater racial equality.

Even though at times the rhetoric had been racist and actions violent and deadly, generally a sense of peace and cooperation had always permeated race relations in Dardanelle. This was typified by the career of Mr. Luther Banks. The son of slaves William and Matilda Banks, who came to Dardanelle in 1852 from Tennessee and 1860 from South Carolina respectively, young Luther worked in the cotton fields of the Bottoms as a young boy. He completed his schooling in the ninth grade and sometime around 1900 began working as a shoe-shine boy in the African American barbershop owned by W. S. Calhoun in Dardanelle. In 1910, he began his career as a barber. For approximately seventy-four years, Luther Banks provided haircuts and shaves to both the white and African American residents of Dardanelle, serving customers from six generations of many Dardanelle families and providing many young children their first haircut. For approximately the last sixty years of his life, his barbershop was located on Market Street. Mr. Banks married Ursie Williams. Together they raised a nephew and had one daughter, who earned a graduate degree and taught school in California.

Banks, known affectionately as "Mr. Luther" by many, worked to within months of his death at the age of ninety-eight in 1984.[230] Luther Banks was not simply a compliant African American who knew and lived within his "place" in Dardanelle, but rather he was a highly successful small businessman who was deeply respected by both African Americans and whites for his numerous kind and humanitarian gestures toward people of both races as well as for his hard work, business acumen, strong family commitment, and personal success. The respect and friendship between Mary Miller Adney, a white beautician, and Luther Banks, an African American barber, beautifully illustrates this point. For several decades Mrs. Adney and Mr. Banks shared adjacent business spaces on the first floor of the Cunningham Building on South Main Street (Market Street), and each had a key to the front door of the other's business. Frequently at the end of a long day's work when Mrs. Adney was exhausted and her feet and legs ached, Mr. Banks, noticing her pain, would urge her to close her shop. He would later go over and mop her floor and clean so that the next morning Mrs. Adney had a clean shop in which to begin that day's work. Mrs. Adney frequently brought vegetables from her large home garden and homemade foods for Mr. Banks and his family and, when needed, she would give Mr. Banks a ride in her car to a place too distant for an easy walk.[231] This was no *quid pro quo* arrangement. It was the stuff of mutual respect and consideration between two hard-working small business owners. It was also the story of two friends, one white and one African American, who saw each other as fellow business owners individually striving to earn a living and not simply as members of the opposite race.

Interracial friendships such as this were not uncommon in Dardanelle. Certainly racism existed as previous examples have illustrated, but there also existed in Dardanelle, at least among some, a core of common decency and respect not altered or determined by race but founded upon the bedrock of appreciation for hard work, honesty, and human kindness. For some in Dardanelle respect, friendship, and cooperation crossed the color line.

Thus while racism existed in Dardanelle and the Bottoms, individuals like Luther Banks, respected for his honesty, work ethic, and genteel manners, undercut at the harshness of race hatred, at least for some. This may have been true primarily because respected African American citizens did not aggressively attempt to alter racial norms.

Perhaps one can best understand the quality of race relations in Dardanelle by examining a 1948 editorial in the *Dardanelle Post-Dispatch*. Arguing that educating Negroes was necessary but that it must occur in separate schools from whites, this writing says that God intended the races to be separate and that mixing them was unwise. While the tone was somewhat thoughtful in its consideration of the race situation, the undertone was strongly negative ending with the then incendiary suggestion of interracial marriage: "I want my grandchildren to be white."[232] Thus, racism was certainly part of the Dardanelle mindset, but it was usually couched in careful phrases and insulting innuendo rather than in blatant defiance. Thus, good men like Luther Banks, who lived peacefully within the status quo racial parameters, could earn a living and become a respected citizen in Dardanelle. What is striking is the circumspect courage of both the African American petitioners and the Dardanelle Board of Education in 1964 and 1965 to integrate the schools. What is surprising is the placidity with which it was accomplished.

## An Era of Change

Throughout the 1950s and 1960s, Dardanelle was changing. These changes were subtle but real. One could still recognize parts of the old town even while these changes were happening. The same could not be said for the Dardanelle Bottoms.

This undertone of change became even more evident to the careful observer during the decade of the 1960s. Agriculture in particular experienced profound changes during the 1960s, a trend that had begun at least a decade earlier. By the 1950s, only a few mules were being used to farm in the Bottoms. Dan Keenan and his son, Bobby, expanded their John Deere farm implement business in 1960, which not only featured farm equipment, but also offered complete service rendered by five factory-trained repairmen, and a sales and parts department. Some 1,000 farmers attended the opening of the expanded implement dealership, which was the largest such business between Little Rock and Oklahoma City.[233] Dan Keenan noted that in 1959, 55 percent of all cotton produced in the Dardanelle Bottoms was harvested by automatic cotton pickers, and that he anticipated that the 1960 harvest would be 85 percent machine harvested. The farm machinery that Dan Keenan and his son sold—in conjunction with their ginning operations—included tractors, air-conditioned combines, and automated cotton pickers. In addition to their cotton interest, the family owned and operated the Keenan Grain Elevator Company, which stored their purchased soybeans and other grain products as well as a complete line of fertilizers. Obviously, agriculture was changing and the Keenans were aggressively working to maintain their position in this changing market.

While crop diversification was expanding, cotton was not completely dead in the Arkansas River Valley. In 1958, Yell County still produced 4,668 bales of cotton, and 9,331 bales were produced in 1959.[234] Still, the chronic problem of farm labor continued to plague Yell County cotton farmers, as elsewhere in Arkansas. Farmer Roy Tillman Jr. firmly believed "the lack of labor ended cotton. Poultry had nothing to do with it."[235] Governor Faubus in 1960 had requested from the US Department of Labor that 2,500 Mexican workers, as part of the Bracero Program, be sent to Arkansas for work in the cotton fields. Although the request netted 1,975 workers for Arkansas, all were assigned to Delta areas.[236]

## Cotton's Death—The 1960s

The profile of the farm operations of Grace and W. H. ("Junior") McClure Jr., Yell County's Farm Family of the Year in 1960, is indicative of the agricultural transitions occurring during the early 1960s.

The McClures farmed 1,490 acres in Lakeview in Carden Bottom and in Riverside, of which 250 acres were devoted to cotton, 720 acres to soybeans, 20 acres to alfalfa, and 80 acres to small grains. The McClures also maintained 110 Hereford cattle on 350 acres of pastureland. "Junior" McClure was the first farmer in Yell County to invest in a combine, a cotton picker, a Hi-boy cotton spray machine, and the first to use chemical pre-emergence control of weeds in cotton. Given this mechanization, by 1960 McClure was using very little hand labor. Other farmers quickly followed McClure's lead as they adopted new farming methods and purchased modern mechanized farm equipment, if they could afford to do so.[237] As farmers mechanized and relied more on fertilizers, many used government programs to farm less land and be paid for doing so. In 1960, 345 Conservation Reserve contracts were in effect in Yell County, which represented the removal of 21,168 acres of farmland from crop production, and which accounted for payments to landowners of $232,000 annually.[238]

These agricultural transitions were not seamless, as farm laborers still working became displaced. By 1962, Yell County had a reported 1,750 persons in the "surplus labor force," and the county's average annual per-person income was $783.[239] The 1965 *Arkansas Business Report* (published in 1966) noted that 5,600 farm laborer jobs were lost during 1965 and that cotton acreage had declined. The report also noted that cotton farmers has a decrease in income, while at the same time, poultry and livestock farmers experienced a rise in income.[240] As leaders discussed the need for future economic development, it was obvious that the long relied upon agricultural backbone of the area was eroding, especially cotton farming.

Nonetheless, growth and transition in Yell County—as indicated in the 1960 to 1965 comparative report of the Arkansas Industrial Development Commission—was highly positive. In Yell County, the population had increased by 8.3 percent, per capita income had increased by 33.5 percent, total bank deposits had increased by 137.9 percent, the value of farm products sold had increased by 76.2 percent, and the average value of farms had increased by 105.9 percent.[241]

Indicative of this transition and the changing attitude toward cotton was an editorial appearing in late 1962 demanding that gin owners in Dardanelle correct the "24 hour a day shower of cotton gin debris" and "the dirty and unhealthy outpouring from our cotton gins."[242] The editorial called for gin operators to resolve the situation or be faced with "the enactment of municipal legislation designed to force the eradication of a public nuisance by popular demand of the citizenry."[243] Gin owner Dan Keenan responded to the public outcry by purchasing and immediately installing lint catching equipment for his cotton gin at a cost of $2,000.[244] Shockingly, Dardanelle's long history of reliance on cotton as its economic backbone was coming to an end.

The public concern voiced against the town's cotton gin smoke, soot, and cotton debris did not end. By 1963, one cotton gin owner offered a blunt reply to the *Dardanelle Post-Dispatch*'s continued pressure for cleaner air and less cotton debris: "if you don't like it, you can move away."[245] The war of words between the general public and the cotton interests in Dardanelle resulted in a chamber of commerce resolution asking the city council and the city health department to "take appropriate action or steps to alleviate the smog conditions arising from some gins."[246]

In July 1964, a petition signed by 124 Dardanelle citizens was presented to Mayor Dana Merritt in a city council meeting asking for immediate city action against the cotton gin owners. Bobby Keenan stated that the gin owners were aware of the problem and were attempting to find a solution. Keenan also noted that the gin operations could save money if proper equipment to limit airborne lint and debris could be installed, but that currently all efforts to find such equipment had failed and previously installed equipment had not satisfactorily solved the problem. Keenan continued: "we feel that the gins contribute to the town's economy and that one problem inherent in the business was the burning of cotton hulls which is required by law to be done on the premises in order to control the pink boll weevil. We are trying to correct this situation, but it may take two or more years to find the 'answer.'"[247] Keenan warned that the cotton gins in Dardanelle served cotton growers from nine counties "who would be scared off by a controversy and would take their cotton elsewhere for ginning . . . cotton farmers are not only customers of the gins but also are customers of other businesses in town."[248] Modernity, with its new emphasis on cleaner air and greater public health precautions, conflicted with the traditional cotton culture and its economic implications, including the reciprocal relationship between the rural and the town. While the gin owners continued their attempts to update their equipment in order to reduce emissions and some town's people continued to be dissatisfied, the mayor and city council attempted to find a middle ground and defuse the controversy. Truth be told, confronting modernity offered little room for compromise.

The flap over cotton gin debris would not long continue primarily because cotton growing continued to decline. A 1967 study of agricultural output for Yell County predicted that by 1975, Yell County would have fewer than 300 acres in cotton production whereas 13,000 acres would be invested in soybeans. Beef cattle and pasture grains were also predicted to increase, but the largest predicted agricultural pursuit would be in poultry production rendering a 1975 production value in Yell County of $50 million.[249] The late 1967 Yell County farming news report submitted by Gene Lowery, the associate county agent, focused entirely on beef cattle and soybeans with no mention of cotton.[250] There was still cotton in the Dardanelle Bottoms, but as the 1960s drew to a close, more and more farmers were producing soybeans.

The decline of the importance of cotton in Dardanelle and the Bottoms can be seen through the career of W. H. Nichols. A Dardanelle resident and business owner, Nichols spent more than fifty years working as a cotton grader. By 1968, he was one of only fifteen cotton graders in Arkansas. A native of Tennessee Nichols began buying cotton in 1925 when 40 million acres of cotton were being grown in the American South and a "small farmer could pay his expenses and have a comfortable living from 3 to 5 bales a season . . . his sole dependence for cash was on a cotton crop."[251] He recalled that the cotton pickers he knew in the 1920s worked for 40 cents per hundred pounds and lived on $10 a month. Nichols credited the demise of cotton to Depression era cotton prices of 5 cents a pound; the development of synthetic fibers, especially nylon, during and just after World War II; and the use of chemicals and mechanized equipment following World War II into the 1950s. By the time of his interview in 1968, only three cotton gins remained in Yell County, all in Dardanelle, whereas once the county had fifty-seven gins. Once over 40 percent of the residents of Yell County were engaged in growing cotton, although by 1968 it had declined to 8 percent.

Still in 1968, Dardanelle remained the largest ginning center between Oklahoma and Pine Bluff. Simultaneously, the days of cotton in the Dardanelle Bottoms were ending as farmers were finding economic security in soybeans.[252] A sign of these new agricultural times was witnessed in December 1969 as the Keenan Grain Warehouse facilities on the north side of the Arkansas River received the first ever barge load of grain shipped up river.

Keenan Gin Company had started construction of their grain elevator and storage facility in late 1964. It contained four storage bins and a conveyor belt system for the loading and unloading of grain from river barges.[253] The first grain received in 1969 was destined for AVI and its poultry farmers. On its return trip, the barge carried soybeans from the Kennan grain storage facility at the Port of Dardanelle.[254] Bobby Keenan built the port facility mainly to ship soybeans, but he was also shipping rubber for the Firestone plant and steel for the steel businesses in Russellville. Within two years of the Keenan port facility's opening, other companies were building their own warehouses and managing their own product shipments. Thus, the Keenan port facility mainly shipped soybeans and was therefore only marginally profitable.[255] The death of cotton, the rise of soybeans, the new dominance of the poultry industry, and shipments via the dams and locks on the Arkansas River all coalesced to create a new reality by 1970, a reality that permanently altered the reciprocity of the Bottoms with Dardanelle.

## Conclusion

After World War II, the New Neely Gin and the cotton gins in the Bottoms—the Cowger and Cotton Town Gins—all closed, as had the Centerville Gin years earlier. In 1969 the McClure Gin in Dardanelle (originally the Farmers' Gin) closed, and one year after Bobby Keenan's death in 1978, his mother, Betty Keenan, and his son, Robert Keenan Jr., sold their ginning operations. Within another year, the operations ceased. Delma Merritt purchased the Yell County Gin on April 1, 1966, ginned cotton from Oklahoma for several years until he was informed that it was illegal to ship cotton across state lines for ginning, and then converted the gin into a farm implement dealership in 1975. Soybeans had proven more profitable than cotton by the 1970s, signaling, as Tomela Wright Keenan noted, that "times had changed."[256]

So it was that cotton in the Dardanelle Bottoms further declined for several reasons in the period from 1945 to 1970. First, the persistent farm labor shortage became chronic after 1955. As rural residents found work in the poultry processing plants and the broiler production phase of the poultry industry, fewer workers were available for cotton's laborious tasks. Second, landowners who could afford to do so invested in expensive mechanized farm machinery, which, as Gordon Crain noted, were not better than mules but they could do the mule's work in one-fourth the time.[257] Third, new pesticides—which were extremely effective against the ravishes of the boll weevil and the Texas cutworms—were as expensive as they were effective, and thus, other crops, particularly soybeans, became a more cost-effective alternative. Fourth, by the 1960s and 1970s, the expansive spaces of the Arkansas Delta could vastly out-produce cotton output from the more geographically restricted Dardanelle Bottoms. Given the rising costs of engaging in cotton farming, this economy of scale was vitally important. Fifth, the last ginning operation in Dardanelle closed in 1979. This closure was the final blow for cotton. Even those loyal cotton farmers who still wanted to raise cotton could not afford to transport their product to ginning operations in Pine Bluff or further south or east. Indeed, times had changed, but what a history cotton had generated.

In the late 1960s, the *Dardanelle Post-Dispatch* ceased carrying a "Carden Bottom" column. Only Carden Bottom's green highway sign remained, and it was removed in 2012. The beauty of the lively little town on the river faded. New folks who had a love for beer, Walmart shopping, and easy pastimes moved to town. The once rich culture of Dardanelle disappeared. Gracious entertainment had given way to Little League games and bingo nights at the American Legion Hut. The world moved on and modernity left little room for Dardanelle and the Bottoms as they once had been. The old reciprocal bond between the Bottoms and the town, which had sustained and enriched both—and ultimately served as their mutual reason for existence—had vanished.

## CHAPTER 7

# Conclusion

*. . . soon now we shall go out . . . into the convulsion of the world, out of history into history and the awful responsibility of Time.*

ROBERT PENN WARREN,
*All the King's Men*

*The modern South completed a circle . . . from undercapitalized colonial dependency to complex, well-capitalized colonial dependence. . . . A new New South had appeared, but whether it was better than the old one was a question not easily and fairly answered.*

JACK TEMPLE KIRBY,
*Rural Worlds Lost: The American South, 1920–1960*

*The world breaks everyone, and afterward, some are strong at the broken places.*

EARNEST HEMINGWAY,
*A Farewell to Arms*

Dardanelle survived the carnage of the Civil War and rebuilt. It bristled with ambitious, hard-driving businessmen and served thousands of farmers as a thriving commercial center for their products and needs. Until the early 1900s Dardanelle had been the largest business center between Little Rock and Fort Smith with two wharfs: one at the river's edge of South Main Street (now Market Street) and the other main wharf at the river's edge of Quay Street. These wharfs received thousands of shipments of goods from steamboats and served as the cotton platforms holding thousands of bales being shipped out by steamboats. Dardanelle had endured the agricultural disruptions following World War I and the trauma of the Great Depression. Following World War II the great change began to happen, slowly and all but undetectable.

In 1948 the chamber of commerce, still reflecting a belief in the indisputable reciprocity of Dardanelle and the Bottoms, issued a statement recognizing "the fact that this is, and probably always will be, a farming community, and that our progress and prosperity depend almost entirely on agriculture."[1] This traditional dynamic, however, changed. The Bottoms slowly, quietly died as its residents moved away. Communities vanished as did schools and churches. Mechanized agriculture and the use of fertilizers brought the end to the tenant farmer, sharecropper, and day laborer. Poultry and soybeans replaced cotton, and cattle farming increased in importance. Dardanelle's entire purpose for existing was undermined. The once vibrant business community dwindled, even though the town's population increased.

Dardanelle in the 1950s and into the 1960s still hummed to the longstanding rhythms of rural/town reciprocity. By the 1970s, all was noticeably changing. Crops changed, cotton gins closed, old families and old established businesses were gone, a new town leadership was coming to the fore, country people had moved to town, and the rural world was being depopulated. Even the physical appearance of Dardanelle and the Bottoms changed. The once beautiful little river town became increasingly poorly maintained. People began parking cars, sometimes numerous cars, sometimes junkers, in front yards. Lawns were not maintained, litter was more evident, and, more and more, one saw indoor furniture on front porches and piles of junk and debris in the yards. A new class of Dardanelle citizens had arrived in town, and they were not always neat and tidy. In the countryside, old houses stood vacant, the vines and trees overtook once clean and swept yards, cropland was turning into pine tree farms, and field turnarounds were growing up with trees and brush. The once black sandy loam of the Bottoms was turned beige, a result of sanding and overuse. The levees were no longer maintained, and trees and weeds grew on their tops and along their bases. Mainly, however, the land was without its people and their instruments of civil society: schools, churches, country stores, and gins. The land was vacant with only a few tractors and combines occasionally working the fields. The people were gone. Seeing cotton pickers in the fields south of Dardanelle during the 1950s was now only a memory that seemed older in its origin than it actually was. Rural road traffic consisted more of fishermen and their boats than of working farmers. The rural world had vanished.

Rural people, whose parents and grandparents had been tenant farmers and farm laborers, now lived in town, worked at the poultry processing plant, and no longer had to worry about the weather, crop prices, and crop financing. They were simply wage earners. For those who remained on the land, the chicken house producing broilers had replaced the cotton patch. The town's sound of the cotton compress—steam/BOOM—fell into silence as the Planters' Compress shut down in 1973. Big landowners more than ever needed a banking/financing relationship to purchase modern equipment and chemicals. Job opportunities in Dardanelle became increasingly limited. Young people left for college or the service and many never returned. "Old Dardanelle," replete with its small, elitist class, had all but vanished. No longer were there elegant social teas and receptions in which young women from important families learned the gracious art of proper entertaining from their mothers. No longer did people dress for church or practice good manners in public. The once-vibrant African American community, both in the Upper Bottoms and in Dardanelle, also declined as its population dramatically decreased.

In short, Dardanelle today is not what it was in the 1950s and 1960s. Few of its citizens know of its rich history and too many seem content to engage in the most pedestrian pleasures. The ambitious, hard-driving impulse to make money has largely been replaced by a desire for relaxation and entertainment. In the 1990s, a grocery store owner noted that each month when the government disability checks arrived, he hired an extra man just to sweep his parking lot because it was littered with empty government envelopes. There is no center of town. Traffic flows through the town on the Highway 7 Bypass. The business community is small and downtown is largely—due to a few absentee and/or uncaring property owners—a collection of ill-maintained, empty buildings. While a few attempt to provide the civic leadership to right the ship and send the town sailing toward a better future, their efforts frequently fall short due to a general lack of interest, will, and civic support.

Of course, rural life in the Bottoms is also drastically different. As mechanization replaced farm laborers and tenant farmers and as expensive chemicals and machinery became a necessary component to farming, the Bottoms began to die. Few families live in the Bottoms. Currently only three families reside in all of Carden Bottom. Most people who farm the Bottoms are absentee farmers or landowners who live in town or somewhere else: Little Rock, Dallas, or Memphis. Beginning in the post–World War II period, as the tenant farmers, sharecroppers, and farm laborers vanished so did Dardanelle's primary purpose for existence. The once proud but hardscrabble life of the Bottoms had become only a memory enshrined in the hearts of those who had lived and survived it.

As mentioned, the last of the area gins closed in 1979 and cotton died. Big landowners worked with banks for financing, and Dardanelle merchants no longer had their "country" customers to whom they extended credit and from whom they garnered much of their retail profits. Walmart came to Dardanelle in the late 1970s and a number of small retail stores closed soon thereafter. McDonalds and other fast food chains opened in the 1980s and local cafes closed. Dardanelle has been carried away and transformed by the contemporary, homogenized world. Dardanelle voted itself dry in the late 1950s and the revenue, which liquor sales had once generated, evaporated and went to nearby "wet" towns. The Joy Theatre closed in the 1970s. Dardanelle was shrinking and changing.

The pride that once was an integral part of being a citizen of Dardanelle became only an occasional, usually sports-related, whoop or holler. The residents of Dardanelle today are more likely to go to the stock car races at Centerville on Saturday night than to attend a cultural event or entertain graciously in their homes. On almost any night one could shoot a shotgun blast down Front Street and be in no danger of harming anyone, except perhaps a stray cat. The only exception to this is bingo night at the American Legion Hut or the auction nights at two antique/junk businesses. The town is no longer vibrant.

Perhaps the recent influx of Hispanic residents will interject some reason for hope as they have opened new businesses and increased the town's population. However, Dardanelle's traditional reason for existing has vanished as the once vibrant Dardanelle Bottoms has become depopulated and left vacant, an empty vessel devoid of its people and its once rich bounty of cotton and jobs.

Before one mourns the death of "old Dardanelle" with its proud elegance, rigid socioeconomic class structure, racism, health problems, and extreme poverty juxtaposed with concentrated wealth, one must examine the comparative profile of the "new Dardanelle" that began to emerge during and after the 1970s. While the town contemporarily lacks much of its old beauty and almost none of its foregone gracious elegance, nonetheless it is somewhat less racist, existing poverty is less severe although still present, general health and educational opportunities are vastly improved, and the socioeconomic differences are less dramatic. The people of Dardanelle now include many former residents of the Bottoms and their descendants. They remain primarily a forthright, strong-willed, and genuine people. Of the descendants of the residents of "old Dardanelle"—the few who remain—some continue to demonstrate a dynamic business acumen and drive for success, some do not. All in all, since the 1970s Dardanelle has experienced a leveling of sorts exhibiting some areas of improvement and some areas of decline. Perhaps this is progress in the modern, homogenized culture or perhaps it represents the loss of identity, a severance from one's past. However one analyzes and interprets these changes, one stark truth remains: "old Dardanelle" and all that it entailed no longer exist. The rural/town reciprocity that functioned so well for a century or more is now simply history.

# APPENDIX

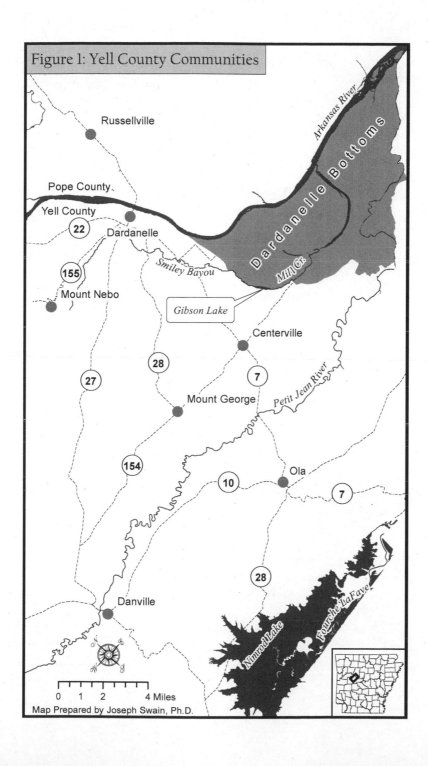

Figure 1: Yell County Communities

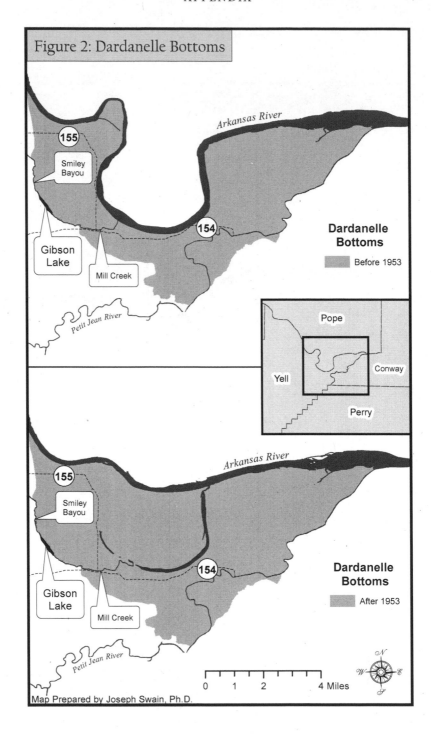

Figure 2: Dardanelle Bottoms

Dardanelle Bottoms

Before 1953

Dardanelle Bottoms

After 1953

Map Prepared by Joseph Swain, Ph.D.

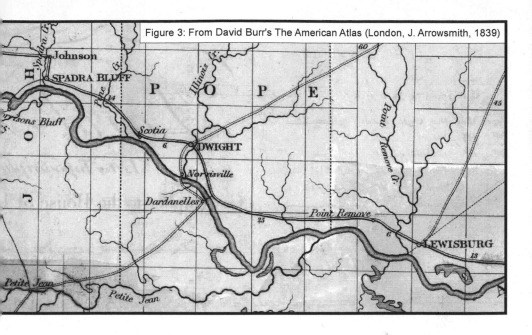

Figure 3: From David Burr's The American Atlas (London, J. Arrowsmith, 1839)

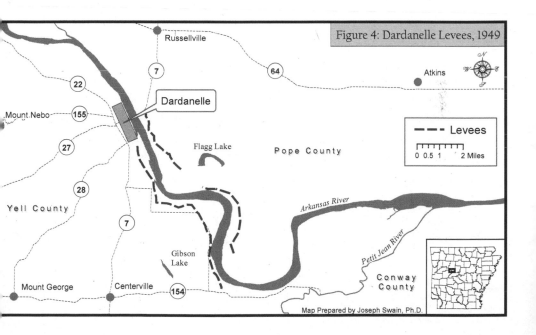

Figure 4: Dardanelle Levees, 1949

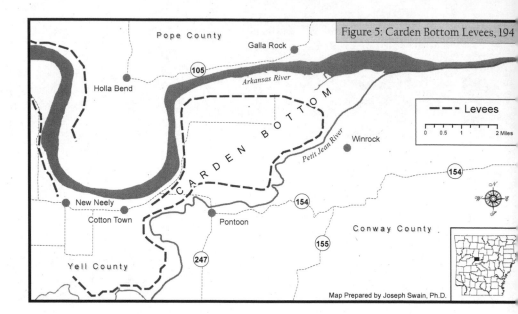

Figure 5: Carden Bottom Levees, 194

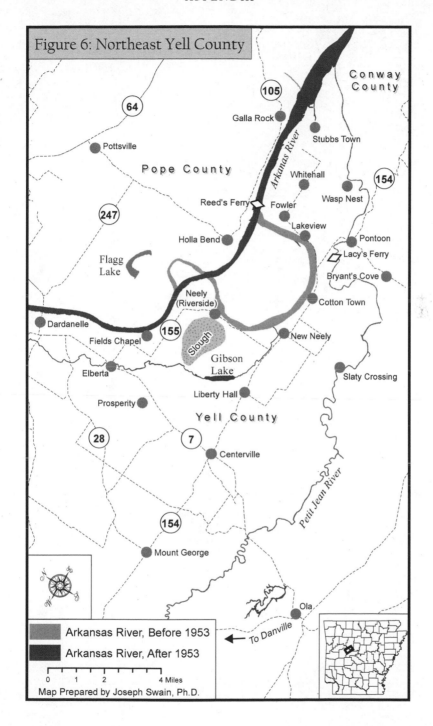

Figure 6: Northeast Yell County

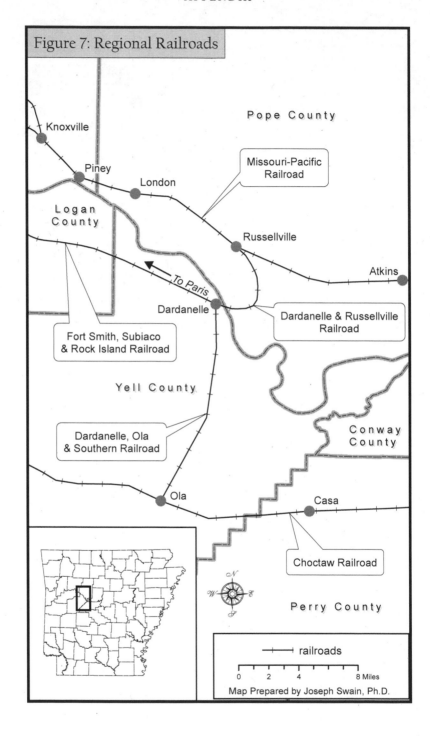

Figure 7: Regional Railroads

# NOTES

## CHAPTER I: The Beginnings, 1819–1879

1. Van Hawkins, "Cotton Industry," *The Encyclopedia of Arkansas History & Culture*.

2. Mrs. Lewis Evans, "A History of Carden Bottoms," *Arkansas Democrat Magazine*, October 19, 1947, 14. John Stroud, interview by author, Atkins, Arkansas, July 15, 2014.

3. Evans, "A History of Carden Bottoms," 14.

4. Leslie Stewart-Abernathy, "Carden Bottom," *The Encyclopedia of Arkansas History & Culture*.

5. Guy Lancaster, "Petit Jean River," *The Encyclopedia of Arkansas History & Culture*.

6. Lancaster, "Petit Jean River."

7. William G. McLoughlin, *Cherokee Renascence in the New Republic* (Princeton, NJ: Princeton University Press, 1986), 216–22, 260–65.

8. Savoie Lottinville, ed., *A Journal of Travels into the Arkansas Territory during the Year 1819* (Fayetteville: University of Arkansas Press, 1999), 131–42.

9. Clara B. Eno, "The History of the Council Oak," *Arkansas Historical Quarterly* 6, no. 2 (Summer 1947): 198–200.

10. John McKay [chief of the Chickamauga Cherokees], interview by author, Dardanelle, Arkansas, March 22, 2014.

11. Wayne Banks, *History of Yell County, Arkansas* (Van Buren, AR: Press-Argus, 1959), 18.

12. Diane Gleason, "Dardanelle," *The Encyclopedia of Arkansas History & Culture*.

13. "Reminiscences," *Dardanelle Post*, December 14, 1882, 1–2.

14. Ernestine Gravley, "Early Twin Cities of Arkansas: Dardanelle and Norristown," *Arkansas Historical Quarterly* 10, no. 2 (Summer 1951): 177–81.

15. Mattie Brown, "River Transportation in Arkansas, 1819–1890," *Arkansas Historical Quarterly* 1, no. 4 (Winter 1942): 342–54.

16. Jeannie Whayne et al., *Arkansas: A Narrative History* (Fayetteville: University of Arkansas Press, 2002), 140–41, 346–49.

17. "Our River in Arkansas and Elsewhere," *Dardanelle Post-Dispatch*, October 27, 1921, 2–6.

18. Brown, "River Transportation," 349–53.

19. Brown, "River Transportation," 351.

20. Georgena Duncan, "'One Negro, Sarah . . . One Horse Named Collier, One Cow and Calf Named Pink': Slave Records from the Arkansas River Valley," *Arkansas Historical Quarterly* 69, no. 4 (Winter 2010): 325–45.

21. John Solomon Otto, "Slavery in the Mountains: Yell County, Arkansas, 1840–1860," *Arkansas Historical Quarterly* 39, no. 1 (Spring 1980): 35–52.

22. Otto, "Slavery in the Mountains," 35–52.

23. Otto, "Slavery in the Mountains," 42–45.

24. Tommy Hunt, interview by author, Dardanelle, Arkansas, July 14, 2008.

25. Otto, "Slavery in the Mountains," 45.

26. Otto, "Slavery in the Mountains," 46–49.

27. Otto, "Slavery in the Mountains," 52–53.

28. Gleason, "Dardanelle."

29. Allen W. Jones and Virginia Ann Buttry, "Military Events in Arkansas during the Civil War, 1861–1865," *Arkansas Historical Quarterly* 22, no. 2 (Summer 1963): 124–70.

30. Mark K. Christ, "Action at Dardanelle and Ivey's Ford," *The Encyclopedia of Arkansas History & Culture.*

31. Ernestine Gravley, "The Presbyterian Church in Dardanelle, Arkansas," *Arkansas Historical Quarterly* 12, no. 3 (Autumn 1953): 274.

32. Thomas Hunt, interview by author, Dardanelle, Arkansas, July 14, 2008.

33. Hunt, interview by author, July 14, 2008.

34. "A War-Time Letter," *Dardanelle Post-Dispatch*, September 14, 1922, 1.

35. Leo E. Huff, "Guerrillas in Northern Arkansas," *Arkansas Historical Quarterly* 24, no. 2 (Summer 1965): 127–48.

36. Banks, *History of Yell County,* 144.

37. "War Time Incident Recalled," *Dardanelle Post-Dispatch,* September 11, 1924, 4; "Recalls Incidents of Knight-Pledger Murder," *Dardanelle Post-Dispatch*, October 16, 1924, 4.

38. Captain J. E. Lindsay, Letter to N. B. (Poly) Eison, March 16, 1866, reproduced in James Reed Eison, ed., "A Letter from Dardanelle to Jonesville, South Carolina," *Arkansas Historical Quarterly* 28, no. 1 (Spring 1969): 72–75.

39. "Texas Visitor Recalls Days of Long Ago," *Dardanelle Post-Dispatch*, April 25, 1929, 6.

40. "A 52 Year Old Dardanelle Newspaper," *Dardanelle Post-Dispatch*, June 26, 1924, 4.

41. See Ken Barnes, *Who Killed John Clayton?: Political Violence and the Emergence of the New South, 1861–1893* (Durham, NC: Duke University Press, 1998).

42. "Reminiscences," *Dardanelle Post-Dispatch*, September 26, 1929, 3.

43. "Reminiscences," *Dardanelle Post-Dispatch*, September 26, 1929, 3.

44. Gleason, "Dardanelle."

45. Gravley, "The Presbyterian Church," 273–77.

46. Lyn Hansen, "David P. Cloyd and the *Dardanelle Independent*," *Arkansas Historical Quarterly* 14, no. 3 (Autumn 1955): 293–300.

## CHAPTER 2: Reestablishment, 1880–1910

1. Diane Gleason, "Yell County," *The Encyclopedia of Arkansas History & Culture.*

2. Jonathan James Wolfe, "Background of German Immigration," *Arkansas Historical Quarterly* 25, no. 4 (Winter 1966): 354–85.

3. Beverly Watkins, "Efforts to Encourage Immigration to Arkansas, 1865–1874," *Arkansas Historical Quarterly* 38, no. 1 (Spring 1979): 32–62.

4. "Yell County: Its Climate, Soil and Productions," *Independent Arkansian*, June 16, 1882, 2.

5. "Yell County: Its Climate, Soil and Productions," *Independent Arkansian*, June 16, 1882, 2.

6. "Yell County: Its Climate, Soil and Productions," *Independent Arkansian*, June 16, 1882, 2.

7. David M. Tucker, *Arkansas: A People and Their Reputation* (Memphis: Memphis State University Press, 1985), 37–38.

8. "Town and Country," *Independent Arkansian*, February 3, 1882, 5.

9. "Town and Country" *Independent Arkansian*, March 24, 1882, 6.

10. Clifton E. Hull and William A. Pollard, *The Dardanelle & Russellville Railroad* (Conway: University of Central Arkansas Press, 1995), 5.

11. "Railroad Meeting," *Independent Arkansian*, October 6, 1882, 2.

12. "Resolution," *Independent Arkansian,* October 6, 1882, 3.

13. Leslie C. Stewart-Abernathy, "Steamboats," *The Encyclopedia of Arkansas History & Culture.*

14. Hull and Pollard, *The Dardanelle & Russellville Railroad*, 4–5.

15. Hull and Pollard, *The Dardanelle & Russellville Railroad*, 8–9.

16. Hull and Pollard, *The Dardanelle & Russellville Railroad*, 16.

17. Hull and Pollard, *The Dardanelle & Russellville Railroad*, 16.

18. Hull and Pollard, *The Dardanelle & Russellville Railroad*, 40–42.

19. "Old Pontoon Bridge Stretched 2,208 Feet," *Yell County Heritage* (Yell County, AR: Yell County Historical & Genealogical Association, 1997), 95.

20. Tucker, *Arkansas,* 55.

21. Tucker, *Arkansas,* 55.

22. "The Local Field," *Independent Arkansian,* March 24, 1882, 6. Also see Gavin Wright, *Old South, New South: Revolutions in the Southern Economy since the Civil War* (Baton Rouge: Louisiana State University Press, 1996).

23. David B. Danbom, *Born in the Country: A History of Rural America*, 4th ed. (Baltimore: Johns Hopkins University Press, 2006), 85. Michael McGerr, *A Fierce Discontent: The Rise and Fall of the Progressive Movement in America* (New York: Oxford University Press, 2003), 20–22.

24. Danbom, *Born in the Country*, 90–95.

25. "Town and Country," *Independent Arkansian*, September 29, 1882, 4.

26. Untitled, *Dardanelle Post,* August 30, 1883, 4.

27. Tucker, *Arkansas,* 123.

28. Advertisement, *Independent Arkansian*, January 6, 1882, 2.

29. "Our Editor's Letter," *Dardanelle Post*, November 15, 1883, 1.

30. "Town and Country," *Independent Arkansian,* February 10, 1882, 5.

31. "Town and Country," *Independent Arkansian,* February 10, 1882, 5.

32. Untitled, *Independent Arkansian,* April 14, 1882, 3 and 6.

33. "Town and Country," *Independent Arkansian*, July 14, 1882, 6.

34. "Town and County," *Independent Arkansian,* February 10, 1882, 5.

35. "Statement," *Dardanelle Post*, November 15, 1883, 3.

36. Carl H. Moneyhon, *Arkansas and the New South, 1874–1929* (Fayetteville: University of Arkansas Press, 1997), 68–70.

37. Matthew Hild, "National Farmers' Alliance and Industrial Union of America," *The Encyclopedia of Arkansas History & Culture*.

38. Judith Barjenbruch, "The Greenback Political Movement: An Arkansas View," *Arkansas Historical Quarterly* 36, no. 2 (Summer 1977): 107–22.

39. Edward J. Chess, "Agricultural Wheel," *The Encyclopedia of Arkansas History & Culture*; F. Clark Elkins, "Arkansas Farmers Organize for Action: 1882–1884," *Arkansas Historical Quarterly* 13, no. 3 (Autumn 1954): 231–48.

40. Elkins, "Arkansas Farmers Organize," 245.

41. Matthew Hild, "Brothers of Freedom," *The Encyclopedia of Arkansas History & Culture*; "Farmers Organize," *Dardanelle Post*, September 27, 1883, 3; Berton E. Henningson Jr., "Northwest Arkansas and the Brothers of Freedom: The Roots of a Farmer Movement," *Arkansas Historical Quarterly* 34, no. 4 (Winter 1975): 304–24; Berton E. Henningson Jr., "Root Hog or Die: The Brothers of Freedom and the 1884 Arkansas Election," *Arkansas Historical Quarterly* 45, no. 3 (Autumn 1986): 197–216.

42. Matthew Hild, "Labor, Third-Party Politics, and the New South Democracy in Arkansas, 1884–1896," *Arkansas Historical Quarterly* 63, no. 1 (Spring 2004): 24–43.

43. Henningson Jr., "Root Hog or Die," 197–216; F. Clark Elkins, "The Agricultural Wheel: County Politics and Consolidation, 1884–1885," *Arkansas Historical Quarterly* 29, no. 2 (Summer 1970): 152–75; F. Clark Elkins, "The Agricultural Wheel in Arkansas, 1887," *Arkansas Historical Quarterly* 40, no. 3 (Autumn 1981): 249–60.

44. Hild, "Labor, Third-Party Politics," 24–43.

45. Thomas S. Baskett Jr., "Miners Stay Away! W. B. W. Heartsill and the Last Years of the Arkansas Knights of Labor, 1892–1896," *Arkansas Historical Quarterly* 42, no. 2 (Summer 1983): 107–33.

46. "Farmers Convention," *Independent Arkansian*, June 2, 1882, 6.

47. Untitled, *Independent Arkansian,* June 2, 1882, 2.

48. "Farmers' Union Resolutions," *Independent Arkansian,* August 11, 1882, 4.

49. Untitled, *Independent Arkansian,* June 21, 1883, 4

50. "Town and Country," *Independent Arkansian,* May 19, 1882, 6; "Gala Rock Township," *Dardanelle Post,* May 3, 1883, 3.

51. "Little Posts," *Dardanelle Post,* May 31, 1883, 3.

52. "Cotton Shipments 82 & 83," *Dardanelle Post,* June 7, 1883, 3; "The Local Field," *Independent Arkansian,* January 6, 1882, 5; "The Local Field," *Independent Arkansian*, February 24, 1882, 5.

53. "Little Posts," *Dardanelle Post*, September 27, 1883, 6.

54. "The Sons of Liberty," *Dardanelle Post*, October 4, 1883, 4.

55. "Farmers' Union," *Dardanelle Post*, September 20, 1883, 3.

56. "Legal Notices," *Dardanelle Post,* December 20, 1883, 3.

57. "To Wheelers of Yell County," *Dardanelle Post*, February 23, 1888, 6.

58. "Cotton Planters' Meeting," *Dardanelle Post-Dispatch*, January 5, 1905, 4.

59. Editorial, *Dardanelle Post-Dispatch*, January 26, 1905, 1.

60. "The Township Meeting," *Dardanelle Post-Dispatch*, February 16, 1905, 2.

61. "Murphy Writes," *Dardanelle Post-Dispatch*, October 24, 1907, 2.

62. "Memphis Cotton Buyers Work with Farmers' Union," *Dardanelle Post-Dispatch,* January 30, 1908, 2.

63. "Union Warehouse Opens," *Dardanelle Post-Dispatch,* May 28, 1908, 5.

64. "A Texan's Plea," *Dardanelle Post-Dispatch,"* February 20, 1908, 4.

65. "Farmers Institute," *Dardanelle Post-Dispatch,* February 6, 1908, 1.

66. "Farmers' Union Campaign Begins," *Dardanelle Post-Dispatch,* July 9, 1908, 1.

67. "Warehouse Ready for Business," *Dardanelle Post-Dispatch,* September 29, 1910, 1.

68. "New Bank and Trust Company," *Dardanelle Post-Dispatch,* June 17, 1909, 1.

69. "A 'Night-Rider' Scare," *Dardanelle Post-Dispatch,* October 8, 1908, 1.

70. "A 'Night-Rider' Scare," *Dardanelle Post-Dispatch,* October 8, 1908, 1.

71. Jeanie Horn, "Night Riders," *The Encyclopedia of Arkansas History & Culture.*

72. "A 'Night-Rider' Scare," *Dardanelle Post-Dispatch,* October 8, 1908, 1.

73. "The Situation Partly Examined," *Dardanelle Post-Dispatch,* October 8, 1908, 1.

74. "The Situation Partly Examined," *Dardanelle Post-Dispatch,* October 8, 1908, 1.

75. "The Situation Partly Examined," *Dardanelle Post-Dispatch,* October 8, 1908, 1.

76. Horn, "Night Riders."

77. "Two Small Fires," *Dardanelle Post-Dispatch,* October 29, 1908, 1.

78. "Fire at Fowler," *Dardanelle Post-Dispatch,* October 7, 1909, 1.

79. "What Builds Up the Country," *Independent Arkansian,* June 9, 1882, 2.

80. "Great Work of Farmers' Union," *Dardanelle Post-Dispatch,* February 24, 1910, 1.

81. "Great Work of Farmers' Union," *Dardanelle Post-Dispatch,* February 24, 1910, 1.

82. "Scientific Farming," *Dardanelle Post-Dispatch,* July 7, 1910, 6.

83. Thomas S. Staples, *Reconstruction in Arkansas, 1862–1874* (New York: Columbia University Press, 1923), 109–14; Thomas S. Staples, *Powell Clayton: The Aftermath of the Civil War in Arkansas* (New York: Neale Publishing Company, 1915), 1–36.

84. John William Graves, "The Arkansas Separate Coach Law of 1891," *Arkansas Historical Quarterly* 32, no. 2 (Summer 1973): 148–65.

85. Graves, "The Arkansas Separate Coach Law of 1891," 150–52.

86. Graves, "The Arkansas Separate Coach Law of 1891," 151–54.

87. Graves, "The Arkansas Separate Coach Law of 1891," 153.

88. Clifton Paisley, "The Political Wheelers and Arkansas' Election of 1888," *Arkansas Historical Quarterly* 30, no. 1 (Spring 1966): 3–21.

89. J. Morgan Kousser, "A Black Protest in the 'Era of Accommodation': Documents," *Arkansas Historical Quarterly* 34, no. 2 (Summer 1975): 149–78.

90. John William Graves, "Negro Disfranchisement in Arkansas," *Arkansas Historical Quarterly* 26, no. 3 (Autumn 1967): 199–225; John William Graves, "Another Look at Disfranchisement in Arkansas, 1888–1894," *Arkansas Historical Quarterly* 69, no. 3 (Autumn 2010): 245–62.

91. Willard B. Gatewood Jr., "Arkansas Negroes in the 1890s: Documents," *Arkansas Historical Quarterly* 33, no. 4 (Winter 1974): 293–325.

92. For a detailed look at the Back-to-Africa movement, see Kenneth C. Barnes,

*Journey of Hope: The Back-to-Africa Movement in Arkansas in the Late 1800s* (Chapel Hill: University of North Carolina Press, 2004).

93. Gatewood, "Arkansas Negroes," 297–300.

94. McGerr, *A Fierce Discontent*, 182–218.

95. Mary Potts Hall, interview by author, Little Rock, Arkansas, October 17, 2009.

96. William F. Holmes, "The Arkansas Cotton Pickers Strike of 1891 and the Demise of the Colored Farmers' Alliance," *Arkansas Historical Quarterly* 32, no. 2 (Summer 1973): 107–19.

97. "Synopsis," *Independent Arkansian*, July 30, 1880, 1.

98. "Hold While We Skin," *Dardanelle Post*, January 18, 1883, 4.

99. Advertisement, *Independent Arkansian*, April 28, 1882, 1.

100. "Fires Twice at Fleeing Negro," *Dardanelle Post-Dispatch*, August 25, 1910, 1.

101. Carl H. Moneyhon, "Black Politics in Arkansas during the Gilded Age, 1876–1900," *Arkansas Historical Quarterly* 44, no. 3 (Autumn 1985): 222–45.

102. Untitled, *Independent Arkansian*, September 8, 1882, 5.

103. Untitled, *Independent Arkansian*, September 22, 1882, 4.

104. "Town and Country," *Independent Arkansian*, May 12, 1882, 6.

105. "One Man Killed and Several Wounded in Faulkner County," *Dardanelle Post*, January 25, 1883, 1.

106. "Town and Country," *Independent Arkansian*, April 14, 1882, 5; see Glenda Elizabeth Gilmore, *Gender and Jim Crow: Women and the Politics of White Supremacy in North Carolina, 1896–1920* (Chapel Hill: University of North Carolina Press, 1996), 91–118.

107. "An Open Letter," *Dardanelle Post-Dispatch*, December 10, 1908, 1.

108. See Willard B. Gatewood Jr., *Aristocrats of Color: The Black Elite, 1880–1920* (Bloomington: Indiana University Press, 1990).

109. "Little Post," *Dardanelle Post*, November 1, 1883, 6.

110. "Little Post," *Dardanelle Post*, October 4, 1883, 7.

111. "The Local Field," *Dardanelle Post-Dispatch*, June 17, 1909, 5.

112. "Nebo News," *Dardanelle Post-Dispatch*, August 4, 1910, 3.

113. "A Tribute to a Passing Type," *Dardanelle Post-Dispatch*, July 1, 1909, 2; see Deborah Gray White, *Ar'n't I a Woman?* (New York: W. W. Norton & Company, 1999), 161–90.

114. "To the Public," *Dardanelle Post-Dispatch*, October 20, 1910, 1.

115. Gatewood Jr., "Arkansas Negroes," 293–325.

116. Scott Branyan, "Floods," *The Encyclopedia of Arkansas History & Culture*.

117. Isodore Thompson, interview by author, Dardanelle, Arkansas, May 20, 2009.

118. "Town and Country," *Independent Arkansian*, February 10, 1882, 5.

119. "Town and Country," *Independent Arkansian*, February 24, 1882, 6.

120. Untitled, *Independent Arkansian*, April 14, 1882, 6; "Ferry Facts," *Dardanelle Post*, November 22, 1883, 4.

121. "The Local Field," *Dardanelle Post-Dispatch*, May 3, 1900, 4.

122. Untitled, *Dardanelle Post-Dispatch*, June 14, 1908, 2.

123. "Arkansas River on Rampage," *Dardanelle Post-Dispatch*, December 3, 1908, 1.

124. "River Improvement Meeting," *Dardanelle Post-Dispatch*, January 14, 1909, 1.

125. "River Improvement Meeting," *Dardanelle Post-Dispatch*, January 14, 1909, 1.

126. Untitled, *Dardanelle Post-Dispatch*, June, 18, 1908, 2.

127. "River Improvement Meeting," *Dardanelle Post-Dispatch*, January 14, 1909, 1.

128. "Notice to Contractors," *Dardanelle Post-Dispatch*, July 22, 1909, 2.

129. "Arkansas River and Tributaries Flood Control Plan," U.S. Engineer Office, Memphis, Tennessee, Sheet no. 36, Appendix No. 1, June 10, 1932.

130. "Contracts for Levee Construction Let," *Dardanelle Post-Dispatch*, August 12, 1909, 1; "The Local Field," *Dardanelle Post-Dispatch*, August 12, 1909, 5.

131. "Lowest Arkansas River Levels Ever," *Dardanelle Post-Dispatch*, November 25, 1909, 1.

132. Untitled, *Independent Arkansian*, January 20, 1882, 1.

133. "Escape from Jail," *Independent Arkansian*, February 24, 1882, 6.

134. "Dardanelle Jail Birds," *Independent Arkansian*, February 10, 1882, 5.

135. Untitled, *Independent Arkansian*, January 20, 1882, 3.

136. Editorial, *Independent Arkansian*, January 13, 1882, 3.

137. "Danville to the Front," *Independent Arkansian*, April 21, 1882, 6.

138. "Terrible Tragedy," *Independent Arkansian*, July 16, 1880, 3.

139. "Another Shooting Affray," *Independent Arkansian*, May 13, 1881, 3.

140. "Another Shooting Affray," *Independent Arkansian*, May 13, 1881, 3

141. "Nearly a Tragedy," *Dardanelle Post*, January 4, 1883, 3.

142. "February Term, 1882," *Independent Arkansian*, February 17, 1882, 4.

143. Untitled, *Independent Arkansian*, May 13, 1881, 3.

144. Cornelia Taylor Daniels, interview by author, Dardanelle, Arkansas, July 1, 2008.

145. "Helphrey's Confession," *Independent Arkansian*, December 2, 1881, 1.

146. "They Lynched Him," *Independent Arkansian*, December 2, 1881, 2.

147. "Note 2," *Independent Arkansian*, December 2, 1881, 1.

148. "James K. P. McGhee," *Dardanelle Post*, February 22, 1883, 2.

149. "James K. P. McGhee," *Dardanelle Post*, February 22, 1883, 2.

150. "J. K. P. McGhee: Sentenced Commuted," *Dardanelle Post*, April 26, 1883, 3.

151. "The Brutal Butchery of a Man," *Dardanelle Post*, September 6, 1883, 3.

152. "Little Posts," *Dardanelle Post*, October 11, 1883, 6.

153. "By the Neck" and "The Crime," *Dardanelle Post Extra Edition*, December 7, 1883, 1–2.

154. "Lynchings," *Dardanelle Post*, January 11, 1883, 1.

155. "February Term, 1882," *Independent Arkansian*, February 17, 1882, 4.

156. Editorial, *Independent Arkansian*, September 13, 1883; "Two Men Killed by Masked Mob," *Dardanelle Post-Dispatch*, April 20, 2016, 1.

157. "Town Talk," *Independent Arkansian*, March 19, 1880, 3.

158. "Town Talk," *Independent Arkansian*, August 6, 1880, 3.

159. Editorial, *Independent Arkansian*, December 3, 1880, 2.

160. "Little Posts," *Dardanelle Post*, October 11, 1883, 5.

161. "Killed by Mistake," *Dardanelle Post-Dispatch*, April 26, 1900, 5.

162. "Town Talk," *Independent Arkansian*, January 16, 1880, 3.

163. "Good Reasons for Not Drinking," *Independent Arkansian*, August 13, 1880, 4.

164. "The Liquor Question," *Independent Arkansian*, September 24, 1880, 3.

165. "Town and Country," *Independent Arkansian,* October 15, 1880, 3.

166. "Liquor and Ferry Licenses," *Independent Arkansian,* January 14, 1881, 3.

167. "Can Druggists Sell Liquor?" *Independent Arkansian,* January 6, 1882, 1.

168. "The Whiskey Law," *Independent Arkansian,* April 15, 1881, 1.

169. "Good Templars," *Independent Arkansian,* April 15, 1881, 3.

170. "King Alcohol," *Independent Arkansian,* January 6, 1882, 8; "Town and Country," *Independent Arkansian,* March 3, 1882, 5.

171. "Town and Country," *Independent Arkansian,* March 10, 1882, 5.

172. "Town and Country," *Independent Arkansian,* March 10, 1882, 5.

173. "The Local Field," *Dardanelle Post-Dispatch,* September 6, 1900, 4.

174. "Liquor at Lacy's Ferry," *Independent Arkansian,* January 25, 1883, 2.

175. "Little Posts," *Dardanelle Post,* May 24, 1883, 3.

176. "Little Posts," *Dardanelle Post,* May 24, 1883, 3.

177. "Run Over at a Horse Race and Killed," *Independent Arkansian,* October 18, 1883, 5.

178. Doris Hundley Hickey, interview by author, Dardanelle, Arkansas, July 9, 2008.

179. "Town and Country," *Dardanelle Post-Dispatch,* November 26, 1908, 3.

180. "Meeting of City Council," *Dardanelle Post-Dispatch,* August 27, 1908, 1.

181. Joe Grimes, interview by author, Dardanelle, Arkansas, June 22, 2009.

182. "Town and Country," *Independent Arkansian,* January 6, 1882, 8.

183. "Town and Country," *Independent Arkansian,* January 6, 1882, 8.

184. Banks, *History of Yell County,* 102-3.

185. "Town and Country," *Independent Arkansian,* November 18, 1881, 3.

186. "Persons Who Can Read and Write," *Independent Arkansian,* December 22, 1882, 2.

187. "Public School Opened Monday," *Dardanelle Post-Dispatch,* October 6, 1910, 1.

188. "School Column," *Dardanelle Post-Dispatch,* January 13, 1910, 2.

189. "Dardanelle Students Away at College," *Dardanelle Post-Dispatch,* January 27, 1910, 2.

190. "Obituaries," *Independent Arkansian,* November 11, 1881, 3; "Town and Country," *Independent Arkansian,* February 3, 1882, 6; "Our Neighbor," *Independent Arkansian,* April 14, 1882, 7.

191. "Suggestions by the State Board of Health," *Independent Arkansian,* January 13, 1882, 1.

192. "Sewerage System Needed," *Dardanelle Post-Dispatch,* July 29, 1909, 1.

193. "Terrible Accident," *Independent Arkansian,* August 20, 1880, 2; "Brief Mention," *Dardanelle Post-Dispatch,* May 17, 1900, 4; "Brief Mention," *Dardanelle Post-Dispatch,* August 9, 1900, 2; "Brief Mention," *Dardanelle Post-Dispatch,* November 17, 1909, 4; and, "Brief Mention," *Dardanelle Post-Dispatch,* January 13, 1910, 2.

194. "Town & Country," *Independent Arkansian,* September 15, 1882, 6.

195. "Mad Dog," *Dardanelle Post,* November 30, 1882, 1.

196. Gravley, "Early Twin Cities," 177-81; Ernestine Gravley, "The Presbyterian Church in Dardanelle, Arkansas," *Arkansas Historical Quarterly* 12, no. 3 (Autumn 1953): 273-77.

197. Janie S. Evins, "Arkansas Women: Their Contribution to Society, Politics, and Business, 1865–1900," *Arkansas Historical Quarterly* 44, no. 2 (Summer 1985): 118–23.

198. Fred Arthur Bailey, "Free Speech and the 'Lost Cause' in Arkansas," *Arkansas Historical Quarterly* 55, no. 2 (Summer 1996): 143–66.

199. Anne Firor Scott, *The Southern Lady: From Pedestal to Politics, 1830–1930,* 2nd ed. (Charlottesville: University Press of Virginia, 1995), 129.

200. Stuart Rockoff, "Jew," *Arkansas Encyclopedia of History and Culture.* Also see Marcia Cohen Ferris and Mark Greenberg, eds., *Jewish Roots in Southern Soil* (Lebanon, NH: University Press of New England, 2006), and Eli Evans, *The Provincials: A Personal History of Jews in the South* (Chapel Hill: University of North Carolina Press, 2005).

201. "History of Mount Nebo," Arkansas State Park Services, Little Rock, Arkansas, 2012; Judy Hamburg Prince, interview by author, Mount Nebo, Arkansas, July 17, 2013.

202. "Joshua W. Toomer," *Independent Arkansian,* January 7, 1881, 3.

203. "Racy Remarks from Colonel Tobey," *Dardanelle Post*, February 8, 1883, 1.

204. Carl H. Moneyhon, "The Creators of the New South in Arkansas: Industrial Boosterism, 1875–1885," *Arkansas Historical Quarterly* 55, no. 4 (Winter 1996): 383–409.

## CHAPTER 3: Growth, 1911–1919

1. "State's Growth Record Is Good," *Dardanelle Post-Dispatch,* May 9, 1912, 2.

2. "The Local Field," *Dardanelle Post-Dispatch*, November 28, 1912, 4; "The Local Field," *Dardanelle Post-Dispatch,* February 20, 1913, 3; "The Local Field," *Dardanelle Post-Dispatch,"* November 6, 1919, 5.

3. "Arkansas Crop and Live Stock Production and Value, Season of 1920," *Dardanelle Post-Dispatch,* March 3, 1921, 2.

4. "Farmers Must Adopt Business Methods," *Dardanelle Post-Dispatch*, July 14, 1921, 4.

5. "The Local Field," *Dardanelle Post-Dispatch*, August 10, 1911, 3.

6. Editorial, *Dardanelle Post-Dispatch,* March 14, 1912, 5.

7. "Splendid Crop on the Cotton Plantation," *Dardanelle Post-Dispatch*, September 4, 1913, 1.

8. "The Local Field," *Dardanelle Post-Dispatch*, September 10, 1914, 5.

9. "Same Old Editor, Luther: Same Old Politics, Too," *Dardanelle Post-Dispatch*, May 11, 1950, 4.

10. "Supplies Should Be Raised at Home," *Dardanelle Post-Dispatch,* May 18, 1911, 1.

11. "Advises Farmers to Use Home Canners," *Dardanelle Post-Dispatch,* July 13, 1911, 1.

12. Advertisement, *Dardanelle Post-Dispatch*, June 22, 1911, 1.

13. "Keep the Garden Working," *Dardanelle Post-Dispatch,* August 23, 1917, 4.

14. "Weekly Letter of Commissioner Page," *Dardanelle Post-Dispatch,* October 21, 1915, 3.

15. "Poultry Raising Is a Source of Profit," *Dardanelle Post-Dispatch*, February 6, 1913, 1.

16. "Building a Poultry House," *Dardanelle Post-Dispatch,* October 17, 1912, 2.

17. "Centerville," *Dardanelle Post-Dispatch*, August 30, 1917, 8.

18. Editorial, *Dardanelle Post-Dispatch*, December 18, 1913, 2.

19. "Plant Nitrogen," *Dardanelle Post-Dispatch*, June 11, 1914, 1.

20. "Cotton Picking Machine Is Invented," *Dardanelle Post-Dispatch,* October 17, 1912, 2.

21. Editorial, *Dardanelle Post-Dispatch,* December 18, 1913, 2.

22. "The Local Field," *Dardanelle Post-Dispatch,* October 5, 1911, 4.

23. "Farmers Union," *Dardanelle Post-Dispatch,* February 15, 1912, 2.

24. Rod Farmer, "Direct Democracy in Arkansas, 1910–1918," *Arkansas Historical Quarterly* 40, no. 3 (Summer 1981): 103.

25. "Would Hold Cotton for 15 Cents Pound," *Dardanelle Post-Dispatch*, October 5, 1911, 6.

26. "The Local Field," *Dardanelle Post-Dispatch*, June 13, 1912, 5.

27. "The Local Field," *Dardanelle Post-Dispatch*, September 12, 1912, 7.

28. "Dardanelle Attracts Trade from Distance," *Dardanelle Post-Dispatch*, November 13, 1913, 1.

29. "The Local Field," *Dardanelle Post-Dispatch,* October 15, 1914, 3.

30. "The Local Field," *Dardanelle Post-Dispatch*, November 13, 1913, 2.

31. "You Can Pay Us in Cotton," *Dardanelle Post-Dispatch,* October 15, 1914, 1.

32. "Additional Local," *Dardanelle Post-Dispatch*, May 29, 1913, 2.

33. "The Local Field," *Dardanelle Post-Dispatch,* July 18, 1912, 5; "Pontoon Items," *Dardanelle Post-Dispatch,* October 2, 1913, 6.

34. "The Local Field," *Dardanelle Post-Dispatch,* October 30, 1913, 5.

35. "Cotton Plantation Notes," *Dardanelle Post-Dispatch,* September 4, 1913, 6; "Cotton Plantation Notes," *Dardanelle Post-Dispatch,* October 23, 1913, 8.

36. Cornelia Daniels, interview by author, Dardanelle, Arkansas, July 1, 2008.

37. "The Local Field," *Dardanelle Post-Dispatch*, April 20, 1916, 5.

38. "The Local Field," *Dardanelle Post-Dispatch*, January 9, 1913, 5.

39. "Farmers Discuss the Present Cotton Crisis," *Dardanelle Post-Dispatch,* October 22, 1914, 1.

40. "Farmers Discuss the Present Cotton Crisis," *Dardanelle Post-Dispatch,* October 22, 1914, 1.

41. "Clarke Suggests Law to Reduce Acreage," *Dardanelle Post-Dispatch,* September 24, 1914, 1.

42. "Centerville," *Dardanelle Post-Dispatch*, February 25, 1915, 5.

43. "The Difference," *Dardanelle Post-Dispatch,* June 17, 1915, 2.

44. "Local News," *Dardanelle Post-Dispatch,* August 19, 1915, 4.

45. George Granville Gleason, conversation with author, Dardanelle, Arkansas, May 11, 1975.

46. "What Do You Think of New Ginning System?" *Dardanelle Post-Dispatch*, October 29, 1915, 1.

47. "The Farmer Deserves All Cotton He Raises," *Dardanelle Post-Dispatch,* November 4, 1915, 1.

48. "Practical Farmers Endorse New System," *Dardanelle Post-Dispatch*, December 16, 1915, 1.

49. "Practical Farmers Endorse New System," *Dardanelle Post-Dispatch*, December 16, 1915, 1.

50. "The Local Field," *Dardanelle Post-Dispatch*, September 3, 1914, 5.

51. "The Local Field," *Dardanelle Post-Dispatch*, September 3, 1914, 5.

52. "Discuss Cotton Crisis at County Meeting," *Dardanelle Post-Dispatch*, September 17, 1914, 1.

53. "Additional Local," *Dardanelle Post-Dispatch*, November 9, 1916, 4.

54. "Hoover Tells of Food Situation," *Dardanelle Post-Dispatch*, August 23, 1917, 6.

55. "Government Experts Will Discuss Farming Problems," *Dardanelle Post-Dispatch*, January 18, 1917, 1.

56. "Centerville," *Dardanelle Post-Dispatch*, March 14, 1918, 6.

57. "The Local Field," *Dardanelle Post-Dispatch*, May 11, 1916, 2–3.

58. "22 Cars of Peaches Shipped This Season," *Dardanelle Post-Dispatch*, August 2, 1917, 1.

59. "Passage of Proposed Arkansas Plant Act Urged," *Dardanelle Post-Dispatch*, January 18, 1917, 1.

60. "To the Farmers of Yell County," *Dardanelle Post-Dispatch*, October 3, 1918, 1.

61. Advertisement, *Dardanelle Post-Dispatch*, December 27, 1917, 3.

62. "Important Meeting Here Next Wednesday," *Dardanelle Post-Dispatch*, May 7, 1914, 1.

63. "The Local Field," *Dardanelle Post-Dispatch*, January 17, 1917, 5; "The Local Field," *Dardanelle Post-Dispatch*, February 1, 1917, 7; "The Local Field," *Dardanelle Post-Dispatch*, December 13, 1917, 8; "The Local Field," *Dardanelle Post-Dispatch*, December 27, 1917, 3; "The Local Field," *Dardanelle Post-Dispatch*, January 3, 1918, 3; "The Local Field," *Dardanelle Post-Dispatch*, January 10, 1918, 3.

64. "Large Crowds Attend the Farming Meetings," *Dardanelle Post-Dispatch*, February 1, 1917, 1.

65. "Weekly Letter of Commissioner Page," *Dardanelle Post-Dispatch*, July 27, 1917, 4.

66. "Weekly Letter of Commissioner Page," *Dardanelle Post-Dispatch*, August 2, 1917, 4.

67. "Cotton Futures Act of 1916," http://www.freebase.com/m/04zzlmx (accessed February 13, 2016).

68. "The Local Field," *Dardanelle Post-Dispatch*, March 6, 1919, 5.

69. "Dardanelle Leads as Cotton Market," *Dardanelle Post-Dispatch*, September 19, 1918, 1.

70. Lu Ann Jones, *Mama Learned Us to Work: Farm Women in the New South* (Chapel Hill: University of North Carolina Press, 2002), 14, 116.

71. "Yell County Farmers Will Study at U. of A.," *Dardanelle Post-Dispatch*, July 17, 1919, 1.

72. "Co-Operative Plan Proves Profitable," *Dardanelle Post-Dispatch*, July 17, 1919, 1.

73. "Farmers to Attend Farm Tractor Demonstration in Little Rock," *Dardanelle Post-Dispatch*, January 1, 1920, 1.

74. Hull and Pollard, *The Dardanelle & Russellville Railroad*, 60; "DO&S Files for Bankruptcy," *Dardanelle Post-Dispatch,* January 12, 1911, 3.

75. Bobby Crow, interview by author, Cotton Town, Arkansas, August 4, 2015.

76. "Charter Is Granted the R.I. & D Railroad," *Dardanelle Post-Dispatch,* October 12, 1911, 1; "Resignations Accepted," *Dardanelle Post-Dispatch,* December 21, 1911, 1.

77. Hull and Pollard, *The Dardanelle & Russellville Railroad*, 61–62.

78. Hull and Pollard, *The Dardanelle & Russellville Railroad*, 62–64.

79. John G. Ragsdale, "Coal Mining," *The Encyclopedia of Arkansas History & Culture.* Also see Gene Hull, "Those Coal Mines at Bernice, Part I," *Pope County Historical Association Quarterly* 30 (September 1996): 4–12; Gene Hull, "Those Coal Mines at Bernice, Part II," *Pope County Historical Association Quarterly* 30 (December 1996): 14–20.

80. Editorial, *Dardanelle Post-Dispatch,* August 19, 1915, 4.

81. "Plan Forty Miles Macadam Highway," *Dardanelle Post-Dispatch,* August 26, 1915, 1.

82. See, among others, Arkansas Supreme Court Opinion in *Lamberson v. Collins,* delivered March 6, 1916. http://opinions.aoc.arkansas.gov/weblink8/0/doc/203371/Electronic.aspx.

83. Robert W. Scoggin, "Roads and Highways," *The Encyclopedia of Arkansas History & Culture.*

84. "Shaping Details for Carden Bottom Road," *Dardanelle Post-Dispatch,* March 15, 1917, 1.

85. "Cost of New Highways Is Less Than Expected," *Dardanelle Post-Dispatch,* July 24, 1919, 1.

86. "Large Crowds Attend Good Roads Meeting," *Dardanelle Post-Dispatch,* September 6, 1917, 1.

87. "Dardanelle Highway to Cost $792,578.20," *Dardanelle Post-Dispatch,* January 22, 1920, 1; "Property Owners Protest against Construction of Proposed Highway," *Dardanelle Post-Dispatch,* May 13, 1920, 1.

88. "Commissioners Stop Work on the Highway," *Dardanelle Post-Dispatch,* May 20, 1920, 1; "Dardanelle Road Improvement District Definitely Abandoned," *Dardanelle Post-Dispatch*, May 27, 1920, 1.

89. "Good Citizens Asked to Improve Streets," *Dardanelle Post-Dispatch,* August 14, 1913, 1; "Good Work Is Done by Volunteer Laborers," *Dardanelle Post-Dispatch*, August 28, 1913, 1.

90. "Three Full Days Work Put in on the Streets," *Dardanelle Post-Dispatch,* September 4, 1913, 1; "Will Complete Work on 2d Street Tuesday," *Dardanelle Post-Dispatch*, September 11, 1913, 1.

91. "Plan to Improve Streets of the City," *Dardanelle Post-Dispatch*, May 24, 1917, 1.

92. Editorial, *Dardanelle Post-Dispatch*, November 9, 1922, 4.

93. "Chamber of Commerce Interested in Paving," *Dardanelle Post-Dispatch,* July 23, 1925, 1; "Paving Project Given Hearty Endorsement," *Dardanelle Post-Dispatch*, October 1, 1925, 1; "Paving of Thirty-Five Blocks Now Assured," *Dardanelle Post-Dispatch*, October 15, 1925, 1; "Paving Petition Filed with the City Council," *Dardanelle Post-Dispatch*, November 12, 1925, 1; "Court's Ruling Boosts Prospects of

Paving," *Dardanelle Post-Dispatch*, March 18, 1926, 1; "The Local Field," *Dardanelle Post-Dispatch*, September 20, 1928, 3.

94. "Pope County Ready to Help Build Free Bridge," *Dardanelle Post-Dispatch*, August 1, 1912, 1; "Plan Free Bridge across River Here," *Dardanelle Post-Dispatch*, January 9, 1913, 1; "Dardanelle Merchants After More Trade," *Dardanelle Post-Dispatch*, January 9, 1913, 1; "Plans for Free Bridge Are Well Under Way," *Dardanelle Post-Dispatch,* February 7, 1913, 1; "Pope County 'Double Crosses' Free Bridge," *Dardanelle Post-Dispatch*, March 1, 1917, 1.

95. Joseph Carruth, "World War I Propaganda and Its Effects in Arkansas," *Arkansas Historical Quarterly* 16, no. 4 (Winter 1997): 385–98.

96. "The Kaiser, The Beast of Berlin," *Dardanelle Post-Dispatch*, August 15, 1918, 1.

97. Carruth, "World War I Propaganda," 388–92.

98. Advertisement, *Dardanelle Post-Dispatch*, November 22, 1917, 1; also see *Dardanelle Post-Dispatch,* December 6, 1917, 1; *Dardanelle Post-Dispatch,* December 20, 1917, 1; *Dardanelle Post-Dispatch,* May 2, 1918, 3; *Dardanelle Post-Dispatch*, October 10, 1918, 7.

99. "The Local Field," *Dardanelle Post-Dispatch*, May 10, 1917, 2.

100. Candice McGee, "American Red Cross," *The Encyclopedia of Arkansas History & Culture.*

101. "Red Cross Chapter Is Organized Here," *Dardanelle Post-Dispatch*, November 15, 1917, 1; "Red Cross Prepares for Effective Work," *Dardanelle Post-Dispatch*, November 29, 1917, 1.

102. "Home for Yell County Red Cross Chapter," *Dardanelle Post-Dispatch*, December 6, 1917, 1.

103. "Red Cross Notes," *Dardanelle Post-Dispatch*, February 28, 1918, 2.

104. McGee, "American Red Cross."

105. "Red Cross Notes" and "Carden Bottom Red Cross," *Dardanelle Post-Dispatch*, March 21, 1918, 1; "Organization and World of County Red Cross," *Dardanelle Post-Dispatch,* March 28, 1928, 1.

106. "Red Cross Notes," *Dardanelle Post-Dispatch,* April 11, 1918, 1.

107. "Centerville," *Dardanelle Post-Dispatch,* May 30, 1918, 2.

108. "Load of Wood Nets Red Cross the Sum of $223," *Dardanelle Post-Dispatch,* November 7, 1918, 5.

109. "Centerville," *Dardanelle Post-Dispatch*, May 23, 1918, 5; "Red Cross Benefit," *Dardanelle Post-Dispatch*, July 4, 1918, 1; "Red Cross Picnic," *Dardanelle Post-Dispatch*, July 25, 1918, 2.

110. "What Has Your Red Cross Money Done?" *Dardanelle Post-Dispatch,* May 23, 1918, 2.

111. See Robert K. Murray, *The Politics of Normalcy: Governmental Theory and Practice in the Harding-Coolidge Era* (New York: W. W. Norton & Company, 1973).

112. Joey McCarty, "The Red Scare in Arkansas: A Southern State and National Hysteria," *Arkansas Historical Quarterly* 37, no. 3 (Autumn 1978): 264–77.

113. "Red Cross Mission Not Ended by Peace," *Dardanelle Post-Dispatch,* July 31, 1919, 1.

114. "Yell County a Leader in Food Conservation," *Dardanelle Post-Dispatch*, April 5, 1918, 1.

115. "Dr. S. E. Miller Named Food Administrator," *Dardanelle Post-Dispatch,* February 21, 1918, 1; "Yell County a Leader in Food Conservation," *Dardanelle Post-Dispatch,* April 5, 1918, 1.

116. Editorial, *Dardanelle Post-Dispatch,* February 28, 1918, 2.

117. "Dardanelle Merchants Are Conserving Fuel," *Dardanelle Post-Dispatch,* December 11, 1918, 1.

118. "Dardanelle Merchants Are Conserving Fuel," *Dardanelle Post-Dispatch,* December 11, 1918, 1.

119. "Two Cent Postage Is Again Effective," *Dardanelle Post-Dispatch,* July 4, 1919, 1; "The Local Field," *Dardanelle Post-Dispatch,* November 1, 1917, 3.

120. "Plant Irish Potatoes," *Dardanelle Post-Dispatch,* July 18, 1918, 1.

121. "The Local Field," *Dardanelle Post-Dispatch,* November 1, 1917, 5; "Centerville," *Dardanelle Post-Dispatch,* October 4, 1917, 8.

122. "Huge Profits in U.S. Industries," *Dardanelle Post-Dispatch,* August 22, 1918, 3.

123. "Sugar for Canning," *Dardanelle Post-Dispatch,* May 2, 1918, 1.

124. "Notice to Sugar Buyers," *Dardanelle Post-Dispatch,* July 18, 1918, 1.

125. "Molasses," *Dardanelle Post-Dispatch,* July 18, 1918, 5.

126. "Centerville Items," *Dardanelle Post-Dispatch,* July 18, 1918, 6.

127. "Centerville," *Dardanelle Post-Dispatch,* February 28, 1918, 6.

128. "Will Urge Need of Growing Food Stuffs," *Dardanelle Post-Dispatch,* March 21, 1918, 1.

129. "Statistics of Cotton, Sugar, and Tobacco," *Agricultural Statistics, 1866–1936* (Washington, DC: US Government Printing Office, 1937), 102–3.

130. "Must Have License to Operate Cotton Gins," *Dardanelle Post-Dispatch,* August 15, 1918, 1.

131. "Yell County 'Goes Over': We've Finished the Job!" *Dardanelle Post-Dispatch,* May 8, 1919, 1.

132. "Third Liberty Loan Drive Starts Saturday, April 6th," *Dardanelle Post-Dispatch,* April 5, 1918, 1; "Yell Over-Subscribes: Total Now Is $181,400," *Dardanelle Post-Dispatch,* May 2, 1918, 1.

133. "War Savings Plan Outlined in Detail," *Dardanelle Post-Dispatch,* December 6, 1917, 1.

134. "County Bought $20,000 W.S.S. Last Saturday," *Dardanelle Post-Dispatch,* March 28, 1918, 1.

135. "The Local Field," *Dardanelle Post-Dispatch,* April 17, 1919, 3.

136. "Robert E. Lee Day," *Dardanelle Post-Dispatch,* January 18, 1917, 4.

137. "Centerville," *Dardanelle Post-Dispatch,* September 13, 1917, 8.

138. "Another Draft Call Probably Necessary," *Dardanelle Post-Dispatch,* August 16, 1917, 1.

139. "Demonstration Marks Departure of Co. C," *Dardanelle Post-Dispatch,* September 13, 1917, 1; "106 Yell County Men Now at Camp Pike," *Dardanelle Post-Dispatch,* September 20, 1917, 1.

140. Editorial, *Dardanelle Post-Dispatch,* October 4, 1917, 4; "129 Yell County Men Called to the Colors," *Dardanelle Post-Dispatch,* June 29, 1918, 1.

141. "More Yell County Boys Arrive in France," *Dardanelle Post-Dispatch,* July 18, 1918, 3.

142. Advertisement, *Dardanelle Post-Dispatch*, July 18, 1918, 1.

143. "The Local Field," *Dardanelle Post-Dispatch*, August 22, 1918, 5.

144. "Our Heroic Dead Are Honored by France," *Dardanelle Post-Dispatch*, February 19, 1920, 1.

145. "Wild Enthusiasm Marks End of War," *Dardanelle Post-Dispatch*, November 14, 1918, 1.

146. "Good Progress Is Made in Jewish Relief Fund," *Dardanelle Post-Dispatch*, May 22, 1919, 1.

147. "The Local Field," *Dardanelle Post-Dispatch*, May 22, 1919, 5.

148. "To Prevent Overflow of the Petit Jean," *Dardanelle Post-Dispatch*, February 2, 1911, 1.

149. "River Survey Ordered," *Dardanelle Post-Dispatch*, February, 1912, 3.

150. "Jacoway on the Job," *Dardanelle Post-Dispatch*, December 12, 1912, 1.

151. Scott Branyan, "Little Rock District U.S. Army Corps of Engineers," *The Encyclopedia of Arkansas History & Culture*.

152. "Jacoway Has Plan to Develop River," *Dardanelle Post-Dispatch*, January 16, 1913, 1.

153. Kay C. Goss, "McClellan-Kerr Arkansas River Navigation System (MKARNS)," *The Encyclopedia of Arkansas History & Culture*.

154. "River on Big Rise," *Dardanelle Post-Dispatch*, May 2, 1912, 1.

155. "Notice: Landowners of Carden Bottom Levee District No. 2," *Dardanelle Post-Dispatch*, June 10, 1915, 1.

156. "Arkansas River Flood Does Serious Damage," *Dardanelle Post-Dispatch*, February 3, 1916, 1.

157. Marie Sheppard Bachman, interview by author, Dardanelle, Arkansas, August 4, 2008.

158. "Blanket of Snow and Ice Covers Arkansas," *Dardanelle Post-Dispatch*, December 13, 1917, 1.

159. "The Local Field," *Dardanelle Post-Dispatch*, January 24, 1918, 3.

160. "The Local Field," *Dardanelle Post-Dispatch*, January 24, 1918, 3.

161. "The Local Field," *Dardanelle Post-Dispatch*, January 24, 1918, 3.

162. "Centerville," *Dardanelle Post-Dispatch*, January 24, 1918, 6.

163. "Children Bitten by Rabid Dog Tuesday," *Dardanelle Post-Dispatch*, August 24, 1911, 1.

164. "The Local Field," *Dardanelle Post-Dispatch*, June 5, 1913, 7.

165. "Popular Russellville Teacher Passes Away," *Dardanelle Post-Dispatch*, October 22, 1914, 1.

166. "The Local Field," *Dardanelle Post-Dispatch*, January 22, 1914, 5.

167. "Centerville," *Dardanelle Post-Dispatch*, December 11, 1919, 8.

168. "Centerville," *Dardanelle Post-Dispatch*, December 11, 1919, 8.

169. "Pellagra," *Dardanelle Post-Dispatch*, July 22, 1915, 1.

170. "Some Reasons Why We Should Be Clean," *Dardanelle Post-Dispatch*, June 17, 1915, 1.

171. "The Removal and Disposal of Sewerage," *Dardanelle Post-Dispatch*, August 24, 1916, 1.

172. "Citizens Petition for Sidewalks and Sewers," *Dardanelle Post-Dispatch*, May 25, 1916, 1; "Improvement District Commissioners Named," *Dardanelle*

*Post-Dispatch*, June 29, 1916, 1; "Work Will Start Soon on New Sewer System," *Dardanelle Post-Dispatch*, July 12, 1917, 1; "Material for Sewer System Now Arriving," *Dardanelle Post-Dispatch*, February 7, 1918, 1.

173. "Water Works System Is Creating a Deficit," *Dardanelle Post-Dispatch*, August 22, 1912, 1.

174. "Plan to Improve Water Works System," *Dardanelle Post-Dispatch*, November 28, 1912; "Overwhelming Vote to Re-Issue Water Bonds," *Dardanelle Post-Dispatch*, January 21, 1915, 1.

175. "Installing New Pump at the Water Station," *Dardanelle Post-Dispatch*, April 24, 1919, 1.

176. "Chamber of Commerce Starts Credit System," *Dardanelle Post-Dispatch*, October 30, 1919, 1.

177. "Chamber of Commerce to Aid Water System," *Dardanelle Post-Dispatch*, November 13, 1919, 1; "Contract Was Let Yesterday for a Guaranteed Adequate Water Supply," *Dardanelle Post-Dispatch*, December 11, 1919, 1.

178. "Lost Pump Material Should Arrive Today," *Dardanelle Post-Dispatch*, February 26, 1920, 1; "Municipal Water Plant Is Operating New Well," *Dardanelle Post-Dispatch*, March 11, 1920, 1.

179. "Plenty of Water Now: Bring on the Banquet," *Dardanelle Post-Dispatch*, March 25, 1920, 1.

180. "Plenty of Water Now: Bring on the Banquet," *Dardanelle Post-Dispatch*, March 25, 1920, 1.

181. "Hookworm a Problem," *Dardanelle Post-Dispatch*, August 28, 1913, 5.

182. "Health Department Will Make Analyses," *Dardanelle Post-Dispatch*, September 4, 1913, 1; "Arkansas Department of Health," *The Encyclopedia of Arkansas History & Culture*.

183. "Watch the Drinking Water," *Dardanelle Post-Dispatch*, August 23, 1917, 1.

184. "Safeguard Public Health," *Dardanelle Post-Dispatch*, August 31, 1922, 1.

185. "To Enforce Vaccination," *Dardanelle Post-Dispatch*, January 3, 1918, 1; "Fields Chapel Items," *Dardanelle Post-Dispatch*, January 3, 1918, 6.

186. "No Smallpox Here," *Dardanelle Post-Dispatch*, January 24, 1924, 1; "Urges Importance of General Vaccination," *Dardanelle Post-Dispatch*, October 9, 1924, 1.

187. "Potts Items," *Dardanelle Post-Dispatch*, May 6, 1926, 2.

188. "Clean Up," *Dardanelle Post-Dispatch*, August 16, 1917, 4.

189. "Influenza Situation," *Dardanelle Post-Dispatch*, October 17, 1918, 1.

190. "Dr. F. A. Outlaw Dead," *Dardanelle Post-Dispatch*, October 10, 1918, 1.

191. "The Local Field," *Dardanelle Post-Dispatch*, October 17, 1918, 5; "Centerville," *Dardanelle Post-Dispatch*, October 24, 1918, 6.

192. "Advice on How to Fight Influenza," *Dardanelle Post-Dispatch*, October 24, 1918, 1.

193. "Health Officer Raises Restrictions," *Dardanelle Post-Dispatch*, February 12, 1920, 1.

194. "Fields Chapel Items," *Dardanelle Post-Dispatch*, February 19, 1929, 2.

195. Carl Zimmer, "In 1918 Flu Pandemic, Timing Was a Killer," *New York Times*, April 30, 2014.

196. "Disastrous Fire Tuesday Morning," *Dardanelle Post-Dispatch*, December 8, 1910, 1.

197. "Disastrous Fire Causes Heavy Loss," *Dardanelle Post-Dispatch*, December 19, 1912, 1.

198. "Ancient Landmarks Are Prey to Flames," *Dardanelle Post-Dispatch*, June 5, 1913, 1.

199. "Flames Claim Another Front Street Building," *Dardanelle Post-Dispatch*, January 28, 1915, 1.

200. "Rock Island Depot Is a Prey to Flames," *Dardanelle Post-Dispatch*, March 11, 1915, 1.

201. "Two Disastrous Fires Occur within a Week," *Dardanelle Post-Dispatch*, March 13, 1919, 1; "Additional Local," *Dardanelle Post-Dispatch*, March 13, 1919, 6.

202. "House Fire in Centerville," *Dardanelle Post-Dispatch*, August 17, 1916, 8; "Woman Incinerated in Early Morning Fire," *Dardanelle Post-Dispatch*, January 31, 1918, 1; "Home of Dr. Sweet Destroyed by Fire," *Dardanelle Post-Dispatch*, December 5, 1918, 1; "Barn Fire on Third Street," *Dardanelle Post-Dispatch*, February 12, 1920, 2.

203. "County Courthouse Destroyed by Fire," *Dardanelle Post-Dispatch*, April 24, 1913, 1.

204. "Dardanelle to Have Fine New Courthouse," *Dardanelle Post-Dispatch*, May 1, 1913, 1.

205. "New $21,800.00 Court House for Dardanelle District of Yell County Is Now Completed," *Dardanelle Post-Dispatch*, August 13, 1914, 1.

206. "Summit Park Hotel Destroyed by Fire," *Dardanelle Post-Dispatch*, May 22, 1919, 1.

207. "Fatal Accident on DO&S RR," *Dardanelle Post-Dispatch*, December 29, 1910, 1.

208. "The Local Field," *Dardanelle Post-Dispatch*, October 27, 1910, 3.

209. "One Killed, Fifteen Injured in Wreck Near Centerville," *Dardanelle Post-Dispatch*, November 20, 1913, 1.

210. "Duke Brown Drowns in Arkansas River Monday," *Dardanelle Post-Dispatch*, July 30, 1914, 1.

211. "Child Missing Near River," *Dardanelle Post-Dispatch*, April 13, 1916, 1.

212. "Additional Local," *Dardanelle Post-Dispatch*, June 12, 1919, 6.

213. Doris Hundley Hickey, interview by author, Dardanelle, Arkansas, July 9, 2008.

214. "The Local Field," *Dardanelle Post-Dispatch*, March 1, 1917, 5; "The Local Field," *Dardanelle Post-Dispatch*, July 5, 1917, 2; "Ordinance no. 244," *Dardanelle Post-Dispatch*, July 11, 1918, 1.

215. "Field Chapel Items," *Dardanelle Post-Dispatch*, April 22, 1920, 2.

216. Jack Guice, telephone interview by author, Dardanelle, Arkansas, March 23, 2013.

217. "J. T. Pickens Killed by Harden George," *Dardanelle Post-Dispatch*, October 27, 1910, 1.

218. Charles F. Robinson, "'Most Shamefully Common': Arkansas and Miscegenation," *Arkansas Historical Quarterly* 60, no. 3 (Autumn 2001): 274.

219. See Glenda Elizabeth Gilmore, *Women and the Politics of White Supremacy in North Carolina, 1896–1920* (Chapel Hill: University of North Carolina Press, 1996).

220. Guy Lancaster, *Racial Cleansing in Arkansas, 1883–1924: Politics, Land, Labor, and Criminality* (New York: Lexington Books, 2014), 8–9.

221. "A Sensational Story," *Russellville Democrat,* March 5, 1885, 1.

222. Lancaster, *Racial Cleansing in Arkansas,* 99–100.

223. Bobby Crow, interview by author, Cotton Town, Arkansas, August 14, 2015.

224. Lonnie Dickens, interview by author, Dardanelle, Arkansas, July 7, 2008.

225. Isodore Thompson, interview by author, Dardanelle, Arkansas, May 20, 2009.

226. Whitey Robinson, telephone interview by author, Dardanelle, Arkansas, September 21, 2009. Also see Todd E. Lewis, "Mob Justice in the 'American Congo': 'Judge Lynch' in Arkansas during the Decade after World War I," *Arkansas Historical Quarterly* 52, no. 2 (Summer 1993): 156–84.

227. Genevieve Grant Sadler, *Muzzled Oxen: Reaping Cotton and Sowing Hope in 1920s Arkansas* (Little Rock: Butler Center Books, 2014), 179.

228. Guy Lancaster, "Night Riding and Racial Cleansing in the Arkansas River Valley," *Arkansas Historical Quarterly* 72, no. 3 (Autumn 2013): 244.

229. See Mitchell Frances Ross, "The New Woman as Club Woman and Social Activist in Turn of the Century Arkansas," *Arkansas Historical Quarterly* 50, no. 4 (Winter 1991): 317–51.

230. Anne Firor Scott, *Making the Invisible Woman Visible* (Chicago: University of Chicago Press, 1984), 220.

231. Nancy Woloch, *Women and the American Experience*, 3rd ed. (New York: McGraw-Hill, 2006), 269–303.

232. "The Local Field," *Dardanelle Post-Dispatch,* October 31, 1912, 4; "Tom Thumb Wedding," *Dardanelle Post-Dispatch,* October 17, 1912, 4.

233. "Colonial Tea," *Dardanelle Post-Dispatch*, February 27, 1913, 1.

234. "The Local Field," *Dardanelle Post-Dispatch,* December 26, 1912, 6; "The Local Field," *Dardanelle Post-Dispatch,* February 24, 1916, 8; "The Local Field," *Dardanelle Post-Dispatch*, October 30, 1919, 4.

235. "History of the First Presbyterian Church," *Dardanelle Post-Dispatch*, May 21, 1914, 1.

236. "Will Build Handsome New Church Edifice," *Dardanelle Post-Dispatch,* April 11, 1912, 1.

237. "Work Started on New M. E. Church Building," *Dardanelle Post-Dispatch*, October 4, 1917, 1.

238. "Handsome New $10,000 First Baptist Church Building Will Be Dedicated Next Sunday, February 12," *Dardanelle Post-Dispatch*, February 9, 1911, 1.

239. "Civic League Proposes a Public Play-Ground," *Dardanelle Post-Dispatch*, March 5, 1914, 1.

240. "Women's Civic League to Start Great Work," *Dardanelle Post-Dispatch,* November 13, 1919, 1.

241. "Anniversary of Cemetery Association," *Dardanelle Post-Dispatch,* May 13, 1915, 1.

242. "Notice," *Dardanelle Post-Dispatch,* July 26, 1917, 6.

243. Paula Kyzer Taylor, "Women's Suffrage Movement," *The Encyclopedia of Arkansas History & Culture.*

244. "Women Must Pay Poll Tax This Week," *Dardanelle Post-Dispatch,*

April 26, 1917, 6; "Attention Ladies!" *Dardanelle Post-Dispatch*, July 18, 1918, 1; "The Local Field," *Dardanelle Post-Dispatch*, March 7, 1918, 3.

245. "Women Vote in Primary," *Dardanelle Post-Dispatch*, May 30, 1918, 1.

246. See Taylor, "Women's Suffrage Movement."

247. "Porch Concert," *Dardanelle Post-Dispatch*, June 8, 1911, 1.

248. "Mrs. Max Kaufman Entertains," *Dardanelle Post-Dispatch,* April 25, 1912, 1.

249. Sadler, *Muzzled Oxen*, 132–33.

250. "High School Opened Last Monday Morning," *Dardanelle Post-Dispatch,* October 5, 1911, 1; "The Local Field," *Dardanelle Post-Dispatch*, November 14, 1912, 8.

251. "Dardanelle Public School Opened Monday," *Dardanelle Post-Dispatch,* October 3, 1912, 1.

252. "Board Apportions $50,000 to Schools," *Dardanelle Post-Dispatch*, May 29, 1913, 5.

253. "The Local Field," *Dardanelle Post-Dispatch,* May 21, 1914, 5.

254. "Untitled," *Dardanelle Post-Dispatch,* September 10, 1914, 6.

255. "Shake-Up in Faculty of Dardanelle School," *Dardanelle Post-Dispatch*, November 4, 1915, 1.

256. "School Opens Next Monday, Sept. 23rd," *Dardanelle Post-Dispatch,* September 19, 1918, 1.

257. "Work Started on New High School Building," *Dardanelle Post-Dispatch,* August 10, 1916, 1.

258. "Bliss Architect for New School Building," *Dardanelle Post-Dispatch,* June 8, 1916, 1.

259. "Work Starts Soon on High School Building," *Dardanelle Post-Dispatch,* June 22, 1916, 1.

260. "The Local Field," *Dardanelle Post-Dispatch*, September 28, 1916, 4.

261. "The Local Field," *Dardanelle Post-Dispatch,* March 1, 1917, 5.

262. "Citizens Want High School Continued," *Dardanelle Post-Dispatch,* June 20, 1918, 1.

263. "Dardanelle School Must Have Increased Revenue or Suspend," *Dardanelle Post-Dispatch,* May 8, 1919, 7.

264. "Voluntarily Assume 17 Mill School Tax," *Dardanelle Post-Dispatch,* June 5, 1919, 1.

265. "The Unselfish Patriots Who Made Our Splendid Schools Possible," *Dardanelle Post-Dispatch,* November 20, 1919, 1.

266. "Neely Items," *Dardanelle Post-Dispatch,* June 21, 1917, 4.

267. "Centerville," *Dardanelle Post-Dispatch,* October 2, 1919, 7; "Centerville," *Dardanelle Post-Dispatch,* November 11, 1920, 1.

268. "Centerville," *Dardanelle Post-Dispatch,* October 18, 1917, 8.

## CHAPTER 4: Hard Times and High Water, 1920–1929

1. "The Local Field," *Dardanelle Post-Dispatch,* November 6, 1919, 5.

2. "Cotton Grower Is Defended in House," *Dardanelle Post-Dispatch,* April 29, 1920, 6.

3. "Yell County Union Met at Ola Last Saturday," *Dardanelle Post-Dispatch*, February 7, 1924, 1.

4. "Notice of Receivers Sale," *Dardanelle Post-Dispatch,* October 23, 1924, 3.

5. "Fred A. Smith Named Master Teacher of the Southern Regional Conference," *Dardanelle Post-Dispatch,* May 2, 1929, 4; "The Local Field," *Dardanelle Post-Dispatch,* October 1, 1925, 3; "Smith Hughes Notes," *Dardanelle Post-Dispatch*, February 17, 1927, 5; "Does Smith Hughes Work Pay?" *Dardanelle Post-Dispatch,* March 10, 1927, 1; "Smith Hughes Notes," *Dardanelle Post-Dispatch*, March 24, 1927, 1; "Fred Smith Discusses Local Dairy Industry," *Dardanelle Post-Dispatch*, March 28, 1929, 3.

6. "Fred A. Smith Named as Master Teacher," *Dardanelle Post-Dispatch*, January 3, 1929, 1.

7. Editorial, *Dardanelle Post-Dispatch*, February 10, 1921, 2.

8. "Quorum Court against Tick Eradication Program," *Dardanelle Post-Dispatch*, November 2, 1922, 1.

9. "49 Counties Are for Demonstration Work," *Dardanelle Post-Dispatch*, November 15, 1923, 3.

10. "County Agent to Have Farm Demonstrator," *Dardanelle Post-Dispatch,* October 23, 1924, 1; "Quorum Court Favors Retiring County Debt," *Dardanelle Post-Dispatch*, October 29, 1925, 1.

11. "Do We Need a County Demonstration Agent?" *Dardanelle Post-Dispatch*, October 21, 1926, 1.

12. "Do We Need a County Demonstration Agent?" *Dardanelle Post-Dispatch*, October 21, 1926, 1.

13. "Quorum Court Favors Demonstration Agent," *Dardanelle Post-Dispatch*, October 28, 1926, 1.

14. "Agricultural Policies for Yell County in 1928," *Dardanelle Post-Dispatch*, November 10, 1927, 2; "County Contest Saturday," *Dardanelle Post-Dispatch*, July 21, 1927, 2.

15. "Home Demonstration Work Means Much to Farm Women," *Dardanelle Post-Dispatch*, June 5, 1924, 3.

16. "Home Demonstration Work Means Much to Farm Women," *Dardanelle Post-Dispatch,* June 5, 1924, 3; Jones, *Mama Learned Us to Work*, 107–38.

17. "Farmers and Business Men Called to Meet," *Dardanelle Post-Dispatch*, January 5, 1928, 1.

18. "Demonstration Work Now Up to Citizens," *Dardanelle Post-Dispatch,* January 12, 1928, 1.

19. "Demonstration Work Will Be Abandoned," *Dardanelle Post-Dispatch*, July 11, 1929, 1.

20. "Don't Burn Stalks: Plow Them Under," *Dardanelle Post-Dispatch*, October 23, 1924, 3; "The Local Field," *Dardanelle Post-Dispatch*, August 25, 1927, 3.

21. "Concerning Improved Roads, Etc.," *Dardanelle Post-Dispatch*, September 30, 1915, 4.

22. "Tick Eradication Work Well Started," *Dardanelle Post-Dispatch*, June 8, 1916, 1; "Centerville," *Dardanelle Post-Dispatch*, June 29, 1916, 8.

23. "Report of County Judge T. E. Wilson," *Dardanelle Post-Dispatch*, November 3, 1921, 3.

24. "Compulsory Dipping Abandoned in County," *Dardanelle Post-Dispatch*, April 13, 1922, 1.

25. "Quorum Court against Tick Eradication Work," *Dardanelle Post-Dispatch*, November 2, 1922, 1.

26. "Meeting to Discuss Tick Eradication," *Dardanelle Post-Dispatch*, March 3, 1923, 1.

27. "Tick Eradication Work to Start March 1st," *Dardanelle Post-Dispatch*, February 18, 1926, 1.

28. "Cattle Must Be Dipped," *Dardanelle Post-Dispatch*, March 4, 1926, 1.

29. "'Suffragette' Opposed Dipping," *Dardanelle Post-Dispatch*, March 11, 1926, 4.

30. "Opposes Cattle Dipping," *Dardanelle Post-Dispatch*, March 18, 1926, 1.

31. J. Blake Perkins, "The Arkansas Tick Eradication Murder: Rethinking Yeoman Resistance in the 'Marginal' South," *Arkansas Historical Quarterly* 70, no. 4 (Winter 2011): 370–74.

32. "Ard Items," *Dardanelle Post-Dispatch*, March 25, 1926, 6.

33. "Opposes Dipping," *Dardanelle Post-Dispatch*, April 8, 1926, 3.

34. "Slaty Branch Items," *Dardanelle Post-Dispatch*, May 13, 1926, 2.

35. "Poultry Association Formed," *Dardanelle Post-Dispatch*, March 15, 1921, 1.

36. "Four Counties in Development Body," *Dardanelle Post-Dispatch*, August 5, 1926, 1.

37. "The Local Field," *Dardanelle Post-Dispatch*, January 27, 1921, 2.

38. "Attention Farmers," *Dardanelle Post-Dispatch*, July 22, 1926, 1.

39. "Dairying and Prosperity," *Dardanelle Post-Dispatch*, June 7, 1928, 1.

40. "Cream Shippers Received $3,981.40 during Year 1925," *Dardanelle Post-Dispatch*, January 7, 1926, 1.

41. "America's Rural Problem and How to Solve It," *Dardanelle Post-Dispatch*, March 22, 1928, 2.

42. "Some Essentials for Successful Hatching," *Dardanelle Post-Dispatch*, January 31, 1924, 5.

43. "Ola Items," *Dardanelle Post-Dispatch*, April 7, 1927, 5.

44. "Says Low Price Due to Too Much Cotton," *Dardanelle Post-Dispatch*, January 13, 1921, 1.

45. "State Conference Adopts Memphis Plan," *Dardanelle Post-Dispatch*, January 20, 1921, 1.

46. Editorial, *Dardanelle Post-Dispatch*, February 10, 1921, 2.

47. Patrick Hagge, "The Decline and Fall of a Cotton Empire: Economic and Land-Use Change in the Lower Mississippi River 'Delta' South, 1930–1970" (PhD diss., Pennsylvania State University, 2013), 46–47.

48. Hagge, "The Decline and Fall of a Cotton Empire," 7.

49. Hagge, "The Decline and Fall of a Cotton Empire," 7

50. Hagge, "The Decline and Fall of a Cotton Empire," 48–49.

51. Hagge, "The Decline and Fall of a Cotton Empire," 50. Also see Carl H. Moneyhon, *Arkansas and the New South, 1874–1929* (Fayetteville: University of Arkansas Press, 1997), 133–35.

52. Donald Holley, *The Second Great Emancipation: The Mechanical Cotton Picker, Black Migration, and How They Shaped the Modern South* (Fayetteville: University of Arkansas Press, 2000), 55.

53. Holley, *The Second Great Emancipation,* 55–56. Also see Sven Beckert, *Empire of Cotton: A Global History* (New York: Alfred A. Knopf, 2014), 395.

54. Hagge, "The Decline and Fall of a Cotton Empire," 7.

55. "Important Meeting Here," *Dardanelle Post-Dispatch,* January 20, 19212, 1; "Cotton Acreage Will Be Greatly Reduced," *Dardanelle Post-Dispatch,* January 27, 1921, 1.

56. "Centerville," *Dardanelle Post-Dispatch,* March 24, 1921, 6.

57. "State Cotton Crop Is Cut 1,000,000 Acres," *Dardanelle Post-Dispatch,* May 19, 1921, 4.

58. "Cotton Prices Next Fall," *Dardanelle Post-Dispatch,* March 31, 1921, 1.

59. "Costs 33 Cents Per Lb. to Grow Cotton," *Dardanelle Post-Dispatch,* April 7, 1921, 1.

60. "Normal Cotton Crop Would Ruin the South," *Dardanelle Post-Dispatch,* May 12, 1921, 1.

61. "Surplus Cotton a Menace to the South," *Dardanelle Post-Dispatch,* March 31, 1921, 2.

62. "Time to Begin New Year's War on the Boll Weevil," *Dardanelle Post-Dispatch,* September 1, 1921, 1.

63. "Cotton Hard Hit by the Army Worm," *Dardanelle Post-Dispatch,* September 1, 1921, 4.

64. "Cotton Condition at Lowest Level," *Dardanelle Post-Dispatch,* October 6, 1921, 1.

65. "The Local Field," *Dardanelle Post-Dispatch,* September 1, 1921, 6.

66. "The Local Field," *Dardanelle Post-Dispatch,* November 6, 1919, 5.

67. "Arkansas Crop Reports," *Dardanelle Post-Dispatch,* September 7, 1922, 6.

68. "The Local Field," *Dardanelle Post-Dispatch,* August 31, 1922, 5.

69. "The Local Field," *Dardanelle Post-Dispatch,* November 9, 1922, 5.

70. "Editorial Remarks," *Dardanelle Post-Dispatch,* August 16, 1923, 4.

71. "Notice to Cotton Growers," *Dardanelle Post-Dispatch,* October 23, 1924, 1.

72. "Old Marketing Plan Is a Failure," *Dardanelle Post-Dispatch,* January 22, 1925, 5.

73. "Cotton States League Urges 30c for Cotton," *Dardanelle Post-Dispatch,* September 24, 1925, 6.

74. "Mill Men Expect Big Cotton Crop in 1926," *Dardanelle Post-Dispatch,* February 18, 1926, 1.

75. "The Local Field," *Dardanelle Post-Dispatch,* September 2, 1926, 3.

76. "Estimate Places 1926 Crop at 18,618,000 Bales," *Dardanelle Post-Dispatch,* December 9, 1926, 1.

77. "The Local Field," *Dardanelle Post-Dispatch,* April 28, 1927, 3.

78. "D & R Depot Consumed by Flames Last Night," *Dardanelle Post-Dispatch,* March 6, 1926, 1.

79. "Ft. S. S. & R. I. Installs New Motor Car," *Dardanelle Post-Dispatch,* October 27, 1921, 1; Shirley Sticht Schuette, "Subiaco," *The Encyclopedia of Arkansas History & Culture.*

80. "Weekly Road Report of Overseer C. L. Russ," *Dardanelle Post-Dispatch,* April 1, 1920, 1.

81. "Tuesday June 15th, Is Road Working Day," *Dardanelle Post-Dispatch*, June 3, 1920, 1; "Road Working Day," *Dardanelle Post-Dispatch*, May 6, 1920, 1.

82. Editorial, *Dardanelle Post-Dispatch*, November 9, 1922, 4; "Carden Bottom Roads," *Dardanelle Post-Dispatch*, June, 19, 1924, 3.

83. "Four Fine Bridges Are Completed," *Dardanelle Post-Dispatch*, February 14, 1924, 1; "Highway Department Begins Big Work Here," *Dardanelle Post-Dispatch*, June 25, 1925, 1; "County Highways to Be Graveled at Once," *Dardanelle Post-Dispatch*, June 14, 1928; "The Local Field," *Dardanelle Post-Dispatch,* June 13, 1929; Tomela Wright Keenan, interview by author, Dardanelle, Arkansas, April 30, 2014.

84. Keenan, interview by author, April 30, 2014.

85. "Highway Department Doing Great Work in Yell County," *Dardanelle Post-Dispatch*, July 23, 1925, 1.

86. "Bad Roads Necessitate Court Postponement," *Dardanelle Post-Dispatch*, February 14, 1929, 1.

87. "Effort Being Made to Improve Bottom Road," *Dardanelle Post-Dispatch*, July 11, 1929, 1.

88. "Tax Payers to Vote on Free Bridge Measure," *Dardanelle Post-Dispatch*, March 26, 1925, 1; "The Free Bridge Bill," *Dardanelle Post-Dispatch*, March 26, 1925, 2.

89. "Pope County for Free Bridge," *Dardanelle Post-Dispatch*, March 26, 1925, 8.

90. "Soundings Completed for New Free Bridge," *Dardanelle Post-Dispatch*, January 28, 1927, 1.

91. "Soundings Completed for New Free Bridge," *Dardanelle Post-Dispatch*, January 28, 1927, 1.

92. "Work on Free Bridge Progressing Rapidly," *Dardanelle Post-Dispatch*, February 23, 1928, 1.

93. "First Bridge Span Was Placed Monday," *Dardanelle Post-Dispatch*, June 14, 1928, 1.

94. "Thousands Attend Big Free Bridge Opening," *Dardanelle Post-Dispatch*, January 24, 1929, 1.

95. "Old Pontoon Bridge Being Salvaged," *Dardanelle Post-Dispatch,* February 21, 1929, 1.

96. "River Damaging Crops in Low Lands," *Dardanelle Post-Dispatch*, May 24, 1923, 1.

97. "Levees Hold, River Falls," *Dardanelle Post-Dispatch*, June 21, 1923, 1.

98. "Low Lands Suffer as Arkansas River Rises," *Dardanelle Post-Dispatch*, October 7, 1926, 1.

99. "Rainfall for Ten Days Amounts to 6.41 Inches," *Dardanelle Post-Dispatch*, January 27, 1927, 1.

100. Nancy Hendricks, "Flood of 1927," *The Encyclopedia of Arkansas History & Culture.*

101. Jeannie M. Whayne et al., *Arkansas: A Narrative History* (Fayetteville: University of Arkansas Press, 2002), 313.

102. John M. Barry, *Rising Tide: The Great Mississippi Flood of 1927 and How It Changed America* (New York: Simon & Schuster Paperbacks, 1997), 188.

103. Pete Daniel, *Deep'n as It Come: The 1927 Mississippi River Flood* (Fayetteville: University of Arkansas Press, 1996), 7.

104. "Unprecedented Flood Devastates Arkansas River Bottom Lands,"
*Dardanelle Post-Dispatch,* April 14, 1927, 1.

105. "Unprecedented Flood Devastates Arkansas River Bottom Lands,"
*Dardanelle Post-Dispatch,* April 14, 1927, 1.

106. "Flood Reaches Crest of 33 Feet, Now Slowly Receding," *Dardanelle Post-Dispatch,* April 21, 1927, 1.

107. "Flood Reaches Crest of 33 Feet, Now Slowly Receding," *Dardanelle Post-Dispatch,* April 21, 1927, 1.

108. "Flood Reaches Crest of 33 Feet, Now Slowly Receding," *Dardanelle Post-Dispatch,* April 21, 1927, 1.

109. "Flood Reaches Crest of 33 Feet, Now Slowly Receding," *Dardanelle Post-Dispatch,* April 21, 1927, 1.

110. "Flood Reaches Crest of 33 Feet, Now Slowly Receding," *Dardanelle Post-Dispatch,* April 21, 1927, 1.

111. Hendricks, "Flood of 1927."

112. Whayne et al., *Arkansas,* 312.

113. Daniel, *Deep'n as It Come,* 8.

114. "Flood Reaches Crest of 33 Feet, Now Slowly Receding," *Dardanelle Post-Dispatch,* April 21, 1927, 1.

115. "Receding Flood Water Shows Havoc Wrought," *Dardanelle Post-Dispatch,* April 28, 1927, 1.

116. Candice McGee, "American Red Cross," *The Encyclopedia of Arkansas History & Culture.*

117. Barry, *Rising Tide,* 369; "Receding Flood Water Shows Havoc Wrought," *Dardanelle Post-Dispatch,* April 28, 1927, 1.

118. "Receding Flood Water Shows Havoc Wrought," *Dardanelle Post-Dispatch,* April 28, 1927, 1.

119. "Rehabilitation Work Now Well Under Way," *Dardanelle Post-Dispatch,* May 5, 1927, 1.

120. "Red Cross Organizes for Effective Relief," *Dardanelle Post-Dispatch,* September 25, 1930, 1.

121. Russell Bearden, "Jefferson County's Worst Disaster: The Flood of 1927," *Arkansas Historical Quarterly* 43, no. 4 (Winter 1984): 337.

122. Hendricks, "Flood of 1927."

123. "Fields Chapel Items," *Dardanelle Post-Dispatch,* May 19, 1927, 5.

124. "The Local Field," *Dardanelle Post-Dispatch,* September 22, 1927, 2.

125. "Bottom Levees Will Be Quickly Rebuilt," *Dardanelle Post-Dispatch,* May 26, 1927, 1.

126. "Precautions to Guard Health Are Economical," *Dardanelle Post-Dispatch,* June 16, 1927, 2.

127. "$10,562.49 Contributed by American Red Cross," *Dardanelle Post-Dispatch,* June 23, 1927, 1.

128. Hendricks, "Flood of 1927."

129. "Pontoon Bridge Out Again," *Dardanelle Post-Dispatch,* June 23, 1927, 1.

130. "Arkansas River Does More Damage to Crops," *Dardanelle Post-Dispatch,* October 6, 1927, 1.

131. "Red Cross Is Again Aiding Flood Victims," *Dardanelle Post-Dispatch*, October 13, 1927, 1.

132. "The Local Field," *Dardanelle Post-Dispatch*, June 23, 1927, 1; "The Local Field," *Dardanelle Post-Dispatch*, November 3, 1927, 2; "Arkansas River Does More Damage to Crops," *Dardanelle Post-Dispatch*, October 6, 1927, 1.

133. "The Local Field," *Dardanelle Post-Dispatch*, October 20, 1927, 3.

134. "Heavy Rains Damage Crops and Highways," *Dardanelle Post-Dispatch*, April 12, 1928, 1.

135. "High Water Damages Crops in Lowlands," *Dardanelle Post-Dispatch*, April 26, 1928, 1.

136. "River Rising Again," *Dardanelle Post-Dispatch*, June 21, 1928, 1.

137. "Levees in Bottoms Prevented Overflow," *Dardanelle Post-Dispatch*, May 23, 1929, 1.

138. "Arkansas Wrapped in Blanket of Snow," *Dardanelle Post-Dispatch*, February 24, 1921, 1.

139. "The Local Field," *Dardanelle Post-Dispatch*, April 8, 1926, 3.

140. "No Actual Famine Exists in the South," *Dardanelle Post-Dispatch*, August 25, 1921, 1.

141. "No Actual Famine Exists in the South," *Dardanelle Post-Dispatch*, August 25, 1921, 1.

142. Gail Stewart, interview by author, Little Rock, Arkansas, July 11, 2014.

143. Cornelia Daniels, interview by author, Dardanelle, Arkansas, July 1, 2008.

144. Sadler, *Muzzled Oxen*, 90–92, 134–35, 198–99.

145. Barry, *Rising Tide*, 387.

146. "Plan to Sell Waterworks," *Dardanelle Post-Dispatch*, May 20, 1920, 1; "Campaign Launches for a Cleaner Town," *Dardanelle Post-Dispatch*, May 20, 1920, 1.

147. "The Local Field," *Dardanelle Post-Dispatch*, July 31, 1919, 4.

148. "$50.00 Reward," *Dardanelle Post-Dispatch*, March 3, 1921, 1.

149. "Water Should Be Boiled," *Dardanelle Post-Dispatch*, September 14, 1922, 1.

150. "The Local Field," *Dardanelle Post-Dispatch*, February 1, 1923, 5.

151. "Plan to Sell Waterworks," *Dardanelle Post-Dispatch*, March 1, 1923, 1; "Ice Company Is Given City Pumping Contract," *Dardanelle Post-Dispatch*, November 29, 1923, 1.

152. "City Retires $8,000 Water District Note," *Dardanelle Post-Dispatch*, February 28, 1924, 1.

153. "The Local Field," *Dardanelle Post-Dispatch*, August 8, 1929, 4.

154. "Influenza in State Now on the Decline," *Dardanelle Post-Dispatch*, February 8, 1923, 5.

155. "Old Neely," *Dardanelle Post-Dispatch*, February 8, 1923, 3; "The Local Field," *Dardanelle Post-Dispatch*, February 1, 1923, 3; "New Neely," *Dardanelle Post-Dispatch*, February 8, 1923, 3.

156. "The Local Field," *Dardanelle Post-Dispatch*, January 3, 1929, 2.

157. "Fields Chapel Notes," *Dardanelle Post-Dispatch*, March 1, 1928, 2; "Liberty Hall Items," *Dardanelle Post-Dispatch*, March 1, 1928, 2; "Liberty Hall Items," *Dardanelle Post-Dispatch*, April 19, 1928, 4.

158. "Health Secretary's Report," *Dardanelle Post-Dispatch,* March 24, 1921, 1; "Health Secretary's Report," *Dardanelle Post-Dispatch,* January 3, 1921, 1.

159. "To Fight Tuberculosis," *Dardanelle Post-Dispatch,* May 12, 1921, 4.

160. "To Fight Tuberculosis," *Dardanelle Post-Dispatch,* May 12, 1921, 4.

161. Nancy Snell Griffith, "Tuberculosis," *The Encyclopedia of Arkansas History & Culture.*

162. "Annual Health Ride to Occur Sunday Evening," *Dardanelle Post-Dispatch,* September 25, 1924, 1.

163. "A Brave Letter," *Dardanelle Post-Dispatch,* July 12, 1923, 2.

164. "A Brave Letter," *Dardanelle Post-Dispatch,* July 12, 1923, 2.

165. Griffith, "Tuberculosis."

166. Griffith, "Tuberculosis."

167. "School Children Should Be Vaccinated Now," *Dardanelle Post-Dispatch,* September 8, 1921, 1.

168. Helen Cole, "Public Health," *The Encyclopedia of Arkansas History & Culture.*

169. "Good Start on Health Plan," *Dardanelle Post-Dispatch,* January 13, 1927, 3.

170. "Yell County's Greatest Problem," *Dardanelle Post-Dispatch,* December 8, 1927, 1.

171. Cole, "Public Health."

172. "County Health Unit Doing Wonderful Work," *Dardanelle Post-Dispatch,* December 15, 1927, 1.

173. "Sanitary Inspector Urges War on Flies," *Dardanelle Post-Dispatch,* July 5, 1928, 1.

174. "Rubbish Being Removed from the River Bank," *Dardanelle Post-Dispatch,* February 9, 1928, 1.

175. "County Health Unit Is Doing Splendid Work," *Dardanelle Post-Dispatch,* May 10, 1928, 1.

176. "Report of Yell County Health Department," *Dardanelle Post-Dispatch,* January 10, 1929, 6.

177. "Centerville," *Dardanelle Post-Dispatch,* September 15, 1921, 3; "Centerville," *Dardanelle Post-Dispatch,* June 22, 1922, 5; "New Neely," *Dardanelle Post-Dispatch,* March 26, 1925, 6; "Mrs. A. L. Martin Dead," *Dardanelle Post-Dispatch,* June 11, 1925, 6; "The Local Field," *Dardanelle Post-Dispatch,* April 8, 1926, 3; "The Local Field," *Dardanelle Post-Dispatch,* January 28, 1926, 3; "The Local Field," *Dardanelle Post-Dispatch,* August 5, 1926, 3; "Local Banker Dies Following Operation," *Dardanelle Post-Dispatch,* July 18, 1929, 1.

178. "The Local Field," *Dardanelle Post-Dispatch,* May 6, 1920, 5.

179. "Grim Tragedy Follows Automobile Accident," *Dardanelle Post-Dispatch,* April 8, 1920, 1.

180. "Tom Holland Narrowly Escapes Serious Injury," *Dardanelle Post-Dispatch,* September 24, 1914, 1; "Jim Cowger Loses Arm in Cotton Gin," *Dardanelle Post-Dispatch,* September 10, 1914, 1.

181. "The Local Field," *Dardanelle Post-Dispatch,* June 17, 1920, 5.

182. "Bohemian Notes," *Dardanelle Post-Dispatch,* June 17, 1915, 6.

183. Lynne Gleason Murphy, personal conversation with author, Dardanelle, Arkansas, June 28, 2012.

184. "The Local Field," *Dardanelle Post-Dispatch*, September 6, 1928, 5.

185. "Child Dies Enroute to Hospital," *Dardanelle Post-Dispatch*, June 16, 1927, 1.

186. See "Red Cross Succors Storm Victims," *Dardanelle Post-Dispatch*, May 5, 1921; "Frank Vaughn Drowned," *Dardanelle Post-Dispatch*, October 20, 1921, 1; "The Local Field," *Dardanelle Post-Dispatch*, April 6, 1922, 1; "Frank Vodrazka Meets Tragic Death," *Dardanelle Post-Dispatch*, November 6, 1924, 1; "Frank Howell Died Following Amputation of Arm," *Dardanelle Post-Dispatch*, September 18, 1924, 1; "Havana Youth Met Tragic Death Sunday," *Dardanelle Post-Dispatch*, August 13, 1925, 1; "Frank Pitts Killed by Fast Train Near Conway," *Dardanelle Post-Dispatch*, September 10, 1925, 1; "Two Bridge Painters Have Narrow Escape," *Dardanelle Post-Dispatch*, January 17, 1929, 3; "Colored Girl Drowns in the Arkansas River," *Dardanelle Post-Dispatch*, July 4, 1929, 1; "Fatal Accident Occurred Saturday," *Dardanelle Post-Dispatch*, October 17, 1929, 1; "Miss Armine Holiman Died in Auto Accident," *Dardanelle Post-Dispatch*, December 19, 1929, 1.

187. "Youth Killed in Card Game at Danville," *Dardanelle Post-Dispatch*, November 20, 1924, 1.

188. "Murder and Suicide Shocks the Community," *Dardanelle Post-Dispatch*, June 17, 1920, 1.

189. "The Local Field," *Dardanelle Post-Dispatch*, November 28, 1912; "Andrew Brown Held on a Serious Charge," *Dardanelle Post-Dispatch*, January 16, 1913, 1; "Bank Robbers Get Two Year Sentences," *Dardanelle Post-Dispatch*, January 1, 1914, 1.

190. "Wife Kills Husband with Automobile Axle," *Dardanelle Post-Dispatch*, April 7, 1921, 1.

191. Bobby Crow, interview by author, Cotton Town, Arkansas, August 4, 2015.

192. "Fall Term of Circuit Court Held This Week," *Dardanelle Post-Dispatch*, September 16, 1926, 1.

193. "Clyde Jones Survives Desperate Wound," *Dardanelle Post-Dispatch*, September 30, 1926, 1.

194. See "Plainview Farmer Killed in Shotgun Duel," *Dardanelle Post-Dispatch*, July 23, 1925, 1; "Aged Hermit Is Found Dead near Delaware," *Dardanelle Post-Dispatch*, November 29, 1928, 1; "The Local Field," *Dardanelle Post-Dispatch*, March 15, 1923, 5; "George Cates Dies of Injuries," *Dardanelle Post-Dispatch*, July 15, 1926, 1; "Ringer's Injuries Serious," *Dardanelle Post-Dispatch*, July 15, 1926, 1; "Two Men Injured in Fight," *Dardanelle Post-Dispatch*, August 22, 1929, 5; "Alton Barnett Victim of Mysterious Death," *Dardanelle Post-Dispatch*, February 2, 1928, 1.

195. "The Local Field," *Dardanelle Post-Dispatch*, December 1, 1927, 4.

196. "The Local Field," *Dardanelle Post-Dispatch*, June 23, 1921, 3.

197. See "Centerville Items," *Dardanelle Post-Dispatch*, January 20, 1921, 6; "Squire Hundley's Store Robbed," *Dardanelle Post-Dispatch*, October 8, 1925, 1; "Local Officers Arrest Ewton Store Robbers," *Dardanelle Post-Dispatch*, January 20, 1927, 1.

198. "Ola Post Office Robbery," *Dardanelle Post-Dispatch*, April 7, 1921, 1.

199. "The Local Field," *Dardanelle Post-Dispatch*, December 1, 1921, 5.

200. "Stole the 'Law's' Fliver," *Dardanelle Post-Dispatch*, November 26, 1925, 1.

201. "Circuit Court in Session," *Dardanelle Post-Dispatch*, September 14, 1922, 1.

202. "Bootlegger Sentenced in Record Time," *Dardanelle Post-Dispatch*, September 22, 1921, 1; "The Local Field," *Dardanelle Post-Dispatch*, October 13, 1921,

3; "Fine Still Captured by Sheriff Joe Gault," *Dardanelle Post-Dispatch,* October 11, 1923, 1; "The Local Field," *Dardanelle Post-Dispatch,* April 27, 1922, 3; "Sheriff Gault Captures Two More Stills," *Dardanelle Post-Dispatch,* May 31, 1923, 1.

203. "Sheriff Joe D. Gault and Volstead Act Make Yell County Literally Dry," *Dardanelle Post-Dispatch*, August 30, 1923, 1; "Twenty-Six Men Are Sentenced to Prison," *Dardanelle Post-Dispatch,* September 20, 1923, 1.

204. "Warns against Sale of Flavoring Extracts," *Dardanelle Post-Dispatch,* May 29, 1924, 1; State of Arkansas, *"Leslie v. State of Arkansas," Arkansas Reports: Cases Determined in the Supreme Court of Arkansas,* Volume 155 (Little Rock: Democrat Printing and Lithographic Company, 1923), 530.

205. "Spring Term Circuit Court Now in Session," *Dardanelle Post-Dispatch*, February 16, 1922, 1; "Fall Term of Circuit Court Adjourned on Saturday," *Dardanelle Post-Dispatch*, September 21, 1922, 6.

206. "Spring Term Circuit Court Now in Session," *Dardanelle Post-Dispatch*, February 11, 1926, 1.

207. "Spring Term Circuit Court Now in Session," *Dardanelle Post-Dispatch*, February 17, 1927, 1.

208. "Fall Term Circuit Court Now in Session," *Dardanelle Post-Dispatch,"* November 3, 1926, 1.

209. "Spring Term Circuit Court Now in Session," *Dardanelle Post-Dispatch,* February 16, 1922, 1.

210. "Centerville," *Dardanelle Post-Dispatch,* August 17, 1922, 2.

211. "Centerville," *Dardanelle Post-Dispatch*, February 25, 1915, 5.

212. "Election Returns Are Finally In," *Dardanelle Post-Dispatch,* October 3, 1912, 6.

213. See Whayne et al., *Arkansas,* 287–88; "Noted Prohibitionist Makes Splendid Talk," *Dardanelle Post-Dispatch,* November 18, 1920, 1.

214. See Jeannie M. Whayne, "Caging the Blind Tiger: Race, Class, and Family in the Battle for Prohibition in Small Town Arkansas," *Arkansas Historical Quarterly* 71, no. 1 (Spring 2012): 44–60.

215. "Klan Initiates Big Class near Havana," *Dardanelle Post-Dispatch,* October 5, 1922, 1; Charles C. Alexander, "White-Robed Reformers: The Ku Klux Klan Comes to Arkansas, 19212–1922," *Arkansas Historical Quarterly* 22, no. 1 (Spring 1963): 21; Brooks R. Blevins, "The Strike and the Still: Anti-Radical Violence and the Ku Klux Klan in the Ozarks," *Arkansas Historical Quarterly* 52, no. 4 (Winter 1993): 407.

216. "Ku Klux Klan Rewards Office for Capturing Still," *Dardanelle Post-Dispatch*, June 8, 1922.

217. "Imperial Wizard Evans Defends Ku Klux Klan," *Dardanelle Post-Dispatch,* December 28, 1922, 1.

218. Alexander, "White-Robed Reformers," 12.

219. "Untitled," *Dardanelle Post-Dispatch*, August 16, 1923, 1.

220. Editorial, *Dardanelle Post-Dispatch*, February 8, 1923, 5.

221. See Donald Holley, "A Look behind the Masks: The 1920s Ku Klux Klan in Monticello, Arkansas," *Arkansas Historical Quarterly* 60, no. 2 (Summer 2001): 131–50; Robert Neymeyer, "The Ku Klux Klan of the 1920 in the Midwest and West: A Review Essay," *Annals of Iowa* 51 (Fall 1992): 625–33; John M. Mecklin, *The Ku Klux Klan: A Study of the American Mind* (New York: Russell & Russell, 1963).

222. Charles C. Alexander, "White Robes in Politics: The Ku Klux Klan in Arkansas, 1922–1924," *Arkansas Historical Quarterly* 22, no. 3 (Fall 1963): 204–8.

223. Charles F. Robinson II, *Dangerous Liaisons: Sex and Love in the Segregated South* (Fayetteville: University of Arkansas Press, 2003), 100; Charles C. Alexander, "Defeat, Decline, Disintegration: The Ku Klux Klan in Arkansas, 1924 and After," *Arkansas Historical Quarterly* 22, no. 4 (Winter 1963): 326–31.

224. Blevins, "The Strike and the Still," 423–25.

225. Joey McCarty, "The Red Scare in Arkansas: A Southern State and National Hysteria," *Arkansas Historical Quarterly* 37, no. 3 (Autumn 1978): 268.

226. "NAACP Report on Lynching," *Arkansas Gazette,* May 3, 1919, 8.

227. "Officers Arrest Seven Alleged Night Riders," *Dardanelle Post-Dispatch,* December 11, 1924, 1.

228. "Alleged Night Riders Waive Examination," *Dardanelle Post-Dispatch,* December 18, 1924, 1.

229. "Alleged Night Riders Waive Examination," *Dardanelle Post-Dispatch,* December 18, 1924, 1; "Night-Riders Threaten Upper Bottom Negroes," *Dardanelle Post-Dispatch,* December 4, 1924, 1.

230. "Alleged Night Riders Waive Examination," *Dardanelle Post-Dispatch,* December 18, 1924, 1.

231. "Night Rider Cases to Be Tried Tomorrow," *Dardanelle Post-Dispatch,* February 12, 1925, 1; "Pleaded Guilty to Night Riding," *Arkansas Gazette,* February 14, 1925, 1.

232. "Night Riding Case," *Arkansas Gazette,* February 10, 1925, 4.

233. "Pleaded Guilty to Night Riding," *Arkansas Gazette,* February 14, 1925, 1.

234. "Pleaded Guilty to Night Riding," *Arkansas Gazette,* February 14, 1925, 1.

235. Guy Lancaster, *Racial Cleansing in Arkansas, 1883–1924: Politics, Land, Labor, and Criminality* (New York: Lexington Press, 2014), 45.

236. Steven Hahn, *A Nation under Our Feet: Black Political Struggles in the Rural South from Slavery to the Great Migration* (Cambridge, MA: Harvard University Press, 2003), 426–28. Also see Guy Lancaster, "Nightriding and Racial Cleansing in the Arkansas River Valley," *Arkansas Historical Quarterly* 72, no. 3 (Autumn 2013): 242–64.

237. Jeannie Whayne, *Delta Empire: Lee Wilson and the Transformation of Agriculture in the New South* (Baton Rouge: Louisiana State University Press, 2011), 121.

238. "Night Riders Threaten Upper Bottoms Negroes," *Dardanelle Post-Dispatch,* December 4, 1924, 1.

239. "Many Negroes Going North," *Dardanelle Post-Dispatch,* May 10, 1923, 2.

240. "Governors Discuss Exodus of Negroes," *Dardanelle Post-Dispatch,* August 9, 1923, 4.

241. Lonnie Dickens, interview by author, Dardanelle, Arkansas, July 7, 2008.

242. "Negroes Returning to the South," *Dardanelle Post-Dispatch,* September 6, 1923, 3.

243. "Public Schools Open Monday, September 14," *Dardanelle Post-Dispatch,* September 3, 1925, 1.

244. "School Books Wanted," *Dardanelle Post-Dispatch,* March 3, 1927, 2.

245. "Public Schools Open Monday, September 14," *Dardanelle Post-Dispatch*, September 3, 1925, 1.

246. "Notice to the White Citizens of Dardanelle," *Dardanelle Post-Dispatch*, April 23, 1925, 4.

247. "Negro Baptists Stage Another Successful Rally," *Dardanelle Post-Dispatch*, December 9, 1926, 1.

248. "St. John's Baptist Church Raises $120.00," *Dardanelle Post-Dispatch*, March 22, 1928, 3.

249. "St. John's Baptist Church Raises $120.00," *Dardanelle Post-Dispatch*, March 22, 1928, 3.

250. "The Local Field," *Dardanelle Post-Dispatch*, November 23, 1922, 3.

251. "'Uncle Dan' Perry Dead," *Dardanelle Post-Dispatch*, February 16, 1928, 1.

252. "Handy Woods Dead," *Dardanelle Post-Dispatch*, May 3, 1928, 1.

253. "'Aunt Mahala' Smith Aged 104, Died Friday," *Dardanelle Post-Dispatch*, December 10, 1925, 1.

254. "'Uncle Eli' Perry Spent Night in Woods," *Dardanelle Post-Dispatch*, July 20, 1922, 1.

255. "The Local Field," *Dardanelle Post-Dispatch*, April 2, 1925, 3.

256. "Baseball Minstrel a Hugh Success," *Dardanelle Post-Dispatch*, January 26, 1922, 1.

257. "New Neely School Notes," *Dardanelle Post-Dispatch*, April 26, 1923, 4.

258. Advertisement, *Dardanelle Post-Dispatch*, December 14, 1922, 8.

259. "The Local Field," *Dardanelle Post-Dispatch*, February 1, 1923, 5.

260. "Flappers," *Dardanelle Post-Dispatch*, August 30, 1917, 4.

261. "What Is a Flapper?" *Dardanelle Post-Dispatch*, July 20, 1922, 1.

262. "Civic Club Program for 1928 and 1929," *Dardanelle Post-Dispatch*, May 31, 1928, 1; "Civic Club Enrolls Many New Members," *Dardanelle Post-Dispatch*, July 19, 1928, 1.

263. "Civic Club Meets," *Dardanelle Post-Dispatch*, June 13, 1929, 1.

264. "The Clean Town," *Dardanelle Post-Dispatch*, July 30, 1925, 2.

265. "The Civic Club," *Dardanelle Post-Dispatch*, April 25, 1929, 1.

266. "Women's Entire Ticket Wins in Mt. Nebo Election," *Dardanelle Post-Dispatch*, June 5, 1924, 1.

267. "Piano Wanted for Mt. Nebo Pavilion," *Dardanelle Post-Dispatch*, June 5, 1924, 1.

268. "Mayor of Mount Nebo Here Monday," *Dardanelle Post-Dispatch*, July 24, 1924, 1.

269. "Mt. Nebo News," *Dardanelle Post-Dispatch*, July 31, 1924, 4.

270. "Mt. Nebo Lady Council Holds Interesting Meeting," *Dardanelle Post-Dispatch*, October 30, 1924, 1.

271. "The Local Field," *Dardanelle Post-Dispatch*, June 7, 1928, 2.

272. "Farmers' Wives Club Will Hold First Sale Saturday," *Dardanelle Post-Dispatch*, September 25, 1924, 3.

273. "Riverside Notes," *Dardanelle Post-Dispatch*, October 21, 1926, 6.

274. "Lakeview Items," *Dardanelle Post-Dispatch*, April 29, 1926, 5.

275. "Centerville," *Dardanelle Post-Dispatch*, April 24, 1924, 3; "Field's Chapel,"

*Dardanelle Post-Dispatch,* March 27, 1924, 4; "Stout-Tucker," *Dardanelle Post-Dispatch*, July 26, 1923, 1.

276. "Riverside Items," *Dardanelle Post-Dispatch*, June 3, 1926, 6.

277. Doris Hundley Hickey, interview by author, Dardanelle, Arkansas, July 9, 2008.

278. Mary Potts Hall, interview by author, Little Rock, Arkansas, October 17, 2009.

279. "Additional Locals," *Dardanelle Post-Dispatch*, September 12, 1929, 4.

280. "Cotton Town Items," *Dardanelle Post-Dispatch*, March 9, 1922, 4.

281. "Centerville," *Dardanelle Post-Dispatch,* July 6, 1922, 2.

282. David D. Dawson, "Baseball Calls: Arkansas Town Baseball in the Twenties," *Arkansas Historical Quarterly* 54, no. 4 (Winter 1995): 409–26.

283. "Local 'Fans' Want Ball Park and Team," *Dardanelle Post-Dispatch,* April 7, 1921, 1.

284. "Ball Park Secured: Fans Are Happy," *Dardanelle Post-Dispatch*, April 21, 1921, 1.

285. "Western Arkansas League Is Organized," *Dardanelle Post-Dispatch,* May 19, 1921, 1.

286. "Board Penalizes Local Baseball Association," *Dardanelle Post-Dispatch*, August 11, 1921, 1.

287. "Dardanelle Wins First of 'World's Series,'" *Dardanelle Post-Dispatch*, July 10, 1924, 1.

288. "The Local Field," *Dardanelle Post-Dispatch,* August 16, 1923, 4.

289. "The Local Field," *Dardanelle Post-Dispatch*, February 18, 1926, 3.

290. "Razorback Nine Plans Spring Vacation Jaunt," *Dardanelle Post-Dispatch*, April 5, 1928, 1.

291. "Churches Condemn Sunday Baseball Law," *Dardanelle Post-Dispatch*, February 17, 1927, 1.

292. "Dardanelle to Have Modern New Theatre," *Dardanelle Post-Dispatch,* September 17, 1925, 1.

293. "New Theatre to Open Next Monday Night," *Dardanelle Post-Dispatch*, October 11, 1928, 1.

294. "McClure Is Installing New Talking Pictures," *Dardanelle Post-Dispatch*, July 11, 1929, 1.

295. "All Talking Program New Theatre Tonight," *Dardanelle Post-Dispatch*, July 25, 1929, 1.

296. "Rains Lower Scores," *Dardanelle Post-Dispatch*, April 7, 1921, 1.

297. "Additional Local," *Dardanelle Post-Dispatch*, July 26, 1923, 4.

298. "Boys Entertain Girls," *Dardanelle Post-Dispatch*, August 30, 1928, 1.

299. "Mrs. Duff at Bridge," *Dardanelle Post-Dispatch,* October 11, 1928, 1; "Miss George Complimented with Bridge," *Dardanelle Post-Dispatch*, October 18, 1928, 1.

300. "Silver Tea a Pleasing Event," *Dardanelle Post-Dispatch*, February 25, 1926, 1.

301. "Boathouse Club Organized," *Dardanelle Post-Dispatch*, December 29, 1921, 1.

302. "Aesthesian Club's Last Summer Meeting," *Dardanelle Post-Dispatch*, June 29, 1922, 3; "The Aesthesians," *Dardanelle Post-Dispatch*, May 26, 1921, 3.

303. See "The Local Field," *Dardanelle Post-Dispatch*, February 17, 1921, 4; "Raising Funds to Finance School Next Term," *Dardanelle Post-Dispatch*, June 30, 1921, 1; "City Schools Opened Last Monday Morning," *Dardanelle Post-Dispatch*, October 6, 1921, 1; "Dardanelle Schools Will Not Be Closed," *Dardanelle Post-Dispatch*, February 9, 1922, 1; "Dardanelle Bank to Rescue of Schools," *Dardanelle Post-Dispatch*, November 16, 1922, 1.

304. "Local High School to Be Advanced to Class A," *Dardanelle Post-Dispatch*, May 26, 1927, 1.

305. "Dardanelle Is Only 'A' School in County," *Dardanelle Post-Dispatch*, August 29, 1929, 1.

306. "New Neely School Opens," *Dardanelle Post-Dispatch*, November 9, 1922, 1.

307. "New Neely," *Dardanelle Post-Dispatch*, November 23, 1922, 5; "New Neely," *Dardanelle Post-Dispatch*, November 30, 1922, 5; "New Neely," *Dardanelle Post-Dispatch*, December 7, 1922, 5; "New Neely," *Dardanelle Post-Dispatch*, March 15, 1923, 5.

308. "New Neely School Items," *Dardanelle Post-Dispatch*, January 4, 1923, 6.

309. "Imposing Ceremonies Mark Dedication of High School," *Dardanelle Post-Dispatch*, November 21, 1929, 7.

310. Roy Tillman Jr., interview by author, Dardanelle, Arkansas, July 8, 2014; Joe Grimes, interview by author, Dardanelle, Arkansas, July 17, 2008.

311. "U. of A. Tuition Free to Seventeen Students," *Dardanelle Post-Dispatch*, July 9, 1914, 1; "Notice," *Dardanelle Post-Dispatch*, August 1, 1918, 2.

312. "Twenty-One Students Leave for College," *Dardanelle Post-Dispatch*, September 13, 1928, 1.

313. "Startling Facts and Figures about Arkansas," *Dardanelle Post-Dispatch*, August 25, 1921, 9.

314. *United States Department of Agriculture, Agricultural Statistics, 1937* (Washington, DC: US Government Printing Office, 1937), 89.

315. Carl H. Moneyhon, *Arkansas and the New South, 1874–1929* (Fayetteville: University of Arkansas Press, 1997), 137.

316. Moneyhon, *Arkansas and the New South,* 136.

317. Moneyhon, *Arkansas and the New South,* 138.

318. See "New Compress Is Now Ready for Business," *Dardanelle Post-Dispatch*, September 13, 1923, 1; "Carden Bottom," *Dardanelle Post-Dispatch*, March 12, 1925, 2; "Another Proof That Paving Means Growth," *Dardanelle Post-Dispatch*, February 17, 1927, 1; "Council Grants New Electric Franchise," *Dardanelle Post-Dispatch*, May 31, 1928, 1; "Radishes to Chicago," *Dardanelle Post-Dispatch,* April 13, 1922, 5; "Gilbert & Yearwood Buy Dardanelle Ice Plant, Neely Gin and Others," *Dardanelle Post-Dispatch*, December 30, 1926, 1; "Miks' Giant Hatchery Moves to Dardanelle," *Dardanelle Post-Dispatch*, September 27, 1928, 1; "Mobley Construction Company Completes Plant," *Dardanelle Post-Dispatch,* September 19, 1929, 1; "Opening of Dardanelle Bank Up to Depositors," *Dardanelle Post-Dispatch*, April 8, 1926, 1.

319. "A New Industry," *Dardanelle Post-Dispatch,* October 24, 1929, 3.

320. "The Retail Outlook for 1921–1922," *Dardanelle Post-Dispatch*, September 8, 1921, 8.

321. "The Local Field," *Dardanelle Post-Dispatch*, December 9, 1926, 4.

322. "Real Cooperation," *Dardanelle Post-Dispatch*, June 10, 1926, 1.

323. "Santa Claus Letters," *Dardanelle Post-Dispatch*, December 20, 1923, 7.


# CHAPTER 5: Deprivation and Survival, 1930–1941

1. Gail S. Murray, "Forty Years Ago: The Great Depression Comes to Arkansas," *Arkansas Historical Quarterly* 29, no. 4 (Winter 1970): 291–307.

2. John L. Smith, "Reminiscences of Farming and Business in the Depression, 1929–1933," *Arkansas Historical Quarterly* 45, no. 4 (Winter 1986): 321–23.

3. Keith J. Volanto, "The AAA Cotton Plow-Up Campaign in Arkansas," *Arkansas Historical Quarterly* 59, no. 4 (Winter 2000): 388.

4. M. S. Venkataramani, "Norman Thomas, Arkansas Sharecroppers, and the Roosevelt Agricultural Policies, 1933–1937," *Arkansas Historical Quarterly* 24, no. 1 (Spring 1965): 3.

5. Pete Daniel, *Breaking the Land: The Transformation of Cotton, Tobacco, and Rice Cultures since 1880* (Urbana: University of Illinois Press, 1986), 91–92.

6. "10 Below Zero Here Last Saturday Morn," *Dardanelle Post-Dispatch*, January 23, 1930, 1.

7. "Weekly Letter from Commissioner Page," *Dardanelle Post-Dispatch*, August 7, 1930, 8.

8. "Wasp Nest Items," *Dardanelle Post-Dispatch*, August 7, 1930, 8.

9. "Red Cross Notes," *Dardanelle Post-Dispatch*, August 14, 1930, 1.

10. "Drouth of 1930 Is the Most Serious in History of South," *Dardanelle Post-Dispatch*, August 21, 1930, 2.

11. "County Drouth Relief Organization Named," *Dardanelle Post-Dispatch*, August 21, 1930, 1.

12. "Smith Urges Planting of Gardens and Pastures," *Dardanelle Post-Dispatch*, August 21, 1930, 1.

13. "County School Notes," *Dardanelle Post-Dispatch*, August 21, 1930, 1.

14. "Weekly Letter from Earl Page," *Dardanelle Post-Dispatch*, September 4, 1930, 7.

15. "Yell County Raising Funds for Red Cross," *Dardanelle Post-Dispatch*, September 18, 1930, 1.

16. "Weekly Letter from Earl Page," *Dardanelle Post-Dispatch*, September 18, 1930, 7.

17. John Spurgeon, "Drought of 1930–1931," *The Encyclopedia of Arkansas History & Culture*.

18. Roger Lambert, "Hoover and the Red Cross in the Arkansas Drought of 1930," *Arkansas Historical Quarterly* 29, no. 1 (Spring 1970): 4–7.

19. Bill Garner, personal conversation with author, Dardanelle, Arkansas, October 19, 2001.

20. Lambert, "Hoover and the Red Cross," 7.

21. McGee, "American Red Cross."

22. Murray, "Forty Years Ago," 296–98.

23. Lambert, "Hoover and the Red Cross," 14–15.

24. Murray, "Forty Years Ago," 298–99.

25. Murray, "Forty Years Ago," 298–99. Also see Nan Woodruff, "The Failure of Relief during the Arkansas Drought of 1930–31," *Arkansas Historical Quarterly* 39, no. 4 (Winter 1980): 301–13.

26. Spurgeon, "Drought of 1930–1931," 2.

27. Lambert, "Hoover and the Red Cross," 17–19.

28. Floyd W. Hicks and C. Roger Lambert, "Food for the Hungry: Federal Food Programs in Arkansas, 1933–1942," *Arkansas Historical Quarterly* 37, no. 1 (Spring 1978): 23–43. Also see Nan Elizabeth Woodruff, *As Rare as Rain: Federal Relief in the Great Southern Drought of 1930–31* (Urbana: University of Illinois Press, 1985).

29. See "Committees Named for RA Drought Relief," *Dardanelle Post-Dispatch,* December 17, 1936, 1.

30. Spurgeon, "Drought of 1930–1931," 1.

31. Spurgeon, "Drought of 1930–1931," 1.

32. Michael B. Dougan, "Business, Commerce and Industry," *The Encyclopedia of Arkansas History & Culture.*

33. Irvin Marion May, "The Paradox of Agricultural Abundance and Poverty: The Federal Surplus Relief Corporation, 1933–1935" (Unpublished PhD diss., University of Oklahoma, 1970), 28–29.

34. "Census Figures Show Loss for Yell County," *Dardanelle Post-Dispatch,* May 29, 1930, 1.

35. "Rainfall This Month Nearly Seven Inches," *Dardanelle Post-Dispatch,* January 21, 1937, 1.

36. "Heat Record Broken," *Dardanelle Post-Dispatch,* July 23, 1936, 4.

37. "The Local Field," *Dardanelle Post-Dispatch,* August 20, 1936, 5.

38. "75 Years Ago," *Dardanelle Post-Dispatch,* June 10, 2015, 3.

39. "Carden Bottom Storm Occasions Severe Loss," *Dardanelle Post-Dispatch,* October 21, 1937, 1.

40. Lola Person Cooper, *Lest We Forget,* Arkansas River Valley Regional Library, Dardanelle, Arkansas (Unpublished Collection, 1972), 75.

41. "Heavy Loss Caused by Sunday Night's Storm," *Dardanelle Post-Dispatch,* May 26, 1938, 1; "Riverside Items," *Dardanelle Post-Dispatch,* May 26, 1938, 8.

42. "Old Home Demolished," *Dardanelle Post-Dispatch,* October 30, 1941, 3; "Dardanelle Commissary Moves to El Dorado Ave.," *Dardanelle Post-Dispatch,* October 30, 1941, 4.

43. "Red Cross Expends $4,693.21 Here during Past Five Weeks," *Dardanelle Post-Dispatch,* December 4, 1941, 1.

44. "Miss Bata Praised for Unusual Courage," *Dardanelle Post-Dispatch,* November 6, 1941, 1.

45. "River Is Falling after High Mark of 24.1 Feet," *Dardanelle Post-Dispatch,* June 6, 1935, 1.

46. "Danger of Overflow Now Appears Averted," *Dardanelle Post-Dispatch,* June 13, 1935, 1; Marie Shepherd Bachman, interview by author, Dardanelle, Arkansas, August 4, 2008; Grace Hatch McClure, interview by author, Dardanelle, Arkansas, June 24, 2008.

47. "At Least 250 Families Driven from River Bottoms in Yell County as Flood Waters Cover 25,000 Acres," *Dardanelle Post-Dispatch,* June 20, 1935, 1.

48. "The Local Field," *Dardanelle Post-Dispatch,* June 20, 1935, 5.

49. "Farmers Returning to Flood Ravaged Homes," *Dardanelle Post-Dispatch,* June 27, 1935, 1.

50. "Crops Recommended for Overflowed Lands," *Dardanelle Post-Dispatch,* July 4, 1935, 1.

51. "Efforts Being Made for Levee Rebuilding," *Dardanelle Post-Dispatch,* July 11, 1935, 1.

52. "Congress Allots $93,200 for Local Levees," *Dardanelle Post-Dispatch,* June 25, 1936.

53. "Rise in Arkansas River Occasions Some Alarm," *Dardanelle Post-Dispatch,* February 17, 1938, 1.

54. "Bottom Lands Flooded But Damage Not Heavy," *Dardanelle Post-Dispatch,* February 24, 1938, 1; "Red Cross Appeals for Funds for Flood Relief," *Dardanelle Post-Dispatch,* February 24, 1938, 1.

55. "The Local Field," *Dardanelle Post-Dispatch,* March 31, 1938, 5.

56. "Heavy Rainfall Causes Serious Loss in County," *Dardanelle Post-Dispatch,* April 20, 1939, 1.

57. "Danger of Overflow Now Appears Ended," *Dardanelle Post-Dispatch,* April 24, 1941, 1; "Carden Bottom Items," *Dardanelle Post-Dispatch,* April 24, 1941, 3; "Riverside Items," *Dardanelle Post-Dispatch,* April 24, 1941, 8.

58. "Disastrous Flood Covers Thousands of Acres of Fertile River Bottom Lands," *Dardanelle Post-Dispatch,* November 6, 1941, 1; "Victims of Flood Returning to Homes," *Dardanelle Post-Dispatch,* November 13, 1941, 1.

59. "Red Cross Expends $4,693.21 Here during Past Five Weeks," *Dardanelle Post-Dispatch,* December 4, 1941, 1.

60. "Red Cross Asks for Surplus Clothing," *Dardanelle Post-Dispatch,* December 11, 1930, 1.

61. "Am I My Brother's Keeper?" *Dardanelle Post-Dispatch,* December 25, 1930, 1.

62. "Red Cross to Provide Employment for Needy," *Dardanelle Post-Dispatch,* January 15, 1931, 1.

63. "Red Cross Aiding 2,338 Yell County Families," *Dardanelle Post-Dispatch,* February 5, 1931, 1.

64. "County School Notes," *Dardanelle Post-Dispatch,* January 29, 1931, 8.

65. "WPA Hot Lunch Project for School Children," *Dardanelle Post-Dispatch,* May 23, 1940, 8.

66. "Yell County Medical Association Meeting," *Dardanelle Post-Dispatch,* February 5, 1931, 1.

67. "Rexall Druggists to Supply Medicine Free," *Dardanelle Post-Dispatch,* February 19, 1931, 1.

68. "Centerville Items," *Dardanelle Post-Dispatch,* October 8, 1931, 8.

69. "Conditions Now Much Better Than Year Ago," *Dardanelle Post-Dispatch,* October 8, 1931, 1.

70. "County Organization Will Urge Self Help," *Dardanelle Post-Dispatch,* January 19, 1933, 1; "Red Cross Relief to Be Curtailed at Once," *Dardanelle Post-Dispatch,* January 26, 1933, 1.

71. Bureau of Economic Analysis, *Personal Income and Employment by Major Component*, Report SA4. Washington, DC.

72. Bureau of Economic Analysis, *Personal Income Summary: Personal Income, Population, Per Capita Personal Income*, Report SA1. Washington, DC.

73. "Committee Votes to Abolish State Bureau," *Dardanelle Post-Dispatch*, February 2, 1933, 1.

74. "Thirty Per Cent Acreage Cut Is Required for Crop Loans," *Dardanelle Post-Dispatch*, March 2, 1933, 1.

75. "Chamber of Commerce Backing Four Projects," *Dardanelle Post-Dispatch*, March 16, 1933, 1.

76. "CWA Workers Are to Register Here Monday," *Dardanelle Post-Dispatch*, November 23, 1933, 1; "CWA Projects Working 245 Men Now," *Dardanelle Post-Dispatch*, December 7, 1933, 1.

77. "CWA Quota for Yell County Is Increased," *Dardanelle Post-Dispatch*, December 14, 1933, 1.

78. "CWA Projects in Yell County Total $126,127," *Dardanelle Post-Dispatch*, January 18, 1934, 1; "CWA Work to Stop in Yell County This Week," *Dardanelle Post-Dispatch*, March 29, 1934, 1.

79. "Home Demonstration Club News and Notes," *Dardanelle Post-Dispatch*, May 21, 1936, 8. Also see Jones, *Mama Learned Us to Work*.

80. "Poultry Pays Club Women," *Dardanelle Post-Dispatch*, June 4, 1936, 1.

81. "Home Improvements by Members of H.D. Club," *Dardanelle Post-Dispatch*, April 21, 1938, 4.

82. "Home Improvements by Members of H.D. Club," *Dardanelle Post-Dispatch*, April 21, 1938, 4.

83. "Home Demonstration Club," *Dardanelle Post-Dispatch*, December 3, 1936, 5.

84. "Carden Bottom Items," *Dardanelle Post-Dispatch*, April 15, 1937, 8.

85. "H.D. Club Sponsoring Better Homes Contest," *Dardanelle Post-Dispatch*, April 8, 1937, 1.; "Special Meeting of H.D. Club Leaders," *Dardanelle Post-Dispatch*, April 15, 1937, 1.

86. "Outstanding Work Done by Miss Lenore Abboud," *Dardanelle Post-Dispatch*, November 23, 1939, 1.

87. "Outstanding Work Done by Miss Lenore Abboud," *Dardanelle Post-Dispatch*, November 23, 1939, 1.

88. "County Will Observe Special Week Arranging Use of Rented Acreage," *Dardanelle Post-Dispatch*, April 11, 1935, 1.

89. "AAA Checks to County Farmers Total $135,000," *Dardanelle Post-Dispatch*, May 13, 1937, 1.

90. "Yell County Farmers to Be Paid $162,000.00," *Dardanelle Post-Dispatch*, March 10, 1938, 1.

91. "AAA Payments to Farmers," *Dardanelle Post-Dispatch*, February 29, 1940, 5.

92. "Farmers Utilizing Production Credit," *Dardanelle Post-Dispatch*, May 3, 1934, 1.

93. "FCA to Make Loans for Winter Grain Crops," *Dardanelle Post-Dispatch*, September 13, 1934, 1. Also see "Crop and Feed Loans for 1940 Now Available," *Dardanelle Post-Dispatch*, November 16, 1939, 1.

94. "Land Bank to Sell All of Its Farms in County," *Dardanelle Post-Dispatch*, October 6, 1938, 1. Also see Advertisement, *Dardanelle Post-Dispatch*, October 6, 1938, 8.

95. "Longer Loan Terms to Yell County Farmers," *Dardanelle Post-Dispatch*, June 6, 1940, 1.

96. See Jack Temple Kirby, *Rural Worlds Lost: The American South 1920–1960* (Baton Rouge: Louisiana State University Press, 1987), 51–79. Also see Daniel, *Breaking the Land*, 98–109.

97. "Work Started on New Armory Here," *Dardanelle Post-Dispatch*, November 28, 1935, 1. Also see "WPA Program Benefits All Parts of County," *Dardanelle Post-Dispatch*, February 1, 1940, 1.

98. "Yell County Sewing Room Project," *Dardanelle Post-Dispatch*, May 23, 1940, 8.

99. "WPA Spent $785,691 in County in 4-Year Period," *Dardanelle Post-Dispatch*, November 2, 1939, 1.

100. "W.P.A. Project Week," *Dardanelle Post-Dispatch*, June 6, 1940, 5.

101. Floyd W. Hicks and Roger Lambert, "Food for the Hungry: Federal Food Programs in Arkansas, 1933–1942," *Arkansas Historical Quarterly* 37, no. 1 (Spring 1978): 26.

102. Bobby Crow, interview by author, Cotton Town, Arkansas, August 4, 2015.

103. "WPA Recreation Project in Yell County," *Dardanelle Post-Dispatch*, May 23, 1940, 8.

104. "WPA Allots $264,818 for Yell County Road Use," *Dardanelle Post-Dispatch*, March 7, 1940, 1.

105. "WPA Doing Lots of Work in Yell County," *Dardanelle Post-Dispatch*, October 31, 1940, 8. Also see "WPA Program Benefits All Parts of County," *Dardanelle Post-Dispatch*, February 1, 1940, 1.

106. "Yell County WPA Commissary," *Dardanelle Post-Dispatch*, May 23, 1940, 8.

107. "Never Too Old to Learn," *Dardanelle Post-Dispatch*, July 3, 1941, 1.

108. "More Pay for 241 Yell County WPA Workers," *Dardanelle Post-Dispatch*, October 23, 1941.

109. "NYA Doing a Splendid Work in Yell County," *Dardanelle Post-Dispatch*, February 18, 1937, 1.

110. "NYA Is Assisting 12,500 Boys and Girls in Arkansas," *Dardanelle Post-Dispatch*, March 2, 1939, 1.

111. "County NYA Students Fund Totals $1,872.00," *Dardanelle Post-Dispatch*, September 7, 1939, 1.

112. "Many Farm Debt Cases Settled during April," *Dardanelle Post-Dispatch*, May 13, 1937, 1.

113. "Debt Adjustment Body to Meet Tuesday," *Dardanelle Post-Dispatch*, January 13, 1938, 1.

114. "New Deal Agencies: Farm Security Administration." http://histclo.com/essay/war/dep/cou/us/nd/agency/nda-fsa.html (accessed May 23, 2015).

115. "Ten More Yell County Families to Buy Farms," *Dardanelle Post-Dispatch*, August 3, 1939, 1. Also see "May File Applications for Farm Tenant Loans," *Dardanelle Post-Dispatch*, May 4, 1939, 1.

116. Venkataramani, "Norman Thomas," 26–27.

117. "Pioneering in 1936," *Dardanelle Post-Dispatch*, March 19, 1936, 1. Also see "Yell County Families Moved to Dyess Colony," *Dardanelle Post-Dispatch*, March 5, 1936, 1.

118. "Yell County Tenant Farmers Number 1741," *Dardanelle Post-Dispatch*, March 4, 1937, 1.

119. Daniel, *Breaking the Land*, 103–5.

120. "Welfare Department Allots County $80,734," *Dardanelle Post-Dispatch*, December 24, 1936, 1.

121. "RA Striving to Raise Standard of Farm Life," *Dardanelle Post-Dispatch*, September 24, 1936, l.

122. "Plan Rural Projects for Relief of Farmers," *Dardanelle Post-Dispatch*, August 25, 1938, 1.

123. "Family Garden Will Protect Farm Income," *Dardanelle Post-Dispatch*, May 18, 1939, 1.

124. "Joe Storment Proves That Diversification Pays," *Dardanelle Post-Dispatch*, February 15, 1940, 4.

125. "Weekly Letter from Commissioner Page," *Dardanelle Post-Dispatch*, September, 25, 1930, 4.

126. "Farmers Now Able to Borrow Money for Food," *Dardanelle Post-Dispatch*, March 12, 1931, 1; "Stoves Wanted," *Dardanelle Post-Dispatch,* November 27, 1930, 8; "Red Cross," *Dardanelle Post-Dispatch,* November 20, 1930, 1.

127. See "Evening School This Year at Riverside" and "Evening School at Fowler," *Dardanelle Post-Dispatch,* January 9, 1930, 2–3; "Weekly Smith-Hughes Notes," *Dardanelle Post-Dispatch*, February 27, 1930, 3; "Riverside Items," *Dardanelle Post-Dispatch,* April 3, 1930, 2; "Important Meeting Here Friday Night," *Dardanelle Post-Dispatch*, September 17, 1931, 1; "Weekly Smith-Hughes Notes," *Dardanelle Post-Dispatch,* July 2, 1931, 4;

128. Advertisement, *Dardanelle Post-Dispatch,* September 10, 1931, 1.

129. "The Trouble with the Cotton Farmer," *Dardanelle Post-Dispatch,* March 12, 1931, 1.

130. "Few Changes Made in 1935 Adjustment Plan," *Dardanelle Post-Dispatch,* February 14, 1935, 1.

131. "Good Progress Made in Acreage Campaign," *Dardanelle Post-Dispatch,* July 6, 1933, 1; "Plan 1,300,000 Acre Cut in State's Cotton Crop," *Dardanelle Post-Dispatch*, September 14, 1933, 1.

132. "Just Notes," *Dardanelle Post-Dispatch,* October 5, 1933, 1; "Attention, Tenants," *Dardanelle Post-Dispatch,* January 3, 1935, 1; "Will Perfect Program Reducing Cotton Crop," *Dardanelle Post-Dispatch,* January 17, 1935, 1.

133. See Volanto, "The AAA Cotton Plow-Up Campaign," 395–406.

134. "Nineteen Arrested for Alleged Night-Riding," *Dardanelle Post-Dispatch*, September 14, 1933, 1.

135. "Carden Bottom Items," *Dardanelle Post-Dispatch*, September 23, 1937, 8.

136. "The Local Field," *Dardanelle Post-Dispatch,* July 5, 1934, 5; "News from the Office of the County Agent," *Dardanelle Post-Dispatch,* April 28, 1938, 1; "Grasshoppers Attacking Young Cotton," *Dardanelle Post-Dispatch,* June 2, 1938, 4; "Poison Bait Effective in Grasshopper Fight," *Dardanelle Post-Dispatch,* June 9, 1938, 1; "Boll Weevil Appears in Sections of County," *Dardanelle Post-Dispatch*, June 23, 1938, 1; "Boll Weevil Present in Parts of County," *Dardanelle Post-Dispatch,* July 10, 1941, 1.

137. "Arkansas Celebrates First Dairy Day in Dardanelle," *Dardanelle Post-*

*Dispatch*, May 23, 1935, 1. Also see "Have We Made Progress?" *Dardanelle Post-Dispatch*, May 23, 1935, 1.

138. "Yell County Poultry Show Here Saturday," *Dardanelle Post-Dispatch*, May 16, 1935, 1.

139. "Just Notes," *Dardanelle Post-Dispatch*, February 13, 1936, 1.

140. "Agriculture in Arkansas Changing Significantly," *Dardanelle Post-Dispatch*, December 28, 1939, 1.

141. "$40,000 Invested in Two New Gins Located in Dardanelle," *Dardanelle Post-Dispatch*, June 12, 1941, 1.

142. "Carden Bottom Folks Desire a Road—They Don't Mean Maybe," *Dardanelle Post-Dispatch*, February 13, 1930, 2.

143. "County Highway Plan Is Adopted 2838 to 67," *Dardanelle Post-Dispatch*, March 27, 1930, 1.

144. "County Judge Report," *Dardanelle Post-Dispatch*, November 13, 1930, 5.

145. Bobby Crow, interview by author, Cotton Town, Arkansas, August 14, 2015; "County School Notes," *Dardanelle Post-Dispatch*, January 21, 1932, 1.

146. "School Faculty, Students and Patrons Work Roads," *Dardanelle Post-Dispatch*, January 21, 1932, 1.

147. "Observin' on Petit Jean," *Dardanelle Post-Dispatch*, September 3, 1936, 5.

148. "Map of Arkansas State Roads," *Dardanelle Post-Dispatch*, July 31, 1930, 4.

149. "Highway Number Seven Association Is Formed," *Dardanelle Post-Dispatch*, May 8, 1930, 1; Keenan, interview by author, April 30, 2014.

150. "Highway Committee Promises Activity," *Dardanelle Post-Dispatch*, February 20, 1930, 1.

151. "Dardanelle-Scranton Line to Be Abandoned," *Dardanelle Post-Dispatch*, February 10, 1938, 1.

152. "Campaign Pledge Redeemed by Gov. Carl E. Bailey—Tax Payers of Free Bridge District Relieved," *Dardanelle Post-Dispatch*, June 30, 1938, 1.

153. David Rison, "Federal Aid to Arkansas Education, 1933–1936," *Arkansas Historical Quarterly* 36, no. 2 (Summer 1977): 192.

154. "Majority for School Consolidation Grows," *Dardanelle Post-Dispatch*, April 24, 1930, 1.

155. "Patrons Overwhelmingly Endorse the Proposed New Consolidated District," *Dardanelle Post-Dispatch*, April 17, 1920, 1; "County Board Perfects Local Consolidation," *Dardanelle Post-Dispatch*, May 22, 1930, 1.

156. "County School Notes," *Dardanelle Post-Dispatch*, June 12, 1930, 7.

157. "Board Asks Bids on New School Building," *Dardanelle Post-Dispatch*, June 26, 1930, 1; "The Local Field," *Dardanelle Post-Dispatch*, June 18, 1931, 5.

158. "Carden Bottom School Has First Graduation," *Dardanelle Post-Dispatch*, June 11, 1931, 1.

159. "County School Notes," *Dardanelle Post-Dispatch*, August 11, 1932, 1.

160. "Hugh Decline Shown in School Revenues," *Dardanelle Post-Dispatch*, October 1, 1931, 1.

161. "Dardanelle Schools Are Forced to Close," *Dardanelle Post-Dispatch*, November 9, 1933, 1; "Dardanelle Schools Re-Opened Wednesday," *Dardanelle Post-Dispatch*, November 30, 1933, 1.

162. "Dardanelle School to Open Next Monday," *Dardanelle Post-Dispatch*,

October 11, 1934, 1; "Heavy Enrollment in Dardanelle Schools," *Dardanelle Post-Dispatch,* October 25, 1934, 1.

163. Lynne Gleason Murphy, personal conversation with author, Dardanelle, Arkansas, June 28, 2012.

164. "Dardanelle School to Continue for Present," *Dardanelle Post-Dispatch,* March 7, 1935, 1; "Hope to Open School about October 15th," *Dardanelle Post-Dispatch,* September 12, 1935, 1; "Dardanelle Schools to Open September 30th," *Dardanelle Post-Dispatch,* September 19, 1935, 1.

165. "School Revenue Grows under Bailey's Regime," *Dardanelle Post-Dispatch,* September 9, 1937, 1.

166. "Local Schools on Tuition Basis," *Dardanelle Post-Dispatch,* April 10, 1941, 1; "Citizens Loyally Support School in Mass Meeting Held Tuesday," *Dardanelle Post-Dispatch,* April 17, 1941, 1.

167. Rison, "Federal Aid to Arkansas Education," 192–200.

168. "Prevention of Typhoid," *Dardanelle Post-Dispatch,* June 19, 1930, 1; "Smallpox and Diphtheria Clinic," *Dardanelle Post-Dispatch,* January 31, 1935, 1.

169. "County Health Unit Makes Annual Report," *Dardanelle Post-Dispatch,* July 24, 1930, 1.

170. "Local Health Unit Is Organized Here," *Dardanelle Post-Dispatch*, May 7, 1931, 1.

171. "Smallpox in County," *Dardanelle Post-Dispatch*, January 23, 1936, 1; "Centerville Items," *Dardanelle Post-Dispatch*, January 12, 1933, 8; "The Local Field," *Dardanelle Post-Dispatch,* December 15, 1932; "Clinic Helping Victims of Trachoma," *Dardanelle Post-Dispatch*, June 27, 1940, 1; "Eleven Here Taking Pasteur Treatment," *Dardanelle Post-Dispatch,* March 28, 1935, 1.

172. "County Health Unit Report," *Dardanelle Post-Dispatch,* January 9, 1936, 8.

173. Christine McKnelly, "Malnutrition," *The Encyclopedia of Arkansas History & Culture.*

174. "Liberty Hall Items," *Dardanelle Post-Dispatch*, November 25, 1937, 5.

175. "The Local Field," *Dardanelle Post-Dispatch*, July 3, 1930, 5; "Civic Club Sponsors City Clean-Up Drive," *Dardanelle Post- Dispatch*, February 25, 1932, 1; "Enthusiastic Meeting of Civic Club Is Held," *Dardanelle Post-Dispatch*, February 4, 1932, 1; "Civic Club Urges a General City Clean-Up," *Dardanelle Post-Dispatch*, March 10, 1932, 1.

176. "U.D.C. Meeting," and "Philharmonic Club," *Dardanelle Post-Dispatch*, October 3, 1935, 2.

177. "Christmas Party," *Dardanelle Post-Dispatch,* December 24, 1931, 1; "Pastor's Wife Honored," *Dardanelle Post-Dispatch,* November 10, 1932, 1.

178. "Philharmonic Club Organized Thursday," *Dardanelle Post-Dispatch,* March 17, 1932, l.

179. "Ola Items," *Dardanelle Post-Dispatch*, August 15, 1935, 4.

180. "Centerville Items," *Dardanelle Post-Dispatch*, November 10, 1932, 2.

181. "Centerville Ladies Shower for Mrs. Percy George," *Dardanelle Post-Dispatch,* February 16, 1933, 1.

182. Doris Hundley Hickey, interview by author, Dardanelle, Arkansas, July 9, 2008.

183. "Deplores the Passing of the 'Good Old Days,'" *Dardanelle Post-Dispatch*, February 6, 1930, 7.

184. "Just Notes," *Dardanelle Post-Dispatch*, June 17, 1937, 4.

185. "Yell County Goes Wet by Majority of 117 Votes," *Dardanelle Post-Dispatch*, July 27, 1933, 1.

186. "Liquor Store Opened Here," *Dardanelle Post-Dispatch*, April 4, 1935, 1.

187. "Drunken Brawl Costs Elmer Coffman Life," *Dardanelle Post-Dispatch*, July 26, 1934, 1.

188. "The Local Field," *Dardanelle Post-Dispatch*, November 10, 1938, 5.

189. "Prosecutor Strikes at Rowdy Beer Joints, Etc.," *Dardanelle Post-Dispatch*, February 9, 1939, 1.

190. "Liquor Permit," *Dardanelle Post-Dispatch*, March 16, 1939, 4.

191. "Local Store Robbed," *Dardanelle Post-Dispatch*, January 7, 1937, 1.

192. "Robbing White Castle," *Dardanelle Post-Dispatch*, August 1, 1925, 1.

193. "Just Notes," *Dardanelle Post-Dispatch*, August 1, 1935, 1.

194. "Capt. Jeff Ellis Fires at Gasoline Thieves," *Dardanelle Post-Dispatch*, June 30, 1932, 1.

195. "J. A. Coleman Kills His Wife and Stepdaughter," *Dardanelle Post-Dispatch*, July 17, 1930, 1.

196. "Kills Self after Shooting at Bride," *Dardanelle Post-Dispatch*, August 17, 1933, 1; "M. T. Thacker Killed by Tom J. Williams," *Dardanelle Post-Dispatch*, January 2, 1930, 1; "Murder Suspected in Death of Local Negro," *Dardanelle Post-Dispatch*, May 4, 1933, 1; "The Local Field," *Dardanelle Post-Dispatch*, October 29, 1936, 5; "Negro Is Fatally Shot by Negress," *Dardanelle Post-Dispatch*, November 18, 1937, 1; "Negress Fatally Shot near City Yesterday," *Dardanelle Post-Dispatch*, July 13, 1939, 1; "Birta Youth Shot by Rival," *Dardanelle Post-Dispatch*, October 17, 1935; "Alleged Rapist Given Three Year Sentence," *Dardanelle Post-Dispatch*, February 18, 1932, 1.

197. "Knife Wound Is Fatal to Lucius Shilling," *Dardanelle Post-Dispatch*, June 14, 1934, 1.

198. "February Term Circuit Court Now in Session," *Dardanelle Post-Dispatch*, February 11, 1932, 1; "'Jelly' Bertram Shot by Intoxicated Miner," *Dardanelle Post-Dispatch*, January 16, 1936, 1; "A. B. Berry Is Victim of Brutal Assault," *Dardanelle Post-Dispatch*, July 23, 1931, 1.

199. "Game Law Violations," *Dardanelle Post-Dispatch*, June 9, 1932, 3.

200. "Giant Still Is Captured by Sheriff's Force," *Dardanelle Post-Dispatch*, January 14, 1932, 1; "Liberty Hall Items," *Dardanelle Post-Dispatch*, September 15, 1932, 8; "Circuit Court in Session," *Dardanelle Post-Dispatch*, February 21, 1935, 1.

201. "Court Now in Session in Danville District," *Dardanelle Post-Dispatch*, August 25, 1932, 1.

202. "The Local Field," *Dardanelle Post-Dispatch*, July 16, 1931, 5.

203. "The Local Field," *Dardanelle Post-Dispatch*, July 16, 1931, 5.

204. "Plans Completed for Red Cross Roll Call," *Dardanelle Post-Dispatch*, October 29, 1931, 1; "Negro School to Sing," *Dardanelle Post-Dispatch*, December 5, 1935, 5.

205. "Colored Citizens Support Red Cross," *Dardanelle Post-Dispatch*, December 19, 1940, 1.

206. "A Whopper," *Dardanelle Post-Dispatch,* July 9, 1931, 1; "This Week's Sad Story," *Dardanelle Post-Dispatch*, January 16, 1941, 4.

207. "Colored Pastor Offers Criticism," *Dardanelle Post-Dispatch,* September 1, 1938, 1; "Riverside Items," *Dardanelle Post-Dispatch,* July 3, 1931, 8; "The Local Field," *Dardanelle Post-Dispatch,* November 5, 1936, 5; "Aged Negroes Lose Home," *Dardanelle Post-Dispatch,* May 7, 1936, 5.

208. "The Local Field," *Dardanelle Post-Dispatch,* October 27, 1938, 5; "Mr. Joseph J. Jackson," *Dardanelle Post-Dispatch,* March 6, 1941, 1.

209. "Civic Club Sponsors an Enjoyable Party," *Dardanelle Post-Dispatch*, May 14, 1931, 1.

210. "Lakeview Sunday School Class Enjoys Outing," *Dardanelle Post-Dispatch*, August 3, 1933, 1.

211. Gordon Crain, interview by author, Dardanelle, Arkansas, July 10, 2008.

212. "Slaty Crossing Items," *Dardanelle Post-Dispatch*, August 13, 1931, 3.

213. Crain, interview by author, July 10, 2008.

214. Joe Grimes, interview by author, Dardanelle, Arkansas, July 17, 2008.

215. Crain, interview by author, July 10, 2008.

216. Crain, interview by author, July 10, 2008.

217. Doris Hundley Hickey, interview by author, Dardanelle, Arkansas, July 9, 2008.

218. Crain, interview by author, July 10, 2008.

219. "Entertains Young Folks," *Dardanelle Post-Dispatch*, April 27, 1933, 1.

220. "Selph Makes White Sox Look Good," *Dardanelle Post-Dispatch*, April 21, 1932, 1; "Dizzy Dean to Spend Winter in Dardanelle," *Dardanelle Post-Dispatch,* October 22, 1931, 1.

221. "Dean Brothers to Play Here Sunday Afternoon," *Dardanelle Post-Dispatch,* November 5, 1931, 1.

222. Grimes, interview by author, July 17, 2008.

223. Thompson, interview by author, May 20, 2009.

224. Thompson, interview by author, May 20, 2009.

225. "Flower Display and Tea of Garden Club," *Dardanelle Post-Dispatch*, May 9, 1940, 1.

226. "The Local Field," *Dardanelle Post-Dispatch,* June 16, 1938, 5.

227. "Will Rogers Greeted by Vast Assemblage," *Dardanelle Post-Dispatch*, February 12, 1931, 1; "Messages to Red Cross Show High Degree of Courage and Optimism," *Dardanelle Post-Dispatch*, February 26, 1931, 1.

228. "Demands on Red Cross Continue to Increase," *Dardanelle Post-Dispatch*, January 22, 1931, 1; "County School Notes," *Dardanelle Post-Dispatch*, February 12, 1931, 4; "Delinquent Tax List Sets Record for Size," *Dardanelle Post-Dispatch*, May 28, 1931, 1; "First National Bank Closed by Withdrawals," *Dardanelle Post-Dispatch*, January 22, 1931, 1.

229. "Farmers Apply for Loans," *Dardanelle Post-Dispatch*, February 12, 1931, 1; "$39,000 in Federal Loans Approved," *Dardanelle Post-Dispatch,* March 26, 1931, 1.

230. "Rexall Stores Are Filling Prescriptions Free," and "County School Notes," *Dardanelle Post-Dispatch*, February 26, 1931, 4.

231. "Col. M. L. Davis Died Last Friday Morning" and "Only 10 Confederate Veterans in County," *Dardanelle Post-Dispatch,* March 26, 1931, 1.

232. "Intermediate Credit Bank to Open April 1" and "Dardanelle Mercantile Company Holds Formal Opening," *Dardanelle Post-Dispatch,* March 26, 1931, 1.

233. "The Local Field," *Dardanelle Post-Dispatch,* April 30, 1931, 5.

234. "Blue Valley Creamery to Open on May 18th," *Dardanelle Post-Dispatch,* May 5, 1932; "Blue Valley Creamery Company to Establish Butter Plant Here," *Dardanelle Post-Dispatch,* March 17, 1932, 1.

235. "Poultry Meeting," *Dardanelle Post-Dispatch,* March 17, 1932, 1.

236. "Cows or Cotton," *Dardanelle Post-Dispatch,* March 24, 1932, 1.

237. "Beautiful Old Home Vacant," *Dardanelle Post-Dispatch,* December 29, 1932, 1.

238. "Digest of Cotton Control Plan Suggested for 1934" and "Ten-Cent Cotton to Be Guaranteed Farmers," *Dardanelle Post-Dispatch,* September 28, 1933, 1.

239. "Slaty Crossing Items," *Dardanelle Post-Dispatch,* September 28, 1933, 2.

240. "1933 Acreage Reduction Nearly Doubles Cotton Income," *Dardanelle Post-Dispatch,* February 8, 1934, 1.

241. "Compress Installing $25,000 Improvements," *Dardanelle Post-Dispatch,* August 29, 1935, 1.

242. Daniel, *Breaking the Land,* 92–96; Julia F. Allen, "One Kind of Pioneer Project," *Arkansas Historical Quarterly* 55, no. 1 (Spring 1996): 8–9; Venkataramani, "Norman Thomas," 5–8; Danbom, *Born in the Country,* 212–16; Tucker, *Arkansas,* 78–81; R. Douglas Hurt, *American Agriculture: A Brief History* (Ames: Iowa State University Press, 1994), 295–99; Ben F. Johnson III, *Arkansas in Modern America, 1930–1999* (Fayetteville: University of Arkansas Press, 2000), 26–28; Paul K. Conkin, *The New Deal,* 3rd ed. (Wheeling, IL: Harlan-Davidson, 1992), 39–45; Kirby, *Rural Worlds Lost,* 60–66.

243. Catherine Barrier, Department of Arkansas Heritage, quotes the Mount Nebo State Park website, noting the Mount Nebo Summer Normal School opened on May 17, 1889, as a training facility for advanced studies for Arkansas teachers prior to it being used by the VCCC group in the 1930s. It burned in 1954.

244. "Conservation Camp to Be Located on Nebo," *Dardanelle Post-Dispatch,* June 8, 1933, 1; "Mt. Nebo V.C.C.C. Notes," *Dardanelle Post-Dispatch,* February 8, 1934, 2; "Notes of V.C.C.C. No. 1780," *Dardanelle Post-Dispatch,* November 2, 1933, 1; "Mount Nebo, Once Famous Summer Resort, Is Rapidly Being Restored," *Dardanelle Post-Dispatch,* February 15, 1934, 1; "Mt. Nebo V.C.C.C. Notes," *Dardanelle Post-Dispatch,* March 22, 1934, 1.

245. "VCCC No. 1780 Has Been on Mt. Nebo One Year," *Dardanelle Post-Dispatch,* July 19, 1934, 1; "Notes of VCCC 1780," *Dardanelle Post-Dispatch,* October 4, 1934, 2.

246. "VCCC 1780 Leaves Nebo State Park Tomorrow," *Dardanelle Post-Dispatch,* October 24, 1935, 1.

247. Cornelia Daniels, ed., *Mt. Nebo: 1900s–2014* (Dardanelle, AR: Yell County Historical Society, 2015), 14; "Donations of Nebo Land," *Dardanelle Post-Dispatch,* March 8, 1934, 1. Also see Arkansas Department of Parks and Tourism, "Arkansas Valley."

248. "Proves Dardanelle Is a Live Town," *Dardanelle Post-Dispatch,* April 9, 1936, 1; "Nation's Business Is Now Best since 1929," *Dardanelle Post-Dispatch,* July 16, 1936, 1; "The Local Field," *Dardanelle Post-Dispatch,* October 22, 1936, 5.

249. Advertisement, *Dardanelle Post-Dispatch*, August 5, 1937, 4–5.

250. "Farmers and Businessmen to Stage Picnic," *Dardanelle Post-Dispatch*, April 22, 1937, 1.

251. "Splendid New Armory Building Is Completed," *Dardanelle Post-Dispatch*, March 18, 1937, 5.

252. "Beautiful New American Legion Hut Will Be Formally Dedicated Tuesday," *Dardanelle Post-Dispatch*, April 25, 1935, 1.

253. "Massive Spring Creek Dam Completed Friday," *Dardanelle Post-Dispatch*, July 15, 1937, 1.

254. "Business Is Good Here," *Dardanelle Post-Dispatch*, June 21, 1934, 1.

255. "Erection of Cannery Is Deferred to 1938," *Dardanelle Post-Dispatch*, August 12, 1937, 1.

256. "Policy of Blue Valley to Continue Unchanged," *Dardanelle Post-Dispatch*, February 23, 1939, 1; "Sugar Creek Creamery Co. Buys Local Plant," *Dardanelle Post-Dispatch*, November 30, 1939, 1.

257. "Census Figures Show Decrease of 27 Here," *Dardanelle Post-Dispatch*, July 4, 1940, 1.

258. "Dr. Millard Moves to New Office Location," *Dardanelle Post-Dispatch*, July 4, 1940, 1.

259. "Crowd of 2,500 Attends Trades Day Wednesday," *Dardanelle Post-Dispatch*, October 20, 1938, 1.

260. "Record Crowd of Shoppers Here Last Saturday," *Dardanelle Post-Dispatch*, September 25, 1941, 1.

261. "Company 'F' Believed to Be Slated for Alaska Duty," *Dardanelle Post-Dispatch*, August 29, 1940, 1.

262. "First Peace Time Draft—October 16 Is Registration Date," *Dardanelle Post-Dispatch*, September 26, 1940, 1.

263. "53rd Infantry, A.N.G. Inducted into Military Service of Nation," *Dardanelle Post-Dispatch*, December 26, 1940, 1; "Soldier Boys Honored on Eve of Departure for Camp Robinson," *Dardanelle Post-Dispatch*, January 2, 1941, 1.

264. "Important to Save All Waste Paper for National Defense," *Dardanelle Post-Dispatch*, December 18, 1941, 1.

265. Hickey, interview by author, July 9, 2008.

## CHAPTER 6: Modernity and Transformation, 1942–1970

1. Marie Shepherd Bachman, interview by author, Dardanelle, Arkansas, August 4, 2008.

2. "Chemical Shortage May Hamper Cotton Seed Treatment," *Dardanelle Post-Dispatch*, March 5, 1942, 1.

3. "Hansen Discusses Planting of Peanuts," *Dardanelle Post-Dispatch*, March 5, 1942, 1.

4. "Centerville News," *Dardanelle Post-Dispatch*, May 21, 1942, 4.

5. "Leaflet Tells How to Save Sugar" and "Stresses Importance of the Dairy Cow," *Dardanelle Post-Dispatch*, April 16, 1942, 1.

6. "Sugar Registration Occurs Next Week" and "Sugar Rationing Plan Explained," *Dardanelle Post-Dispatch*, April 30, 1942, 1.

7. "Rationing," *Dardanelle Post-Dispatch*, September 10, 1942, 1.

8. "Kroger Aids in Saving Paper for U. S." and "Help Win the War! Leave Tooth Paste and Shaving Cream Tubes at Local Drug Stores," *Dardanelle Post-Dispatch*, March 19, 1942, 1.

9. "Shortage of Scrap Metal Threatens Production," *Dardanelle Post-Dispatch*, September 24, 1942, 1; "Junk Needed for War," *Dardanelle Post-Dispatch*, October 1, 1942, 1; "Citizens Respond Nobly in Drive for Scrap Metal Needed for War," *Dardanelle Post-Dispatch*, October 8, 1942, 1.

10. "Enthusiasm Marks Shipment of Scrap," *Dardanelle Post-Dispatch*, October 15, 1942, 1.

11. "Proves Patriotism by Collecting Keys," *Dardanelle Post-Dispatch*, October 15, 1942, 1.

12. "Cooking Utensils Curtailed by War," *Dardanelle Post-Dispatch*, August 27, 1942, 1.

13. "Rubber Famine Sure to Be Felt Soon," *Dardanelle Post-Dispatch*, April 9, 1942, 1.

14. "Gas Ration Books to Be Issued," *Dardanelle Post-Dispatch*, October 8, 1942, 1.

15. "Old Cannons to Be Their Part in War against Axis," *Dardanelle Post-Dispatch*, July 9, 1942, 1.

16. "Announces Postponement of County Fair," *Dardanelle Post-Dispatch*, July 23, 1942, 1.

17. Lonnie Dickens, interview by author, Dardanelle, Arkansas, July 7, 2008.

18. "Riverside Items," *Dardanelle Post-Dispatch*, June 18, 1942, 1.

19. "Henry Cooper Wins First Bale Awards," *Dardanelle Post-Dispatch*, August 27, 1942, 1.

20. "Date School to Open Not Yet Decided," *Dardanelle Post-Dispatch*, September 17, 1942, 1.

21. "Dardanelle Public Schools to Open Next Monday Morning, October 12," *Dardanelle Post-Dispatch*, October 8, 1942, 1.

22. "Sees Farm Labor Shortage," *Dardanelle Post-Dispatch*, October 8, 1942, 4.

23. "Full Use of Manpower on Farms Essential," *Dardanelle Post-Dispatch*, August 27, 1942, 1.

24. "Yell County Crop Spoilage Can Be Halved," *Dardanelle Post-Dispatch*, August 13, 1942, 1.

25. "FSA to Finance Needy Farmers," *Dardanelle Post-Dispatch*, December 3, 1942, 1.

26. "Locals," *Dardanelle Post-Dispatch*, April 23, 1942, 3.

27. "Centerville Items," *Dardanelle Post-Dispatch*, July 9, 1942, 4.

28. "Locals," *Dardanelle Post-Dispatch*, July 9, 1942, 3.

29. "Carden Bottom Items," *Dardanelle Post-Dispatch*, December 3, 1942, 2.

30. "Local Men Go to Maine to Harvest Irish Potato Crop," *Dardanelle Post-Dispatch*, September 16, 1943, 1.

31. "Carden Bottoms Items," *Dardanelle Post-Dispatch*, June 13, 1946, 4.

32. "Red Cross Roll-Call to Be Held in March," *Dardanelle Post-Dispatch*, July 2, 1942, 1–2; "Red Cross Active in Contacting Soldiers" and "One Hundred and Thirty Knitters Needed," *Dardanelle Post-Dispatch*, July 2, 1942, 1–2.

33. "Red Cross Pleads for Women Workers," *Dardanelle Post-Dispatch*, July 23, 1942, 2; "Women Volunteer Wanted," *Dardanelle Post-Dispatch*, July 30, 1942, 1; "Red Cross First Classes by Dr. Gavlas," *Dardanelle Post-Dispatch*, December 3, 1942; "County Chapter Met Here Yesterday," *Dardanelle Post-Dispatch*, August 20, 1942, 1; "Red Cross Chapter Fills August Quota," *Dardanelle Post-Dispatch*, August 20, 1942, 1; "Red Cross Surgical Dressing Room Will Open Here January 4," *Dardanelle Post-Dispatch*, December 31, 1942, 1.

34. "Partial Report on Local Bond Pledges," *Dardanelle Post-Dispatch*, June 11, 1942, 1.

35. "Yell County Schools Successfully Conduct War Bond Campaign," *Dardanelle Post-Dispatch*, December 17, 1942, 1.

36. "Three Yell County Boys Now Missing," *Dardanelle Post-Dispatch*, June 18, 1942, 1.

37. "Local Boy Taken by Japs at Corregidor," *Dardanelle Post-Dispatch*, May 14, 1942, 1.

38. "Former Local Boy Lost Aboard 'Jarvis,'" *Dardanelle Post-Dispatch*, October 1, 1942, 1.

39. "Local Board Gives Serial Numbers to Feb. 16 Registrants," *Dardanelle Post-Dispatch*, March 12, 1942, 1.

40. "Another Dardanelle Colored Boy Joins U. S. Navy," *Dardanelle Post-Dispatch*, March 12, 1942, 1.

41. "Navy Needs Men: Lowers Restrictions," *Dardanelle Post-Dispatch*, July 9, 1942, 1.

42. "Men 45 to 65 to Register April 27th," *Dardanelle Post-Dispatch*, April 23, 1942, 1; "Married Men with Children May Be Called for Service," *Dardanelle Post-Dispatch*, September 17, 1942, 1.

43. "115 Yell County Men to Be Inducted into Army Next Week," *Dardanelle Post-Dispatch*, October 15, 1942, 1; "Another 125 Yell County Men Drafted" and "18 Year Old Registration Begins December 11," *Dardanelle Post-Dispatch*, November 19, 1942, 1.

44. "December Army Quota for Yell County Totals 328 Men," *Dardanelle Post-Dispatch*, December 10, 1942, 1.

45. "Few Negroes Volunteer," *Dardanelle Post-Dispatch*, October 8, 1942, 4.

46. "Yell County Exceeds War Bond Quota," *Dardanelle Post-Dispatch*, January 7, 1943, 1; "Red Cross War Fund Oversubscribed," *Dardanelle Post-Dispatch*, March 25, 1943, 1.

47. "Yell County Exceeds Red Cross Quota," *Dardanelle Post-Dispatch*, April 8, 1943, 1; "Red Cross War Fund Continues to Grow," *Dardanelle Post-Dispatch*, April 1, 1943, 1.

48. "Yell County 'Over Top' in Bond Drive," *Dardanelle Post-Dispatch*, April 22, 1943, 1.

49. "Yell County Exceeds War Bond Quota," *Dardanelle Post-Dispatch*, October 7, 1943, 1.

50. "Women Needed for Red Cross Work," *Dardanelle Post-Dispatch*,

January 28, 1943, 1; "Need Is Urgent for Surgical Dressings," *Dardanelle Post-Dispatch,* March 4, 1943, 1.

51. "Weekly Report of Red Cross Workers," *Dardanelle Post-Dispatch,* April 15, 1943, 1.

52. "Soldiers and Sailors Will Long Remember These Noble Women," *Dardanelle Post-Dispatch,* August 19, 1943, 1; "These Are 'Backing the Boys Over There,'" *Dardanelle Post-Dispatch,* November 18, 1943, 1.

53. "These Are Heroines of the Home Front," *Dardanelle Post-Dispatch,* December 2, 1943, 1.

54. "Female Stenographers and Typists Wanted," *Dardanelle Post-Dispatch,* February 4, 1943, 1; Keenan, interview by author, April 30, 2014; "Locals," *Dardanelle Post-Dispatch,* May 13, 1943; "Locals," *Dardanelle Post-Dispatch,* April 29, 1943, 1; "Centerville Girl Meets Tragic Death," *Dardanelle Post-Dispatch,* July 1, 1943, 1.

55. "Women Needed for Work on Farms," *Dardanelle Post-Dispatch,* July 15, 1943, 3.

56. "Information on Rationing to Date," *Dardanelle Post-Dispatch,* April 22, 1943, 1.

57. "Fewer Shoes for Civilian Use," *Dardanelle Post-Dispatch,* September 30, 1943, 1.

58. "Expect Further Cuts in Civilian Use of Gasoline," *Dardanelle Post-Dispatch,* October 14, 1943, 1.

59. Jack Guice, telephone interview by author, Pensacola, Florida, March 23, 2013.

60. "County's Army Quota to Report March 5," *Dardanelle Post-Dispatch,* February 25, 1943, 1; "Recruiter Says Navy Needs 17-Year-Olds," *Dardanelle Post-Dispatch,* April 29, 1943, 1; "July Draft Quota Calls for 126 Men," *Dardanelle Post-Dispatch,* June 10, 1943, 1; "65 Yell County Men to Be Inducted," *Dardanelle Post-Dispatch,* August 5, 1943, 1; "Married Men with Children to Be Called to Army," *Dardanelle Post-Dispatch,* August 26, 1943, 1.

61. "Gratifying—But Not Surprising," *Dardanelle Post-Dispatch,* October 7, 1943, 1; "Ninety County Men Sent for Induction," *Dardanelle Post-Dispatch,* December 2, 1943, 1.

62. "Negro Registrants to Be Inducted December 20th," *Dardanelle Post-Dispatch,* December 17, 1942, 3; "Four Colored Registrants to Be Inducted March 22," *Dardanelle Post-Dispatch,* March 4, 1943, 1; "Colored Registrants Leave Saturday," *Dardanelle Post-Dispatch,* October 21, 1943, 1; "Army Accepts Nine Yell County Men," *Dardanelle Post-Dispatch,* June 24, 1943, 1.

63. "Locals," *Dardanelle Post-Dispatch,* November 4, 1943, 3.

64. "County Exceeded Quota in Fourth War Bond Sale," *Dardanelle Post-Dispatch,* March 16, 1944, 1.

65. "Yell County over Top in 5th Bond Sale," *Dardanelle Post-Dispatch,* July 6, 1944, 1; "Yell County Exceeds 6th War Bond Quota," *Dardanelle Post-Dispatch,* December 14, 1944, 1.

66. "Dardanelle Territory Is Way over the Top in the Mighty 7th War Bond Sale!" *Dardanelle Post-Dispatch,* June 28, 1945, 1.

67. "Yell County Is over the Top in Red Cross Drive," *Dardanelle Post-Dispatch,* March 30, 1944, 1, 4–5.

68. "An Urgent Appeal to the Women of Dardanelle," *Dardanelle Post-Dispatch*, April 6, 1944, 2; "Workers Needed at Red Cross Room," *Dardanelle Post-Dispatch*, November 2, 1944, 1; "Helpers Are Needed at the Red Cross Room," *Dardanelle Post-Dispatch*, December 14, 1944, 1.

69. "Locals," *Dardanelle Post-Dispatch*, March 16, 1944, 8; "Eight Men Called to Armed Forces," *Dardanelle Post-Dispatch*, July 6, 1944, 1.

70. "Miss Kitty Jo Clark," *Dardanelle Post-Dispatch*, July 19, 1945, 1.

71. "Mother Opens Paper, Sees Son's Picture," *Dardanelle Post-Dispatch*, July 19, 1945, 8.

72. "27 Registrants Will Take Pre-Induction Examination Sunday," *Dardanelle Post-Dispatch*, February 17, 1944, 1; "Twenty-Five Yell County Men to Be Inducted March 6," *Dardanelle Post-Dispatch*, March 2, 1944, 1; "Yell County Sends Sixty-Five More Young Men to Army," *Dardanelle Post-Dispatch*, April 12, 1944, 1; "Twenty-Five Men to Enter Army Monday," *Dardanelle Post-Dispatch*, May 11, 1944, 1; "Thirty-Four Men to Enter Armed Forces," *Dardanelle Post-Dispatch*, June 15, 1944, 1; "11 Local Men Are Called for Induction," *Dardanelle Post-Dispatch*, August 10, 1944, 1; "Nineteen Men to Enter Army," *Dardanelle Post-Dispatch*, August 31, 1944, 1; "19 Local Men Called for Induction Friday," *Dardanelle Post-Dispatch*, September 21, 1944, 1; "Six Men to Army Monday, Nov. 13th," *Dardanelle Post-Dispatch*, October 26, 1944, 1; "21 Yell County Men to Enter Armed Forces December 11," *Dardanelle Post-Dispatch*, November 23, 1944, 1; "27 Men to Enter Armed Forces Jan. 9," *Dardanelle Post-Dispatch*, January 4, 1945, 1; "Thirty-Seven Men to Enter Armed Forces," *Dardanelle Post-Dispatch*, March 8, 1945, 1; "Four Local Men Are Called for Induction," *Dardanelle Post-Dispatch*, April 12, 1945, 1; "Twenty-Seven Men to Enter Armed Forces," *Dardanelle Post-Dispatch*, May 19, 1945, 1; "17 Men Will Be Inducted July 16th," *Dardanelle Post-Dispatch*, July 12, 1945, 1; "Twelve Men to Enter Armed Forces Aug. 16," *Dardanelle Post-Dispatch*, August 9, 1945, 1.

73. "County Sends 42 Men to U.S. Navy," *Dardanelle Post-Dispatch*, April 13, 1944, 1.

74. "Locals," *Dardanelle Post-Dispatch*, April 20, 1944, 8.

75. "Dardanelle Sergeant Missing in Action," *Dardanelle Post-Dispatch*, June 15, 1944, 8.

76. "Lt. John P. Cowger Missing in Action," *Dardanelle Post-Dispatch*, August 10, 1944, 1.

77. "Pfc. Stanley W. Wesley A German War Prisoner," *Dardanelle Post-Dispatch*, August 3, 1944, 1.

78. "Lt. Col. Thomas Willson Released from Japanese POW Camp," *Dardanelle Post-Dispatch*, February 8, 1945, 1.

79. "Pfc. Charles McClure Is Killed in Action," *Dardanelle Post-Dispatch*, July 13, 1944, 1.

80. "Foy Marion Clark Gives His Life for His Country," *Dardanelle Post-Dispatch*, August 10, 1944, 1; "Dardanelle Flier Killed in Alaska," *Dardanelle Post-Dispatch*, December 6, 1944, 1; "Locals" and "Carden Bottom Items," *Dardanelle Post-Dispatch*, January 11, 1945, 8; "Centerville Items," *Dardanelle Post-Dispatch*, January 18, 1945, 8; "Battle Wounds Fatal to Private Elbert Garrett," *Dardanelle Post-Dispatch*, February 8, 1945, 1; "Yell County Youth Killed in Action," *Dardanelle*

*Post-Dispatch*, February 24, 1944, 1; "Major Cunningham Meets Tragic Death in Pacific Theatre," *Dardanelle Post-Dispatch*, March 22, 1945, 1; "Locals," *Dardanelle Post-Dispatch*, May 10, 1945, 8; "Sgt. George R. Pfeifer Killed in Action" and "Carden Bottoms Items," *Dardanelle Post-Dispatch*, May 17, 1945, 1, 8; "First Sgt. Wilson Word Killed on Okinawa May 31," *Dardanelle Post-Dispatch*, June 28, 1945, 1; "Maj. Bill Dawson Died When Jap Prison Ship Was Torpedoed off Luzon," *Dardanelle Post-Dispatch*, August 2, 1945, 1; "A Beautiful Tribute to Local Lad Who Lost Life on Okinawa," *Dardanelle Post-Dispatch*, August 23, 1945, 1.

81. "Pfc. Grady Merritt Loses Life While a Prisoner of Japanese," *Dardanelle Post-Dispatch*, August 30, 1945, 1.

82. "Arkansas' Army Dead Totals 3,814," *Dardanelle Post-Dispatch*, July 4, 1946, 1.

83. "Locals," *Dardanelle Post-Dispatch*, June 28, 1945, 8. Also see "Jack Scott Escapes Suicide Bombers," *Dardanelle Post-Dispatch*, June 28, 1945, 8; "Carden Bottom Items," *Dardanelle Post-Dispatch*, February 8, 1945, 8; "Locals," *Dardanelle Post-Dispatch*, February 22, 1945, 8; "Local Colored Boy Helped Save Carrier 'Saratoga,'" *Dardanelle Post-Dispatch*, July 5, 1945, 1.

84. "Sgt. 'Buck' McConnell Automobile Fund," *Dardanelle Post-Dispatch*, July 11, 1946, 1; "Locals," *Dardanelle Post-Dispatch*, September 5, 1946, 5.

85. "Germany Surrenders," *Dardanelle Post-Dispatch*, May 10, 1945, 1.

86. "Japs Surrender!" *Dardanelle Post-Dispatch*, August 16, 1945, 1.

87. "Welfare Department Distributing Potatoes," *Dardanelle Post-Dispatch*, April 20, 1944, 1; "Eggs for the Needy," *Dardanelle Post-Dispatch*, March 2, 1944, 8.

88. "Local Commissary Received Commodities Worth $3,996.45 during Month of January," *Dardanelle Post-Dispatch*, March 12, 1942, 1.

89. "Farm Labor Committee Active," *Dardanelle Post-Dispatch*, February 24, 1944, 1.

90. "Farm Labor Committee Active," *Dardanelle Post-Dispatch*, February 24, 1944, 1.

91. "First Cotton Bloom Received June 20," *Dardanelle Post-Dispatch*, February 24, 1944, 1.

92. "Dardanelle Schools to Open October 16th," *Dardanelle Post-Dispatch*, October 5, 1944, 1.

93. "Farm Credit Bureau Opens Office in Dardanelle," *Dardanelle Post-Dispatch*, July 13, 1944, 1.

94. "Honorably Discharged from Armed Forces," *Dardanelle Post-Dispatch*, September 20, 1945, 1; "Locals," *Dardanelle Post-Dispatch*, August 1, 1946, 5; "10 Men Will Be Inducted Sept. 16th," *Dardanelle Post-Dispatch*, September 13, 1945, 1; "Five Men Will Be Inducted October 23," *Dardanelle Post-Dispatch*, October 18, 1945, 1; "Memorial to Honor Corporal Marze Waid," *Dardanelle Post-Dispatch*, September 27, 1945, 1; "Yell Is Champion War Bond County," *Dardanelle Post-Dispatch*, December 6, 1945, 1.

95. "School to Open for 1945–46 Term Next Monday, Sept. 17," *Dardanelle Post-Dispatch*, September 13, 1945, 1.

96. "Centerville Items," *Dardanelle Post-Dispatch*, August 23, 1945, 8.

97. "All-Time River High of 33.8 Feet Set Here Last Friday," *Dardanelle Post-Dispatch*, May 20, 1943, 1.

98. "He Don't Mean Maybe," *Dardanelle Post-Dispatch*, May 20, 1943, 1.

99. Tommy Hunt, interview by author, Dardanelle, Arkansas, July 14, 2008.

100. "Arkansas River Raging in Greatest Flood Ever Known," May 13, 1943, 1; "River Set New High Record Mark of 34.05 Feet Tuesday," *Dardanelle Post-Dispatch*, May 27, 1943, 1.

101. "Ask Donations of Surplus Garden Seed," *Dardanelle Post-Dispatch*, May 27, 1943, 1.

102. Joe Grimes, interview by author, Dardanelle, Arkansas, August 3, 2015.

103. Lynne Gleason Murphy, personal conversation with author, Dardanelle, Arkansas, June 28, 2012.

104. "Bottom Farmers Resuming Operations," *Dardanelle Post-Dispatch*, June 10, 1943, 1.

105. "Army Completes Rehabilitation Work in Flooded District," *Dardanelle Post-Dispatch*, August 5, 1943, 1.

106. "Red Cross Relief to Flood Victims Totals $10,225.13," *Dardanelle Post-Dispatch*, July 1, 1943, 1.

107. Crain, interview by author, July 10, 2008.

108. Crain, interview by author, July 10, 2008.

109. "Caudle Reports on Hearing on Fort Gibson Dam Project," *Dardanelle Post-Dispatch*, March 2, 1944, 1.

110. "Vital River Meeting to Be Held March 12," *Dardanelle Post-Dispatch*, March 8, 1945, 1.

111. "Arkansas River Floods Bottom Lands," *Dardanelle Post-Dispatch*, April 20, 1945, 1; "Red Cross Flood Relief Work Ends," *Dardanelle Post-Dispatch*, May 24, 1945, 1.

112. "Rich Bottom Lands Again Inundated," *Dardanelle Post-Dispatch*, June 14, 1945, 1.

113. "Flood Waters Destroy Carden Bottom Crops," *Dardanelle Post-Dispatch*, October 4, 1945, 1.

114. Grimes, interview by author, August 3, 2015.

115. "GIs Out to Reform County Politics," *Dardanelle Post-Dispatch*, August 8, 1946, 1.

116. "GIs of Yell County Perfect Organization," *Dardanelle Post-Dispatch*, August 15, 1946, 1.

117. "GI Rally Held Here Last Friday Night," *Dardanelle Post-Dispatch*, October 24, 1946, 1.

118. "GIs to Announce Full Ticket at Big Mass Meeting Friday Night," *Dardanelle Post-Dispatch*, August 22, 1946, 1.

119. Jay Barth, "Election Fraud," *The Encyclopedia of Arkansas History & Culture*. Also see C. Fred Williams, "GI Revolt," *The Encyclopedia of Arkansas History & Culture*.

120. "GIs Cite Laws Governing Elections," *Dardanelle Post-Dispatch*, September 12, 1946, 1.

121. Johnson III, *Arkansas in Modern America*, 20. Also see Patsy Hawthorn Ramsey, "A Place at the Table: Hot Springs and the GI Revolt," *Arkansas Historical Quarterly* 59, no. 4 (Winter 2000): 407–28.

122. "Democratic Ticket Wins in County," *Dardanelle Post-Dispatch*, November 7, 1946, 1.

123. "Yell County Now Has Fewer Farms," *Dardanelle Post-Dispatch*, August 22, 1946, 1.

124. Grimes, interview by author, August 3, 2015.

125. "Carden Bottom Items," *Dardanelle Post-Dispatch,* December 2, 1948, 4; "Families Leaving Carden Bottom," *Dardanelle Post-Dispatch,* February 21, 1946, 1; "Locals," *Dardanelle Post-Dispatch,* January 19, 1950, 5.

126. "Population of Yell County Shows Decline," *Dardanelle Post-Dispatch,* June 15, 1950, 1.

127. "52 Carden Bottom Residents Picnic," *Dardanelle Post-Dispatch*, July 22, 1965, 1.

128. "Fourth Annual 'Old Timers' Reunion," *Dardanelle Post-Dispatch,* August 17, 1967, 1.

129. "Carden Bottom," *Dardanelle Post-Dispatch*, March 2, 1967, 8.

130. Joe Grimes, "Carden Bottom Reunion Program," Dardanelle, Arkansas, October 19, 2008.

131. Letter to the Editor, *Dardanelle Post-Dispatch,* June 12, 1969, 6.

132. "Many Matters Discussed at Chamber of Commerce Meet," *Dardanelle Post-Dispatch,* March 17, 1949, 1; "Rural Telephone Surveys Completed," *Dardanelle Post-Dispatch,* March 24, 1949, 1.

133. Roy Tillman Jr., interview by author, Dardanelle, Arkansas, July 9, 2014.

134. "Bottom Road to Be Constructed," *Dardanelle Post-Dispatch,* January 27, 1944, 1.

135. "Members of Highway Commission Pay Visit to City," *Dardanelle Post-Dispatch,* June 21, 1945, 1.

136. "County Judge Jack White Greatly Improving Roads," *Dardanelle Post-Dispatch,* June 7, 1945, 1.

137. "Carden Bottom Road Improvement Sought," *Dardanelle Post-Dispatch,* June 24, 1954; Delma Merritt, interview by author, Dardanelle, Arkansas, July 9, 2014.

138. Hickey, interview by author, July 9, 2008; "Road in Bottom to Receive Coat of Oil," *Dardanelle Post-Dispatch*, July 1, 1954, 1.

139. "Kil-o-Watts," *Dardanelle Post-Dispatch,* March 3, 1955, 1.

140. "To Dedicate New Highway June 28," *Dardanelle Post-Dispatch,* June 18, 1959, 1.

141. Hickey, interview by author, July 9, 2008.

142. "Paving Job Will Start Immediately," *Dardanelle Post-Dispatch,* May 4, 1950, 1.

143. "Cattle Good Property," *Dardanelle Post-Dispatch,* June 8, 1944, 1.

144. "Locals," *Dardanelle Post-Dispatch,* April 26, 1945, 8.

145. "Locals," *Dardanelle Post-Dispatch,* February 15, 1945, 8; "Clement-Byrd Store Is Moved to Russellville," *Dardanelle Post-Dispatch*, November 19, 1953, 1.

146. "Keenans Purchase Russellville Business," *Dardanelle Post-Dispatch,* July 28, 1949, 1.

147. Advertisement, *Dardanelle Post-Dispatch,* January 5, 1950, 8; "John Deere Day Friday, February 24," *Dardanelle Post-Dispatch,* February 23, 1950, 1.

148. "Splendid New Gin Now in Operation," *Dardanelle Post-Dispatch,* September 1, 1949, 1.

149. "Over $2 Million Cotton Crop Ginned Here This Year," *Dardanelle Post-Dispatch,* November 5, 1953, 1.

150. "Keenan Gin Adds Storage for Beans" and "Building New Grain Elevator," *Dardanelle Post-Dispatch,* August 18, 1955, 1.

151. "Farmers Urged to Attend 'Corn' Meeting Here Tonight," *Dardanelle Post-Dispatch*, January 28, 1954, 1.

152. "Cotton Labor Drive for Native Workers," *Dardanelle Post-Dispatch,* August 18, 1955, 2; "Kil-o-Watts," *Dardanelle Post-Dispatch*, October 20, 1955, 1.

153. "Produces 26 Bales of Cotton on 11 Acres," *Dardanelle Post-Dispatch,* November 29, 1956, 1.

154. "Malaria Control Unit Using New Chemical," *Dardanelle Post-Dispatch,* May 18, 1950, 1; "Fly-Killing Crew Is Now in Dardanelle," *Dardanelle Post-Dispatch*, June 22, 1950, 1.

155. "Airplanes Used in Fighting Boll Weevils," *Dardanelle Post-Dispatch,* July 27, 1950, 1.

156. "Say Dusting Cotton Causing Complaints," *Dardanelle Post-Dispatch,* August 4, 1955, 1.

157. "Man Heavily Fined for Shooting Geese from an Airplane," *Dardanelle Post-Dispatch,* November 10, 1949, 1.

158. "Kil-o-Watts," *Dardanelle Post-Dispatch,* August 4, 1955, 1.

159. "Survey to Be Made for Broiler Business," *Dardanelle Post-Dispatch,* November 1, 1945, 1; "Great Interest in New Broiler Industry," *Dardanelle Post-Dispatch,* April 11, 1946, 4; "Efforts to Secure Broiler Industry Now near Success," *Dardanelle Post-Dispatch,* January 6, 1949, 1.

160. "Establishment of Broiler Industry Here by First of February Now Seems Certain," *Dardanelle Post-Dispatch,* January 13, 1949, 1; "First Chicks Placed in New Broiler Houses," *Dardanelle Post-Dispatch*, February 24, 1949, 1.

161. "Broiler Dinner Tomorrow Night," *Dardanelle Post-Dispatch,* July 14, 1949, 1.

162. "New Feed Mills Will Mean Much to This Section of Arkansas," *Dardanelle Post-Dispatch*, February 27, 1947, 1.

163. "Local Feed Mills Rapidly Expanding," *Dardanelle Post-Dispatch,* January 8, 1948, 1.

164. "Rain Cuts Attendance at C. of C. Meeting," *Dardanelle Post-Dispatch,* June 16, 1949, 1.

165. "Arkansas Valley Feed Mills to Again Produce Own Feed," *Dardanelle Post-Dispatch,* January 28, 1960, 1; "AVI Declares Liberal Dividend," *Dardanelle Post-Dispatch,* September 29, 1960, 1.

166. "Ken Parker Joins AVI; To Live Here," *Dardanelle Post-Dispatch,* September 8, 1960, 1; "Dr. Treat Joins AVI as Nutritionist," *Dardanelle Post-Dispatch,* September 15, 1960, 1; "Stanfield Joins AVI as Personnel Director," *Dardanelle Post-Dispatch,* November 15, 1960, 1.

167. "Will Sign Contract for New Processing Plant This Afternoon," *Dardanelle Post-Dispatch*, June 14, 1951, 1; "Chamber of Commerce Is Successful in Securing Large New Industry for Dardanelle," *Dardanelle Post-Dispatch*, August 2, 1951, 1.

168. "Processing Plant to Begin Operations on or before April 2," *Dardanelle Post-Dispatch,* March 13, 1952, 1.

169. Jack Temple Kirby, *Rural Worlds Lost: The American South, 1920–1960* (Baton Rouge: Louisiana State University Press, 1987), 355–57.

170. "Locals," *Dardanelle Post-Dispatch,* July 12, 1951, 5.

171. "Over 4½ Million Broilers Processed Here in '53," *Dardanelle Post-Dispatch,* March 4, 1954, 1; "Kil-o-Watts," *Dardanelle Post-Dispatch,* March 18, 1954.

172. "Fox DeLuxe Plants to Be Enlarged; To Increase Help," *Dardanelle Post-Dispatch,* August 28, 1958, 1.

173. "Fox DeLuxe Plant Reaches New High in Production," *Dardanelle Post-Dispatch,* January 15, 1959, 1.

174. "Citizens Vote $450,000 Bond Issues by Overwhelming Margin," *Dardanelle Post-Dispatch*, December 29, 1960, 1.

175. "AVI Begins Operations of Three Poultry Plants Feb. 27," *Dardanelle Post-Dispatch,* February 16, 1961, 1.

176. "Dardanelle in Enthusiastic Display of 'Appreciation' for Ark. Valley Ind., Inc.," *Dardanelle Post-Dispatch,* March 30, 1961, 1.

177. "Proposed Ark Valley Bank Charter Up for Approval," *Dardanelle Post-Dispatch,* April 13, 1961, 1; "AVI Home Offices Locate in Downtown Dardanelle," *Dardanelle Post-Dispatch,* April 13, 1961, 1.

178. "Harold D. Gooden Manager Waldron AVI Plant," *Dardanelle Post-Dispatch,* September 14, 1961, 1.

179. "Harold Snyder Says—'Crop Contracts' the Only Salvation for Farmers," *Dardanelle Post-Dispatch,* February 28, 1963, 1.

180. "AVI Name Changed to VALMAC," *Dardanelle Post-Dispatch,* August 6, 1970, 1.

181. Kirby, *Rural Worlds Lost,* 358–59.

182. Kirby, *Rural Worlds Lost,* 358–59. Also see http://www.nationalchicken council.org/industry-issues/vertical-integration/ and http://www.growwithtyson. clomn/chicken-production-process.

183. "The Multiple-Purpose Plan for the Arkansas River," *Dardanelle Post-Dispatch,* June 29, 1950, 2–3; "Col. Clema Outlines Arkansas River Development Program," *Dardanelle Post-Dispatch,* October 15, 1953, 1.

184. "Congressman Says Dam Will Be Built," *Dardanelle Post-Dispatch,* October 5, 1950, 1.

185. "President Signs Waterways Bill," *Dardanelle Post-Dispatch,* October 25, 1951, 1.

186. "Arkansas River Program Is Again Going Forward," *Dardanelle Post-Dispatch,* November 1, 1951, 1.

187. "Emergency Aid Being Sought to Save Rich Bottom Lands," *Dardanelle Post-Dispatch,* January 24, 1952, 1.

188. "Holla Bend Cut Off Work to Begin Early Next Spring," *Dardanelle Post-Dispatch,* December 4, 1952, 1.

189. "Holla Bend Refuge, An Island to Itself Created by Rerouting a River Channel," *Dardanelle Post-Dispatch,* February 29, 1968, 1.

190. "Holla Bend Refuge, An Island to Itself Created by Rerouting a River Channel," *Dardanelle Post-Dispatch,* February 29, 1968. 6.

191. "Holla Bend Lands Go to Wildlife Service," *Dardanelle Post-Dispatch,*

July 18, 1957, 1. The name "Holla Bend" was known in the nineteenth century as Holly Bend, which came from an 1830 surveyor of the area, Mr. Holly Bend.

192. "2,284 Acres Sought for Holla Bend," *Dardanelle Post-Dispatch,* August 22, 1968, 6.

193. Reba Thone, interview by author, Dardanelle, Arkansas, July 10, 2008.

194. "Congress Votes $450,000 for Dardanelle Dam," *Dardanelle Post-Dispatch,* June 23, 1955, 1.

195. Dardanelle Lock & Dam (Dardanelle Lake), Lakes Online.com. http://dardanelle.uslakes.info/DamInfo.asp?DamID=100071.

196. "Land in Lake Must Be Vacated Sept. 30, 1964," *Dardanelle Post-Dispatch,* October 24, 1963, 1.

197. "Bright Sunshine Ushers in Ground Breaking," *Dardanelle Post-Dispatch,* June 13, 1957, 1; "Lands Being Taken in Dardanelle Dam Area," *Dardanelle Post-Dispatch,* June 13, 1957, 1.

198. "Dam Dedication Set for May 13," *Dardanelle Post-Dispatch,* March 1, 1966, 1.

199. "Third Bridge to Span River," *Dardanelle Post-Dispatch,* November 9, 1967, 1; "River at Dardanelle," *Dardanelle Post-Dispatch,* November 9, 1967, 1.

200. "First Cars Cross New Bridge: Dec. 8, 1970," *Dardanelle Post-Dispatch,* December 10, 1970, 1

201. "Levee Breaks in Dardanelle Bottom When River Goes on Rampage at 33 Feet," *Dardanelle Post-Dispatch*, May 30, 1957, 1; Grace Hatch McClure, interview by author, Dardanelle, Arkansas, June 24, 2008; "Water Receding from Two Bottoms," *Dardanelle Post-Dispatch*, June 6, 1957, 1.

202. "Flood Disaster Meeting Held Here," *Dardanelle Post-Dispatch*, June 6, 1957, 1.

203. "Conway Firm Is Low Bidder on Levee," *Dardanelle Post-Dispatch,* July 25, 1957, 1.

204. "Locals," *Dardanelle Post-Dispatch,* May 22, 1947, 5.

205. Tillman Jr., interview by author, July 8, 2014.

206. "New Telephones Installed in Rural Areas; Dials Here Soon," *Dardanelle Post-Dispatch,* July 4, 1957, 1.

207. Corey Thone, interview by author, Russellville, Arkansas, August 9, 2010.

208. "Les Thone to Run for Twp. Constable," *Dardanelle Post-Dispatch*, June 30, 1966, 1.

209. "Carden Bottom Votes against Annexation," *Dardanelle Post-Dispatch*, December 6, 1962, 1.

210. "Carden Bottom Schools to Open September 3," *Dardanelle Post-Dispatch*, August 29, 1963, 1; "Dardanelle Enrolls 1,049 Students," *Dardanelle Post-Dispatch,* September 5, 1963, 1.

211. "Basic Education and Secretary Training at Carden Bottom," *Dardanelle Post-Dispatch,* September 1, 1966, 1; "Who Attends and What Goes on at Carden Bottom Adult Education School," *Dardanelle Post-Dispatch,* September 8, 1966, 1.

212. Keenan, interview by author, April 30, 2014.

213. "Rollow H. Carden," *Dardanelle Post-Dispatch,* April 9, 1964, 5.

214. "Area Native Writes about 'Good Old Days,'" *Dardanelle Post-Dispatch,* August 22, 1968, 6.

215. Donald Holley, "The Second Great Emancipation: The Rust Cotton Picker

and How It Changed Arkansas," *Arkansas Historical Quarterly* 52, no.1 (Spring 1993): 45.

216. Holley, "The Second Great Emancipation," 44–77.

217. "Local," *Dardanelle Post-Dispatch,* June 3, 1948, 5; "Progress Calls for Demise of Dardanelle's Jacoway Mansion," *Dardanelle Post-Dispatch,* September 23, 1965, 1.

218. "By-Pass Work to Begin after 4th of July," *Dardanelle Post-Dispatch,* June 28, 1961, 1.

219. https://alfred.stlouisfed.org.

220. Bureau of Economic Analysis, "Personal Income and Employment by Major Component." Index. Washington, DC.

221. Dickens, interview by author, July 7, 2008.

222. Roy Reed, *Faubus: The Life and Times of an American Prodigal* (Fayetteville: University of Arkansas Press, 1997), 173.

223. Marie Williams, "The Road to the Central High Crisis: Jim Johnson's Manipulation of the Southern Red Scare in Arkansas and the Integration of Hoxie" (Master's thesis, Arkansas Tech University, 2014), 51–52.

224. Williams, "The Road to the Central High Crisis," 52.

225. See Jeff Woods, *Black Struggle, Red Scare: Segregation and Anti-Communism in the South, 1948–1968* (Baton Rouge: Louisiana State University Press, 2004).

226. "Dardanelle Colored Families Ask for Admittance of High School Students," *Dardanelle Post-Dispatch,* April 16, 1964, 1.

227. "Russellville-Dardanelle-Danville Schools Integrate," *Dardanelle Post-Dispatch,* May 28, 1964, 1.

228. "One Elementary School This Year: Douglas Closed," *Dardanelle Post-Dispatch,* August 12, 1965, 1.

229. "Kil-o-Watts," *Dardanelle Post-Dispatch,* June 10, 1954, 1.

230. "Luther Banks, A Barber Here for Fifty-Eight Years," *Dardanelle Post-Dispatch,* October 24, 1968, 1.

231. Janelle Searcy Menick, telephone interview by author, Dardanelle, Arkansas, July 28, 2016.

232. "Just in Passing," *Dardanelle Post-Dispatch,* February 26, 1948, 3.

233. "Keenan Implement to Hold Formal Opening Saturday," *Dardanelle Post-Dispatch,* March 10, 1960, 4; "Keenan Opening Well Attended," *Dardanelle Post-Dispatch,* March 17, 1960, 1.

234. "Ginners of Cotton Shows Increase for County," *Dardanelle Post-Dispatch,* March 31, 1960, 8.

235. Tillman Jr., interview by author, July 9, 2014.

236. "Cotton Crops," *Dardanelle Post-Dispatch,* June 16, 1960, 6.

237. "Elected Farm Family of Year," *Dardanelle Post-Dispatch,* October 6, 1960, 1.

238. "No Soil Bank Signup This Fall," *Dardanelle Post-Dispatch,* October 6, 1960, 1.

239. "County Development Assn. Organized," *Dardanelle Post-Dispatch,* March 15, 1962, 1.

240. "State of Arkansas Business Report for '65," *Dardanelle Post-Dispatch,* March 10, 1966, 11.

241. "5 Year Statistics, 1960 through 1965, for Yell County," *Dardanelle Post-Dispatch,* August 3, 1967, 1.

242. Editorial, *Dardanelle Post-Dispatch,* October 18, 1962, 4.

243. Editorial, *Dardanelle Post-Dispatch,* October 18, 1962, 4.

244. "Thanks," *Dardanelle Post-Dispatch,* November 22, 1962, 1.

245. Editorial, *Dardanelle Post-Dispatch,* October 17, 1963, 1.

246. "C of C Asks Cotton Smog Relief," *Dardanelle Post-Dispatch,* October 17, 1963, 1.

247. "City Council Hears Citizens Protest to Stop Cotton Debris," *Dardanelle Post-Dispatch,* July 30, 1964, 1.

248. "City Council Hears Citizens Protest to Stop Cotton Debris," *Dardanelle Post-Dispatch,* July 30, 1964, 8.

249. "County Agent Predicts Big Growth in Agriculture Here," *Dardanelle Post-Dispatch,* October 5, 1967, 1.

250. "Yell County Farming News," *Dardanelle Post-Dispatch,* October 26, 1967, 6.

251. "W. H. Nichols of Dardanelle Is One of States 15 Remaining Cotton Graders," *Dardanelle Post-Dispatch,* March 21, 1968, 1.

252. "W. H. Nichols of Dardanelle Is One of States 15 Remaining Cotton Graders," *Dardanelle Post-Dispatch,* March 21, 1968, 1.

253. "Keenan Gin Coop. to Build River Wharf," *Dardanelle Post-Dispatch,* July 23, 1964, 1.

254. "Historic Shipment Reaches Dardanelle," *Dardanelle Post-Dispatch,* February 5, 1970, 1.

255. Keenan, interview by author, April 30, 2014.

256. Keenan, interview by author, April 30, 2014; Delma Merritt, interview by author, Dardanelle, Arkansas, July 9, 2014; Crow, interview by author, August 4, 2015.

257. Crain, interview by author, July 10, 2008.

## Chapter 7: Conclusion

1. "First Definite Move Made in Better Farm Community Plan," *Dardanelle Post-Dispatch,* July 22, 1948, 1.

# SOURCES

## Personal Conversations and Interviews

Bachman, Marie Shepherd. Interview by author. Dardanelle, AR, August 4, 2008.

Crain, Gordon. Interview by author. Dardanelle, AR, July 10, 2008.

Crow, Bobby. Interview by author. Cotton Town, AR, August 4, 2015.

Crow, Bobby. Interview by author. Cotton Town, AR, August 14, 2015.

Daniels, Cornelia. Interview by author. Dardanelle, AR, July 1, 2008.

Dickens, Lonnie. Interview by author. Dardanelle, AR, July 7, 2008.

Garner, Bill. Conversation with author. Dardanelle, AR, October 19, 2001.

Gleason, George Granville. Conversation with author. New Neely, AR, May 11, 1975.

Grimes, Joe. Interview by author. Dardanelle, AR, July 17, 2008.

Grimes, Joe. Interview by author. Dardanelle, AR, June 22, 2009.

Grimes, Joe. Interview by author. Dardanelle, AR, August 3, 2015

Guice, Jack. Telephone interview by author. Dardanelle, AR, March 23, 2013.

Hall, Mary Potts. Interview by author. Little Rock, AR, October 17, 2009.

Hickey, Doris Hundley. Interview by author. Dardanelle, AR, July 9, 2008.

Hunt, Tommy. Interview by author. Dardanelle, AR, July 14, 2008.

Keenan, Tomela Wright. Interview by author. Dardanelle, AR, April 30, 2014.

McClure, Grace Hatch. Interview by author. Dardanelle, AR, June 24, 2008.

McKay, John. Interview by author. Dardanelle, AR, April 26, 2014.

Menick, Janelle Searcy. Telephone interview by author. Dardanelle, AR, July 25, 2016.

Merritt, Delma. Interview by author. Dardanelle, AR, July 9, 2014.

Murphy, Lynne Gleason. Conversation with author. Dardanelle, AR, June 28, 2012.

Pitts, Bill. Conversation with author. Dardanelle, AR, November 2, 1997.

Prince, Judy Hamburg. Interview by author. Mount Nebo, AR, July 17, 2013.

Robinson, Whitey. Telephone interview by author. Dardanelle, AR, September 21, 2009.

Stewart, Gail. Interview by author. Little Rock, AR, July 11, 2014.

Stroud, John. Interview by author. Atkins, AR, July 9, 2014.

Thompson, Isodore. Interview by author. Dardanelle, AR, May 20, 2009.

Thone, Corey. Interview by author. Russellville, AR, August 9, 2010.

Thone, Reba. Interview by author. Dardanelle, AR, July 10, 2008.

Tillman Jr., Roy. Interview by author. Dardanelle, AR, July 8, 2014.

Tillman Jr., Roy. Interview by author. Dardanelle, AR, July 9, 2014.

Tillman, Wanda Lee. Interview by author. Dardanelle, AR, July 8, 2014.


## Newspapers

*Arkansas Democrat* (Little Rock)

*Arkansas Gazette* (Little Rock)

*Dardanelle Post*

*Dardanelle Post-Dispatch*

*Independent Arkansian* (Dardanelle)

*New York Times*

*Russellville Democrat*


## Secondary

Alexander, Charles C. "Defeat, Decline, Disintegration: The Ku Klux Klan in Arkansas, 1924 and After." *Arkansas Historical Quarterly* 22, no. 4 (Winter 1963): 311–21.

Alexander, Charles C. "White-Robed Reformers: The Ku Klux Klan Comes to Arkansas, 1921–1922." *Arkansas Historical Quarterly* 22, no. 1 (Spring 1963): 8–23.

Alexander, Charles C. "White Robes in Politics: The Ku Klux Klan in Arkansas, 1922–1924." *Arkansas Historical Quarterly* 22, no. 3 (Fall 1963): 195–214.

Allen, Julia F. "One Kind of Pioneer Project." *Arkansas Historical Quarterly* 55, no. 1 (Spring 1996): 1–25.

"Arkansas Department of Health." *The Encyclopedia of Arkansas History & Culture.*

Arkansas, State of. Division of State Parks, Arkansas Department of Parks and Tourism. "History of Mt. Nebo." Little Rock, 2012.

Arkansas, State of. "*Leslie v. State of Arkansas.*" *Arkansas Reports: Cases Determined in the Supreme Court of Arkansas,* Volume 155. Little Rock: Democrat Printing and Lithographic Company, 1923.Bailey, Fred Arthur, "Free Speech and the 'Lost Cause' in Arkansas." *Arkansas Historical Quarterly* 55, no. 2 (Summer 1996): 143–66.

Banks, Wayne. *History of Yell County, Arkansas.* Van Buren, AR: Press-Argus, 1959.

Barjenbruch, Judith. "The Greenback Political Movement: An Arkansas View." *Arkansas Historical Quarterly* 36, no. 2 (Summer 1977): 107–22.

Barnes, Ken. *Journey of Hope: The Back-to-Africa Movement in Arkansas in the Late 1800s.* Chapel Hill: University of North Carolina Press, 2004.

Barnes, Ken. *Who Killed John Clayton?: Political Violence and the Emergence of the New South, 1861–1893.* Durham, NC: Duke University Press, 1998.

Barry, John M. *Rising Tide: The Great Mississippi Flood of 1927 and How It Changed America.* New York: Simon & Schuster Paperbacks, 1997.

Barth, Jay. "Election Fraud." *The Encyclopedia of Arkansas History & Culture.*

Bashaw, Carolyn T. "'One Kind of Pioneer Project': Julia F. Allen and the Southern Tenant Farmers' Union College Student Project, 1938." *Arkansas Historical Quarterly* 55, no. 1 (Spring 1996): 1–25.

Baskett Jr., Thomas S. "Miners Stay Away! W. B. W. Heartsill and the Last Years of the Arkansas Knights of Labor, 1892–1896." *Arkansas Historical Quarterly* 42, no. 2 (Summer 1983): 107–33.

Bearden, Russell. "Jefferson County's Worst Disaster: The Flood of 1927." *Arkansas Historical Quarterly* 43, no. 4 (Winter 1984): 324–38.

Blevins, Brooks R. "The Strike and the Still: Anti-Radical Violence and the Ku Klux Klan in the Ozarks." *Arkansas Historical Quarterly* 52, no. 4 (Winter 1993): 405–25.

Branyan, Scott. "Floods." *The Encyclopedia of Arkansas History & Culture.*

Branyan, Scott. "Little Rock District U.S. Army Corps of Engineers." *The Encyclopedia of Arkansas History & Culture.*

Brown, Mattie. "River Transportation in Arkansas, 1819–1890." *Arkansas Historical Quarterly* 1, no. 4 (December 1942): 342–54.

Bureau of Economic Analysis. "Personal Income and Employment by Major Component." Report SA4, Washington, DC, 2016.

Bureau of Economic Analysis. "Personal Income Summary: Personal Income, Population, Per Capita Personal Income." Report SA1, Washington, DC, 2016.

Carruth, Joseph. "World War I Propaganda and Its Effects in Arkansas." *Arkansas Historical Quarterly* 16, no. 4 (Winter 1997): 385–98.

Chess, Edward J. "Agricultural Wheel." *The Encyclopedia of Arkansas History & Culture.*

Christ, Mark K. "Action at Dardanelle and Ivey's Ford." *The Encyclopedia of Arkansas History & Culture.*

Clayton, Powell. *The Aftermath of the Civil War, in Arkansas.* New York: Neale Publishing Company, 1915.

Cole, Helen. "Public Health." *The Encyclopedia of Arkansas History & Culture.*

Conkin, Paul K. *The New Deal,* 3d ed. Wheeling, IL: Harlan-Davidson, 1992.

Cooper, Lola Person. "Lest We Forget." Unpublished Collection. Dardanelle, AR: Arkansas River Valley Regional Library, 1972.

"Cotton Futures Act of 1916." http://www.freebase.com/m/04zzlmx (accessed February 13, 2016).

Danbom, David B. *Born in the Country: A History of Rural America.* 2d ed. Baltimore: Johns Hopkins University Press, 2006.

Daniel, Pete. *Breaking the Land: The Transformation of Cotton, Tobacco, and Rice Cultures since 1880.* Champagne-Urbana: University of Illinois Press, 1986.

Daniel, Pete. *Deep'n as It Come: The 1927 Mississippi Flood.* Fayetteville: University of Arkansas Press, 1996.

Daniels, Cornelia. *Mt. Nebo: 1900s–2014.* Dardanelle, AR: Yell County Historical Society, 2015.

Dawson, David D. "Baseball Calls: Arkansas Town Baseball in the Twenties." *Arkansas Historical Quarterly* 54, no. 4 (Winter 1995): 409–26.

Dougan, Michael B. "Business, Commerce, and Industry." *The Encyclopedia of Arkansas History & Culture.*

Duncan, Georgena. "One Negro, Sarah . . . One Horse Named Collier, One Cow and Calf Named Pink: Slave Records from the Arkansas River Valley." *Arkansas Historical Quarterly* 69, no. 4 (Winter 2010): 325–45.

Economic Research Division, Federal Reserve Bank of St. Louis. "Per Capita Personal Income in Arkansas Vintage: 2015-06-22, Dollars, Annual, Not Seasonally Adjusted." Report ARPCPI-20150622. https://afred.stlouisfed.org (accessed July 22, 2016).

Economic Research Division, Federal Reserve Bank of St. Louis. "Per Capita Personal Income in United States Vintage: 2016-03-25, Dollars, Annual, Not Seasonally Adjusted." Report A792RC0A052NBEA. https://afred.stlouisfed.org (accessed July 22, 2016).

Elkins, Clark. "Arkansas Farmers Organize for Action: 1882–1884." *Arkansas Historical Quarterly* 13, no. 3 (Autumn 1954): 231–48.

Elkins, F. Clark. "The Agricultural Wheel: County Politics and Consolidation, 1884–1885." *Arkansas Historical Quarterly* 29, no. 2 (Summer 1970): 152–75.

Elkins, F. Clark. "The Agricultural Wheel in Arkansas, 1887." *Arkansas Historical Quarterly* 40, no. 3 (Autumn 1981): 249–60.

Eno, Clara B. "The History of the Council Oak." *Arkansas Historical Quarterly* 6, no. 2 (Summer 1947): 198–200.

Evans, Lewis (Mrs.). "A History of Carden Bottoms." *Arkansas Democrat Magazine,* October 19, 1947.

Evins, Janie Synatzske. "Arkansas Women: Their Contribution to Society, Politics, and Business, 1865–1900." *Arkansas Historical Quarterly* 44, no. 2 (Summer 1985): 118–33.

Farmer, Rod. "Direct Democracy in Arkansas, 1910–1918." *Arkansas Historical Quarterly* 40, no. 3 (Summer 1981): 99–118.

Foti, Thomas. "Arkansas Valley." *The Encyclopedia of Arkansas History & Culture.*

Gatewood Jr., Willard B. *Aristocrats of Color: The Black Elite, 1880–1920.* Bloomington: Indiana University Press, 1990.

Gatewood Jr., Willard B., ed. "Arkansas Negroes in the 1890s: Documents." *Arkansas Historical Quarterly* 33, no. 4 (Winter 1974): 293–325.

Gilmore, Glenda Elizabeth. *Gender and Jim Crow: Women and the Politics of White*

*Supremacy in North Carolina, 1896–1920.* Chapel Hill: University of North Carolina Press, 1996.

Gleason, Mildred Diane. "Dardanelle." *The Encyclopedia of Arkansas History & Culture.*

Gleason, Mildred Diane. "Yell County." *The Encyclopedia of Arkansas History & Culture.*

Goss, Kay C. "McClellan-Kerr Arkansas River Navigation System (MKARNS)." *The Encyclopedia of Arkansas History & Culture.*

Graves, John William. "Another Look at Disfranchisement in Arkansas, 1888–1894." *Arkansas Historical Quarterly* 69, no. 3 (Autumn 2010): 245–62.

Graves, John William. "The Arkansas Separate Coach Law of 1891." *Arkansas Historical Quarterly* 32, no. 2 (Summer 1973): 148–65.

Graves, John William. "Negro Disfranchisement in Arkansas." *Arkansas Historical Quarterly* 26, no. 3 (Autumn 1967): 199–225.

Gravley, Ernestine. "Early Twin Cities of Arkansas: Dardanelle and Norristown." *Arkansas Historical Quarterly* 10, no. 2 (Summer 1951): 177–81.

Gravley, Ernestine. "The Presbyterian Church in Dardanelle, Arkansas." *Arkansas Historical Quarterly* 12, no. 3 (Autumn 1953): 273–77.

Griffith, Nancy Snell. "Tuberculosis." *The Encyclopedia of Arkansas History & Culture.*

Grimes, Joe. "Carden Bottom Reunion Program." October 19, 2008. Dardanelle, Arkansas.

"Grow with Tyson." http://www.growwithtyson.com/chicken-production-process/ (accessed July 24, 2016).

Hagge, Patrick. "The Decline and Fall of a Cotton Empire: Economic and Land-Use Change in the Lower Mississippi River 'Delta' South, 1930–1970." PhD diss., Pennsylvania State University, 2013.

Hahn, Steven. *A Nation Under Our Feet: Black Political Struggles in the Rural South from Slavery to the Great Migration.* Cambridge, MA: Harvard University Press, 2003.

Hansen, Lyn. "David P. Cloyd and the Dardanelle Independent." *Arkansas Historical Quarterly* 14, no. 3 (Autumn 1955): 293–300.

Hawkins, Van. "Cotton Industry." *The Encyclopedia of Arkansas History & Culture.*

Hendricks, Nancy. "Flood of 1927." *The Encyclopedia of Arkansas History & Culture.*

Henningson Jr., Berton E. "Northwest Arkansas and the Brothers of Freedom: The Roots of a Farmer Movement." *Arkansas Historical Quarterly* 34, no. 4 (Winter 1975): 304–24.

Henningson Jr., Berton E. "'Root Hog or Die': The Brothers of Freedom and the 1884 Arkansas Election." *Arkansas Historical Quarterly* 45, no. 3 (Autumn 1986): 197–216.

Hicks, Floyd W., and C. Roger Lambert. "Food for the Hungry: Federal Food Programs in Arkansas, 1933–1942." *Arkansas Historical Quarterly* 37, no. 1 (Spring 1978): 23–43.

Hild, Matthew. "Brothers of Freedom." *The Encyclopedia of Arkansas History & Culture.*

Hild, Matthew. "Labor, Third-Party Politics, and the New South Democracy in Arkansas, 1884–1896." *Arkansas Historical Quarterly* 63, no. 1 (Spring 2004): 24–43.

Hild, Matthew. "National Farmers' Alliance and Industrial Union of America." *The Encyclopedia of Arkansas History & Culture.*

Holley, Donald. "A Look behind the Masks: The 1920s Ku Klux Klan in Monticello, Arkansas." *Arkansas Historical Quarterly* 60, no. 2 (Summer 2001): 131–50.

Holley, Donald. *The Second Great Emancipation: The Mechanical Cotton Picker, Black Migration, and How They Shaped the Modern South.* Fayetteville: University of Arkansas Press, 2000.

Holley, Donald. "The Second Great Emancipation: The Rust Cotton Picker and How It Changed Arkansas." *Arkansas Historical Quarterly* 52, no.1 (Spring 1993): 44–77.

Holmes, William F. "The Arkansas Cotton Pickers Strike of 1891 and the Demise of the Colored Farmers' Alliance." *Arkansas Historical Quarterly* 32, no. 2 (Summer 1973): 107–19.

Horn, Jeanie. "Night Riders." *The Encyclopedia of Arkansas History & Culture.*

Huff, Leo E. "Guerrillas, Jayhawkers, and Bushwhackers in Northern Arkansas during the Civil War." *Arkansas Historical Quarterly* 24, no. 2 (Summer 1965): 127–48.

Hull, Clifton E. "Prosperity Rolls across Arkansas." *Arkansas Historical Quarterly* 34, no. 4 (Winter 1975): 325–32.

Hull, Clifton E., and William A. Pollard. *The Dardanelle and Russellville Railroad.* Conway: University of Central Arkansas Press, 1995.

Hull, Gene. "Those Coal Mines at Bernice, Part I." *Pope County Historical Association Quarterly* 30 (September 1996): 4–12.

Hull, Gene. "Those Coal Mines at Bernice, Part II." *Pope County Historical Association Quarterly* 30 (December 1996): 14–20.

Humphrey, Mary Vinson, and Doyle Traxler. "Links That Bind Yell County, Arkansas." Dardanelle: Unpublished Collection, Arkansas River Valley Regional Library, 1980.

Hurt, R. Douglas. *American Agriculture: A Brief History.* Ames: Iowa State University Press, 1994.

Johnson III, Ben F. *Arkansas in Modern America, 1930–1999.* Fayetteville: University of Arkansas Press, 2000.

Jones, Allen W., and Virginia Ann Buttry. "Military Events in Arkansas during the Civil War, 1861–1865." *Arkansas Historical Quarterly* 22, no. 2 (Summer 1963): 124–70.

Jones, Lu Ann. *Mama Learned Us to Work: Farm Women in the New South.* Chapel Hill: University of North Carolina Press, 2002.

Kirby, Jack Temple. *Rural Worlds Lost: The American South, 1920–1960*. Baton Rouge: Louisiana State University Press, 1987.

Kousser, J. Morgan. "A Black Protest in the 'Era of Accommodation': Documents." *Arkansas Historical Quarterly* 34, no. 2 (Summer 1975): 149–78.

Lambert, Roger. "Hoover and the Red Cross in the Arkansas Drought of 1930." *Arkansas Historical Quarterly* 29, no. 1 (Spring 1970): 3–19.

Lancaster, Guy. "Nightriding and Racial Cleansing in the Arkansas River Valley." *Arkansas Historical Quarterly* 72, no. 3 (Autumn 2013): 242–64.

Lancaster, Guy. "Petit Jean River." *The Encyclopedia of Arkansas History & Culture*.

Lancaster, Guy. *Racial Cleansing in Arkansas, 1883–1924: Politics, Land, Labor, and Criminality*. New York: Lexington Books, 2014.

Lewis, Todd E. "Mob Justice in the 'American Congo': 'Judge Lynch' in Arkansas during the Decade after World War I." *Arkansas Historical Quarterly* 52, no. 2 (Summer 1993): 156–84.

Lindsay, Captain J. E. to Major N. B. (Poly) Eison. Dardanelle, AR. March 16, 1866. Reproduced in James Reed Eison, ed. "A Letter from Dardanelle to Jonesville, South Carolina." *Arkansas Historical Quarterly* 28, no. 1 (Spring 1969): 72–75.

Lottinville, Savoie, ed. *A Journal of Travels into the Arkansas Territory During the Year 1819*. Fayetteville: University of Arkansas Press, 1999.

May, Irvin Marion. "The Paradox of Agricultural Abundance and Poverty: The Federal Surplus Relief Corporation, 1933–1935." PhD diss., University of Oklahoma, 1970.

McCarty, Joey. "The Red Scare in Arkansas: A Southern State and National Hysteria." *Arkansas Historical Quarterly* 37, no. 3 (Autumn 1978): 264–77.

McGee, Candice. "American Red Cross." *The Encyclopedia of Arkansas History & Culture*.

McGerr, Michael. *A Fierce Discontent: The Rise and Fall of the Progressive Movement in America*. New York: Oxford University Press, 2003.

McLoughlin, William G. *Cherokee Renascence in the New Republic*. Princeton, NJ: Princeton University Press, 1986.

Mecklin, John M. *The Ku Klux Klan: A Study of the American Mind*. New York: Russell & Russell, 1963.

Moneyhon, Carl H. *Arkansas and the New South, 1874–1929*. Fayetteville: University of Arkansas Press, 1997.

Moneyhon, Carl H. "Black Politics in Arkansas during the Gilded Age, 1876–1900." *Arkansas Historical Quarterly* 44, no. 3 (Autumn 1985): 222–45.

Moneyhon, Carl H. "The Creators of the New South in Arkansas: Industrial Boosterism, 1875–1885." *Arkansas Historical Quarterly* 55, no. 4 (Winter 1996): 383–409.

Murray, Gail S. "Forty Years Ago: The Great Depression Comes to Arkansas." *Arkansas Historical Quarterly* 29, no. 4 (Winter 1970): 291–312.

Murray, Robert K. *The Politics of Normalcy: Governmental Theory and Practice in the Harding-Coolidge Era*. New York: W. W. Norton & Company, 1973.

National Chicken Council. "Vertical Integration." http://www.nationalchicken council.org/industry-issues/vertical-integration/ (accessed July 24, 1016).

"New Deal Agencies: Farm Security Administration." http://histclo.com/essay/war/ dep/cou/us/nd/agency/nda-fsa.html (accessed May 23, 2015).

Neymeyer, Robert. "The Ku Klux Klan of the 1920 in the Midwest and West: A Review Essay." *Annals of Iowa* 51 (Fall 1992): 625–33.

"Old Pontoon Bridge Stretched 2,208, Feet." *Yell County Heritage*. Yell County Historical & Genealogical Association. Bedford, TX: Curtis Media, 1997: 95.

Otto, John Solomon. "Slavery in the Mountains: Yell County, Arkansas, 1840–1860." *Arkansas Historical Quarterly* 39, no. 1 (Spring 1980): 35–42.

Paisley, Clifton. "The Political Wheelers and Arkansas' Election of 1888." *Arkansas Historical Quarterly* 25, no. 1 (Spring 1966): 3–21.

Perkins, J. Blake. "The Arkansas Tick Eradication Murder: Rethinking Yeoman Resistance in the 'Marginal' South." *Arkansas Historical Quarterly* 70, no. 4 (Winter 2011): 363–97.

Ragsdale, John G. "Coal Mining." *The Encyclopedia of Arkansas History & Culture*.

Ramsey, Patsy Hawthorn. "A Place at the Table: Hot Springs and the GI Revolt." *Arkansas Historical Quarterly* 59, no. 4 (Winter 2000): 407–28.

Rison, David. "Federal Aid to Arkansas Education, 1933–1936." *Arkansas Historical Quarterly* 36, no. 2 (Summer 1977): 192–200.

Robinson II, Charles F. *Dangerous Liaisons: Sex and Love in the Segregated South*. Fayetteville: University of Arkansas Press, 2003.

Robinson II, Charles F. "'Most Shamefully Common': Arkansas and Miscegenation." *Arkansas Historical Quarterly* 60, no. 3 (Autumn 2001): 265–83.

Ross, Mitchell Frances. "The New Woman as Club Woman and Social Activist in Turn of the Century Arkansas." *Arkansas Historical Quarterly* 50, no. 4 (Winter 1991): 317–51.

Sadler, Genevieve Grant. *Muzzled Oxen: Reaping Cotton and Sowing Hope in 1920s Arkansas*. Little Rock: Butler Center Books, 2014.

Schuette, Shirley Sticht. "Subiaco." *The Encyclopedia of Arkansas History & Culture*.

Scoggin, Robert W. "Roads and Highways." *The Encyclopedia of Arkansas History & Culture*.

Scott, Anne Firor. *Making the Invisible Woman Visible*. Chicago: University of Chicago Press, 1984.

Scott, Anne Firor. *The Southern Lady: From Pedestal to Politics, 1830–1930*, 2nd ed. Charlottesville: University Press of Virginia, 1995.

Smith, John L. "Reminiscences of Farming and Business in the Depression, 1929–1933." *Arkansas Historical Quarterly* 45, no. 4 (Winter 1986): 321–29.

Spurgeon, John. "Drought of 1930–1931." *The Encyclopedia of Arkansas History & Culture*.

Staples, Thomas S. *Reconstruction in Arkansas 1862–1874*. New York: Columbia University Press, 1923.

Stewart-Abernathy, Leslie C. "Carden Bottom." *The Encyclopedia of Arkansas History & Culture.*

Stewart-Abernathy, Leslie C. "Steamboats." *The Encyclopedia of Arkansas History & Culture.*

Taylor, Paula Kyzer. "Women's Suffrage Movement." *The Encyclopedia of Arkansas History & Culture.*

Tucker, David M. *Arkansas: A People and Their Reputation.* Memphis: Memphis State University Press, 1985.

US Army Corps of Engineers. "Arkansas River and Tributaries Flood Control Plan," sheet no. 36, appendix no. 1. Memphis, TN: 1932.

US Department of Agriculture. *Agricultural Statistics, 1866–1936.* Washington, DC: US Government Printing Office, 1937.

Venkataramani, M. S. "Norman Thomas, Arkansas Sharecroppers, and the Roosevelt Agricultural Policies, 1933–1937." *Arkansas Historical Quarterly* 24, no. 1 (Spring 1965): 3–28.

Volanto, Keith J. "The AAA Cotton Plow-Up Campaign in Arkansas." *Arkansas Historical Quarterly* 59, no. 4 (Winter 2000): 388–406.

Watkins, Beverly. "Efforts to Encourage Immigration to Arkansas, 1865–1874." *Arkansas Historical Quarterly* 38, no. 1 (Spring 1979): 32–62.

Whayne, Jeannie M. "Caging the Blind Tiger: Race, Class, and Family in the Battle for Prohibition in Small Town Arkansas." *Arkansas Historical Quarterly* 71, no. 1 (Spring 2012): 44–60.

Whayne, Jeannie M. *Delta Empire: Lee Wilson and the Transformation of Agriculture in the New South.* Baton Rouge: Louisiana State University Press, 2011.

Whayne, Jeannie M., Thomas A. DeBlack, George Sabo III, and Morris S. Arnold. *Arkansas: A Narrative History.* Fayetteville: University of Arkansas Press, 2002.

White, Deborah Gray. *Ar'n't I a Woman?: Female Slaves in the Plantation South.* New York: W. W. Norton & Company, 1999.

Williams, C. Fred. "GI Revolt." *The Encyclopedia of Arkansas History & Culture.*

Williams, Marie. "The Road to the Central High Crises: Jim Johnson's Manipulation of the Southern Red Scare in Arkansas and the Integration of Hoxie." MA thesis, Arkansas Tech University, 2014.

Wolfe, Jonathan James. "Background of German Immigration, Part III." *Arkansas Historical Quarterly* 25, no. 4 (Winter 1966): 354–85.

Woloch, Nancy. *Women and the American Experience,* 3rd ed. New York: McGraw-Hill, 2006.

Woodruff, Nan Elizabeth. *As Rare as Rain: Federal Relief in the Great Southern Drought of 1930–31.* Urbana: University of Illinois Press, 1985.

Woodruff, Nan. "The Failure of Relief during the Arkansas Drought of 1930–31." *Arkansas Historical Quarterly* 39, no. 4 (Winter 1980): 301–13.

Wright, Gavin. *Old South, New South: Revolutions in the Southern Economy since the Civil War,* 2nd ed. Baton Rouge: Louisiana State University Press, 1996.

Yell County Historical and Genealogical Association. "Yell County Heritage." Dardanelle, AR: 1997.

Zimmer, Carl. "In 1918 Flu Pandemic, Timing Was a Killer." *New York Times*, April 30, 2014.

## Map Sources and Boundary Files

ADEQ Water Base Layer (2015), Arkansas Department of Environmental Quality, Arkansas Geographic Information Office, www.gis.arkansas.gov.

Arkansas Road Inventory (2014), Arkansas Highway and Transportation Department, Arkansas Geographic Information Office, www.gis.arkansas.gov.

Communities (1981, updated 2014), US Board of Geographic Names, Arkansas Geographic Information Office, www.gis.arkansas.gov.

Cultural Feature (1981, updated 2014), US Board of Geographic Names, Arkansas Geographic Information Office, www.gis.arkansas.gov.

High Resolution: National Hydrography Dataset Flowline Feature (2013, updated 2014), Earth Science Information Center, US Geological Survey, Arkansas Geographic Information Office, www.gis.arkansas.gov.

High Resolution: National Hydrography Dataset Waterbody Feature (2014), Earth Science Information Center, US Geological Survey, Arkansas Geographic Information Office, www.gis.arkansas.gov.

Highwater Maintenance: Cardens Bottom Drainage District No. 2 (1946, updated 1949), Corps of Engineers, US Army, Little Rock District, Little Rock, Arkansas.

Highwater Maintenance: Near Dardanelle Levee Project (1946, updated 1949), Corps of Engineers, US Army, Little Rock District, Little Rock, Arkansas.

Historic Feature (1981, updated 2014), US Board of Geographic Names, Arkansas Geographic Information Office, www.gis.arkansas.gov.

Landform (1981, updated 2014), US Board of Geographic Names, Arkansas Geographic Information Office, www.gis.arkansas.gov.

NAIP Imagery 2006 (2007, updated 2014), US Geological Survey, Arkansas Geographic Information Office, www.gis.arkansas.gov.

Places (2010, updated 2014), US Department of Commerce, US Census Bureau, Geography Division, Geographic Products Management Branch, Arkansas Geographic Information Office, www.gis.arkansas.gov.

Railway Distance Map of the State of Arkansas (1934), American Hotel Register Co., David Rumsey Historical Map Collection, www.davidrumsey.com.

Rand McNally and Company Shippers' Railroad Map (1909), David Rumsey Historical Map Collection, www.davidrumsey.com.

2000 County Boundaries (2013), Arkansas Highway and Transportation Department, Arkansas Geographic Information Office, www.gis.arkansas.gov.

# INDEX

MILDRED DIANE GLEASON is an Associate Professor of History at Arkansas Tech University. She is the co-author of *Warren G. Harding: Harbinger of Normalcy.*